THE COMPLETE BOOK OF OPENING LEADS

by Easley Blackwood

Published by
Devyn Press
Shelbyville, Kentucky

Cover by Bonnie Baron Pollack

Copyright © 1983 by Devyn Press

All rights reserved. No part of this
book may be reproduced in any form
without the permission of Devyn Press.

Printed in the United States of America

Devyn Press
1327 Walnut Street
Shelbyville, KY 40065

ISBN 0-910791-05-8

THE COMPLETE BOOK OF OPENING LEADS

Table of Contents

INTRODUCTION

It is generally agreed that there are three aspects to the game of bridge. There is bidding, there is the declarer's play of the hand (generally called "dummy play"), and there is defense. Each of these is necessary to be a consistent winner, but of the three, defensive play is the most difficult and most important.

Unless you are a hand hog, you defend approximately twice as often as you play the dummy. You would expect for your side to be declarer about half the time and be defenders the other half of the time. However, when your side is playing the hand, it will be your partner half the time who plays the hand while you simply sit there as dummy. This does not prove that defensive play is twice as important as dummy play, but it does point out to you where you are going to be spending the greater part of your time as far as the play of the cards is concerned.

You will usually find that the greatest advantage you can have over your opponents is in the area of defense. Most bridge players do everything else better than they defend, and this makes it highly profitable for you to excel in this particular department of the game. The next time you have a 60% or better score in a duplicate game, count the number of hands your side played, and the number you defended. You might be surprised to find how many you defend when you have your best games.

There are several reasons why defensive play is more difficult than dummy play. The declarer, before he plays a card, gets to see his twenty-six cards in combination. The cards which show up in the dummy are his cards and go with his thirteen. At first glance, the defenders get to see their own thirteen cards and the thirteen which belong to the declarer's dummy. It is true that this gives the defenders some advantages which declarer does not have, but they are not nearly so great as those which accrue to the declarer himself. Many of the technical plays which are available to the declarer are also available to the defenders, but not seeing their two hands in combination, they don't know that they can make these plays. The defenders may be able to get a suit established, they may be able to pick up extra tricks by ruffing, they have available holdup plays or unblocking plays, they may even have available a throw-in play and a squeeze play; but they cannot do this nearly so well as can declarer when he has these plays available. As an obvious example, take the following card combination:

Q 10 2
K J 4 3

If it is the declarer who holds this combination in his two hands, he knows that by giving up a trick to the ace he can establish three tricks. He sees three cards in the dummy and four in his own hand. However, if it is the two defenders who hold this combination of cards, each of them may be afraid to lead the suit, fearing it may give the declarer a trick which he could not otherwise take.

This volume is dedicated to the unfortunate player who has to make the opening lead. He has fewer clues than he or any other player will have on any subsequent play. He has heard the bidding, but has seen only his own thirteen cards. Immediately after he leads, thirteen additional cards are going to be placed on the table for everyone to see, and, in addition, the card which he had led should tell something about the opening leader's holding in the suit led. But lead he must.

Before playing a card he should have some notion about the number of high-card points which his partner holds. This is information which he can get from the way the opponents bid, or from some bids his partner may have made. The more bids your opponents make, the more information you get. Even when their bidding sequence is short and sweet, the final contract should give you some idea of how many of the forty high-card points they have. The majority of hands played at four of a major suit will have about 24 high-card points. Slams in suit contracts will have about 30 high-card points. This estimate plus or minus two points will usually be correct. If your opponents are playing notrump, your estimate will be even closer. When they are playing three notrump, count on them for 26 high-card points, and if they bid six notrump, estimate 32. You will usually be right to within one point. Should they stop in two of a suit

6

after finding a fit, the high-card points will be found to be not far from 20 for each side. When they stop in any other part score, they may hold a few more than half.

Your estimate of the high-card points the opponents have added to those in your own hand, and subtracted from 40 will tell you about what you expect your partner to hold. After the opening lead you will see the dummy, and can revise your estimate if there are any surprises there. As the play develops, you may have to make further revisions, but most of the time you will find that your original estimate was correct.

We no longer have to theorize about opening leads—or about many other aspects of bidding and play. There is enough data available to look at the record and see what has actually worked in practice. Is it true, for instance, that it works out better to lead low from three to the king, queen, jack or ten than it does to lead "the highest card in the suit bid by partner?" Is it as bad to underlead aces against suit contracts as claimed by the conventional wisdom? How does it work out to make aggressive leads against small slams in a suit contract, while going conservative when leading against a grand slam or a small slam in notrump? How about leading aces against slam contracts?

A study of the record shows that while most of the conventional wisdom is correct, some of it is not. In those cases where the generally accepted lead has lost more than it has gained, I recommend the adoption of the lead which, in actual play, has won more than it has lost. Let those who say I am wrong take a look at the record.

In this book, I am going to use some hands which were constructed to illustrate a point, because they make good teaching hands. The majority of the hands I am going to use, though, are from the published accounts of hands played by the world's best players in actual competition.

PART ONE:

CHOOSING
THE
CARD

CHAPTER 1:
THE OPENING LEAD
AS A SIGNAL

The player who is making the opening lead has less information to go on than he, or any other player, will have thereafter. The dummy does not come down until after he has led. There are going to be times when, after seeing the dummy, he will wish he could take his lead back and start over.

But he is not without resource. He has heard the bidding, and he can make a tentative appraisal of the high-card strength held by the opponents and, therefore, the high-card strength held by his partner. Similarly, he can make a preliminary diagnosis of the distribution which the opponents have described in their bidding. He may change his mind about some of this after he sees the dummy, but, more often than not, he can be pretty close in his original estimate. As play proceeds, the evidence is going to build until, at some point in the play, it will become conclusive.

LONG SUIT LEADS

The card chosen by the opening leader has a dual purpose. It is designed to set into motion the procedure which will allow the defenders to take the desired number of tricks, and it is the first of a number of signals given by the defenders to help overcome their disadvantage at not being able to see all twenty-six of their cards in combination.

First, let us consider the opening lead as a signal. Here we are talking about side suits. We will get to opening leads of trumps later.

More often than not, when the opening leader has led an honor card, he is telling his partner something about the high cards he has in the suit led. This is especially true when he is leading a suit which his partner has not bid. Generally speaking, when he leads a "spot" card, the emphasis is on telling his partner how many cards he has in the suit led, rather than what specific high cards he is holding.

Let us take a good look at the information conveyed by the opening lead of an honor card in a suit not bid by the partner of the opening leader.

Leads From A Sequence

Cards in the same suit which are next to each other in rank, and hence of equal trick-taking value, are called cards in sequence. The term "a sequence" is generally used only when there is at least one of the five honor cards in the sequence. For the time being, we are going to stick with that definition.

It is customary in the United States (and in many other countries as well) to lead the king when you hold the ace and king, unless you have the A-K doubleton. Therefore, the lead of the ace tells your partner you do not have the king. There are some exceptions to this, but now we are just laying down the basic principles. We will get around to the exceptions later on.

When your sequence does not include the ace and is three cards long or longer, it is customary to lead the highest card in the sequence.

<u>K</u>QJx   <u>Q</u>J104   <u>J</u>109x   <u>1</u>098x

The underlined card is accepted as the proper lead when there are three cards or more in the sequence, no matter how many small cards go along with the sequence. You will notice that the lead of the queen denies the king. If you lead the queen and your partner cannot find the king in either his hand or the dummy, he will know that the declarer has it. He has now accounted for three of the HCPs advertised by the declarer in his bidding.

With two-card sequences, you have a different situation:

<u>K</u>Qx   <u>Q</u>J4   <u>J</u>104   <u>1</u>09x

If there are no more than a total of three cards, as shown above, the high card is still the proper lead. But, it is when you get to four or more cards the problem arises.

KQ632   QJ632   J10632   109632

If you are going to lead this suit, and are defending against a trump contract, the highest card is still the best lead. However, if you are defending against a notrump contract, your best chance is to lead the fourth-best card in the suit. In the illustrations shown above, this would be the three-spot in each case.

"Almost" sequences (like the following), where the third ranking card misses being in the sequence by just one gap, are sometimes called broken sequences:

KQ10x   QJ9x   J108x

With these holdings, the standard lead is the highest card, whether you are defending notrump or a suit contract. For myself, I must say that I am not in love with the leads from these holdings, and make them only when other choices seem worse. It seems to me that too often the missing intermediate card turns up in the dummy, allowing the declarer to take a trick he could not otherwise have taken. Maybe it is just my bad luck that I have situations like the following so often:

K1043

QJ96   872

A5

The lead of the queen allows the declarer to take three tricks which he could not possibly have taken had I never led the suit.

I have noticed that this problem plagues other players also. This hand caused the famous Italian Blue Team to come a cropper. The hand is from the match of North America vs. Italy in the 1976 World Championship.

```
              NORTH
            ♠ K 10 4 2
            ♡ A 10 7
            ◇ A 10 7
            ♣ A Q 9
WEST                        EAST
♠ Q J 7 5                   ♠ 8
♡ Q J 9 8 4 3              ♡ 5
◇ Q 8                       ◇ J 9 6 4 2
♣ J                         ♣ 8 7 5 4 3 2
              SOUTH
            ♠ A 9 6 3
            ♡ K 6 2
            ◇ K 5 3
            ♣ K 10 6
```

Fred Hamilton, South for North America, played in four
spades. In spite of a combined holding of 30 HCPs, the absolutely square distribution in both his hand and dummy's suggested that he might have problems taking ten tricks. You can
see that he had a loser in each of the red suits. If he took the first
spade trick with dummy's king, he would lose two trump tricks
as well. Well, he misguessed the spades, but he didn't go set.
The reason? Antonio Vivaldi, for Italy, led the queen of hearts.
Now, Hamilton had no heart losers. He won the first trick in his
hand with the king and led a small spade to dummy's king. A
lead back to his ace revealed the bad break. He quit leading
trumps. He finessed dummy's ten of hearts, cashed the ace of
hearts, cashed the ace-king of diamonds, and started cashing
clubs. It would have done Vivaldi no good to ruff, so Hamilton
took all of his club tricks and ended up losing only the last three
tricks.

Of course, I know that there are two players, other than dummy, who could hold those pesky ten-spots, and that even when
the ten is to my left it could be doubleton. I even know, in
theory at least, the lead of the queen will work out well more
often than not. Nonetheless, whenever I have that holding, I
look around to see if I can justify a lead from any other suit. It
may be that my feeling about this particular combination is just
my own superstition.

There is still one more form of sequence to be considered. This is generally called an intermediate or interior sequence. You have a sequence, but there is one card in the suit which is higher than the cards in the sequence:

AQJ10   AJ109   KJ109   Q1098

Leading against a notrump contract, the standard lead is the highest card which is in the sequence. That would be the queen in the first illustration, the jack in the second and third, and the ten in the last.

Leading against a suit contract, if you must lead the suit when you hold the ace, the best bet is to lay down the ace. Underleading aces against suit contracts is not generally a paying proposition on opening lead. However, if you are leading from one of the suits headed by the king or queen, then the highest card in the sequence is the standard lead.

Now, for an exception. I don't think you are going to have many opportunities to lead from this combination against a notrump contract, but it may happen. Say you hold:

AKJ6432

but have no outside entry. The book play is to lead the ace. This asks your partner to play any high honor (jack or better) which he holds. Of course, with this particular holding, it could only mean the queen. You don't want to find that your partner started with three cards to the queen and that the suit blocks when he plays high low. Should that be the case, you want him to get that queen out of his hand to unblock the suit. On the other hand, you don't want to lead low and let the declarer win a cheap trick with a doubleton queen. This old convention, that the lead of an ace against a notrump calls for your partner to play the highest card he holds, would serve you well with this particular holding, should he happen to hold the queen. When partner does not have the high honor, he signals the number of cards he has in the suit. Holding an even number of cards, this signal is given by playing first a high card and then a lower one. With an odd number of cards, the signal is given by first playing a small card and then a higher one.

Opening Leads Without A Sequence

I like to call the spot cards (two through nine) the signal cards. As long as you aren't giving up any trick-taking potential, they can be used to give your partner useful information. Usually, the honor cards themselves cannot be spared for this purpose, and even the nines and eights sometimes become too useful to be spent giving signals. But the very small cards can frequently be used for this purpose, and when there are several cards in sequence, such as 7-6-5, they are all of equal value in taking tricks. If you are playing them, you might as well play them in the order that gives your partner the greatest amount of useful information. There is a code concerning the order in which the signal cards are played which is in general use today.

When holding a four-card or longer suit without a sequence, the standard lead is the fourth-best card in the suit. This lead allows your partner (and declarer as well) to use the Rule of Eleven, which we will talk about later. We call suits of four or more cards "long suits". Four is not all that long, but it is a little more than your average share.

An exception to this fourth-best rule is when you are leading against a suit contract, and the suit contains the ace. If you lead the suit, it is best to lead the ace against a suit contract. The fourth-best is led against a notrump contract, whether or not you hold the ace.

Usually, when you lead fourth-best, you have an honor in the suit. Problems arise when you have a four-card holding without an honor, such as 8-6-4-2. Usually, the lead of a small signal card implies to your partner that you would like this suit led back, while the lead of a high signal card implies that you prefer a shift. So the question is, when you lead such a miserable suit, do you want your partner to continue your suit or not?

When you're defending against a suit contract, you're trying to cash or develop high-card tricks. Your chances of taking long-card tricks—that is, tricks with small cards after the opponents have no more cards in the suit—are poor when they have trumps. So the best bet in defending against a suit contract would be the lead of the six-spot to indicate to your partner that you have no interest in having the suit returned.

Defending against notrump creates extra problems. If you think that your partner has length in your four-card suit, it generally will pay you to tell him how many you have by leading fourth-best. Certainly, if your partner has bid the suit, the small card is correct. At other times, the bidding will suggest that he probably has length in the suit. However, when you elect to lead from a bad four-card suit against notrump, merely to be passive, it is best to lead your second highest, unless your two top cards are touching in rank, in which event the highest is the best choice. This tells partner that there is no future in the suit, and will suggest that he return something else when he gets the lead.

A small card probably should be led from a suit headed by a ten or better, in some hope you can build up a high-card winner. Otherwise, lead high.

Lead Of The Fourth-Best—The Rule Of Eleven

Below is a list of the bits of information that you can learn when partner leads a fourth-best card. Assume that he has led a five-spot.

1. Your partner does not have an honor sequence in the suit which would justify the lead of a high card.

2. If you are playing against a suit contract, your partner will not underlead an ace. If you don't see the ace in the dummy, or in your hand, you can be assured declarer has it.

3. The cards are numbered from two through fourteen. As a result, subtract two from the number on the card led, and that will tell you how many cards there are in the deck lower than the card led. For example, if your partner has led a five, there are three cards in that suit lower than the five. If you can see all three of them, you know your partner has led from a four-card suit.

4. If you subtract the numeral on the card led from fourteen, you will know how many cards there are in the deck higher than the one led. For example, if your partner has led the five, there are nine cards in that suit which are higher than the five.

5. Your partner has three of these cards which are higher than the five.

6. As your partner holds three of the cards in the suit higher than the one led, you can determine how many are in the other three hands combined by subtracting the number on the

card led from eleven. For example, if the card led is the five, of the nine cards higher in the suit, three are in your partner's hand, and the other six are in the other three hands. The short-cut method is simply to subtract five from eleven and you get the same answer of six. You can see two of these three hands, namely the dummy and your own, and therefore can tell how many cards higher than the card led are in the declarer's hand.

So, the lead of the fourth-best is a definite signal which has many implications. However, there are times when this information will be more helpful to the declarer than to your partner. Tough luck. On balance, the information is much more valuable to the defense.

There are some players who lead the smallest card from a long suit, and there are others who use different methods. Some lead third-best when they have an even number of cards, and low when they have an odd number of cards. Proponents of these various methods will construct hands to show you where their choice of leads gives some extremely interesting information. In real life they often give more interesting information than a fourth-best lead. However, it is seldom that they will give more USEFUL information. Bridge is not a game for those who like to play with codes and see how much information they can get through their use. Signals are supposed to give partner information which will help him take tricks.

Before we begin looking at example hands, here is one little bit of information which might come in handy. As a general rule, the highest card which can be led as a fourth-best is the eight-spot. When the nine is the fourth-best card in the suit, there are only five higher cards in the suit. They must be held in such a manner that there is a sequence. The top of the sequence is a superior lead to the lead of fourth-best. So when your partner leads an eight or smaller card, it may or may not be fourth-best. It's up to you to come to a decision about it. But when he leads a nine or higher, it almost certainly is not.

Let's start by looking at some teaching hands. In this way we can see how to use the information given by the lead of the fourth-best in the simplest form possible.

Both vul., dealer South.

NORTH
♠ 8 6 3
♡ A Q 10 9
◇ K 6 5
♣ K 8 3

WEST
♠ Q 10 2
♡ J 7 3
◇ Q 10 8 7
♣ J 7 5

EAST
♠ J 9 7 4
♡ K 5 2
◇ A J 9 3
♣ 9 4

SOUTH
♠ A K 5
♡ 8 6 4
◇ 4 2
♣ A Q 10 6 2

The bidding:

SOUTH	WEST	NORTH	EAST
1 ♣	Pass	1 ♡	Pass
1 NT	Pass	3 NT	Pass
Pass	Pass		

West leads the seven of diamonds. East sees dummy, and examines the dummy's diamond holding. There is no reason to think that the seven is anything other than a fourth-best lead. Seven from eleven leaves four. There are four diamonds higher than the seven which are not in the West hand. They are, therefore, in the North hand, plus the East hand, plus the South hand. East can see one of them in the dummy. In his own hand he can see three. This means that South has no diamonds higher than the seven. If dummy plays the five or six, East plays the three, confident that West will hold the first trick with the seven. The defenders take the first four diamond tricks, and, as declarer has only eight tricks, he is going to have to try the heart finesse. This would be a very poor teaching hand if the heart finesse worked, so we have the satisfaction of defeating the hand through the use of the Rule of Eleven. Of course, if East

17

had played any diamond other than the three, declarer could have made the hand with five club tricks, two spade tricks, and two heart tricks.

Before we go on, let's see just what information we can get from the fourth-best lead, be it useful or not. Even if it is not useful on this hand, the principle might be useful on some hand in the future.

Is the lead of the seven-spot from just a four-card suit, or is it from a five- or six-card suit? There are five cards smaller than the seven. East could see three of these; two were missing. If West had one of these, South has a singleton. If West has a six-card suit, South has no diamonds at all. South's rebid of one notrump indicated he does not have a singleton in his hand. So, let's assume that South has both of these missing diamonds, and that West started with only a four-card diamond suit. This means that he almost certainly does not have a five-card suit anywhere in his hand. It is also unlikely that he has four spades of any quality, because he probably would have preferred to lead a major suit.

How about the cards higher than the seven-spot? West had three of these. Looking at the dummy and at his hand, East could see exactly what these three higher diamonds were. The only three which were not in evidence were the Q, 10, and 8. So, East knew his partner's exact holding in the diamond suit.

Unfortunately, this scenario is not too realistic. It is rare that you can be sure you can let your partner win the first trick with his lead of the seven. But, if that is all we have learned from our study of the fourth-best lead, we have cheated ourselves badly. There is much more than that to it. The next hand will add another element.

Both vul., dealer South.

NORTH
♠ J 8 3
♡ Q 10 5 2
◊ 8 6 5
♣ A K 2

WEST
♠ K 10 7 6
♡ 7 3
◊ K 10 4 2
♣ 9 7 6

EAST
♠ Q 9 5
♡ 9 6
◊ Q J 9 7
♣ Q 8 4 3

SOUTH
♠ A 4 2
♡ A K J 8 4
◊ A 3
♣ J 10 5

SOUTH	WEST	NORTH	EAST
1 ♡	Pass	2 ♡	Pass
4 ♡	Pass	Pass	Pass

Some people think the fourth-best lead is useful only against notrump contracts. Not so. When you lead from a four-card or longer suit, headed by an honor but without a sequence, the fourth-best should be chosen, whether the opponents are playing with a suit as trumps or at notrump. On this hand, West held only six high-card points. He decided that an attacking lead was a good gamble. The chances were excellent his partner would have support cards for his kings. The opposing bidding had been unrevealing. West had no way of knowing whether either opponent had a long suit on which they could discard losers. Had he chosen to lead a small diamond, his partner would have had no problem at all. However, he decided that it is usually better to lead a major suit than a minor in these circumstances, so he led the six of spades.

Dummy played low. East now had a golden opportunity to hand the declarer his contract on a silver platter by playing third hand high. But, East did no such thing. How did he know that he should not play his queen?

Of the five spades higher than the six, East could see two in the dummy and two in his own hand. This meant that South had exactly one spade higher than the six. What was that one card? Either East needed a new partner, or it was the ace. Good partners do not underlead aces on opening lead against suit contracts. If the only card South had which could beat the six was the ace, all East had to do to force the ace was cover whatever card dummy played. When dummy played the three, his five was sufficient. Had dummy played the eight, he would have played the nine. By the use of the fourth-best signal he was able to avoid disaster, and the defenders now were sure to get two spade tricks. They also took a club and a diamond to set the hand. Had East followed the old third-hand-high adage and played his queen, the defenders would have taken only one spade trick, and the declarer would have fulfilled his contract.

In 1964, a group of young American players presented Journalist Leads to bridge players. Many of the methods used today derive from Journalist Leads. These leads follow one pattern when leading against a notrump contract, and a different pattern when used against suit contracts.

A young friend of mine gave me the next hand to explain why he had abandoned Journalist Leads after trying them for several months.

NORTH
♠ K Q 5
♡ Q 7 2
♢ 10 7 2
♣ A 7 4 3

WEST
♠ 7 6
♡ 6 3
♢ A Q 9 6 3
♣ K J 8 2

EAST
♠ J 10 8 2
♡ J 10 9 4
♢ J 8 4
♣ 10 9

SOUTH
♠ A 9 4 3
♡ A K 8 5
♢ K 5
♣ Q 6 5

My friend sat West in a Swiss Team match. Defending against notrump contracts, playing Journalist leads, you lead your lowest card from a suit you want your partner to return, instead of leading fourth-best. Therefore, my friend led the three of diamonds. Dummy played small, East the jack, and South won the king. South was looking at ten tricks if both major suits were three-three, and nine tricks if either one broke. He tried spades first, but on the third spade, West discarded a club. Next he cashed the queen, ace and king with the same result. West discarded another club. The remaining chances for taking nine tricks were not too good, but South decided to take the one which offered the best prospect. He led a small diamond, hoping that West had the king of clubs and only four diamonds left in his hand. After failures in both major suits, South found his success in the minor suits. West cashed his four diamond tricks, but declarer kept two clubs in each hand and took the last two tricks.

Possibly, East should have played the eight of diamonds at trick one, but if there is a way to arrive at that conclusion, East did not find it. In the other room, where East and West were playing fourth-best leads, it was easy. This time, West led the six of diamonds. On examining the dummy, East was able to see that South had just one diamond higher than the six. Was there some way to figure out which one it was? Well, he could not quite do that, but East did find a way to figure out which one it was not. Of the eight diamonds higher than the six, East could see the J-10-8-7. The other four which he could not see were the A-K-Q-9. The one card South could not hold was the nine, because if South had the nine, then West held the A-K-Q. From that holding, he would not be leading the six-spot. So, East didn't play the jack. It seems that declarer made a feeble effort by putting on dummy's seven, and East covered with the eight. Now declarer no longer had the throw-in play available. When he led a diamond, East won the trick with his jack. Declarer could take only eight tricks.

On the next hand, West led the four of spades against a three notrump contract. South won with the ace. East got the lead at trick two when declarer finessed the queen of diamonds. If West held the king of spades, East thought it worthwhile to continue the suit. If South held the king of spades, giving him three stoppers in that suit, East thought it time to shift. Let's see how the fourth-best signal gave him the information he needed to arrive at a decision.

```
                        NORTH
                        ♠ Q 8 5
                        ♡ K J 4
                        ◇ A J 9 2
                        ♣ 8 6 2
        WEST                          EAST
        ♠ J 10 7 4                    ♠ 9 3 2
        ♡ Q 6 2                       ♡ A 10 8 3
        ◇ 7 6 4                       ◇ K 8 3
        ♣ K 7 5                       ♣ 10 4 3
                        SOUTH
                        ♠ A K 6
                        ♡ 9 7 5
                        ◇ Q 10 5
                        ♣ A Q J 9
```

Examining the dummy, East could tell that West had only four spades and, therefore, that South had three spades. As East could see all of the spades smaller than the four-spot, he didn't even have to use the Rule of Eleven to know that all of South's spades were higher than the four-spot. So, he set out to see if he could determine which high cards his partner held. Noting that South had used the ace to cover the nine, it seemed that South did not have either the jack or the ten, as surely he would have won with one of those two cards if he could. East therefore placed the jack and ten in his partner's hand. If his partner also held the king, his holding would have been K-J-10-4. East decided that with that interior sequence West would have chosen the jack as his opening lead. Therefore, West did not have the king, and that card must be in the South hand.

East looked for a more profitable lead than a spade return. Prospects were not too good. But, there was a possibility in the heart suit. If his partner had the queen of hearts and an entry, there was a chance. Holding only seven HCPs himself, he knew that West's hand was approximately as good as his own, and that most of his points were outside of the spade suit. He thought there was a reasonable chance West held an entry. So instead of woodenly returning his partner's suit, he led the three of hearts, and was delighted to see the queen come from his partner's hand. South had a pretty good idea what was going on, and let the queen hold the trick, hoping that West had started with only two hearts. But it was not to be. West continued with the six of hearts. This time, East held up and let declarer win with the jack. Declarer had only eight tricks without the club finesse. When he took the finesse, West won. His heart lead let East take two heart tricks to set the contract. Had East continued spades after he won the king of diamonds, declarer would have had time to get his club tricks established.

Since the days of whist, card players have been trying to find out what players held which cards. Today, these efforts have acquired a fancy new name: "Discovery". Only the name is new—the principle is as old as card games.

Let's watch East let the fourth-best signal give him an opportunity for some high-class discovery on the next hand.

Both vul., dealer South.

                    NORTH
                    ♠ J 2
                    ♡ Q 10 6
                    ◇ 8 6
                    ♣ A Q 10 7 5 4
    WEST   EAST
    ♠ 8 7 5 3   ♠ 10 9 6 4
    ♡ J 9 8 5 4   ♡ A 7 3
    ◇ A Q 4   ◇ J 10 5
    ♣ 2   ♣ K 8 3
                    SOUTH
                    ♠ A K Q
                    ♡ K 2
                    ◇ K 9 7 3 2
                    ♣ J 9 6

The bidding:

SOUTH	WEST	NORTH	EAST
1 NT	Pass	3 NT	Pass
Pass	Pass		

West led the five of hearts and declarer played the six from dummy. The Rule of Eleven told East that South had just one heart higher than the five-spot. The question: Which higher heart did he hold? If he held the king, then he had the heart suit stopped twice. If he held the jack or any lower card, then West held the king; and if the hearts were a five-card suit, East could lay down the ace of hearts when he got the lead, and his partner could take all the rest of the heart tricks. East had an idea he was going to be on lead shortly. It looked like declarer would have to bring in the club suit to get the tricks, and East was quite proud of that king of clubs in his hand. So he covered dummy's six with his seven. He soon discovered declarer had two heart tricks.

South won with the king and led the jack of clubs for a finesse. East won and, holding only eight HCPs himself, knew that his partner held some high cards somewhere. They were not in hearts and they were not in clubs. The most likely prospect seemed to be diamonds. East led the jack of diamonds. South let that hold the trick, and now East decided his best play was to take the ace of hearts before continuing with diamonds. So the defenders took three diamonds, a club, and a heart.

On the next hand, East used the Rule of Eleven to figure out that he had nothing to lose and everything to gain by unblocking in his partner's suit.

Neither vul., dealer North.

```
                    NORTH
                    ♠ 7 6 4
                    ♡ A 9 6
                    ◊ A
                    ♣ A Q 9 7 5 3
        WEST                      EAST
        ♠ 10 5 3                  ♠ Q J 9 2
        ♡ 7 5 4                   ♡ Q 10 8 3
        ◊ Q 9 8 7 2               ◊ K 10 3
        ♣ 8 2                     ♣ K 4
                    SOUTH
                    ♠ A K 8
                    ♡ K J 2
                    ◊ J 6 5 4
                    ♣ J 10 6
```

The bidding:

SOUTH	WEST	NORTH	EAST
		1 ♣	Pass
2 NT	Pass	3 ♣	Pass
3 NT	Pass	Pass	Pass

West led the seven of diamonds. The Rule of Eleven told East that South had exactly one diamond higher than the seven. The diamonds missing which were higher than the seven were the Q-J-9-8. Of these four cards, South had one, while West had the other three. It wasn't difficult to figure out that East had nothing to lose by playing his ten on the first trick. If the one card held by South was the jack, he might have a great deal to gain by getting that ten out of his hand. Declarer came to his hand with the ace of spades to finesse clubs. East won the king of clubs and led the king and a small diamond. East's foresight had paid off. The defenders took four diamond tricks. Had East not unblocked the ten, South could have let the ten hold the trick when it was led, and there would have been no way for the defenders to get four diamond tricks.

Sometimes I think those of us who teach bridge overemphasize the point that when your partner leads fourth-best, you can tell how many cards declarer has which are higher than the card led by your partner. Sometimes the information your partner needs is how many cards declarer has in the suit, period. What we want to do with our signaling is give our partner information which will be useful, not just information which is interesting.

Take a look at the next hand.

Both vul., dealer South.

```
                    NORTH
                    ♠ J 9 8 2
                    ♡ J 6
                    ◊ Q 9 2
                    ♣ A K 8 3
        WEST                        EAST
        ♠ K 7 5                     ♠ Q 10 6 3
        ♡ A 3                       ♡ 9 8 7 5 2
        ◊ 10 8 7 3                  ◊ A 5
        ♣ 9 7 5 2                   ♣ 10 6
                    SOUTH
                    ♠ A 4
                    ♡ K Q 10 4
                    ◊ K J 6 4
                    ♣ Q J 4
```

The bidding:

SOUTH	WEST	NORTH	EAST
1 NT	Pass	2 ♣	Pass
2 ♡	Pass	3 NT	Pass
Pass	Pass		

Like a good partner, West led the fourth-best of his longest and strongest suit. That turned out to be the diamond suit. Down comes the dummy, and East sees that West started with only a four-card suit. This means that South also started with four diamonds, and any diamond tricks the defenders have are high-card tricks, not long-card tricks. East was not enthralled

26

by the idea of working on a suit in which the opponents had more cards than the defenders. He looked around for something better to do. Reviewing the bidding, East noticed that South had also said that he had four hearts. That took care of the two red suits. East now knew that South had only five cards in the black suits. In one of these suits, South had a doubleton. Could it be clubs? If South started with only a doubleton club, then West would have had five cards in the suit and would have led a club, rather than a diamond. So East decided that South probably had three clubs. That left him with two spades. East had the advantage of location over the dummy in the spade suit. He decided to explore that avenue of tricks, rather than continue diamonds. He led the three of spades.

South ducked, West won the king and then returned the seven of spades. Dummy played the eight, but East did not cover with the ten. East stood by his conviction that South had started with only two spades and played the six. South had to win his ace. Declarer could not get nine tricks without a heart. He led a small heart toward dummy's jack, hoping he might steal a trick, but West would have none of it. He went up with the ace and led the five of spades. Now East took his two spade tricks. This gave the defenders a total of three spade tricks, and the two red aces.

It is obvious that had East woodenly returned the diamond, declarer would have established hearts while he still had control of the first round of spades. He would have taken eleven tricks.

East had information about the distribution of the hands which West could not have. That is frequently true, because on opening lead, it is the leader who has given the signal, but his partner who has received it. When you have information not available to your partner, you may be able to save him from making a losing play. Look at the next hand.

27

Both vul., dealer West.

NORTH
♠ Q 9
♡ 9 4 3
◇ K Q 10 6
♣ K J 9 4

WEST
♠ K J
♡ Q 10 8 2
◇ J 9 7
♣ A 8 5 2

EAST
♠ None
♡ K J 7
◇ A 8 5 4 3 2
♣ Q 10 6 3

SOUTH
♠ A 10 8 7 6 5 4 3 2
♡ A 6 5
◇ None
♣ 7

The bidding:

SOUTH	WEST	NORTH	EAST
	Pass	Pass	Pass
4 ♠	Pass	Pass	Pass

West led the two of hearts. When the dummy came down, East had no doubt about the heart distribution. His partner had four and everybody else had three. This was information West could not possibly have.

East played the king and South won with the ace. South laid down the ace of spades, and, of course, East showed out. Now West knew that South had started with nine spades, but that information wasn't too useful. There wasn't anything he could do about it. East had a pretty good idea that South started with nine spades, but conceivably he could have had the king in his hand and could have started with ten. In any event, South had at most one card, outside of the major suits. So what was there to fear?

The fear was that if South led a club, West might duck, hoping declarer would play the jack from the dummy. How could East protect his partner? He found a way. On the ace of spades,

28

he discarded his queen of clubs. Now when South led the seven of clubs, West knew what to do. He played the ace. He also knew better than to lead a second club. He continued hearts and the defenders got all of their tricks. This turned out to be one trump, two hearts, and the ace of clubs.

See what a little bit of simple counting did for the defenders on this hand.

Both vul., dealer South.

```
                    NORTH
                    ♠ K 5 2
                    ♡ 10 7 6 5
                    ◇ K J 6 5
                    ♣ A Q
        WEST                    EAST
        ♠ Q 10 8 4              ♠ J 9 3
        ♡ Q 9 8 2              ♡ A J 4 3
        ◇ 4                    ◇ Q 10 3
        ♣ 8 5 4 2              ♣ J 10 3
                    SOUTH
                    ♠ A 7 6
                    ♡ K
                    ◇ A 9 8 7 2
                    ♣ K 9 7 6
```

The bidding:

SOUTH	WEST	NORTH	EAST
1 ◇	Pass	1 ♡	Pass
2 ♣	Pass	3 ◇	Pass
3 NT	Pass	Pass	Pass

Against the three notrump contract, West led the four of spades. East examined the dummy and took note of two matters which he tucked away in his memory, in case they might be useful later on. First, West probably held about four high-card points. Second, West had exactly four spades. East could see the two spades smaller than the four-spot in his hand and the dummy. So far, none of this did him any good, but when dummy played low, he just played the jack and South won with the ace. South now laid down the ace of diamonds and a small diamond. On the second diamond, West discarded a small club. Now East knew something else about his partner's hand. He had started with a singleton diamond. The pieces began to fall in place. After losing one diamond trick, South could take four diamond tricks, two spade tricks, and there were two club tricks for him in the dummy. He had bid clubs and probably had the king of clubs for his ninth trick. Continuing spades was not going to get the defense anywhere. But, West's distribution was an open book. If spades were his longest suit, then his longest suit was four cards long. And, he had started with a singleton. What is the distribution where you have no suit longer than four cards and a singleton? The only possible distribution is 4-4-4-1. As that left West with four hearts, the distribution of the heart suit was also 4-4-4-1, with South holding the singleton. Unless this analysis of the distribution was accurate, there seemed to be no way to keep declarer from taking nine tricks. On the second diamond lead, declarer put in dummy's jack, and East won with the queen. Now he laid down the ace of hearts. He didn't care what heart South had, if it was a singleton. When South played the king, West was able to judge the situation and saw he could not spare a high heart for a signal. In spite of his play of the two, East continued with the three of hearts to the queen. The return of the nine of hearts gave the defenders four heart tricks to add to their diamond trick.

On the next hand, East knew about the heart suit, but he also knew that his partner could not know about the heart suit. East found a way to tell him about it.

Both vul., dealer South.

```
                    NORTH
                    ♠ K J 3
                    ♡ 5 3
                    ◇ Q J 10 6 5 3
                    ♣ A 5
      WEST                        EAST
      ♠ 9 6 2                     ♠ 10 8 7 5
      ♡ A 9 8 7 4                 ♡ Q J 10
      ◇ K 7 4                     ◇ 8
      ♣ K 6                       ♣ J 10 9 8 2
                    SOUTH
                    ♠ A Q 4
                    ♡ K 6 2
                    ◇ A 9 2
                    ♣ Q 7 4 3
```

The bidding:

SOUTH	WEST	NORTH	EAST
1 NT	Pass	3 NT	Pass
Pass	Pass		

West led the seven of hearts, and East used the Rule of Eleven to conclude that South held just one heart higher than the seven. It did not tell him which one. East played the ten, and when South won with the king, East knew that South had no more hearts higher than the seven. This meant that West could take tricks with each of the hearts he had in his hand which were higher than the seven-spot. If West happened to hold five or six hearts, it meant that West could take a trick with every heart he had. The trouble was that while East knew this, West did not. South very well may have held the king and queen of hearts, leaving East with the ten and jack. East's prospects for getting the lead so he could clarify the situation were bleak, but he did find a way to be helpful. Holding only four HCPs, he thought his partner held somewhere around ten. This made it likely West would gain the lead before too long.

At trick two, South went to the dummy by leading the four of

31

spades to the jack, and led the queen of diamonds for a finesse. West declined that trick. Declarer happily led a second diamond to take another finesse, but his happiness disappeared when East discarded. His discard gave West cause for thought. East discarded the queen of hearts.

South no longer could have held the king and queen of hearts. As a matter of fact, it was easy to see that East must hold the jack as well, otherwise East would have played the queen on the first trick. The situation was now pretty clear to both South and West, but there wasn't anything South could do about it. He couldn't come anywhere near nine tricks without some more diamond tricks, so he decided to limit his losses. He took the ace of diamonds and then surrendered a diamond to West. West cashed the ace of hearts and then took his three remaining heart tricks. Now South had the balance for down one.

Against a suit contract, Journalist leaders show count when they have nothing but spot cards. From an odd number of cards the lowest is led; from an even number of cards the third-highest is led. Proponents of these leads can construct some beautiful hands to demonstrate how these length signals on opening leads are more helpful to the defenders than they are to the declarer. Hands in which you have a direct comparison are not easy to come by. I did, however, find one which was played in the 1977 Trials to select the American Contract Bridge League Team for the World Championship. Let's take a look at it and examine just what the partner of the opening leader could determine from the lead, compared to what the declarer could learn, where one used fourth-best signals and the other used Journalist signals.

E-W vul., dealer West.

```
                    NORTH
                 ♠ K J 8 2
                 ♡ Q 4
                 ◊ K J 4 2
                 ♣ A Q 5
    WEST                        EAST
 ♠ 10 9 6 5 3               ♠ A 7 4
 ♡ J 9                      ♡ K 8 2
 ◊ 10 6 5 3                 ◊ A Q 9 8 7
 ♣ 10 3                     ♣ 9 7
                    SOUTH
                 ♠ Q
                 ♡ A 10 7 6 5 3
                 ◊ None
                 ♣ K J 8 6 4 2
```

Room 1

SOUTH	WEST	NORTH	EAST
Cohen	Wolff	Katz	Hamman
	Pass	1 NT	Pass
3 ♡	Pass	3 NT	Pass
4 ♣	Pass	4 ♡	Pass
5 ♣	Pass	6 ♣	All Pass

Room 2

SOUTH	WEST	NORTH	EAST
Eisenberg	Mohan	Kantar	Rosenkranz
	Pass	1 NT	Pass
2 ◊	Pass	2 ♡	Pass
3 ♣	Pass	3 NT	Pass
4 ♣	Pass	5 ♣	Pass
6 ♣	All Pass		

There was a slight difference in the bidding which did not affect either the final contract or the opening lead. Eisenberg and
Kantar used a transfer sequence where Eisenberg's two-

diamond response showed a heart suit, while Cohen and Katz had a natural sequence. In both rooms, the opening lead was a diamond.

In Room 1, Wolff led the three of diamonds. As dummy has the two, this was obviously the smallest diamond Wolff had. If it was a singleton, South would have started with three small diamonds. Not only had South bid like a man who did not hold three worthless cards in any suit, he had also bid like a man who had at least eleven cards between hearts and clubs. This meant he didn't have three of anything else. Neither did Hamman have any trouble deciding the lead was not small from three to the queen. If the lead were a fourth-best, then Hamman didn't need any Rule of Eleven to decide that Cohen was void in diamonds. Hamman was looking at nine of the diamonds between his hand and the dummy. If you care to go through the Rule of Eleven just for practice, in his own hand Hamman had five of those cards higher than the three-spot, while in the dummy he saw three more, and that accounted for all eight of them. This meant that declarer had no diamonds higher than the three-spot, and as the two was showing in the dummy, he didn't have any lower either. So all Hamman had to do was cover whatever card dummy played without fear that South would turn up with a higher card to win the trick. This would be easy for those of us who lead high from three small, but if Wolff had led low from three small, it would not have been so easy for Hamman to be sure South did not have the singleton ten. However, he soon found out about that.

Now let's look at what South could learn from this lead of the three. It wasn't hard for him to come to the conclusion that West probably had four diamonds and East had five, but that information was of no help to him at all. He did not know whether the highest card in the West hand was or was not the queen. Neither did he know whether the lead happened to be from three cards to the queen. Apparently, Cohen decided that his best bet was that Wolff had led from the queen, and he inserted dummy's jack. This solved any problems Hamman might have had left. He covered the jack with the queen and Cohen trumped. From here on, Cohen did the best he could, but that was not good enough. He went to the dummy with a trump and led the queen of hearts, which would work out if West held the singleton jack and only one trump. Hamman covered with the king, and now the jack of hearts in West looked like a sure trick. Cohen went back to the dummy with trumps and led the four of hearts. When Hamman played the two, he finessed the seven and Wolff now had his trick with the jack of hearts. Wolff wasn't about to let Cohen discard all of his spades on the established hearts, and so he led a spade and the hand was set.

In Room 2, the defenders were playing Journalist leads. Against suit contracts, Journalist leaders lead small from an odd number of cards, and high from an even number of cards. With two spot cards, they lead the higher. With four or six, they lead the third-best. Holding four diamonds, Mohan led the five.

Now let's see what Dr. George Rosenkranz, of Mexico, could make out of that lead. It may have been the top card of a doubleton, in which event South would hold the ten-spot. Also, it could have been just what it was. There was no way for Rosenkranz to know.

Look at the lead of the five-spot from the view of Billy Eisenberg, with the South hand. He couldn't tell whether it was the top of a doubleton or third-best from four, any better than Rosenkranz could. As far as Eisenberg was concerned, it could have been third-best from a suit headed by the queen. However, Eisenberg also knew that Rosenkranz could not tell. So he decided to let Rosenkranz do the guessing. He just played the two from the dummy.

I wasn't there and I don't know how long it took Rosenkranz to play the queen, but that's what he finally did. Now Eisenberg was able to get to the dummy two times with clubs to establish a diamond and cash a diamond trick, discarding the queen of spades. There was still a trump left in the dummy to establish hearts, and let Eisenberg bring home his slam.

The fourth-best signal is not limited to opening leads. Whenever either defender leads low from a long suit, he should give a signal by leading his fourth-best. For example, whenever the partner of the opening leader returns his partner's original suit, he should lead his original fourth-best when he holds four or more cards in the suit. This can best be illustrated by an example.

Both vul., dealer South.

NORTH
♠ A 10 6 5
♡ A 5 4 3
◇ 6
♣ K 5 4 3

WEST
♠ 7 4 3
♡ J 8 7
◇ K 10 7 4 2
♣ 8 7

EAST
♠ K 8 2
♡ Q 10 9
◇ Q 8 5 3
♣ J 10 6

SOUTH
♠ Q J 9
♡ K 6 2
◇ A J 9
♣ A Q 9 2

The bidding:

SOUTH	WEST	NORTH	EAST
1 NT	Pass	2 ♣	Pass
2 ◇	Pass	3 NT	All Pass

Against the three notrump contract, West led the four of diamonds. East played the queen and South decided his best chance would be to take the trick with the ace. Maybe the spade finesse would be right. If not, maybe East had either the king or the ten of diamonds. Had he guessed that I prepared this hand to demonstrate a point, he would have known better, but it still would have done him no good. He couldn't gain by holding off, as East held more diamonds than he did.

At trick two, he led the queen of spades and finessed. East lost no time winning with the king and returning a diamond. The important point is that he returned the correct diamond.

Had East started with three diamonds, it would have been incumbent upon him to return the middle one. The play of the smallest one is reserved for a holding of either two or four. So when the three came back, West knew that it was one or the other. This is that famous "two-card difference", but here it's

not too difficult to determine which it is. If East started with only two diamonds, South would have started with five. South
surely had the jack, else East would have played it at trick one.
Why then would South be playing the nine if he had two smaller
cards to play on the return? West won with the ten and decided
he could now take the balance of the diamond tricks. The jack
was alone in the South hand.

When he led the king, East decided he had better get out of
the way with his eight-spot, or he might end up holding the trick
with that card. That enabled West to cash the seven and two for
the setting tricks.

It is rare that the opening leader cannot tell when his partner
returns a suit whether it is a two-card suit, a three-card suit, or a
four-card or longer suit. He just has to be careful to examine the
situation and account for the missing cards. Here are two examples. In each case, third hand won the first trick with the ace.
On one hand, he returned the five, and on the other the four.

Example A

10 3

K 8 7 6 2   A 5

Q J

You led the six from the West hand, and dummy has come
down with the doubleton 10-3. Your partner has played the ace
and declarer has played the jack. Your partner has returned the
five and declarer has played the queen. What is going on?

There are still two cards unaccounted for. They are the 9 and
the 4. One card your partner should not have is the nine. If he
had A-9-5, he would have returned the nine and not the five. If
he had a A-9-5-4, his return would have been the four. Well, if
East doesn't have the nine, then South does. It looks like East
started with A-5-4, and South with Q-J-9, and that the declarer
is trying to hornswoggle you into playing your king , so that
after he wins the third trick in the suit, East will have no more.
If you don't have a side entry, you had better duck and hope
your partner can get in. When he regains the lead, you will expect him to continue with the four, and declarer to find the nine
in his hand, and you can take the rest of the tricks.

Now look at Example B.

Example B

```
                10 3
K 8 7 6 2                 A 4
                Q J
```

Here, everything is the same, except that this time your partner has returned the four. That is not from a three-card suit, as you can see both the two and the three between your hand and the dummy. It is either a four-card suit or a two-card suit. Which is it?

If it is a two-card suit, then South holds both of the missing cards. They are the 9-5. Just why would South, with Q-J-9-5, throwing away the queen and jack to limit himself to one trick in the suit, when by simply playing a small card he could assure two tricks. The answer is that this time, East not only has the nine, he also has the five. Go ahead and win the trick with the king and continue the suit. You should lead the two, which should make it easy for him to play his nine and return the five for you to overtake.

You can construct a hand where unblocking and trying to signal at the same time create problems. Look at the next hand.

Both vul., dealer South.

```
                    NORTH
                    ♠ A K 8 5
                    ♡ K 10 7
                    ◇ J 10 8 4 2
                    ♣ 4
        WEST                      EAST
        ♠ Q J                     ♠ 10 9 4 3 2
        ♡ Q 8 6 2                 ♡ J 4 3
        ◇ 6 5                     ◇ 9
        ♣ K J 7 6 3               ♣ A 10 9 2
                    SOUTH
                    ♠ 7 6
                    ♡ A 9 5
                    ◇ A K Q 7 3
                    ♣ Q 8 5
```

The bidding:

SOUTH	WEST	NORTH	EAST
1 ◇	Pass	1 ♠	Pass
1 NT	Pass	3 ◇	Pass
3 NT	All Pass		

The normal lead against three notrump is the six of clubs, and the normal play is for East to play the ace. Now what club should East return? Looking at all four hands, you and I can see that he had better lead the ten or nine, else the suit is going to become blocked. Let's look at the situation from the viewpoint of East, who cannot see the hidden cards in the South and West hands. What can he tell about the possibility of the suit becoming blocked?

One of the cards smaller than the six has not shown up, and there is a good chance West has it, though this is by no means sure. However, it is sure that West holds at least one, but not as many as all three of the missing cards higher than the ten-spot in the East hand. If West had held the K-Q-J, he would have led the king, and not the six. However, of the spot cards higher than the six, the only ones which East has not seen are the seven and eight, and as West holds three cards higher than the six, at least one of them must be a face card. However, West could just as easily hold two of the face cards. East can tell that if he returns the two of clubs he is likely to be on lead to the fourth club trick, with whatever cards West has that are higher than the ten-spot having been played. And if it seems likely West has five clubs in his hand, then East will have blown a trick by failing to unblock. So the answer is not too difficult for East. It's poor West who is going to have problems.

West will have a better chance to spot the return of the ten as an unblocking card than he would have should East return the nine. Of course, if South is napping and merely plays the eight when East returns the ten, there will be no problems. The matter will be cleared up when East continues with the nine. If, however, South is on his toes, he will play the queen when East leads the ten. Let's see what West can do if declarer makes the superior play of playing the queen at trick two.

Did East start with only two clubs? That is not likely, for then South would have had five clubs and the bids he made would have made no sense.

Could East have held only three clubs? The only small cards missing after trick two would be the nine, eight and deuce. This would leave East with A-10-9, A-10-8, or A-10-2. In any event, the entryless West player would have to let declarer hold the queen if he wanted to try for four club tricks. This illustrates the disadvantage under which the defenders work in not being able to see their hands in combination, as can the declarer.

There are other holdings third hand may have which make it imperative for him to unblock and difficult for his partner to read. Holdings such as A-J-10-2, or Q -J-10-2, or even K-8-7-2, may need to be unblocked. The best bet is to agree that when East fears he may block the suit because of such holdings, he returns specifically the highest card remaining in his hand after the first trick. On the hand in question, the return of the ten should suggest to West the possibility that East is unblocking with a four-card holding. If he thought it likely that his partner had another entry, he might let South's queen hold the trick. However, on this hand, West's best chance to beat 3NT is to win the queen with the king, play the jack, and hope for the best.

I have deliberately made this hand difficult. In real life, it is seldom so difficult. Here is a deal in which Charles Goren and his partner were able to solve the unblocking problem without difficulty.

In 1957, when he visited England, Goren joined with three British stars to play a Team-of-Four match against a Scottish team at Aberdeen, Scotland. When the British pair played the North and South hands, they reached a contract of five clubs and took eleven tricks.

None vul., dealer North.

```
                    NORTH
                    ♠ A
                    ♡ A K 9 7
                    ◇ A Q 9 8
                    ♣ K 8 5 3
     WEST                           EAST
     ♠ Q 8 7 6 5                    ♠ K 10 9 2
     ♡ J 4 2                        ♡ Q 10 6
     ◇ 7 6 4                        ◇ 10 3 2
     ♣ A 7                          ♣ J 10 4
                    SOUTH
                    ♠ J 4 3
                    ♡ 8 5 3
                    ◇ K J 5
                    ♣ Q 9 6 2
```

When the Scots played the hand, they bid to a contract of three notrump with South as declarer. Leslie Dodds led the six of spades, and when North won the trick with the ace, Goren played the ten-spot. This served the double purpose of unblocking the suit, and asking for the suit to be continued. The Rule of Eleven showed the wisdom of unblocking the suit. Of the five cards higher than the six, Goren could see one of them in the dummy and three in his own hand. This left just one for South. Looking for the missing cards, Goren could see that the only cards higher than the six outstanding were the Q-J-8-7. Of these cards, South had one, while West had three. No matter which of these four cards South held, unblocking was a no-lose play, while if South happened to hold the jack, it was necessary for Goren to unblock to bring in all of the defensive spade tricks. West soon got the lead with the ace of clubs, and the spade continuation brought the defenders an additional four tricks.

Had Goren failed to play the nine or ten on the first spade lead, the suit would have become blocked. When West got in with the ace of clubs, he would lead a spade to Goren's king, and when Goren led a third spade, South would have to play the jack, as that would be the only spade he had. The high spade would be left in the East hand and there would be no way to give West the lead again. Declarer could not get home with four diamond, one spade, two heart, and two club tricks.

Here is a hand in which one pair took two more tricks than the other by working out an unblocking play after a fourth-best lead signal return.

Both vul., dealer South.

```
                    NORTH
                    ♠ J 7 5
                    ♡ A 7 5
                    ◇ Q 10
                    ♣ A 9 6 3 2
        WEST                    EAST
        ♠ 8 6 3                 ♠ A 10 9 2
        ♡ 9 8 6 2               ♡ K 4
        ◇ A J 6 5 4             ◇ K 8 7 2
        ♣ 8                     ♣ 7 5 4
                    SOUTH
                    ♠ K Q 4
                    ♡ Q J 10 3
                    ◇ 9 3
                    ♣ K Q J 10
```

Table 1

SOUTH	WEST	NORTH	EAST
Wolff	Rubin	Hamman	Becker
1 ♡	Pass	2 ♣	Pass
2 NT	Pass	3 NT	All Pass

Table 2

Passell	Lazard	Brachman	Levitt
1 ♣	Pass	3 ♣	Pass
3 NT	All Pass		

This hand came up in the semi-finals of the Vanderbilt Cup Match in 1978. In both rooms, West led the five of diamonds, declarer played the queen from the dummy, and the first trick was won by East with the king. At this point, East knew, by the Rule of Eleven, that South had one diamond higher than the five-spot. The diamonds missing were the A-J-9-6. Of these four cards, South held one and West held three.

What were the chances of a blockage in view of the fact that East held the eight and seven? The queen and ten in the dummy, which had to be played on the first two tricks, indicated that the intermediate cards were going to be promoted very quickly. Between his hand and the dummy, East could see three of the six diamonds higher than the eight-spot, leaving three divided between South and West. East could choose between giving a false count by returning the eight, hoping the situation might be worked out, or he could give true count by leading the deuce, again hoping things could be worked out. In both cases, East returned the deuce, and West won with the jack.

Now came the parting of the ways. East had played the king followed by the deuce, and that indicated that he had started with an even number of cards. Obviously this was two or four. This is what many bridge players refer to as "the two-card difference" in signaling, and some of them claim that you can always work out which it is. Whether you can or not, Ron Rubin, at Table 1, did arrive at the correct decision. He saw that if he cashed the ace, the suit would become blocked. So he led the four of diamonds to the seven in his partner's hand, and then overtook the eight with his jack to cash a fifth diamond. On this trick, Mike Becker discarded the two of spades, so Rubin led a heart. Declarer had no choice but to duck, as that was his only chance to take more than six tricks, and East won with the king. Wolff won only six tricks after all, as Becker now cashed the ace of spades, and the defenders had won seven tricks before Wolff even gained the lead.

At Table 2, Sidney Lazard decided there was no way to tell whether his partner had started with two diamonds or with four, and so he cashed the jack of diamonds. East had to win the lead of the fourth diamond. There was no way West could regain the lead to cash his fifth diamond. So the defenders were limited to four diamond tricks plus the ace of spades, and Mike Passell got out for down one.

All in all, it looks like the return of the eight might have had the best chance to succeed, and that East, after viewing that dangerous dummy holding in the diamond suit, should have protected his partner by returning the eight. If West read that as a three-card suit, he would go ahead and cash his jack. Only if West read partner to hold a doubleton diamond would there be any question whether he should cash the jack or not. If East held a doubleton, then South held 9-7-3-2. From that holding, South would not be likely to play the three and then the nine. All of which goes to show that signals cannot always be as clear and precise as the textbooks would like to make us believe.

It may be difficult for the opening leader to work out the return of a ten, but don't think it's any easier for him to solve the puzzle of a return of the fourth-best when that interior sequence is held. Look at the tragedy which befell Billy Eisenberg and Ira Rubin in the 1972 Vanderbilt Team-of-Four match.

None vul., dealer South.

                        NORTH
                        ♠ A J 9 6 3 2
                        ♡ K 8 7 5
                        ◊ 5 2
                        ♣ 5
        WEST   EAST
        ♠ Q 10 5   ♠ 8 4
        ♡ 10 9 4   ♡ A 6 3 2
        ◊ 7 6   ◊ 4 3
        ♣ K Q 6 3 2   ♣ A 10 9 8 4
                        SOUTH
                        ♠ K 7
                        ♡ Q J
                        ◊ A K Q J 10 9 8
                        ♣ J 7

South opened the bidding with a gambling three notrump.
Eisenberg, West, led the three of clubs. Rubin won with the ace,
and either because he does not return the top of an interior sequence, or for some reason of his own, he returned the eight,
which was his original fourth-best. The jack was played by
South, Eisenberg won with the queen, and now faced his problem. As I pointed out earlier, the largest card which can be a
fourth-best is an eight, and frequently that card itself will be involved in a sequence. There were six cards higher than the eight,
and after South played the jack, Eisenberg has seen four of
them. The two missing were the nine and ten. Who had them?
Was it possible that South had opened a gambling three
notrump with a seven-card diamond suit and J-10-9-7 of clubs?
That may have been an unlikely holding, but it was not an impossible holding. So, fearing that Rubin had started with A-8-4
of clubs, Eisenberg switched to the queen of spades. The
declarer was not unhappy to see that switch.

Suppose your partner wins your opening lead with an ace or
king, when he started with a three-card holding with the ten as
his second-highest. When he leads back the ten, can you tell
whether he is unblocking from an interior sequence, or whether
he is leading the ten simply to show you that he does not have

four cards?

Usually you can. If you see the nine either in your hand or in the dummy, the answer is obvious. On the next hand, Victor Mitchell could not see the nine, but still came up with the right answer. The hand was played in the finals of the 1964 World Championship in the match between Italy and the United States.

E-W vul., dealer East.

```
                        NORTH
                        ♠ K J 10 8
                        ♡ A 10
                        ◇ 4
                        ♣ A K 10 9 6 5
        WEST                            EAST
        ♠ 9                             ♠ A 7 5 3 2
        ♡ Q 9 8 7 5                     ♡ K 4 3
        ◇ K J 8 7 3                     ◇ A 10 2
        ♣ J 7                           ♣ 8 2
                        SOUTH
                        ♠ Q 6 4
                        ♡ J 6 2
                        ◇ Q 9 6 5
                        ♣ Q 4 3
```

The bidding:

SOUTH	WEST	NORTH	EAST
Avarelli	Mitchell	Belladonna	Stayman
			Pass
Pass	Pass	1 ♠	Pass
1 NT	Pass	3 ♣	Pass
3 NT	All Pass		

Frequently, the Italians do very well bidding three notrump with long minor suits and considerably fewer than twenty-six HCPs. This time, they simply did not have the wherewithal. Victor Mitchell, West, led the seven of diamonds. Sam Stayman won the ace, South playing the five. Stayman returned the ten, and Avarelli played his queen. Mitchell won with the king. If Stayman had started with the nine, the suit was solid. If Stayman had started with A-10-x, Mitchell would give Avarelli a diamond trick if he continued the suit. Which was it?

The evidence seemed to indicate that Avarelli still had the guarded nine. The missing card was the two. Of course, Avarelli might have false-carded with something like Q-5-2. If Stayman had the two, he could hold A-10-9-2, or just A-10-2. However, Mitchell held only seven HCPs and it appeared the Italians were in one of those club notrump hands with considerably fewer than twenty-six HCPs. Mitchell, therefore, took the view that it didn't matter whether Stayman had the nine or not, as it was unlikely that Avarelli could run away with nine tricks. All he had to do was find an entry to Stayman's hand, and then it wouldn't make any difference who had the nine. Mitchell led the nine of spades to the ace, and when Stayman continued with the diamond two, the defenders had the first six tricks for a two-trick set.

Now let's look at a deal in which third hand wins the first trick, returns the smallest card possible, and opening leader has to decide whether he started with two or four cards in the suit.

Both vul., dealer South.

```
                    NORTH
                    ♠ J 5
                    ♡ K 8 7 5 2
                    ◇ Q J 10 8
                    ♣ A 9
      WEST                          EAST
      ♠ K 8 7                       ♠ 10 4 3 2
      ♡ Q 9 3                       ♡ A 10 6 4
      ◇ 7 4                         ◇ K 3 2
      ♣ 10 8 7 5 2                  ♣ K 3
                    SOUTH
                    ♠ A Q 9 6
                    ♡ J
                    ◇ A 9 6 5
                    ♣ Q J 6 4
```

The bidding:

SOUTH	WEST	NORTH	EAST
1 ◇	Pass	1 ♡	Pass
1 ♠	Pass	3 ◇	Pass
3 NT	All Pass		

This time, let's follow the reasoning from the West position, as it is he who is going to have to make the killing play. Holding only five HCPs, and the opponents arriving at three notrump, he knew his partner had something like nine HCPs. The opponents had bid every suit except clubs, so he hopefully led the five of clubs. Declarer played low from the dummy and East won the king and promptly returned the three of clubs.

Looking at the two in his hand, that return of the three of clubs had to be either from a doubleton or from a four-card suit. Could West tell which it was? This time the answer turns out to be easy. On the two club leads, South has played the four and six, and so every club from the two through the ten has been accounted for. If East started with four clubs, in addition to his king and three, he had to hold the queen and jack. If he had that holding, he would have won the first trick with the jack and then continued with the king.

Dummy won the ace and led the queen of diamonds, on which East gave his partner count, showing an odd number of diamonds by playing the two. Declarer then led the jack of diamonds and East completed the signal by playing the three. Unless East had decided not to signal on this hand, he still had a diamond left and it looked like it was probably the king. It was not surprising that South held four diamonds. He certainly would not have opened one diamond with only a three-card suit when holding four clubs.

So West had a pretty good idea about South's holding in the minor suits. And now he remembered that South had bid spades. It sounded like he had four spades as well as four diamonds and four clubs. If that was his distribution, any mystery about the number of hearts he held was dissipated. After winning two diamonds in the dummy, declarer led the jack of spades and let it ride. West won with the king, and now he knew what to do. If the one heart South held was the ace, then it made no difference which heart he led, as his partner had the jack and ten. If the one card South held was a small one, then the defenders could gather in quite a few heart tricks, provided West led specifically the queen so that he could retain the lead. If the one heart South held was either the jack or the ten, then the queen lead was necessary to pin that card, but in that event, the defense would still get three heart tricks to add to the two tricks they had won with the black kings. So with nothing to lose, West led the queen of hearts. The declarer could not avoid losing three heart tricks.

On the next hand, inadequate attention to the fourth-best signal let Sam Stayman confuse the issue and steal a hand from Eric Murray and Sammy Kehela.

E-W vul., dealer South.

```
                    NORTH
                    ♠ 9
                    ♡ 7 6 4 3 2
                    ◊ A 10 7 5 3
                    ♣ A J
        WEST                        EAST
        ♠ 8 7 4 3                   ♠ A 10 6 5 2
        ♡ K J 8                     ♡ A 9 5
        ◊ J 6 4                     ◊ K 9 2
        ♣ Q 10 6                    ♣ 4 3
                    SOUTH
                    ♠ K Q J
                    ♡ Q 10
                    ◊ Q 8
                    ♣ K 9 8 7 5 2
```

The bidding:

SOUTH	WEST	NORTH	EAST
Stayman	Murray	Mitchell	Kehela
1 ♣	Pass	1 ♡	1 ♠
Pass	2 ♣	3 ◊	Pass
3 NT	Pass	Pass	Pass

In 1965, there was a match between four players representing traditional styles, and four players representing modern styles, who were scientific players. Each team was trying to prove that its bidding methods were better than the other. For most of the match, the traditionalists led, but right at the finish, the scientists surged ahead and won the match. On examining the hands, we find that bidding had very little to do with the results. The results were largely determined by dummy play and by defense. This hand contributed to the victory of the modern, or scientific, team.

Murray led the three of spades, Kehela played his ace, and Stayman dropped the queen. At this point, an alert East would have known that that queen was not the smallest spade South held. Just the fourth-best signal without bothering about the complications of the Rule of Eleven was enough to tell him that. Murray had raised spades, and obviously his three-spot was not a singleton. Neither could it be a five-card suit, as Kehela held the two in his own hand. If it was a fourth-best, then simply counting the thirteen spades in the deck told him that Stayman held three spades. I don't know whether Murray leads low from three small, but if he does after he has supported a suit, then Stayman could have started with four spades.

Kehela led back his original fourth-best spade, the five. Stayman won with the king. At this point, an alert West would also know that Stayman was not out of spades. If the five was Kehela's fourth-best, and Murray has the four and three, then Kehela could not have more than five spades. Again, simply counting up to thirteen and looking at the dummy and his own hand would tell Murray that Stayman had started with at least three spades. Probably the exact number was three, as Kehela would need a five-card suit to overcall.

What was the third spade Stayman held? It didn't seem likely that he held anything like the K-Q-2, and had deliberately thrown away a trick after Kehela won with the ace. About the only explanation was that Stayman still held the jack. What was he trying to do? It should have been obvious to both players that he was trying to get the defenders to continue spades. And why would he want that done? Could it have to do with entries into his hand?

Stayman's chances didn't look good, but he definitely made

the best of them. He led a small club and finessed dummy's jack. The finesse worked. Next, he laid down the ace of clubs, and when both followed, his remaining problem was how to get back to his hand to cash four good club tricks. Technically, about his only chance was to lead a diamond and find the king in Kehela's hand. The trouble with that procedure was that, whoever won the diamond trick, the defenders would almost be forced into tackling hearts to get whatever tricks there were in that suit. So Stayman decided to cloud the issue a bit further. Acting like a man holding some important hearts, he led a small heart from the dummy and, when East played low, he played his queen. Murray won, and had he played a diamond, the defenders could have taken a total of one diamond, one spade, and three heart tricks. But, after winning a heart trick, Murray continued the spades. There was that entry Stayman wanted! He now had six club tricks, two spade tricks, and the ace of diamonds for his contract.

It was a long match, and I suspect all of the players were affected by fatigue, that terrible enemy of bridge players. It can get to even the sturdiest man. Murray and Kehela had not played their usual sharp game on this deal. I might add that playing against this pair for stakes would be a poor way to try to get rich.

To help overcome weariness, I urge all of my pupils to look for my energy-saving devices. As far as reading the fourth-best signal is concerned, this says that you first see "how many", and then look for "which ones" only when it is necessary.

Before I finish this section, I must remind you that the fourth-best signal, like all other signals, is plagued by the fact that it sometimes helps the declarer more than it helps the defenders. The next hand is an example.

E-W vul., dealer North.

NORTH
♠ K 8
♡ 7 3
♢ A 10 9 6 2
♣ A Q 9 7

WEST
♠ 9 7 6 3
♡ K 9 5
♢ 3
♣ K J 8 6 4

EAST
♠ 10 5 2
♡ A Q J 10
♢ K 8 7 5 4
♣ 2

SOUTH
♠ A Q J 4
♡ 8 6 4 2
♢ Q J
♣ 10 5 3

The bidding:

SOUTH	WEST	NORTH	EAST
		1 ♢	Pass
1 ♡	Pass	2 ♣	Pass
2 NT	Pass	3 NT	Pass
Pass	Pass		

Opening lead: ♣6

Had West led a heart or a spade, declarer would surely have taken the diamond finesse. East would have won the king of diamonds, and quickly cashed four heart tricks to beat 3 NT clubs. This time, neither the fourth-best rule nor the Rule of Eleven did East a bit of good, but it was a bonanza for the declarer. The Rule of Eleven told him that if this was a fourth-best lead, East had no club higher than the six. Therefore, declarer played a low club from dummy, overtook the seven with his ten, and led another club to dummy's nine. Eventually he took four clubs, four spades, and the ace of diamonds. Things like this will happen from time to time, but in the long run, the fourth-best signal will be helpful to the defenders much more often than it will help the declarer. Unfortunately, the defenders seldom have a way to judge when the signal will help the declarer more than themselves on opening lead. However, they might be able to judge this after they have had a look at the dummy and several tricks have been played. Take a look at this hand, which was played in the 1977 Grand National Team of Four. Only an additional undertrick was involved, but the hand does illustrate the principle very clearly. And it turned out that one trick made a tremendous difference.

E-W vul., dealer West.

```
                    NORTH
                    ♠ A 8 2
                    ♡ 9 7 3
                    ◇ Q 5 4
                    ♣ K 8 7 6
        WEST                    EAST
        ♠ K 4                   ♠ 10 9 6
        ♡ K 10 4                ♡ J 8 6 5
        ◇ K 10 7 3              ◇ A 6 2
        ♣ J 10 9 3              ♣ A Q 5
                    SOUTH
                    ♠ Q J 7 5 3
                    ♡ A Q 2
                    ◇ J 9 8
                    ♣ 4 2
```

The bidding:

SOUTH	WEST	NORTH	EAST
Smith	Lipsitz	Wold	Parker
	Pass	Pass	1 ♣
1 ♠	2 ♣	2 ♠	All Pass

The 1977 Grand Nationals started with 7,970 teams from all over the North American continent vying for the championship. After months of play, it had come down to a team from the Washington, D.C., area against a Texas team. The finish was one of the closest on record.

Eddie Wold and Curtis Smith had the North and South hands for Texas. Bob Lipsitz and Steve Parker had the East and West hands for the District of Columbia and Virginia team. At first glance, it looked like Smith must be set two tricks in his two-spade contract. He should lose a trump trick, and two tricks in each of the other three suits. However, due to some mix-up in signaling, Smith went set only one trick. Had the defenders taken all seven of their tricks, the match of sixty-four boards would have ended in a dead tie, instead of ending with the Texas team one international matchpoint ahead.

Here is how it went. West led the jack of clubs and continued with a small club. After winning the queen of clubs, East switched to a heart.

Looking at the dummy, a heart lead was called for. The question is, which heart? Had East been leading a heart on opening lead, there is no doubt he should lead the five. But having seen trick one and the dummy, East could make a more informed decision than he could on opening lead. In this situation, you lead a small card to suggest to your partner that he return the suit, and you lead a high card when you don't want him to return the suit. When you simply want to tell him how many cards you have in this suit, and not what you want him to do, you lead fourth-best. Had East been underleading a king or a queen, he would have led the five. As he was underleading a jack, the eight would have made it perfectly clear he did not care to have the suit returned. West would have had no trouble deciding that the eight was not fourth-best. Between his hand and the dummy, he was looking at three of the six hearts which are higher than the eight-spot, and if East was leading fourth-best, he would have to hold the other three. Therefore, the eight could only be fourth-best if East held A-Q-J-8. With that holding, he would hardly be leading low. I must tell you, however, that East led neither the five nor the eight, but the six. Just what form of signaling they were using where the six was the proper lead, I do not know; possibly it was Journalist, where you lead third-highest from a four-card suit against a suit contract. Whatever it was, it did not work. Smith played the two from his hand and Lipsitz won with the ten. Apparently he felt that a heart return was safe, for he led back the king right into the arms of the ace and queen. There went one of the defenders' heart tricks.

Had East led the eight, West almost certainly would have

switched to a diamond, and the defenders would have gotten their seven tricks for a two-trick set. As it was, they only took six of these tricks for a one-trick set. This overtrick represented the entire margin of victory for the Texans.

LEADING FROM A SHORT SUIT

Whenever you have only one or two cards in a suit, it is a short suit. If you decide to lead a suit in which you hold one card, there is no problem about choosing "which card" to lead. Really, there isn't much problem when you hold two cards. The standard accepted lead is always to lead the higher card of a two-card suit, no matter what it is, and no matter whether it does or doesn't have a sequence. If your partner leads the ace and then the king against a trump contract, he is telling you he has no more and that if you can gain the lead, he can trump whatever card you may lead in that suit.

Leading minor honor card doubletons, such as Qx or Jx, in a suit your partner has not bid, is not likely to pay you dividends except in those rare cases where the bidding by the opponents simply screams for the lead of that suit. This lead should seldom be made as an opening lead. There are times later in the play when it becomes apparant that a suit where the holding is Qx or Jx is called for. At times, it may be desirable to make the deceptive lead of low from Qx. We will discuss those situations when we get to the subject of deceptive leads. Right now, let's stick to the standard lead of two-card suits. If your partner's lead is from a short suit, when he plays the six and then the two, he is out of the suit. With 6-4-2, his second play would be the four.

Opening Leads With A Three-Card Holding

In the suit which you have decided to lead, you hold the 7-5-2. Do you lead the deuce to indicate to your partner that you have four or more cards in the suit, or do you lead the seven and indicate to your partner that you are short in the suit? Standard procedure is to lead the seven to tell your partner you have no desire to have that suit continued if he gains the lead. After you have led the seven, the next time you play a card from that suit, you must be careful to play the five-spot and not the two. Should you play the two the second time, your partner will assume you are out. If you lead the seven and later on play the five, your partner may be able to work it out that the missing two is in your hand, and that you have led from a three-card suit. This lead from the highest of three spot cards is generally called "the top of nothing".

How about a lead from a three-card suit which holds one or more honors? First, let's consider the ace with two small cards. If you are going to lead from this combination against a NT contract, it usually will be right to lead the small card. The chances are that when you lead from this combination against NT, you do so because your partner has bid the suit. The player to your right is obviously the NT bidder or you would not be on lead. And, he has advertised that he has some high cards in the suit your partner bid. Your low lead is calculated to keep a high card in back of whatever high cards the declarer holds.

However, there are times when the evidence calls for a lead from this combination, even though your partner has not bid it. Let's see just what evidence Jim Jacoby picked up from the bidding on the hand which enabled him to make the devastating lead of a small spade:

N-S vul., dealer North.

```
                    NORTH
                    Barros
                    ♠ Q 9 8 7
                    ♡ 2
                    ◇ A 5 4
                    ♣ A K J 6 5
        WEST                        EAST
        Jacoby                      Wolff
        ♠ A 4 2                     ♠ K J 10 5 3
        ♡ J 7 6 3                   ♡ K 8
        ◇ 6 3 2                     ◇ J 10 9 8
        ♣ 10 8 3                    ♣ Q 4
                    SOUTH
                    Ferreir
                    ♠ 6
                    ♡ A Q 10 9 5 4
                    ◇ K Q 7
                    ♣ 9 7 2
```

The bidding:

NORTH	EAST	SOUTH	WEST
1 ♠	Pass	2 ♡	Pass
3 ♣	Pass	3 NT	Pass
Pass	Pass		

This hand was played by North America against Brazil in the Round Robin of the 1970 World Championship.

The Brazilian players were using a canape style of bidding where the second suit bid is longer than the first. This alerted Jim Jacoby that North's club suit was longer than his spade suit. Jacoby was well-acquainted with this style of bidding, as he and Wolff often used the canape principle themselves. He also knew that the first suit bid could be a very weak four-card major.

On the sequence of bidding, the defenders were entitled to have about fourteen high-card points, plus or minus one or two. With only five points in his own hand, Jacoby knew that Wolff had some good cards somewhere. The question was, where was his long suit? The bidding indicated that it was not in hearts—South holding length in that suit—nor was it in clubs where North held length. While you might be happy to lead through dummy's strength, it usually a pretty good idea to stay as far away as possible from dummy's length, especially when defending against a notrump contract. Knowing that the dummy probably was going to have presicely four spades, Jacoby knew that there would be six spades divided between the East and South hands. He decided to try to establish the spade tricks where he had a high card to help, rather than diamond tricks where he had zilch.

Bobby Wolff won the first spade trick with the ten, and had no trouble determining the true situation. Surely Jacoby had not led a singleton spade, and even had he done so, South would have started with three to the ace and would have had no reason to refuse the first trick. Wolff led back the five to Jacoby's ace and the next spade lead, by Jacoby, gave the defenders the first five tricks. Bobby Wolff, in the East, then decided to have his bit of fun. He led the eight of hearts and put declarer to the test. South decided that the club finesse would give him the balance of the tricks, so he rose with the ace of hearts and cashed the ace of clubs. He then returned to his hand with a diamond, led a second club and took the finesse. Wolff took the queen of clubs and the king of hearts and the hand was set three tricks.

In the room where the Americans had the North and South hands, Bob Goldman, North, played 3 NT. He took nine tricks.

How about these opening leads from the ace and two small against a suit contract? If the suit is trumps, the lead of a small one frequently will work out quite well. But, if it is a side suit, and you decide to lead the suit, I recommend that you lay down the ace. This may not be the greatest lead in the world for, as the old saying goes, aces were meant to catch kings and queens, and the opponents are likely to put their twos and threes on aces when you lead them. However, leading the ace works out well more often than underleading it. Yes, I know there are times when underleading an ace will be a killing play. You may catch your partner with a doubleton king and be able to give him a quick ruff. You may even run into the following situation:

```
                    DUMMY
                    K x
    WEST                        EAST
    A x x x                     Q x x x
                    SOUTH
                    J x x
```

Declarer, after the lead of your small card, will decide you surely could not have underled the ace. He will duck in dummy, hoping you have underled the queen, and your partner's queen will win. You win two tricks where declarer would almost surely have led small from his hand and played the king, had you left him to his own devices. You might even find your partner with a doubleton queen, in which event he will win the first trick with the queen, you win the second with the ace, and then he will win the third by ruffing. The trouble with all of these brilliances is that you cannot know when to make them until after the opening lead. I am not saying "don't underlead aces against suit contracts." I am saying "don't underlead them on *opening* lead." For every time you gain a trick by doing so, you probably will lose two and even three. It is uncanny how often you will lose that trick because the declarer to your right happened to have the singleton king of your suit. Yes, I also know that sometimes the leading experts do underlead aces against suit contracts, as the best of a bad lot of opening leads. Generally, they do this not as an attacking move, but as a passive move, hoping that it will do no harm and that it may enable them to get a look at the dummy while keeping control of the suit.

Here is one where Ira Rubin underled his aces, not once, but twice. The underlead of the ace on opening lead did no harm, but the second underlead, after he had a chance to count out the hand, brought in an extra defensive trick. However, I must warn you that Ira Rubin has the reputation of finding the right time to do the right thing. He has an uncanny ability to make the anti-percentage bid or play when the odds are going to fail, but the bid or play is going to succeed. On this hand, he lived up to his reputation.

E-W vul., dealer East.

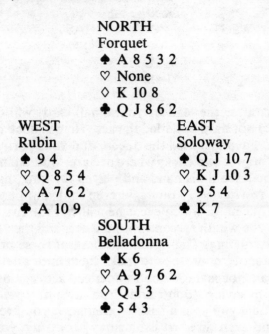

NORTH
Forquet
♠ A 8 5 3 2
♡ None
◇ K 10 8
♣ Q J 8 6 2

WEST
Rubin
♠ 9 4
♡ Q 8 5 4
◇ A 7 6 2
♣ A 10 9

EAST
Soloway
♠ Q J 10 7
♡ K J 10 3
◇ 9 5 4
♣ K 7

SOUTH
Belladonna
♠ K 6
♡ A 9 7 6 2
◇ Q J 3
♣ 5 4 3

The bidding:

EAST	SOUTH	WEST	NORTH
Pass	Pass	Pass	1 ♠
Pass	2 ♡	Pass	Pass
Pass			

This hand was played in the finals of the 1976 Bermuda Bowl
World Championship. The Italians were playing the Precision
Club, so Forquet, North, was unable to open the bidding with
one club, as that bid was reserved for a hand with sixteen or
more HCPs. Holding the spade suit and an average hand in high
cards, Forquet thought he might have a good chance for a part
score. When Belladonna responded two hearts, he saw it would
be easy to get in trouble. He decided to pass before he got into
deeper water.

Now put yourself in Rubin's seat. Despite all of the hands we
writers and teachers give you with nice opening leads, the dealer
frequently gives you hands with horrible choices in all four

suits. Leading dummy's five-card suit is not often a paying proposition, nor is leading from the queen of trumps. That left the
two minor suits. Rubin led the two of diamonds. At least, that
left him in control of the suit. Belladonna won with the queen
and promptly led a small diamond back. As Soloway might
have the jack, Rubin ducked, and the picture was clear when
dummy's ten-spot won the trick. Belladonna now led a spade to
his king and a spade to dummy's ace. He led a third spade to
ruff it and the roof showed signs of caving in. Rubin overtrumped. In the meantime, he had learned a good bit about the
hand. He was looking at ten HCPs in his own hand and another
ten in the dummy. Belladonna had passed once and then
responded two hearts, so it sounded as though he had ten or
eleven points. Presto—Soloway also had either an average hand
or close to it. Where were his points? He was known to have
three HCPs in spades and none in diamonds. At least six or
seven points had to be in hearts and clubs. The only high card
missing in clubs was the king. Rubin could almost see that card
in Soloway's hand. The question was, how many clubs did
Soloway hold? Rubin was looking at eight clubs in his hand and
the dummy, leaving a 3-2 split likely. If Soloway has three, a
club lead would be harmless. But if he had only a doubleton
king, then Rubin had a fine chance to pick up a trick by
underleading his ace of clubs. He struck gold when Soloway
won the king, returned a club to Rubin's ace, and ruffed on the
third club. Now, to apply the axe, Soloway led his last spade.
Once more, Rubin overruffed declarer, cashed the ace of
diamonds, and led a diamond for Soloway to apply an upper-
cut.

Whether Belladonna could have played differently to save a
trick or two didn't make any difference at this stage. The
recorded score was that he won two spades, two diamonds, and
only one trump trick, going down three.

Another trouble about underleading aces on opening leads
against suit contracts is that your partner just won't believe that
you did it. If you make the lead to fool somebody, you may well
succeed—but your partner may be the victim. Look at what
happened to two of the world's greatest players in the semi-
finals of the 1975 World Championship when the famous
Italians played the Indonesians:

NORTH
- ♠ J 7 5
- ♡ K Q 9
- ◊ A K J 2
- ♣ Q 7 5

WEST
Garozzo
- ♠ A 6 3
- ♡ 8 5
- ◊ 10 9 5
- ♣ A 8 6 4 3

EAST
Belladonna
- ♠ K 10 4 2
- ♡ J 7 2
- ◊ 8 4 3
- ♣ K 9 2

SOUTH
- ♠ Q 9 8
- ♡ A 10 6 4 3
- ◊ Q 7 6
- ♣ J 10

It's easy to see that four tricks are there for the taking, against a four-heart contract. However, the great Italian pair of Garozzo and Belladonna managed to take only three. For his opening lead, Garozzo led the three of spades. Just what he had in mind, I do not know, but if he hoped to fool someone, he did. He fooled Belladonna. On the small spade from the dummy, Belladonna played his ten. The Indonesian declarer gratefully won with the queen, and took nine tricks in the two red suits before relinquishing the lead. If a pair whom many consider the greatest in the world are unable to successfully lead aces on open leads against suit contracts, I suggest you and I give it up and look for other ways to take tricks.

How about the A-Q-x? When the bidding indicates that the lead should be from a suit where you have this holding, which card to you lead? When the suit is trumps, the lead of the ace has a lot going for it. However, we are now talking about leads of suits which are not trumps. In the textbooks, there will be long tables telling you what to lead from most combinations, but this one is absent from most such tables. I suppose the theory is that you simply do not lead from this holding. Not so. There are times when the bidding indicates that you need to lead from a suit where you hold precisely these cards.

There are a few books which recognize the fact that you may

need to lead from such a suit. They will tell you that if you are leading against a suit contract, you should lead the ace. But when it comes to leading against a NT contract, most will tell you to lead the queen. I have looked long and hard to find a case where the defenders scored a triumph by making this lead, but I have been unable to find one. I did find a hand where the lead was made, but I can't exactly call it a triumph. Here it is:

None vul., dealer West.

<pre>
                    NORTH
                    ♠ J 8 6
                    ♡ 9 4
                    ◇ A J 10 8 7 3
                    ♣ 9 5
      WEST   EAST
      ♠ A Q 4   ♠ 10 9 7 2
      ♡ A 10 7   ♡ J 8 6 5 2
      ◇ 9 5   ◇ Q 4
      ♣ K J 7 4 2   ♣ 6 3
                    SOUTH
                    ♠ K 5 3
                    ♡ K Q 3
                    ◇ K 6 2
                    ♣ A Q 10 8
</pre>

The bidding:

WEST	NORTH	EAST	SOUTH
Schenken	Delmouly	Sobel	Bourchtoff
1 ♣	2 ◇	Pass	3 NT
Pass	Pass	Pass	

The hand was played in the 1960 World Championship, where the Americans played against the French. Howard Schenken, on the American Team, was playing in the closed room, and his opening lead was the queen of spades. No other lead would have permitted the declarer to take two spade tricks by force. This lead, of course, gave the declarer an easy time of it. He won the king, led the king of diamonds, and finessed a diamond. Helen Sobel, East, won with the queen and shifted to a small heart. When declarer put up the queen, Schenken won the ace and returned the ten of hearts. Declarer won the king and cashed four diamond tricks. Schenken had to make four discards. He discarded two clubs, a heart, and a spade. The four cards he had remaining were the ace of spades and three clubs. South kept two spades and two clubs. Bourchtoff, the declarer, decided it was time to go after his second spade trick. He led a spade, and when Schenken won with the ace, he had nothing left to lead but clubs. This gave declarer two club tricks plus the jack of spades. He took a total of ten tricks.

In the open room, the American, Paul Allinger, North, over-called only one diamond. Lew Mathe, South, jumped to 3NT. Pierre Jais, West, led the dull, unimaginative, and successful fourth-best club. Maybe he was working on the theory that if they are good enough to bid they are good enough to lead. This lead gave Mathe two club tricks, but he took only eight tricks in all. Dummy's nine won the first trick. Mathe also took the king of diamonds and finessed dummy's ten-spot. East won and con-tinued clubs. Mathe played the queen. West won the king and switched to a small heart. Easy played the jack and Mathe won the queen. He now cashed his four diamonds, discarding two spades and a club from his hand. West discarded three clubs and a spade. Finally, Mathe led the king of spades. Instead of winning two spade tricks, as the French declarer had done in the closed room, he won no spade tricks at all. West won his two spade tricks and the ace of hearts. The defenders took two spades, and one trick in each of the other suits, to beat the con-tract.

I did find two additional hands from World Championships where the defenders decided to lead from a three-card suit head-ed by the ace and queen against 3NT. In neither instance did they lead the queen. The first was played way back in 1953 be-tween the American and the Swedish teams.

N-S vul., dealer West.

```
                    NORTH
                    ♠ K Q J 9 8
                    ♡ K 9 8
                    ◇ A J 6 3
                    ♣ J
     WEST                          EAST
     ♠ 10 6 3                      ♠ A 7 2
     ♡ A Q 4                       ♡ 10 7 6 2
     ◇ 9 4 2                       ◇ 7
     ♣ K 10 7 5                    ♣ Q 9 8 6 4
                    SOUTH
                    ♠ 5 4
                    ♡ J 5 3
                    ◇ K Q 10 8 5
                    ♣ A 3 2
```

The bidding:

CLOSED ROOM

WEST	NORTH	EAST	SOUTH
Lilliehook	Crawford	Anulf	Rapee
Pass	1 ♠	Pass	2 ◇
Pass	3 ◇	Pass	3 NT
Pass			

OPEN ROOM

WEST	NORTH	EAST	SOUTH
Stayman	Wohlin	Becker	Larsen
Pass	1 ♠	Pass	2 ◇
Pass	3 ◇	Pass	3 ♡
Pass	3 ♠	Pass	3 NT
Pass	Pass	Pass	

In the closed room, the opponents had bid spades and diamonds and it would seem that Lilliehook had only hearts and clubs to consider for his opening lead. He decided that the weakish four-card minor suit was not as attractive a lead as the unbid major. He led the heart ace. Looking at the dummy and his hand, it was not difficult for Anulf to decide that this was not one of those situations where his partner had some six-card suit and wanted him to play the highest card he had. Were that true, South would have had no hearts at all, as Anulf and the dummy had seven between them. He indicated his lack of interest in the heart suit by playing the two. After seeing the dummy, Lilliehook changed his mind about the desirability of club leads. He led the five of clubs. Dummy's jack was covered by the queen, but Rapee held up his ace until the third lead of the suit. In the meantime, West had unblocked by getting the king and ten out of his hand. Rapee now had a total of only seven tricks without relinquishing the lead to the opponents, but he cashed five diamonds to see if he could get any favorable discards. East was under some pressure and finally did discard one club. He still had a club left to defeat the contract when Rapee led a spade.

I shudder to think what would have happened if Lilliehook had started proceedings by leading the queen of hearts. Declarer could have won with dummy's king and immediately established spades. Now declarer would take eleven tricks.

In the open room, Stayman also found the lead of the ace of hearts in spite of the fact that Larsen had bid hearts during the auction. When Becker played the two-spot, Stayman also switched to clubs and took all doubt out of the matter by leading the king. Larsen, South, also held up until the third club lead, but immediately led a spade before he ran his diamonds. This enabled the defenders to take all four of their club tricks and, with the two major suit aces, they set the hand two tricks.

For the next hand, we have to skip all the way up to 1976. This time it is North America versus Italy.

Both vul., dealer East.

```
                    NORTH
                    ♠ K
                    ♡ Q J 9 5
                    ◇ A Q J 10 7
                    ♣ K 4 3
    WEST                            EAST
    ♠ J 9 8 7 4                     ♠ A Q 6
    ♡ 8 4 2                         ♡ K 10 6 3
    ◇ K 6 2                         ◇ 9 8 5 4
    ♣ Q 9                           ♣ 8 6
                    SOUTH
                    ♠ 10 5 3 2
                    ♡ A 7
                    ◇ 3
                    ♣ A J 10 7 5 2
```

The bidding:

CLOSED ROOM

EAST	SOUTH	WEST	NORTH
Hamilton	Vivaldi	Eisenberg	Pittala
Pass	Pass	Pass	1 ◇
Pass	1 ♠	Pass	2 ♡
Pass	2 NT	Pass	3 NT
Pass	Pass	Pass	

OPEN ROOM

Franco	Soloway	Garozzo	Rubin
Pass	Pass	Pass	1 ♡
Pass	2 ♣	Pass	2 ◇
Pass	2 ♠	Pass	3 NT
Pass	Pass	Pass	

In the closed room, Eisenberg decided to lead the seven of spades, and it was fortunate that he led that suit. Had Vivaldi, South, been able to get the lead, he would have had six clubs, the two red aces and, with both red kings favorably placed for him, would have had no trouble picking up a ninth trick. However, Hamilton won the first trick with the ace, continued with the queen and a small spade, so the defenders took the first five tricks. Vivaldi had a lot of trouble finding good discards from the dummy and actually ended up going set two tricks.

In the open room, East was on lead. The bidding here made it even clearer than in the closed room that a spade lead was the best chance. After some thought, Franco laid down the ace. Maybe those books saying the queen should be led from this combination have not been translated into Italian. You can see that had he led any other card in his hand, Rubin would have had no trouble taking nine tricks. Actually, the defenders took only the first five tricks, but that was enough to set the hand.

So in the hands that I have discovered, the score is three to nothing in favor of leading the ace from this combination rather than the queen. Yes, I can construct the hand where the queen would be the killing lead, but apparently the dealers have trouble dealing such a hand. I am going to go along with leading the ace from A-Q-x against a notrump contract.

This brings us to a three-card suit headed by the king and without a sequence. Almost any textbook you read will tell you that with this holding you lead the small card, and they will not admit any exceptions. You are told to expect a setup like the following:

$$
\begin{array}{ccc}
 & 6\ 3 & \\
\text{K 4 2} & & \text{A J 10 9 8} \\
 & \text{Q 7 5} & \\
\end{array}
$$

More often than not, when you are leading from this holding, it is because your partner has bid the suit. It is certainly true that your best shot is to lead the small card when it is your right-hand opponent who has shown strength in the suit. The idea is to keep your high cards back of declarer's high cards to that you can play after the strong opposing hand has played. In my files of hands, I find this illustration:

None vul., dealer East.

```
                    NORTH
                    ♠ 7
                    ♡ A Q 5
                    ◇ Q 10 9 6 2
                    ♣ 10 9 4 2
        WEST                    EAST
        ♠ K 8 2                 ♠ Q J 9 6 5
        ♡ 8 7 4 3 2             ♡ J 9 6
        ◇ 5                     ◇ A 7 4
        ♣ 8 7 6 3              ♣ A J
                    SOUTH
                    ♠ A 10 4 3
                    ♡ K 10
                    ◇ K J 8 3
                    ♣ K Q 5
```

The bidding:

EAST	SOUTH	WEST	NORTH
1 ♠	1 NT	Pass	2 NT
Pass	3 NT	Pass	Pass
Pass			

This hand was played in a matchpoint duplicate game. Very few of the North-South players found the five-diamond contract. Generally, the bidding went as shown.

When the only card in your hand worth having led up to is the king of your partner's suit, it will sometimes prove better to lead that king instead of a small one for two reasons. You hope your king will hold the lead and let you have a look at the dummy before deciding how to proceed. In addition, if your partner has too many high cards, you may have him end-played at trick two if you lead small and give him the lead. This is not one of those hands. You have two cards which you would like to have led up to. The king of spades is one of them and the eight is the other. Those spot cards can be very important.

A few players did, in fact, lead the king of spades, and the declarer had no trouble taking nine tricks. Declarer won the ace and promptly established diamonds. If East cashed his two high spades, he would establish one for declarer, and that would give declarer two spade, three heart, and four diamond tricks. Declarer could find no way to take nine tricks against defenders who started with the two of spades. This held him to only one spade trick no matter how he played. Adding the spade trick to seven tricks in the red suits gave him a total of only eight. When he tried to establish a ninth trick in clubs, the defenders could cash enough tricks to set him.

Most of the textbooks admit no exceptions. They simply tell you that when you have three to the king, the opening lead should be the small one. They must be written for teachers who are trying to tell beginners how to play bridge by rote, rather than by thinking. The publishers should recall all of these books. They have a serious flaw. There are many exceptions in a variety of situations. Here is an example from the qualification rounds of the 1976 World Olympiad:

```
                       NORTH
                       ♠ J 5 4 2
                       ♡ K 2
                       ◇ K 8 5 2
                       ♣ 10 9 2
          WEST                        EAST
          ♠ K 9 6                     ♠ A 10 8 7 3
          ♡ Q 8 7 6 3                 ♡ 10 9
          ◇ Q 6 4 3                   ◇ 9 7
          ♣ 3                         ♣ J 6 5 4
                       SOUTH
                       ♠ Q
                       ♡ A J 5 4
                       ◇ A J 10
                       ♣ A K Q 8 7
```

In the qualifying round, all boards were duplicated and each hand was played 44 times by the 45 teams who had entered the event (one team having a bye each round). When North and South reached 3NT played by North, East usually opened a small spade, and the defenders proceeded to cash the first five tricks. However, 3NT was played by South at 11 tables. At ten of these tables, the contracts were made. In the Poland versus Greece match, the Polish player in the East seat got in an over-call of one spade, and the bidding made it crystal-clear that the outstanding spade length was in the North hand. Julian Klukowski, called by the 1976 World Championship Book, "...a veteran performer...", took that fact into account in choosing his opening lead. Here is the way the bidding went:

WEST	NORTH	EAST	SOUTH
		Pass	1 ♣
Pass	1 ◊	1 ♠	2 ♡
2 ♠	Double	Pass	3 NT
Pass	Pass	Pass	

One of the reasons for ignoring the "rule" (lead low from three to the king), is the knowledge that the opponents' chief length in the suit is on your left, so that your partner's strength in that suit is over the strength held by the opponents. Thanks to his partner's bid of one spade and North's double of his two-spade raise, Klukowski had no trouble placing the chief length the opponents held in that suit. He led the king of spades and was the only successful defender of 3NT where the lead had to come from West.

While the old saying, "You should lead an ace so you can see the dummy" has been discredited, it still may be true more often than we like to think. Even more frequently, it would prove wise to lead the king of the suit your partner bid so that you can see the dummy. That is exactly what Ira Rubin did on the next hand, which is from the 1977 World Championship:

E-W vul., dealer West.

NORTH
♠ 10 8 6 5
♡ K Q 6 2
◇ 10 9 7 6
♣ 8

WEST
♠ K J 2
♡ A J 10 9 8 3
◇ K
♣ 6 3 2

EAST
♠ A 9 7 4 3
♡ None
◇ Q J 5 3 2
♣ Q J 10

SOUTH
♠ Q
♡ 7 5 4
◇ A 8 4
♣ A K 9 7 5 4

The bidding:

WEST	NORTH	EAST	SOUTH
		Von Der	
Rubin	Swanson	Porten	Soloway
1 ♡	Pass	1 ♠	3 ♣
Pass	Pass	Double	Pass
Pass	Pass		

In the closed room, Bobby Wolff, East, had struggled mightily with a contract of four spades doubled. The defense won the first three tricks by taking the ace and king of clubs and trumping a club, but from there on, Wolff never got his hand on the wrong card and managed to escape for down one.

Ira Rubin and Ron Von Der Porten got more mileage out of the hand when Paul Soloway, holding the South hand, made a jump overcall of three clubs. It is not clear from reading an account of the bidding methods they used just what this three-club bid meant, but I presume the three players at the table knew what it meant. At any rate, Rubin and Von Der Porten knew what to do about it. Rubin refused to rebid his six-card suit with a minimum hand and Von Der Porten's double ended the bidding.

Let's see if we can justify Rubin's lead of the king of spades rather than the small one. It would be rare for a good player to jump to three clubs when he held spade length over a spade bid to his right. If this three-club bid said anything at all about Soloway's spade holding, it said he didn't have many of them. This indicated that any length held by the opponents was probably held by North. Rubin's lead of the king also enabled him to retain the lead and get a good look at the dummy before proceeding with the defense.

Von Der Porten followed with the three of spades. According to the system of signaling they were using, this indicated to his partner that he had an odd number of cards in the suit and made Soloway look like an honest man when he played the queen. To justify his double of three clubs, Von Der Porten had to have something other than the ace five times of spades and a few clubs, so Rubin tried the king of diamonds. Von Der Porten played the two-spot on that, again showing that he had an odd number of diamonds. If that odd number was only three diamonds, then Soloway would have had five, and probably would have jumped to 2NT to show length in both minor suits. Soloway could have saved some tricks by taking the king of diamonds with his ace and leading the ace, king and a small club. However, the situation was far from clear, especially concerning the distribution of the opposing clubs and he let the king of diamonds hold the trick.

If Von Der Porten had five spades and five diamonds, he was unlikely to have many hearts. Rubin, therefore, led the ace and another heart. Now the defenders had a crossruff going and, when the smoke cleared away, Soloway was down three tricks doubled.

Many years ago I learned—the hard way—of the other situation where it's better to lead the king from the king third in partner's suit. Here is the hand:

```
                    NORTH
                    ♠ Q J 8
                    ♡ Q 7 6
                    ◇ A J 2
                    ♣ K J 7 4
        WEST                        EAST
        ♠ 9 6 2                     ♠ 5
        ♡ K 5 3                     ♡ A J 10 9 8 2
        ◇ 9 6 4 3                   ◇ K Q 10
        ♣ 9 8 6                     ♣ Q 10 3
                    SOUTH
                    ♠ A K 10 7 4 3
                    ♡ 4
                    ◇ 8 7 5
                    ♣ A 5 2
```

This hand was played in rubber bridge. At that time, I had
read a great many books on bridge but had not played much.
My partner, sitting East, opened the bidding with one heart, but
the opponents got to a four-spade contract. I did just what the
books told me I should do. I led the three of hearts. My partner
won that one neatly with his eight, but then was stymied as he
had no killing return. When the clubs broke favorably for the
declarer, he discarded one of his diamonds on one of dummy's
long clubs, and ended up losing one trick in hearts, one in
diamonds, and one in clubs. My more experienced partner
pointed out that I should have led the king of hearts. After I saw
the dummy and his signal, he explained, I should switch to a
diamond. After a diamond switch at trick two, the contract
would probably fail.

I made a record of this hand and put it in my files to give me
time to decide what it was about my hand that made it proper to
ignore the advice to lead a small heart rather than the king. I
think I finally found the answer, and I am passing it on to you.
When I lead a small card in my partner's suit, it is in hopes of
giving him the lead. If I have some very nice combination, like
A-Q-J, in some suit, and declarer has the king, my partner
might figure out that it's best for him to lead the suit up to my
strength. Looking at my West hand in the illustration above,
there was no suit where I had high cards in any suit that I

wanted my partner to lead to. But, my partner had opened the bidding, the dummy has been active in the bidding, and it was likely that my partner had some suits where he would like to play after dummy. This was the actual case. We could gain only if I led diamonds, not if my partner led diamonds. Therefore, I should have retained the lead until I got a look at dummy, hoping that I would be able to work out just what suit to lead.

To make my story complete, here is a hand where the opening leader had a suit he wanted led up to and chose to lead a small card from three to the king for that reason. This hand is taken from the 1957 World Championship, which was called the United States versus Europe, but was actually the U.S. versus Italy.

None vul., dealer South.

```
                    NORTH
                    ♠ A Q 9 8 3
                    ♡ 9 4
                    ◇ A 8 7 3
                    ♣ J 8
        WEST                        EAST
        ♠ 7 5 2                     ♠ K J
        ♡ K J 3                     ♡ A 10 7 6 5 2
        ◇ 10 9                      ◇ 6
        ♣ A Q 10 5 3                ♣ 7 6 4 2
                    SOUTH
                    ♠ 10 6 4
                    ♡ Q 8
                    ◇ K Q J 5 4 2
                    ♣ K 9
```

75

The bidding:

SOUTH	WEST	NORTH	EAST
Chiaradia	Leventritt	D'Alelio	Sobel
1 ◇	2 ♣	3 ♣	4 ♡
Pass	Pass	4 ♠	5 ♣
Pass	Pass	Double	Pass
5 ◇	Pass	Pass	Double
Pass	Pass	Pass	

In the closed room, where the Americans were North and South, Belladonna and Avarelli, of the Italian Team, passively allowed Harold Ogust, North, to buy the hand for three spades. They set him two tricks for 100 points.

In the open room, where the Americans had the East and West hands, things were more lively. After Peter Leventritt overcalled with two clubs, Mrs. Sobel bid four hearts, which she could make with an extra trick. Then she bid five clubs, which would also make. The Italians decided it was in order to sacrifice. They would have done better to let the Americans score their game, as Leventritt and Sobel picked the hand clean as plucking feathers off a goose.

With his lively holding in clubs, Leventritt led the three of hearts and Helen won with the ace. Back came the deuce of clubs, and Leventritt won the queen and ace of clubs and the king of hearts. Next, he led the two of spades. Chiaradia, South, played low from dummy, Mrs. Sobel winning the jack. She then led a diamond, leaving it up to Chiaradia to decide what to do about the spades. He decided wrong and finessed again, and Helen got her king of spades as well. Down 700, giving the American team a net score of plus 600.

Let me show you a couple of hands from my files where the king was led from the king three times for different reasons. In neither case had the suit been bid at all.

N-S vul., dealer South.

NORTH
♠ 7 5
♡ Q 8 3
♢ 3 2
♣ A K Q 9 7 5

Mrs. Rupp
WEST
♠ K J 4
♡ A 10 9 6 5
♢ J 10 9 4
♣ 2

EAST
♠ Q 9 8 6 3 2
♡ 2
♢ 8 5
♣ J 10 6 3

Me
SOUTH
♠ A 10
♡ K J 7 4
♢ A K Q 7 6
♣ 8 4

The bidding:

SOUTH	WEST	NORTH	EAST
1 ♢	1 ♡	2 ♣	Pass
2 NT	Pass	3 NT	Pass
Pass	Pass		

Mrs. Virgil Rupp, of Indianapolis, is known throughout the Middle West as an aggressive bidder. What is not so well known is that she is also an aggressive defender. I was the victim of her opening lead on this hand.

Because of the weakness of her heart suit and the opponents' willingness to play notrump after she overcalled, she decided not to lead a heart. I had bid diamonds and my partner clubs, and Mrs. Rupp saw no need to give us an assist by leading one of our suits. The only suit left was spades. Neither my partner no I had bid spades. Therefore, she decided that her partner probably had some length in that suit. So, she chose spades for her attack, deciding at the same time that she had better start unblocking the suit in view of the fact that her partner was unlikely to have many entries. As you can see, the king of spades lead was devastating. Had she led anything except one of the high spades, I would certainly have taken at least nine tricks by conceding a club trick as a safety play. I would have had five clubs, three diamonds, and a spade. If hearts had been led, I would have picked up a few more. As it was, when clubs and diamonds both failed to break, I was down two tricks.

On the next hand, the king was led for a different reason. The results were sensational.

None vul., dealer East.

```
                    NORTH
                    ♠ 5
                    ♡ Q
                    ◇ K Q 10 8 7 4
                    ♣ A K J 8 4
        WEST                    EAST
        ♠ A Q 8 7               ♠ 6 4 3 2
        ♡ K 7 3                 ♡ J 10 6 4 2
        ◇ A 6 2                 ◇ 9
        ♣ 10 7 6                ♣ 9 3 2
                    SOUTH
                    ♠ K J 10 9
                    ♡ A 9 8 5
                    ◇ J 5 3
                    ♣ Q 5
```

The bidding:

EAST	SOUTH	WEST	NORTH
Pass	Pass	1 ♠	2 ◇
Pass	2 NT	Pass	3 ♣
Pass	3 NT	Pass	Pass
Pass			

Holding 13 HCPs himself, West figured his partner could have at most one or two HCPs. Still, he needed partner's help to set 3NT. One thing seemed sure: he didn't have five tricks in his own hand. West decided that any chance he had to set the hand

was to lead the unbid suit. Looking for an entry to partner's hand so that East could lead back a spade to his ace-queen, he decided to lead the king of hearts. South did the best he could by letting the king hold the trick. West continued with the seven, and this time South won his ace, fearing that a spade lead through his king-jack might be fatal. Counting on five club tricks, he had a total of only six tricks without losing the lead. So, he led a diamond. West rose with the ace, and the returned the three of hearts to the jack in the East hand. The order in which he played the heart suit indicated that he had started with only three, so East got the point and shifted to a spade. This gave the defenders two spade tricks, two heart tricks, and a diamond trick, leaving declarer only eight tricks.

This lead of the king from a suit which your partner has not bid must be rated a high-risk lead and is not for everyday use. I would say there are four requirements to make this lead. They are:

1. The situation is desperate
2. You have paid close attention to the bidding
3. You are a brave person
4. You have an understanding partner

If one of my students asks me what to lead from three to the king, I will have to say, "Usually the small one will work out best, but not all the time." I think I would sum it up this way:

1. When it is a suit my partner has bid, I mentally review the bidding to see whether either of the opponents has indicated strength in his suit. Should it be the opponent to my left, I will lead the king.
2. When there is nothing to indicate which opponent might hold strength in my partner's suit, I tend to lead small except when I have virtually no potential winners in my hand outside the king of my partner's suit. When that is true, I lead the king, hoping a look at the dummy and my partner's signal will give me some suggestions as to whether I should continue his suit or lead through some strength in the dummy.
3. When the bidding by the opponents virtually demands the lead of a suit where I have three to the king, I will lead low if my

purpose is to get our high cards established and cash them
before the opponents discard on a long side suit. Likewise, I will
lead low if I have no indication as to which opponent holds
strength in that particular suit, and if the strength between my
hand and partner's hand seems to be evenly divided.

Opening Leads From Qxx

Unless you believe it is the opponent to your left who holds
strength in the suit, the odds favor leading the small card. Lou
Watson, in *Play of the Hand,* gives this classic illustration:

```
                          4 3
        Q 8 6                          A 10 9 7 5
                          K J 2
```

It is obvious that with this combination, South can always get
two tricks should West lead the queen, and will always be held
to one trick in the suit if South leads the small one.

In the 1967 World Championship, a hand was dealt which
had almost this exact pattern. Although the heart suit was not
bid, hearts were led.

N-S vul., dealer North.

```
                       NORTH
                       ♠ A Q 9 6
                       ♡ 5 4
                       ◇ 5
                       ♣ Q J 10 9 8 4
        WEST                         EAST
        ♠ 10 5 3                     ♠ J 8 4
        ♡ Q 7 2                      ♡ A 10 9 8 3
        ◇ J 8 7 3                    ◇ 6 2
        ♣ A 7 2                      ♣ K 6 5
                       SOUTH
                       ♠ K 7 2
                       ♡ K J 6
                       ◇ A K Q 10 9 4
                       ♣ 3
```

The bidding:

NORTH	EAST	SOUTH	WEST
Belladonna	Roth	Avarelli	Root
Pass	Pass	1 ◊	Pass
1 ♡	Pass	3 ◊	Pass
3 NT	Pass	Pass	Pass

CLOSED ROOM

NORTH	EAST	SOUTH	WEST
Kaplan	Garozzo	Kay	Forquet
Pass	Pass	1 ◊	Pass
2 ♣	Pass	3 NT	Pass
Pass	Pass		

In the open room, Belladonna and Avarelli were playing the Roman System. In that system, a one-heart response to a one-diamond opening bid shows fewer than nine HCPs. I presume Belladonna thought his nine HCPs were a poor nine points when he responded one heart, but in any event, his bid showed nothing about a heart suit, and only indicated that he was responding on minimum values. Avarelli's jump rebid of three diamonds indicated that he had a solid or semi-solid suit, with only five losers in his hand.

Alvin Roth, East, had no trouble leading a heart. Belladonna tried the jack, but Bill Root, West, won with the queen and continued the suit. The distribution was cruel. The spade suit, which could furnish only four tricks, did break 3-3, while the diamond suit, which could have furnished six tricks, broke 4-2. In addition to his heart trick, Belladonna got only his four spade tricks and three diamond tricks before he had to relinquish the lead, and those eight tricks were all he took.

In the closed room, the 3NT contract was bid by Norman Kay, South, and the heart lead was not so obvious from the West seat. The lead from three to the queen in an unbid suit is considered by many to be a doubtful lead. However, the opponents had bid both minor suits and Forquet must have thought a major suit lead was called for. He did not know in

which major his partner had length. That was a guess. However,
if his partner had spade length, his ten of spades might not be
enough to help establish the suit. So even if his partner had
spade length, the lead of the suit might not help. In hearts, the
presence of the queen made it more likely that, if his partner
had length, the suit could be established. Garozzo won the first
trick with the ace and continued with the ten. Kay tried the jack,
but of course he got the same bad diamond break which
Belladonna got, and ended up with the same eight tricks.

It is of passing interest to note that if East had no entry outside of the heart suit, South could have frustrated the defense if
he had taken the right view in the heart suit. He could have
played the king, which would have blocked the suit. Of course,
that would not have worked on this hand, as East did have
another entry with the king of clubs.

There are combinations other than this where leading low
from the queen third will be the proper lead. Here is a hand
where the heart suit was led by West because his partner had bid
the suit:

N-S vul., dealer North.

```
                    NORTH
                    ♠ A 9
                    ♡ J 9 2
                    ◇ J 7 3
                    ♣ K Q J 10 5
        WEST                    EAST
        ♠ J 7 6 3               ♠ Q 5 4
        ♡ Q 5 3                 ♡ K 10 8 7 6
        ◇ 10 9 8 4              ◇ K 6 2
        ♣ 7 3                   ♣ A 6
                    SOUTH
                    ♠ K 10 8 2
                    ♡ A 4
                    ◇ A Q 5
                    ♣ 9 8 4 2
```

The bidding:

NORTH	EAST	SOUTH	WEST
1 ♣	1 ♡	1 ♠	Pass
2 ♣	Pass	3 NT	Pass
Pass	Pass		

The heart overcall by East is not the sort of bid which teachers regularly recommend to their pupils. The heart suit is sometimes considered to be too weak for an overcall. Nevertheless, it is the sort of an overcall that experts often make. In this case, it made it easy for West to make the only lead which would defeat the contract.

It was the player to his right who jumped to 3NT, and so West had no trouble coming to the conclusion that the proper heart to lead was the small one. All East had to do was cover whatever heart declarer played from the dummy and declarer could take the ace or hold up one trick, whichever he preferred. In any event, he was doomed to lose four heart tricks, plus a trick to the ace of clubs.

Had West led the queen of hearts, declarer would win with the ace, and when East got in with the ace of clubs, he could not continue hearts without giving the declarer another trick in the suit. Any attempt to give his partner the lead so he could lead another heart would be futile. With the defenders only entitled to about 14 points, and with East himself holding 12 HCPs, he would have known that the queen which his partner led was his only significant high card.

Still, there are times when the bidding indicates that the queen itself should be led.

Both vul., dealer South.

```
                        NORTH
                        ♠ K 9 5
                        ♡ 8 7 2
                        ◇ A J 8 2
                        ♣ Q J 8
        WEST                        EAST
        ♠ Q 8 3                     ♠ A J 10 7 4 2
        ♡ 10 9 5 4                  ♡ 3
        ◇ 7 6 3                     ◇ K 9 5 4
        ♣ 6 5 4                     ♣ A 3
                        SOUTH
                        ♠ 6
                        ♡ A K Q J 6
                        ◇ Q 10
                        ♣ K 10 9 7 2
```

The bidding:

SOUTH	WEST	NORTH	EAST
1 ♡	Pass	2 ◇	2 ♠
3 ♣	Pass	3 NT	Pass
4 ♡	Pass	Pass	Pass

It looks like the declarer can take five tricks in hearts, four in clubs after giving one up to the ace, and the ace of diamonds, for an easy ten tricks, while the defenders are taking one spade trick, one diamond trick, and one club trick. That is exactly what would happen if West opened the three of spades. East could win with the ten, but now would have no good play. However, West did not lead the three of spades. The bidding and his hand called for the lead of the queen, not in hopes of retaining the lead to look the dummy over, but in the hope that he could avoid putting his partner on the spot. North, the player to his left, had bid NT, but South would have none of it. This placed the spade strength in the hand to the leader's left. In addition to that, he had nothing in his hand which he would liked to have led up to. So he led the queen of spades and one of declarer's tricks disappeared.

Whether dummy covered or not, the spade suit would be continued, and sooner or later South would have to trump or he would be set before he got started. That would reduce his number of trumps to the same number as West. Declarer would discover this when he led the ace and king of hearts. He could not go ahead and take West's trumps away from him while the ace of clubs was outstanding. Should he do that, the defenders would cash a lot of spade tricks when they won a trick with the ace of clubs.

So, declarer would have to stop after leading two trump tricks and see what he could do about clubs. East would win and continue with yet another spade. When South trumped, West would have more trumps than South, and West would be sure to come to a trump trick. So on the probable line of play, the defenders would still get their trick in spades, diamonds, and clubs, but, in addition, would get a trick in trumps and down would go McGinty.

One of the things that makes bridge so fascinating is that there are exceptions to exceptions. While leading high from the king or queen with two small cards in a suit your partner has bid will frequently work out well when you have little or nothing in outside suits, there are holdings where this lead will turn out badly. One of these combinations is where the dummy holds the ace and jack with one or more small cards, and your partner holds the balance of the high cards. Suppose you run into this situation:

$$\text{A J 5}$$

$$\text{Q 4 3} \qquad \text{K 10 9 7 2}$$

$$\text{8 6}$$

Swap the king and queen and the situation would be the same. Of course, the declarer might decide that you have only a doubleton in the suit and that his best play is to hold up and let you win the trick, in which event everything will be just lovely. Conceivably, if it is the king you have led, he could decide that you have both honors and could let you win the first trick, planning to finesse the second time around. This is not too likely when your partner has bid the suit. It is more probable that he will think you led from a doubleton, and go up with the ace.

With the miserable hand which would cause you to lead the king or queen, you are not likely to have an entry to lead the suit again, and your partner cannot lead the suit without giving declarer another trick. Had you led small, East could simply have played the nine-spot if the dummy played low, or played the king if dummy played the jack, and the suit would be established with the declarer winning only one trick.

Once again we see how much better informed we would be if we could only see the dummy before we lead. However, the rules don't allow this, and so we just have to make the play that is most likely to succeed most of the time.

Before we leave this subject, I must point out that leading from three to the queen in an unbid suit is a worse gamble than leading from three to the king. There is an old saying that when you give your opponents a trick by leading from a king, you often will get it back. But when you give them a trick by underleading a queen, you seldom will get it back. I certainly agree that there are many situations where underleading a king will be called for, even though your partner has not bid the suit, but that underleading a queen in a suit your partner has not bid should be made only in those cases where leading the suit in question is clear-cut. In looking through World Championship hands, I have tried to find a hand which demonstrated this point. While I did not find one which quite does that, I did find one which demonstrates the horrible disasters which can occur when you decide to underlead a queen of a suit your partner has not bid. It occurred in the match between North America and the Netherlands in the World Championship of 1966. Here is it:

E-W vul., dealer West.

NORTH
♠ K J
♡ 10 8 2
♢ K 9 4 2
♣ A 9 7 3

WEST
♠ A 8 7 6 5 4 2
♡ None
♢ Q 8 5
♣ K 6 2

EAST
♠ Q 9
♡ A 7 5 4
♢ 10 7 3
♣ Q J 8 5

SOUTH
♠ 10 3
♡ K Q J 9 6 3
♢ A J 6
♣ 10 4

The bidding:

OPEN ROOM

WEST	NORTH	EAST	SOUTH
Kehela	Kreyns	Murray	Slavenburg
1 ♠	Pass	1 NT	2 ♡
2 ♠	3 ♡	3 ♠	4 ♡
Pass	Pass	Double	Pass
Pass	Pass		

CLOSED ROOM

WEST	NORTH	EAST	SOUTH
Oudshoorn	Feldesman	Boender	Rubin
2 ♠	Pass	Pass	3 ♡
Pass	4 ♡	Pass	Pass
Pass			

Kehela and Murray, in the Open Room, played the Acol
System, which does not use weak two-bids, but does open
distributional hands which other systems might pass. Kehela,
West, chose to bid one spade. You will see that Slavenburg ended up playing four hearts doubled. Kehela led the ace of spades

and continued a spade to dummy's king. South started leading trumps. Murray won the third round and shifted to a club.

Slavenburg won the king with his ace and led a club. Murray, East, won and got off lead with his last trump. Slavenburg finally had to lose a trick to the queen of diamonds and ended up losing one trick in each suit for down one.

In the closed room, Oudshoorn was playing weak two-bids and opened two spades with the West hand. Ira Rubin, for the USA, ended up playing four hearts from the South hand, and Oudshoorn did not seem inclined to lead the ace of his suit. If he didn't want to lead spades, he had to choose between diamonds and clubs. Just why he decided to lead from his queen of diamonds rather than his king of clubs is not clear to me, but that is what he did. The result was that Rubin lost no tricks in either minor suit and made five on the hand. He won the opening lead with the jack of diamonds and started leading trumps. Boender, the Netherlands East player, won the second heart and switched to a club. It was too late. Rubin won the ace and continued pulling trumps until they were exhausted. He then led the ace and one diamond. When diamonds broke 3-3, he was able to discard one of his clubs on the dummy's diamonds. He then trumped a club to get back to his hand. When he led a spade, he had no trouble guessing to play the king in view of the bidding.

The example you find in the textbook to demonstrate that the proper lead from the jack and two small in your partner's suit is the small one will probably look something like this:

$$10\ 9\ 4$$
$$J\ 8\ 3 \qquad\qquad A\ K\ 7\ 5\ 2$$
$$Q\ 6$$

Obviously, if West leads the jack, declarer will collect a trick with dummy's ten-spot which he could not get if West led the three. There are many other combinations of cards where the winning lead is small from three to the jack. For example, look at this one:

$$Q\ 6$$
$$J\ 3\ 2 \qquad\qquad K\ 10\ 8\ 7\ 5$$
$$A\ 9\ 4$$

This one is even more typical because you need to keep the jack behind declarer's nine-spot. If you lead the jack, it would be covered by the queen, king and ace, and then the declarer could go to the dummy and lead towards the nine-spot for another trick. Should you lead the two, your partner would play the king if dummy played the queen, but otherwise he would play the ten. In either event, declarer would get only one trick.

Those instances where the winning lead is the jack are few and far between, but they do exist.

```
                    K 9 4
        J 6 3                   A Q 10 7 2
                     8 5
```

Against notrump with this particular combination, the defense can take the first five tricks, provided the jack is led. But should the small one be led and West have no other entries, the defense would be stymied. Unless the bidding sequence makes it perfectly clear that the only strength in your partner's suit is held to your left, the odds are going to greatly favor leading the small card rather than the jack.

As a general rule, a lead from Jxx should be made only when you have reason to believe you are leading your partner's suit. This usually means that your partner has bid the suit. Otherwise, the chances that you are going to build up tricks for your side by leading from three to the jack are pretty farfetched. Usually, when you are on opening lead, the opponents have more high cards than your side, and to hope that your partner has something like the king and queen of your suit is on the optimistic side. However, if the bidding indicates that the lead in the other suits will probably be worse than leading the suit where you have this holding, you have little choice. There was an occasion in the 1958 World Championship where the bidding pointed directly to the lead of such a suit and, by avoiding a couple of worse leads, enabled the defenders to defeat the contract. It was in the match of the Argentine versus Italy.

Both vul., dealer North.

```
                        NORTH
                        ♠ 9 6 4
                        ♡ 5
                        ◊ Q 10 7 5 3 2
                        ♣ J 4 3
        WEST                            EAST
        ♠ J 7 5                         ♠ K 8 3 2
        ♡ 3 2                           ♡ J 8 7 6
        ◊ J 8                           ◊ K 9 6 4
        ♣ A Q 10 9 8 6                  ♣ 7
                        SOUTH
                        ♠ A Q 10
                        ♡ A K Q 10 9 4
                        ◊ A
                        ♣ K 5 2
```

NORTH	EAST	SOUTH	WEST
Belladonna	Cabanne	Avarelli	Lerner
Pass	Pass	1 ♣	Pass
1 ◊	Pass	2 ♡	Pass
2 ♠	Pass	3 ♣	Double
3 ◊	Pass	3 NT	Pass
4 ◊	Pass	4 ♡	Pass
Pass	Pass		

Belladonna and Avarelli, the Italian North and South, were bidding the Roman system, so some explanation is in order. The one-club opening bid could have been any one of several different-type hands. The one-diamond response showed seven HCPs or less. The two-heart rebid clarified the opening bid, saying it was a game going hand with a heart suit and asking Belladonna to describe his support in that suit. Belladonna's response of two spades said that he had either a void or a small singleton in hearts. The three-club bid by Avarelli asked his partner to tell him what controls were held in the club suit. The three-diamond bid by North said that he had no controls—no ace, no king, no singleton, no void—in clubs. If my understanding of the system is correct, the four-diamond bid showed a diamond suit.

Avarelli knew he had to be satisfied with a game bid, as his partner had none of the cards which would have given him any sort of play for a slam. His partner was very short in hearts and had no club controls. The trouble was that Lerner, in the West seat, who had the opening lead, knew all of this, too. These beautiful descriptive sequences are no doubt excellent in locating specific cards for slam contracts, but there is a price to pay. Descriptive bids not only help the declarer reach the right spot, but they also help the defenders find the right defense.

By process of elimination, Lerner came to the conclusion that the spade suit would be the proper suit to lead. With the dummy holding not more than one small trump, there was a good chance his partner held several of them and that the only way he could fail to get a trump trick would be for Lerner to lead trumps. Avarelli had indicated that he had a control in clubs which needed some help, and Belladonna had shown that he had nothing in the suit, so that ruled out a club lead. The fact that Belladonna had shown the only suit he had was diamonds made a lead of diamonds doubtful. As a matter of fact, a diamond lead would have done no harm, but had declarer had a small diamond to go with his ace, it would have been a different story. The spade lead gave declarer an extra spade trick, but that was not the game going trick. The king went to declarer's ace and declarer led four rounds of hearts, giving the lead to East. East exited with a club and West won the ace and queen and then gave the lead back to declarer by playing a third round of clubs to South's king. The defenders now had their book of three tricks and Lerner still had to win a trick with his jack of spades to set the contract one trick.

In the other room, the bidding was not so revealing. Castro, playing for the Argentine team in the South seat, opened the bidding with two hearts. When his partner bid 2NT, he jumped straight to four hearts. This natural bidding system didn't describe all of these details either to his partner or to his opponents. Chiaradia of the Italian team held the West hand, and was on opening lead. Having nothing to guide him, he laid down the ace of clubs and continued a second club. He gave his partner a ruff which his partner didn't need. His partner had a natural trump trick anyway, which had now disappeared.

D'Alelio, the Italian East, put declarer to the test right away by leading a low spade. Castro promptly passed the test by playing the queen. He then led out all of his trumps, and the good king of clubs, and let the opponents guess what to discard. It was not a good day for guessing. They held onto their diamonds for dear life and discarded too many spades. When Castro finally cashed his ace of spades, his ten became a trick and he took eleven tricks, compared to the nine taken by Avarelli in the other room.

In the 1934 edition of Lou Watson's great book on play of the hand, he said that with all the holdings of three cards headed by the ten or lower, you should lead the highest card. Today, the lead of the small card holding three to the ten is considered standard. I am sure today's methods are technically superior. The ten-spot is high enough that it may be needed in back of declarer. You may run into this sort of combination:

$$\begin{array}{ccc} & \text{Q 3} & \\ \text{10 4 2} & & \text{A J 8 7 6} \\ & \text{K 9 5} & \end{array}$$

If you lead the two, declarer can be held to one trick. If dummy plays small, your partner should play the jack and declarer will win the king, but he is now out of business. If the queen is played, your partner wins with the ace, leads the seven back, and there sits your ten right over declarer's nine. Should you, on the other hand, lead the ten, declarer can get two tricks simply by playing dummy's queen. If your partner wins with the ace, his jack is now finessable because your precious ten is now gone with the wind.

Personally, I always hate to lead from this combination. My partner seems always to expect me to hold something higher than the ten, and I am distressed by the reproachful look he gives me when he finds the best I have to offer is the lowly ten-spot. Nonetheless, I am a great believer in leading suits my partner has bid, and if he has bid this suit, I am probably going to lead it. If I hold the ten and two small ones, I am going to lead the small one unless there is simply overwhelming evidence that all strength in that suit is to my left.

Leading from the ten and two small cards when there is

nothing in the bidding to indicate that that particular suit needs to be led must be a bad lead. I have had trouble finding a hand where it was even tried, but did finally find one in the 1964 World Championship. This was the hand from the match of Italy versus Sweden.

NORTH
♠ J 3
♡ 7 5 4
♢ 10 5 2
♣ Q 10 9 7 3

WEST
♠ 9 7 4
♡ 10 3 2
♢ Q 8 4
♣ K J 8 6

EAST
♠ Q 10 8 5
♡ K Q 6
♢ 9 7 6 3
♣ 5 4

SOUTH
♠ A K 6 2
♡ A J 9 8
♢ A K J
♣ A 2

As in all team games, this hand was played twice, once with the Italians being on lead from the West hand, and again with the Swedes being on lead. In both rooms, the bidding simply said that South had a whale of a big hand and North had very little, but in neither did it say much about the distribution. It was up to West to pick the opening lead against three notrump with little to guide him.

When the Italians were playing East and West, Belladonna sat West and led the three of hearts. I am not sure just what the lead of the three indicated. From the way the play went, I'm not sure East knew either. East played his queen and Holmgren, the Swedish declarer, won with the ace and led a small spade toward dummy's jack. There was no good news there as Avarelli in the East seat won the queen. He continued with the king and a small heart. The Swedish player got his good news when he won with the jack and Belladonna's ten fell out, establishing another heart trick. Holmgren now proceeded to cash his good heart, the ace and king of spades, and the ace of clubs. Then he handed Belladonna the lead by leading the two of clubs. Belladonna won the king and had nothing to lead except minor suit cards. He settled on the small diamond, and that gave Holmgren three tricks in diamonds to add to his three hearts, two spades, and the ace of clubs, making a total of nine tricks.

In the other room, Berglund of Sweden was on lead. He elected to lead his fourth-best club. Leading from a four-card suit headed by the king-jack is not considered the greatest lead in the world, but neither was a lead from any other suit he held. For my book, leading either red suit simply had to be wrong, making the choice between one of the black suits. With the defenders entitled to somewhere around 14 HCPs, it seems to me that West should not be faulted for leading clubs. His partner was bound to have something in the neighborhood of eight HCPs, and maybe that would turn out to include either the ace or queen of clubs. As a matter of fact, his partner had neither, and the first trick was won by Garozzo, the Italian South, with dummy's nine of clubs. But declarer still did not manage to maneuver nine tricks. His first play was to lead the four of hearts from the dummy and finesse his nine-spot. That precious ten from which West had refused to lead now won a trick. The report says that West continued hearts. Garozzo won the ace and then conceded a heart to East to get his long heart established. East switched to a diamond. Garozzo played his ace and led a spade toward dummy's jack. He too got the bad news that the jack of spades was not going to take a trick. East won with the queen and continued diamonds. Garozzo had reached the point of no return. If the diamond finesse didn't win, he was going to be set. He played the jack of diamonds and the diamond finesse did not win. West won the queen and handed the lead back to Garozzo by continuing diamonds. Garozzo still had a spade to lose, going down one, losing in all two tricks in spades, two in hearts and one in diamonds.

SIGNALS WHEN LEADING TRUMPS

When you are leading from three small cards in a suit which is not trumps, the chances that the highest card of the three might take a trick if you keep it are negligible. You can construct the hand where you should not lead the eight-spot because of its trick-taking value, but you just about never are dealt such a hand in real life. When leading trumps, however, the situation is different. Due to its overruffing potential, high spot cards in trumps are much more likely to take tricks than are high spot cards which are not trumps. Because of this, it is conventional to lead the smallest card from three small trumps and, as a generalization of that theory, you lead the smallest card when whatever trumps you have are all small, whether that be from a two-, three-, or four-card holding.

There are players who like to tell their partners (and their opponents) how many trumps they have when they lead trumps. I haven't seen this method make anybody rich, but you might find a hand where it is useful if you like to use these methods. The idea is that when you have three trumps, you first play the middle and then the small one.

You will also adopt this method if you happen to hold five trumps. The play of a higher trump followed by a smaller one indicates the holding of an odd number of trumps. Contrariwise, if you hold two or four trumps and you decide to lead the suit, you first lead the small one and then a higher one.

The problem with this form of signaling, as well as with all forms of signaling, is that the question arises whether the information you give is more useful to your partner or the declarer. If you are not convinced either way, I would just recommend that you go ahead and lead small no matter how many you have.

CHAPTER 2:
OTHER METHODS

Ace From AKx

The conventions concerning opening leads, and generally of signals as well, largely go back to the days of whist. Today, many theorists and players think that some of these can be improved upon, and we are going through a period of experimentation. It is not within the scope of this book to tell all of the things which are being tried, but I do want to touch at least briefly on those which have received enough acceptance to make it quite likely that you will run into them if you play very much bridge.

In the United States, we lead the ace from an ace-king only when those are the only two cards held in the suit. When there are three or more cards in the suit, we lead the king. This means that we may lead the king from KQxx, as well as from AKxx. This sometimes creates problems for our partner. If, for instance, he has J-7-2, he will want to play the seven to encourage us to continue the suit when we have led from KQxx, but might want to play the two-spot to show no interest in the suit if we have led from AKxx. Of course, if either the ace or queen shows up in the dummy, he has a pretty good idea what combination we led from, but if the missing card is in the closed hand, he will have no way of knowing.

In many other countries, they tried to solve this problem by leading the ace from the ace-king when other cards are held in the suit and showing a doubleton in the suit by leading the king and then playing the ace. A number of American tournament bridge players are using this procedure. While it does solve one problem, it creates another. There are times when the lead of a suit headed by an ace without the king is called for by the bidding. If the partner of the opening leader happens to hold the Q-7-2, he will want the suit continued if the ace is led from AKxx, but would prefer a switch if the lead is from Axxx.

Which method is better? The records I have examined reveal nothing. If there has been a case in World Championship play where points have been won because of the use of either method, I have overlooked it. Any prolonged debate about which is better seems to me to fall in the category of majoring in minors.

The most appealing ideas I have seen about choosing whether to lead the ace or the king when you have both have come from the Academic Bridge Club at the University of Oslo. They have been presented in publication by Helge Vinje. At the time of writing, there is little or no record of what these leads have achieved in competition, but the ideas which they present are intriguing, and, if you choose to use them, you might keep a copy of the results to see just what flaws show up, if any.

The first convention is simple enough. If you are on lead against a slam in a suit and are fortunate enough to hold both the ace and king of a side suit, always lead the king. Your partner should give a count signal, playing high-low with an even number of cards in the suit and low-high with an odd number. Suppose, for instance, your opponent has become overenthusiastic and has reached a six-spade contract, when the diamond suit is distributed in this fashion:

$$\diamond \text{ Q 8 5 3}$$
$$\diamond \text{ A K 10 9 6} \qquad \diamond \text{ 7 2}$$
$$\diamond \text{ J 4}$$

West leads the king of diamonds, and now needs to know whether he can or cannot cash the ace. If South started with a singleton diamond, West should not play the ace and establish the queen in the dummy. And if South started with more than one diamond, West surely would like to know that his ace is good for a trick.

East gives West the answer to this when he plays the seven, and it makes no difference whether South plays the jack or the four. The seven cannot be a small card from a three-card holding. Of the seven diamonds which are higher than the seven, West is looking at four of them in his own hand and two in the dummy, making it impossible for East to have two diamonds higher than the seven. Presto—the seven is either a

Vinje's book, *New Ideas in Defense,* is available from the publisher for $11.95, including shipping charges.

singleton or from an even number of cards, and when South follows suit, the seven cannot be from a four-card holding, as that would have left South with no diamonds at all.

Against a suit contract of anything less than a slam, the procedure becomes cuter, and at the same time more complicated. If your lead is from an even number of cards you lead the ace, while if it is from an odd number of cards you lead the king. You can remember that the ace is really number fourteen in the deck, an even number, while the king is really number thirteen. And now we come to quite a few ifs, ands, and buts. I'm not going to give you all of these, but will give you some of the more interesting ones.

When the dummy shows up with as many as three cards, including the queen, third hand gives count indicating whether he has an even or an odd number of cards in the suit. With an odd number of cards he always plays low. With an even number of cards he plays high, then low. With only two cards he plays the higher, while with four he plays the third-lowest. You will notice that the third-lowest is also the second-highest.

If the dummy does not have the queen of the suit with two or more cards, it is up to third hand to tell his partner how many tricks the defenders can take in the suit, RELATIVE TO THE NUMBER HELD IN THE CLOSED HAND. High-low shows an even number of defensive tricks; low-high an odd number. For example, West has bid in a manner to show length in a suit and leads an ace showing an even number. East can take this to indicate a six-card holding. Suppose this is the situation:

8 4

A K 10 7 6 3   9 2

Q J 5

East plays the two, indicating that, compared to the South hand, he has three tricks. West continues the suit, and even if East cannot overtrump the dummy the defenders have killed the established queen in the South hand by ruffing it.

Those of us accustomed to attitude signals are going to have trouble playing the nine with this holding.

```
                      8 6 4
      A K 7 3                        9 5 2
                      Q J 10
```

West leads the ace to show an even number and, helped along by the bidding, East reads that as a four-card suit. The defenders have only two tricks in the suit and so it is incumbent upon East to play his third-lowest. That turns out to be the nine.

In my next illustration, West leads the king of a suit to indicate an odd number of cards.

```
                      J 7 2
      A K 3                        Q 10 6 4
                      9 8 4
```

East will read that as either three or five cards, and in either event will play his lowest card to indicate that the defenders can take an odd number of tricks. If West has led from a three-card holding, then the defenders can take three tricks, while if West has led from a five-card holding, the defenders can take one trick.

Only time will tell whether this method of signaling will add to or subtract from the number of tricks the defenders take. Is the information given more helpful to the declarer or to the defenders? Can the defenders really distinguish what is called the "two-card difference": whether an even signal is two or four, or an odd signal is three or five, or whether it might even be a singleton, and whether or not these methods are accident-prone?

RUSINOW LEADS

A less-complicated way of solving the problem of whether an ace or a king in a side suit should be led is the use of Rusinow leads.

With these leads, the second ranking honor is led. Thus from A-K, the king would be the lead, while from KQx, the queen would be the lead. This second-best of touching honors goes right on down as long as either card in a sequence is an honor, until finally the 9 is led from 10-9. Today, most of those who use Rusinow leads use them only against suit contracts, and use other methods against notrump contracts. The second-highest honor is led even if there are more than two honor cards in the sequence. From Q-J-10-9, the jack would still be the proper lead.

Holding only two cards in the suit, the order of leading is reversed. Thus, using Rusinow leads, the higher honor is led followed by the lower in order to show a doubleton.

Rusinow leads generally are used only on opening lead, and only in a suit the leader's partner has not bid. After the opening lead, the highest of touching honors is led. Likewise, should the opening leader have touching honors in a suit his partner has bid, he would lead the higher card.

Using Rusinow leads, the nine becomes the ambiguous lead rather than the king. With standard leads, the lead of the king could be either from A-K, or K-Q. With Rusinow leads, the lead of the nine could be from either 10-9 or 9-8.

In theory, Rusinow leads must be superior to standard opening leads. The ambiguity that goes with the lead of a king in standard leads is transferred down to the nine-spot with Rusinow leads. With standard leads, the lead of a king can be from AKx or from KQx. With Rusinow leads, the lead of a nine can be from 10-9 or 9-8. The ambiguity of the nine lead certainly must be less harmful than the ambiguity of a king lead. For example, there are times when your partner would want to trump your opening lead of a king if it was from KQx, but not if it was from AKx.

In spite of this, Rusinow leads have made little headway with American players. Probably the reason is that it is extremely difficult to find the deal where the third hand had problems with the lead of a king. If standard leads practically never create the problems which Rusinow leads are supposed to correct, why bother with them?

JOURNALIST LEADS

Journalist leads, which were presented to American players in the mid-1960s, adopted Rusinow opening leads against suit contracts. Advocates of Journalist leads also recognize the great difference between the best methods to use against suit contracts as compared with those to use against notrump contracts. In addition to using Rusinow leads against suit contracts, they lead third-best from an even number of cards, and smallest from an odd number of cards. From Q-8-6-2 or from Q-8-6-5-4-2, they would lead the six. From Q-6-2, Q-10-6-4-2, or Q-9-7-5-4-3-2, they would lead the deuce.

Here are the procedures which many users of Journalist leads apply when leading against notrump contracts:

The lead of an ace asks partner to unblock any picture card he holds, otherwise to play low with an odd number of cards or begin an echo with an even number of cards.

The lead of the king asks partner to encourage or discourage with normal high-low signals depending on his holding.

The lead of the queen is either the top of a sequence, or is from K-Q-10-9, and asks the partner to unblock the jack if he holds it.

The lead of the jack is the top of a sequence, and denies a higher honor.

The ten is a strong card. Leading it guarantees a higher honor or honors.

The lead of the nine promises the ten, but no higher honors.

When leading spot cards, the lead of a small card encourages the return of the suit, while the lead of a high spot card discourages the return of the suit.

Whether these leads are an improvement in practice as well as in theory is yet to be determined. They, like other opening leads, at times are more helpful to the declarer than to the defenders. Clever declarers can false-card against them effectively and there are ambiguous situations with Journalist leads just as with all others. Searching the record, it is hard to see whether their use has done either much good or much harm.

Try them if you like, but I suggest you keep a record of the tricks won and the tricks lost. See how you come out over a period of time before you decide whether to adopt them permanently.

MODERN METHODS OF OPENING LEADS

Some time ago, some of my bridge-playing friends started using what they call the "Modern Method" of opening leads from suits that have an interior sequence. This method called for the lead of the second card in the sequence. For instance, the nine would be led from K1098xx, or K109xx, while the ten would be led from AJ10xx or KJ10xx. This method has been adopted by a number of leading players and is sometimes described as "Zero or Two Higher" leads. The idea is that the lead of the ten or nine promises either zero or two higher honors in the suit, while the lead of the jack denies any higher honors. I don't think the description usually given for this method of leading is correct, as these players will also lead the nine-spot from AK109x or from AQ109x, calling these leads "exceptional" cases. To me, the best explanation to give opponents of this method is to state that you lead second-highest from an interior sequence. This seems to cover all the bases.

Some players have added the jack to those leads which show both zero or two higher, and would lead the jack from AQJxx. I notice that the American Contract Bridge League book covering the 1977 World Championship says that the winners of that event, Paul Soloway and Paul Swanson, agreed that the lead of the queen showed either zero or two higher cards. I suppose this would mean they would lead the queen from AKQxx.

Many years ago, I failed to win a tournament because I led the jack from the KJ109x, and when my partner gained the lead, he simply did not believe I had the king. So he switched to a different suit. Had he continued my suit, we would have won the event. I was delighted that these "Modern Methods" cleared up that ambiguity and promptly took up this method myself, insofar as the lead of the nine and ten were concerned, confident that never again would my partner and I have a misunderstanding when a lead was from an interior sequence. After partner led the ten, we would examine the dummy and, if the jack was in sight, it was obvious that our partner had not led second-highest from an interior sequence. We would then know that any missing honors were held by the declarer. Likewise, if we could see the ace and king between our hands and the dummy, we would know the same thing, for the only honors higher than the ten left would be the queen and jack, and with the Q-J-10, partner would not have led the ten-spot. Oh, there might occasionally be a case where the matter was not cleared up because even though we saw neither the jack nor the ace-king, partner's ten-spot was simply the highest card he held, with the declarer holding the missing cards. In those cases, we hoped the bidding would help clarify the matter for us. Likewise, when our partner led the nine-spot and we could see the ten-spot, we would know that he had no higher cards than the nine. Of course, the same would be true if we happened to see the three top honors. In those cases where we could not see the critical cards, we again hoped the bidding would help us clarify the matter.

Considerable time elapsed and I was still waiting for all those matchpoints I was going to pick up through use of these modern methods. I was beginning to become nervous about the whole business. First, I noticed that in many instances where my opponents used this type opening lead I, as the declarer, felt extremely comfortable about the whole thing when they led a nine or ten. Next, it began to occur to me that while I knew what my partner was doing when he led a nine or ten, so did the declarer, and that often it seemed to help the declarer more than it helped me. For instance, I ran across this hand.

```
                    NORTH
                    ♠ Q 10 7 5
                    ♡ A 7 4 3
                    ◇ 5
                    ♣ Q 7 4 3
WEST                                EAST
♠ A 6                               ♠ 8 3 2
♡ Q 9 6                             ♡ J 10 8 5
◇ Q 9 6 2                           ◇ K J 10 4 3
♣ J 10 9 8                          ♣ K
                    SOUTH
                    ♠ K J 9 4
                    ♡ K 2
                    ◇ A 8 7
                    ♣ A 6 5 2
```

My partner and I were playing the new method so that the lead of the jack guaranteed no higher cards in the suit. Sitting West, I led the jack of clubs against a four-spade contract. After seeing the dummy, my partner knew the declarer had the ace, and declarer knew my partner had the king. This information did my partner no good, as the only way not to play the king was to revoke, but it made life easy for the declarer.

He played low from the dummy. If East played low, he meant to win the trick with the ace and eventually to lead a small club from both hands, hoping I had started with three and that the king, known to be in my partner's hand, was doubleton. When my partner played the king, he thought the matter over again. Now it was obvious my partner's king was a singleton. Declarer had two club losers, so he decided to lose one of them right now. He let the king hold the trick. He didn't know who had the ace of trumps, but if I had it, he didn't want to take that first trick with the ace of clubs and have the good queen of clubs in the dummy ruffed out. If East was going to trump any clubs, he wanted him to trump losing clubs and not winning clubs.

Seeing the singleton diamond in the dummy, my partner returned a trump. I led a second club, and, sure enough, my partner got a ruff, but declarer simply played small clubs from both hands, and now had his two good club tricks. The defenders had run out of anything good to do. Declarer had disposed of the three losers he had in the black suits. One lead pulled trumps, and declarer was able to claim.

I don't know how declarer would have played had my lead of the jack not made it clear that I did not have the king. At the very least, that information kept him from making a mistake. I prefer to give my opponents every possible opportunity to make mistakes.

In spite of this and other hands, it seemed to me that the new method must be an improvement, and I continued to look for those matchpoints it was going to bring me. As time went on and nothing good happened, I decided to look through the literature and see what I could find. I found this hand played in the 1969 Spingold Team-of-Four Match.

None vul., dealer South.

                        NORTH
                        ♠ A Q
                        ♡ A Q 6 4
                        ◇ 10 8 4
                        ♣ K 10 9 2
        WEST   EAST
        ♠ None   ♠ 8 7 6 4 3
        ♡ J 10 9 5 3 2   ♡ K 7
        ◇ 7 2   ◇ A Q 9 6 5
        ♣ A Q 5 4 3   ♣ 6
                        SOUTH
                        ♠ K J 10 9 5 2
                        ♡ 8
                        ◇ K J 3
                        ♣ J 8 7

The bidding:

SOUTH	WEST	NORTH	EAST
Rubin	Lawrence	Feldesman	Hamman
2 ♠	3 ♡	4 ♠	Double
Pass	Pass	Pass	

Mike Lawrence led the jack of hearts. As you can see, had Ira Rubin tried a finesse, he would not have made his contract. Bob Hamman would win with the king and return a club. He would now get a ruff, and the ace of diamonds would be enough to set the contract. But it never occurred to Ira Rubin to finesse hearts. Lawrence and Hamman were playing that the lead of the jack guaranteed no higher card. Rubin went right up with the ace.

He led the ace of spades and then overtook the queen and pulled trumps. A trick-by-trick record of the play is not available, but the record shows that Rubin made an extra trick, and presumably he lost only to the two minor suit aces.

As for the notion that not only the nine or ten, but also the jack or queen showed two or none higher, let's look at this hand from the 1967 World Championship, where a declarer from

Thailand could have come up with a sensational play against Venezuela.

```
                    NORTH
                    ♠ K 3
                    ♡ J 10 6
                    ♦ K Q 6 2
                    ♣ Q 7 4 3
        WEST                        EAST
        ♠ Q J 9 8 7 4 2             ♠ A 10
        ♡ Q 5 3                     ♡ 9 8 7 2
        ♦ 4                         ♦ J 8
        ♣ 8 5                       ♣ K J 9 6 2
                    SOUTH
                    ♠ 6 5
                    ♡ A K 4
                    ♦ A 10 9 7 5 3
                    ♣ A 10
```

In the room where the Thai players were North-South, the contract was 3NT played by North. East led a small club and declarer took no chances. He was looking at six tricks in diamonds, and two in hearts, plus the ace of clubs, and he decided to take them before they got away from him. He didn't want to lose the lead to West and have a spade come through, so he played dummy's ace and cashed his nine tricks.

In the other room, the Venezuelan team also got to 3NT, but this time it was played by South. West led the queen of spades. Of course, it could have been the top of an interior sequence or it could have been just what it was. The official report of that World Championship said that the declarer took the percentage play and covered the queen with his king. The result was that the defenders took the first seven tricks and set the hand three tricks. Had East and West been playing that version of the modern method where the lead of the queen guaranteed two or none higher, declarer would have known that the ace was with East. He was looking at the king in the dummy which made it impossible for West to have two spades higher than the queen. Knowing the futility of playing the king, declarer would have played the three. Then the suit would have been handsomely blocked and he would have had no trouble taking nine tricks.

Today I am convinced that these new leads cost the defenders more than they gain. I have long been a believer that proper signaling on the part of the defenders is more helpful to the defenders than it is to the declarer, but there must be an exception to everything. I predict other players are going to find the same thing as they go along, and that these modern methods will disappear from serious bridge before too long. For those who think otherwise, I suggest they keep books on the subject and compare their gains with their losses.

There is one more which comes from the old so-called "Journalist Leads" of the mid-1960s. The standard lead from K-Q-10-9 is the king. The Journalist lead calls for the queen, with instructions for partner if he has the jack to play it. If you hold the queen instead of the ace, he does want the suit continued, but if you hold the ace and king without the queen, he may want you to switch. However, when you lead the queen and he holds the jack, he will know you have not led from the Q-J-10, and as the queen is seldom led unless it is the top card of a sequence, he will know that you have led from the K-Q-10-9. If he has the jack he will play it, and you will know you can continue the suit without running into the ace-jack in declarer's hand. If he doesn't play the jack, you will know that you had better switch if the declarer lets you hold the trick.

Some use this convention when defending against notrump, and others whenever they are leading a suit no matter what the contract is. Personally, I like it no matter what the contract is, assuming that it is the lead of a suit which my partner has not bid.

Back in 1934, Ely Culbertson, in his red book on play, said that when you hold A-Q-10-9 or longer, and are defending against notrump, you should lead the ten-spot. However, in a footnote, he says, "If bidding indicates the king in dummy, lead the queen." That advice has been given repeatedly since then, both in books and in articles in bridge magazines. For instance, the *Bridge World* gave this example in May, 1952:

```
                    NORTH
                    ♠ K 7 3
                    ♡ K Q J 7
                    ◇ A Q 10
                    ♣ K Q J
        WEST                      EAST
        ♠ A Q 10 6 2              ♠ 9 8
        ♡ A 9 5                   ♡ 8 3 2
        ◇ 8 7 4 3                 ◇ K 9 5
        ♣ 8                       ♣ 10 9 7 4 3
                    SOUTH
                    ♠ J 5 4
                    ♡ 10 6 4
                    ◇ J 6 2
                    ♣ A 6 5 2
```

The 1952 story is that North dealt and bid one heart, South responded 1NT, and North jumped to 3NT. I rather suspect that today North would be playing notrump and not South, because North would probably open the bidding with 2NT. Be that as it may, the author goes on to say that the strong bidding by North indicated that he probably held the king of spades. The author uses this hand as an example where the lead of the queen from AQ10xx will defeat 3NT, whereas if West led his fourth-best, the declarer would win the first trick with the jack and end up with ten tricks. Personally, I would feel better about the lead if West didn't have that blooming ace of hearts. Holding ten points himself, West's partner has about four points. Since it is necessary for him to gain the lead for the ploy of the queen lead to be successful, I would have grave doubts in real life that he had an entry so that he could continue spades. However, the author (even as we teachers all do) proved his point by putting the king of diamonds with East and making it necessary for the declarer to bring in two diamond tricks to fulfill his contract. When the diamond finesse is finally taken and fails, East can still have a spade to lead to his partner to scuttle the contract.

I have searched the records long and hard trying to find a hand which demonstrates a victory for this lead of the queen, and the best I have been able to do is find the reverse of that.

My finding is that you don't lead the queen unless you are pretty darn sure the king is going to show up in the dummy. This exhibit is not the greatest hand I ever used to illustrate a point, because Dorothy Hayden (now Dorothy Truscott) was destined to make her contract of 3NT no matter what they led. The only problem was managing to bid 3NT. The Italian pair of Avarelli and Belladonna, in the other room, were not up to it. They not only let Peter Leventritt play three spades, but also let him make it as well. However, for what it's worth, here is the hand, from the 1965 World Championship.

N-S vul., dealer East.

```
                    NORTH
                    ♠ J 5 4
                    ♡ J 9 7 4
                    ◇ Q 10
                    ♣ Q 8 7 2
        WEST                        EAST
        ♠ A Q 10 9 3 2              ♠ 8 7 6
        ♡ Q 8 2                     ♡ K 6 5 3
        ◇ 6 2                       ◇ J 9
        ♣ 9 3                       ♣ A J 10 4
                    SOUTH
                    ♠ K
                    ♡ A 10
                    ◇ A K 8 7 5 4 3
                    ♣ K 6 5
```

The bidding:

EAST	SOUTH	WEST	NORTH
Garozzo	Hayden	Forquet	Becker
Pass	1 ◇	1 ♠	Pass
Pass	2 ◇	Pass	Pass
2 ♠	Pass	Pass	3 ◇
Pass	3 NT	Pass	Pass
Pass			

I have named all of the players to let you know that this was a star-studded cast in the drama to follow. It looks like Garozzo went to the well once too often. When Dorothy found out that her partner, B. J. Becker, had some diamond support, she was pretty sure she was looking at eight running tricks in the two red suits. All she needed to do was pick up one trick in one of the black suits and it seemed more than likely she could do that.

Just what sort of subtle thinking convinced Forquet that Dorothy had gone to 3NT because she decided her partner had a spade stopper is not clear, but anyway he led the queen of spades. That's the play that allowed me to make my point. Dorothy won that lead with her singleton king, and now any further spade leads by her opponents would make the jack of spades good in the dummy. There was now ample time to establish a club trick, and Dorothy ended up taking ten tricks in all. While Forquet's lead gave her only an extra trick, the hand does illustrate the point that with the lead of any spade other than the queen, the declarer would have been held to only one spade trick.

Culbertson, and others since him, seem to have overlooked the fact that when the suit is six cards long, and you have an entry, the best lead is the ace. That caters not only to a singleton king or jack, but also to Kx or Jx. Without an entry, the ten is still the best bet.

There are players who feel that leading fourth-best from a long broken suit aids the declarer too often, and that something better should be found. One of the suggestions is to lead the smallest card you have from a long suit. The smaller the card led, the more interested you are in having the suit returned. The higher the spot card, the less interest you have in the suit. I have found a couple of examples where this procedure may have affected the final result, but I have found nothing to endear me to the idea of leading the small card. Here is an example which goes all the way back to 1957.

None vul., dealer East.

```
                    NORTH
                    ♠ A Q 8 4
                    ♡ A K Q 9 6
                    ◊ 6 3
                    ♣ K 9
        WEST                    EAST
        ♠ K 10 9 5              ♠ J 7 6
        ♡ 5 3                   ♡ 8 4 2
        ◊ K 9 8                 ◊ 4
        ♣ J 10 8 4              ♣ A Q 6 5 3 2
                    SOUTH
                    ♠ 3 2
                    ♡ J 10 7
                    ◊ A Q J 10 7 5 2
                    ♣ 7
```

The bidding:

CLOSED ROOM

EAST	SOUTH	WEST	NORTH
Seamon	Forquet	Leventritt	Siniscalco
Pass	2 NT	Pass	3 NT
Pass	Pass	Pass	

OPEN ROOM

EAST	SOUTH	WEST	NORTH
Chiaradia	Koytchou	D'Alelio	Ogust
Pass	3 ◊	Pass	3 NT
Pass	Pass	Pass	

The 2NT bid by Forquet in the closed room is a specialized bid in the Italian system, showing the seven-card suit which is either solid or has only one loser. Siniscalco thought he had enough to justify a bid of 3NT. There is nothing about the results to make you fall in love with Forquet's conventional call. Peter Leventritt started proceedings by leading the jack of clubs. Forquet put on dummy's king and Billy Seamon, East, won the ace and led back the five, carefully returning the card which was his original fourth-best card. Things went swimmingly from there on for the defenders, who took the first six tricks, finally leaving Forquet his five heart tricks plus his two side aces.

In the open room, Koytchou had no convention bid for the South hand, so he made the natural bid of three diamonds. Harold Ogust, North, also decided he had enough for 3NT. Chiaradia, East, led a club, but he chose the two. Ogust won the ten-spot with the king and promptly led a diamond and finessed the ten. D'Alelio made the mistake of allowing the ten to win. That suited Ogust just fine. Having won a club trick, and looking at five heart tricks and a spade trick, all he needed was two diamond tricks to bring him home. He gave up all ideas of doing any more finessing and simply took his nine tricks.

If Chiaradia had led the five of clubs instead of the two, would his partner have had a better chance to make the winning play? I don't know what he would have done, but I do know what he should have done. The rule of eleven would have told him that Ogust had only one more club higher than the five. Unless that one card was the ace, East could now take a trick with each club in his hand. All signs pointed to East as the player with the ace. With the two and three missing, the probability was high that he had enough clubs to set the hand right now. Even in bridge, a bird in the hand may be worth more than one in the bush.

Now we jump all the way up to 1977. For the first time, the World Championship was a contest between two teams from North America, one known as the defenders, and one as the challengers. On my next hand, the challengers picked up 12 International Match Points.

Both vul., dealer South.

NORTH
♠ K J 7 6 5 4
♡ A K
◇ J 9
♣ J 7 6

WEST   EAST
♠ A 8   ♠ Q 10 3
♡ Q J 9 6 3   ♡ 8 7
◇ 7 3   ◇ A 8 6 5 2
♣ 9 8 4 2   ♣ Q 5 3

SOUTH
♠ 9 2
♡ 10 5 4 2
◇ K Q 10 4
♣ A K 10

The bidding:

OPEN ROOM

SOUTH	WEST	NORTH	EAST
		Von Der	
Rubin	Swanson	Porten	Soloway
1 ♡	Pass	1 ♠	Pass
1 NT	Pass	3 ♠	Pass
3 NT	Pass	Pass	Pass

CLOSED ROOM

SOUTH	WEST	NORTH	EAST
Hamman	Ross	Wolff	Paulson
1 ♡	Pass	1 ♠	Pass
1 NT	Pass	2 ♣	Pass
2 ◇	Pass	3 NT	Pass
Pass	Pass		

The bidding indicates that neither Rubin, in the South seat for the defenders, nor Hamman, in the South seat for the challengers, adheres to five-card major suits for opening bids. Both opened the South hand with one heart. It is also of interest

113

that this opening bid kept neither Swanson nor Ross from finding the heart opening lead with the West hand. However, there was a difference. Swanson led the six of hearts while Ross led the three of hearts.

In the open room, where Swanson led the six of hearts, Rubin won dummy's king and led the jack of diamonds. Soloway, East, rose with his ace and returned a heart. Even with the club finesse working, Rubin could take only eight tricks before giving up the lead to Swanson's ace of spades. Swanson took the rest of the tricks with his hearts.

In the closed room, where Ross led the three of hearts, things turned out differently. Hamman led the nine of diamonds from dummy rather than the jack. Paulson played low and Hamman played the queen. When the queen held the trick, he decided that East, rather than West, had the ace. He played for split aces and led a small spade toward dummy, and, when Ross played low, he went up with dummy's king. Having this spade trick in the bank, he reverted to diamonds, getting that suit established. When the club finesse worked for him, he had nine tricks.

Of course, Paulson could have defeated this had he gone up with the ace of diamonds and returned a heart. You will have to ask Paulson whether the fact that his partner led the three of hearts rather than the six had anything to do with his decision. The analyst in the official World Championship Book says of Paulson, "...he may have felt Ross had only a four-card suit as a result of the lead." Certainly it is true when partner leads from a long suit that the lead of a higher spot card, like the six, suggests strongly that the suit is more than four cards long, while the lead of a small one, like the three, makes it appear more likely that the suit is only four cards long.

Whatever may have motivated Paulson, I have failed to find any examples where leading the small card from a five-card or longer suit has won any points which could not have been won by leading the fourth-best. However, I have found two hands where success did not follow the lead of a card other than fourth-best.

THE LEAD FROM FOUR SMALL

I have suggested that when you hold four small cards against a suit contract that you lead second-highest. When you're leading from this suit against notrump, it depends upon whether you have reason to think your partner has length in the suit.

Should you hold ♠Q108, ♡8642, ◇AJ9, ♣KJ4, I think you would want to make a passive lead against three notrump when you have no reason to believe your partner has length in hearts. Your partner is not going to be leading too many times anyway, because he only has a few high card points, but when he does, you would like for him to lead anything except hearts. Certainly, had your right-hand opponent made some strong bid, such as two notrump, you would not want to lead from any of those suits against any game contract. In this case, the opening lead of the six of hearts would be the best way to get him to lead something other than hearts, should he win a trick somewhere during the proceedings.

However, holding such a weak suit where you believe your partner has length in the suit, I believe the best bet is to lead the fourth-best and let him know how many you have. You do that when you hope that your side is going to have some long card tricks in the suit. Many authorities do not agree with me, and think that the second-highest should be led, whether your partner has or has not bid the suit. The high qualification of some of the authorities who hold a view different from mine has caused me to search the records. My first exhibit goes all the way back to 1953, with the United States playing against the Swedish team.

E-W vul., dealer South.

NORTH
♠ A 7 5
♡ 4
◇ K Q 9 5 4 2
♣ 9 8 7

WEST
♠ Q J 6 3
♡ 8 7 5 3
◇ 8 7
♣ 10 5 4

EAST
♠ 9 8 2
♡ A Q J 9 6
◇ A J 3
♣ J 6

SOUTH
♠ K 10 4
♡ K 10 2
◇ 10 6
♣ A K Q 3 2

The bidding:

OPEN ROOM

SOUTH	WEST	NORTH	EAST
Werner	Crawford	Koch	Stayman
1 ♣	Pass	1 ◇	1 ♡
1 NT	Pass	2 ◇	Pass
2 NT	Pass	3 NT	Double
Pass	Pass	Pass	

CLOSED ROOM

SOUTH	WEST	NORTH	EAST
Schenken	Anulf	Lightner	Lilliehook
1 ♣	Pass	1 ◇	1 ♡
1 NT	Pass	3 ◇	Pass
3 NT	Pass	Pass	Pass

In the open room, things went along smoothly for the Americans. Stayman's double insisted that Crawford lead hearts, and Crawford duly led the three. Put yourself in Stayman's place in the East seat, and I think after you have had a look at the dummy, you would have no trouble deciding that

116

the three was not a singleton or the high card from a doubleton. South's bidding certainly was not the bidding of a man who had a five- or six-card heart suit. I think you would decide that it was either small from an honor, or else that it was small from a four-card suit. The way to find out whether it was low from the king was to put in the jack, and that is what Stayman did. Werner won the king, but then he only had seven more tricks without giving up the lead. He cashed his five club tricks and two spade tricks, but when he finally had to lead a diamond, Stayman won the ace and had four good heart tricks.

In the closed room, the Swedish player, Anulf, also led his partner's suit, but he led the eight instead of the three. The strangest things happened. East played the six and the first trick was won by Schenken in the South with the ten. Before anything could be clarified, Schenken led a diamond and Lilliehook, East, won the ace. He returned the queen of hearts, and Schenken played the deuce, leaving his king bare. However, that turned out all right as Lilliehook continued with the jack. Schenken won his now-singleton king and had no trouble taking the rest of the tricks for a score of 430 points.

Did I hear you say that was a long time ago? Let's see what happened in 1977. This time, the lead was made from four small cards in a suit which had not been bid, but the bidding strongly suggested that there was no length in the suit, either in the declarer's hand or in the dummy. This deal is from the match between Taiwan and Argentina in the World Championship.

None vul., dealer South.

NORTH
♠ Q 2
♡ J 3 2
◇ 10 2
♣ A K 9 8 6 5

WEST
♠ 7 6 4 3
♡ K 5
◇ A J 8 6
♣ Q 4 3

EAST
♠ A J 9 8 5
♡ 10 8 7
◇ Q 9 5 3
♣ 10

SOUTH
♠ K 10
♡ A Q 9 6 4
◇ K 7 4
♣ J 7 2

The bidding:

SOUTH	WEST	NORTH	EAST
Santamarina	Lin	Attaguile	Tai
1 ♡	Pass	2 ♣	Pass
2 NT	Pass	3 NT	Pass
Pass	Pass		

Lin, sitting West, led a spade. Three tricks later, he was on lead with the king of hearts, and he led another spade. Would you believe that Santamarina, South, won two spade tricks, and that the way the hand developed, the only chance the defenders had to set the hand was for Tai, East, to discard his ace of spades?

Could the fact that Lin led the seven of spades have had anything to do with it?

On the first spade trick, East properly played the jack and South won the king. Santamarina played his two high clubs from the dummy and, when nothing good happened, he led a small heart and finessed the queen. Lin, of course, won with his king. At this point, the defenders could have taken four spade tricks, four diamond tricks, and a club trick, to add to the trick

118

they already had for a total of ten tricks. But they didn't do that. Lin continued spades by leading the six. Apparently, Tai decided that Santamarina must have started with K10x and he ducked this trick, letting dummy's queen win. Santamarina now cashed his hearts, and the defenders discarded badly. Five tricks had been played in hearts, two in spades, and two in clubs, for a total of nine. Of these, the declarer had won eight and the defenders had won only one trick. Here are the four cards which everyone had left:

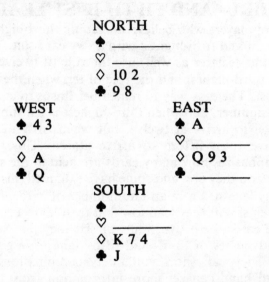

It was Santamarina's lead from the South hand. Whatever he led, the defenders could take the last four tricks and still set him. Had he led the jack of clubs, that probably is what they would have done. West would have led another spade, which East would have had to win, because he only had the ace left, and then the ace of diamonds would serve as the re-entry to the West hand to cash the good spade. But while the defenders seemed to have been confused, Santamarina was not. He led the four of diamonds, taking that entry out of the West hand. West won the diamond ace, cashed the queen of clubs, and East had one more chance. If he discarded that ace, West could still win all the tricks. He didn't discard the ace. He discarded the nine of diamonds. Apparently, he still could not bring himself to believe that his partner had started with four spades and that

Santamarina had no spades left. If his partner has started with only three spades, then Santamarina had one left. Now it was too late and West led a spade. This gave East his trick, but that last trick went to Santamarina when East had to lead back to his king of diamonds.

At the other table, the Taiwan pair played four hearts and were set two tricks, with the defenders getting one spade, two diamonds, the king of hearts, and a club ruff.

THIRD- AND FIFTH-BEST LEADS

There are players who believe in leading third-highest with a four-card suit and fifth-highest with a five-card suit. Their partners (and the declarer as well) use the rule of twelve when the lead is the third-highest and the rule of ten when the lead is the fifth-highest. The easy way to remember this is to count fifteen as the key number, and when third-highest is led subtract three from fifteen to arrive at twelve, but when fifth-highest is led subtract five from fifteen to arrive at ten. This method of leading emphasizes how many cards are held in the suit, rather than how good they are, and some have extended this to include suits of any length. From an odd number of cards, be it three, five, or even seven, they lead low and then high. From an even number of cards, be it two, four, or six, they play high-low.

Most advocates of third- and fifth-highest are genuine true believers. They can show you many combinations of cards where third hand can get more information from these leads than any other way. This might be an example:

```
                  10 7
(1) K 9 5 4                   A 8 6
(2) K 9 5 4 3
              (1) Q J 3 2
              (2) Q J 2
```

With (1), West would lead the five. East would win with the ace and would have no trouble telling that West had started with a four-card suit. He does this by first testing to see whether it could have been a five-card suit. In other words, he subtracts five from ten. If the five-spot is from a five-card suit, then the dummy plus third hand plus declarer have five cards higher than the five. Between his hand and the dummy, East can see five cards higher than the five, which leaves none with South. In that event, West would have started with the K-Q-J and would not have led low. Therefore, if the suit is a long suit, it is a four-card suit, and South has as many cards in the suit as does West.

With (2), West would lead the three. After the appearance of the two, East will know that the lead is from an odd number of cards, and if it is from a long suit, that number is five. Suppose South false-cards with the queen or jack at trick one? Could West have a six-card suit, leaving South only the doubleton queen-jack? Not with those players giving count whenever they have an even number of cards. These players, when they have a four-card suit, lead the third-highest, which is also the second-lowest, but when they have a six-card suit, lead the third-lowest. That means they will have two cards smaller than the one they led, and there is no way West can have two cards smaller than the three.

East wins the first trick with the ace and, knowing his partner has five, continues with the eight. If West is without an entry, he can let South win that trick. When East gains the lead, he will continue the suit and the defenders will come to four tricks.

Bridge hands can be constructed to demonstrate almost anything you want to demonstrate. The basic question is, in real life, do these methods gain more tricks than they lose?

Looking for records on these third- and fifth-best and related leads, I found where, in the 1979 World Championship, the three pairs on the Central American-Caribbean Zone (CAC) Team used these methods. They did not qualify for the finals, but the ACBL World Championship Book does give 105 deals they played from the qualifying rounds. In these 105 deals, they did not have very many opportunities to lead low from long suits, but on those where they did, I failed to find any hand where these methods either gained or lost a trick which would not have been gained or lost by leading fourth-best.

There are players who have no objection to third-best leads against suit contracts, but who are reluctant to lead them against notrump contracts for fear of wasting a valuable spot card. True Believers say that there is a compensation for this because there are times when leading third-best unblocks a suit.

Max Hardy, a tournament director for the ACBL, a publisher, and writer on bridge, as well as an experienced player, says that he has been using third- and fifth-best leads for more than twenty years. In the Pilgrim Open Pairs game in the 1981 North American Summer Championship, Hardy found a hand where the unblocking aspect of the third-best lead might have been helpful. The hand is rather inconclusive, but it is the best real hand I have been able to find in support of these leads.

```
                      NORTH
                      ♠ 9
                      ♡ J 10 6
                      ◇ A Q 10 9 7 3
                      ♣ A J 5
        WEST                        EAST
        ♠ K Q 5 4 3 2               ♠ 8 6
        ♡ Q 9 8 2                   ♡ A 7 5 4 3
        ◇ 4                         ◇ K 6 5
        ♣ 9 6                       ♣ Q 8 4
                      SOUTH
                      ♠ A J 10 7
                      ♡ K
                      ◇ J 8 2
                      ♣ K 10 7 3 2
```

The bidding:

SOUTH	WEST	NORTH	EAST
	Pass	1 ◇	Pass
1 ♠	Pass	2 ◇	Pass
3 ♣	Pass	3 ◇	Pass
3 NT	Pass	Pass	Pass

When this hand came up Max was playing, not directing. The bidding called for the lead of a heart, and he led the third-best, the eight, with considerable success. East won with the ace and returned the suit. Max won with the queen and led the nine, conceding a heart to the dummy. Declarer did not have nine tricks without developing some suit, and elected to go after diamonds. When he came to his hand and led a diamond to

East's king, East was able to cash his two heart tricks because the heart remaining in Max's hand was the lowly deuce.

In the analysis of the hand in the Daily Bulletin during that tournament, it was pointed out that if the deuce had been led, the defense would still have had a chance. East would have to duck the first round of diamonds so that West could jettison his blocking heart on the second round. However, South could still counter that by taking the diamond ace on the second lead of diamonds and guessing the queen of clubs to come to nine tricks.

Hands which are constructed to prove a point seem much more clear-cut. On such hands, the analysts seldom can find a way for the victim to escape the superiority of the methods being recommended. However, even these hands sometimes present unexpected problems. Here is an example by a well-known writer demonstrating the superiority of third-best leads.

NORTH
♠ K 9 8
♡ A Q J 4
◊ Q 7 6
♣ 10 5 2

WEST
♠ 5 4
♡ 8 6 2
◊ K 10 8 4
♣ A Q J 9

EAST
♠ 7 3 2
♡ 10 7 3
◊ A J 9 3
♣ 8 4 3

SOUTH
♠ A Q J 10 6
♡ K 9 5
◊ 5 2
♣ K 7 6

Defending against three spades, West led the eight of diamonds, his third-best. This obviously is not fifth-best. If it were, West would have four diamonds higher than the eight. Looking at the dummy and his own hand, East can see four of the six diamonds higher than the eight. Therefore, West can have only two diamonds higher than the eight. So, East decided the eight-spot was third-best. For third-best, you use the Rule of

123

Twelve. Eight from twelve leaves four, so there were four diamonds not in the West hand which were higher than the eight-spot. East saw three of these in his own hand and one of them in the dummy. By this reasoning, he arrived at the conclusion that South had no diamonds higher than the eight. The bidding is not given, but we must assume that something in the bidding had indicated that West had not started with a doubleton diamond.

East won the first trick with his nine and then, faithful to the rule of leading third-best, returned the three of clubs. West won with the jack and led the four of diamonds. He now knew that a third diamond would be ruffed, and so he did not try to cash the ace. Instead he led a small club, and as West knew that East had started with only three clubs, he also knew that he should not try to cash a diamond before taking both of his club tricks.

I have found only one hand from real life where leading fifth-best made a difference. This time, the lead helped the declarer rather than the defenders. That is a charge often leveled against the lead of fourth-best, but the matter would have been much less clear had the opening lead been fourth-best. The hand is from the 1981 European Championship, with Norway playing Israel.

NORTH
♠ 7 4
♡ Q 3 2
♢ K Q 9 8 2
♣ 8 5 3

WEST
♠ Q 10 8 5 3
♡ 10 8 4
♢ 7 6 5 3
♣ Q

EAST
♠ J 9
♡ J 9 7 6 5
♢ A J 10
♣ 9 7 4

SOUTH
♠ A K 6 2
♡ A K
♢ 4
♣ A K J 10 6 2

Leif-Eric Stabell, of Norway, reached six clubs with this

hand. The Israelis were using third- and fifth-best leads. West led the three of spades. Declarer won, and laid down the ace of clubs. From the lead of the three, he was confident that West had an odd number of spades and when West showed up with a singleton club, declarer decided that the spade holding was five in West and hence only two in East. This meant that the obvious play of trying to trump a spade would not work, as East would overtrump. So, Stabell cashed the ace and king of spades and the ace and king of hearts. He then led a diamond. East won with the ace, but he had no more spades to lead. Any card he led from any of the three suits he held would give the dummy the lead, and declarer could discard two spades on the two high red cards in the dummy.

Had West led the five of spades rather than the three, and had he then refused to complete count by playing the three of spades, declarer would have been in doubt whether he could or could not trump a spade in dummy and discard another on dummy's queen of hearts. As a matter of fact, in the other room the contract was also six clubs, and that is exactly what the declarer tried to do. Of course, he went down one trick.

If there is enough data available to tell us whether these third- and fifth-best leads have gained or lost tricks, I have not found it. The number of times it has done either are insufficient for making a judgment. Until more history on this subject is available, we might try to take a look at the theoretical pros and cons of these leads. After all, each partnership has to make a decision whether to use them or not.

LEADS FROM THREE SMALL CARDS

The two most basic signals in bridge are the attitude and count signals. Attitude is shown by playing a high card followed by a lower card to encourage a continuation of the suit. The play of a low card followed by a higher card discourages a continuation. Count is shown by playing high and then low to show an even number of cards in the suit, while low and then high shows an odd number of cards. These signals often apply to opening leads as well as later in the hand. Some extremists try to use one exclusively. With some players, every signal is showing count, and attitude is never shown. With others, attitude is nearly always shown and count is given only in a few situations. These extremists do not seem to be winning many championships. The successful players use both depending on the situation. The important thing is that each partnership agrees which signal is proper in each situation.

Opening fourth-best or third- and fifth-best are two different attempts to combine both attitude and count. For attitude players, the lead of a small card indicates an interest in the suit. Choosing precisely the fourth-, third- or fifth-best starts telling the story about the number of cards held in the suit.

The chief advantage of leading third- and fifth-best is that your partner frequently knows the number of cards held in the suit quite early—sometimes at trick one. The disadvantage is that the declarer also knows, and it is very difficult in subsequent plays to deceive the declarer about the number held should that be deemed desirable. A second disadvantage is that the lead of the third-best card frequently wastes a valuable spot card.

The main disadvantage of fourth-best leads is that it may not be until the second or even the third play from the suit before your partner can get the count. The advantage is that should you think it desirable that count not be given, you can withhold count.

Leading low from three small cards instead of the old-fashioned top of nothing lead is also a form of giving count. It has the advantage of doing away with the lead of the high card where the partner may have difficulty deciding in time whether the lead is from a doubleton or a three-card holding. On the other hand, partner cannot tell whether the leader wants the suit continued. For those of us who like to give attitude on opening lead, the lead of third-best can itself be ambiguous. When an intermediate card like a five or six is led, we are going to have trouble deciding whether the lead is top of a short suit or third-best from a four-card suit. Should we decide to adopt third- and fifth-best leads, we probably should abandon top of nothing from three small, and go along with the many leading players who lead small from three small cards.

Let's take a special look at this problem of leads from three small. It is still considered standard to lead high from three small cards, but many of the world's leading players lead small.

126

From 7-5-2 these players would not lead the seven, but would lead the deuce. There are good arguments for both sides with this holding. Those who lead high say that leading the seven would indicate to your partner that you had no honor in the suit, and that you were not interested in having it continued. The advocates of leading small say that when you lead high, your partner may be able to judge it is not a fourth-best and that you do not have an honor, but that he will not know whether you have a three-card holding or a two-card holding. Usually he can tell when you play the second card, but sometimes he can't tell even then, and that may be too late for the information to be helpful. So they claim that with this holding it is better to lead the deuce, hoping that your partner can work it out that you do not have an honor. However, there are two sides to this question. While when you lead high your partner frequently cannot tell whether you have two or three, when you lead low your partner frequently cannot tell whether you have three or four. Look at the trouble George Rapee and Edgar Kaplan had in the 1968 Spingold Championship team game.

E-W vul., dealer north.

```
                    NORTH
                    ♠ A 9 7 3
                    ♡ 7
                    ◇ A 6 4 3
                    ♣ A J 8 4
      WEST                        EAST
      ♠ J 5 2                     ♠ Q 8 4
      ♡ A 8 5 2                   ♡ K Q J 9 4 3
      ◇ Q 10 7                    ◇ 9 2
      ♣ Q 7 2                     ♣ 9 3
                    SOUTH
                    ♠ K 10 6
                    ♡ 10 6
                    ◇ K J 8 5
                    ♣ K 10 6 5
```

The bidding:

SOUTH	WEST	NORTH	EAST
	Rapee		Kaplan
		1 ♣	Pass
1 NT	Pass	Pass	2 ♡
2 NT	Pass	Pass	Pass

Fred Karpin reports this hand in the *Bridge World* magazine, and, unfortunately for the record, does not tell us who the North and South players were. Rapee led the two of hearts, and Kaplan won with the jack. A sadist would now sit back and enjoy watching just what declarer discarded from his hand and the dummy on the run of six heart tricks by the defenders. However, we will never know just what a mess they would have gotten into with these discards, for they did not have to make them. After winning with the jack, Kaplan returned the queen, and Rapee played the eight. This pair leads small from three small cards, and it now became apparent to Kaplan that Rapee had started with 8-5-2, leaving South with A-10-6. As Kaplan had no entry for his heart suit, he saw no future in leading it, and so he tried shifting to a small spade.

That gave declarer his opportunity. Rapee played the jack of spades. Declarer promptly finessed Kaplan's queen. Eventually he guessed to play the clubs right, and when play had ended he had taken four spades, four clubs, and two diamonds. Instead of losing the first six tricks and getting into a mess discarding, he'd come home with ten tricks.

Had the defenders been playing that they led high from three small, Kaplan would have known that Rapee did not start with three small cards when he led the deuce. He either had three to an honor, or else he had four. On the second lead when South played the ten, the only three to an honor Rapee could have had was three to the ace, as all of the other honors had appeared. And if that had been his holding, he would have played the ace at trick two to unblock.

George Rapee and Edgar Kaplan are two bridge players who command maximum respect, and they went on to win the event in which they played this hand.

Seeking a perfect solution to this problem of leading from

three small cards, some players have adopted the practice of leading the middle one. For the second lead, they play the highest and finally the smallest, and because of this sequence of plays, this method of leading has become known as MUD, for middle, up, down. The leader always reserves the right of playing the small card second in case he concludes it is to his advantage to deceive the declarer. They point out that with this method, if your partner leads a nine, it cannot be the middle of a three-card suit, for with three to an honor the small card would be led. Even if the leader leads the eight and the nine appears, his partner will know that it is either a singleton or a two-card suit. The trouble with this method is that the five can be led from 7-5-2, 5-2, Q-7-5, K-10-7-5, as well as from a singleton. It is putting an awful burden on your partner to try to figure out which of these combinations you have led from when you lead the five, and because of this, a number of players who tried MUD have quit using it.

If you haven't had a lot of discussion with your partner on the subject, I suggest you stick to standard leads. That will be the easy part. Now, we get to the tough part that requires thinking. How do we decide not what card to lead, but which suit to lead?

PART TWO:

CHOOSING THE SUIT

CHAPTER 3:
WHEN TO LEAD SHORT SUITS

When you are using standard leads, the choice of which card to lead after you have decided on a suit is virtually automatic. This decision will not always enable you to make good leads. The decision as to which suit you should lead is not so automatic. That requires looking at all available evidence before making a choice. You can get evidence not only from looking at the cards you hold, but also from what you have heard in the bidding.

When a beginner is defending against a trump contract, you can pretty well guess that the opening lead is from the shortest side suit in his hand. The defensive maneuver we all learned first was that of trying to score a trick by trumping and our method of trying to do that was to get rid of all the cards in some side suit in our hand. I even knew one player who had two singletons in his hand, one of them being the ace of trumps. He had become so used to leading singletons when he had them that he automatically led the other singleton. Leading singletons in short suits practically amounts to a compulsion with inexperienced players. No matter how often teachers tell them that on occasion leading long suits can be better, they cannot resist grabbing a card from the shortest suit in their hand. The oldest known written instructions from a teacher to a pupil were published in Maxims from the Crown Coffeehouse in London in 1728. One of them read, ''...Lead from the strong suit, study your partner's hand, and attend to the score.'' Today, we might substitute for this (or add to it) an admonition to study the bidding. In 1728, they played whist, and there was no bidding.

There will be times when you lead a singleton and find your partner with the ace in the suit you led and you will get an immediate ruff. This is a very dramatic start, and it is obvious to everyone just what has happened, even if that one trick does not set the contract. Unfortunately, many a declarer has had his contract handed to him by the lead of that singleton, even if it

131

did secure a ruff. This is not nearly so dramatic or so easy to see. After the hand is over, the cards are shuffled and redealt and no one is ever the wiser that the lead of a long suit might not have gotten that immediate ruff, but would have defeated the contract.

Getting in that ruff with a small trump does its best job when you have your book in high cards but need just one more trick to set the contract. No person alive can always tell when this is the case, but there are situations that strongly suggest that it might be. When you lead a small singleton, you expect to surrender the lead to the declarer, but you hope to regain it before your trumps are gone, find an entry into your partner's hand, and score with one of otherwise worthless trumps. If you can spot those situations where these circumstances are likely to exist, you can lead these short suits with the odds in your favor instead of leading them with the odds against you.

Let us list the three circumstances which are needed to help you take a trick with that small trump:

1. YOU HAVE AN OTHERWISE WORTHLESS TRUMP. Of course, if you hold precisely the Q-J-10, the holding is no more worthless than the holding of the singleton ace, as you are bound to take one trick no matter what you do with this trump suit. You do not gain anything by trumping with this holding unless you can trump more than once, and it is not often that you can give your partner the lead two times to make two trumps with this holding. It seems pretty obvious that holding high cards which will take tricks under their own power does away with any advantage to leading short suits, but it is not so obvious that holding four small trumps sometimes can do the same thing for you. Let's look at a hand:

None vul., dealer South.

```
                    NORTH
                    ♠ K 6
                    ♡ J 10 4
                    ◊ A Q 10 8 2
                    ♣ Q 8 3
      WEST                      EAST
      ♠ 8 7 4 2                 ♠ 9 5
      ♡ K 6 3                   ♡ 8 7 2
      ◊ 3                       ◊ K 7 6 4
      ♣ K J 9 6 4               ♣ A 10 5 2
                    SOUTH
                    ♠ A Q J 10 3
                    ♡ A Q 9 5
                    ◊ J 9 5
                    ♣ 7
```

The bidding:

SOUTH	WEST	NORTH	EAST
1 ♠	Pass	2 ◊	Pass
2 ♡	Pass	2 NT	Pass
3 ◊	Pass	3 ♡	Pass
3 ♠	Pass	4 ♠	Pass
Pass	Pass		

Looking at the North and South hands, it seems obvious that declarer can take five spade tricks and five tricks in the red suits with no problem. If West is a new player who is not aware of the requirements for leading singletons, he leads the three of diamonds. Then declarer would indeed go ahead and take his ten tricks without difficulty. He would rise with dummy's ace of diamonds and pull four rounds of trumps. He would then offer East the king of diamonds by leading the nine and overtaking with dummy's ten. If East chooses to take the trick, declarer would have four diamond tricks and a heart trick. If East declines the offer of the king of diamonds, declarer finesses hearts and establishes three heart tricks.

But let's say that West is a player who knows about *the forc-*

ing game. The bidding tells him this is an ideal situation for a forcing defense. South bid three suits, but indicated he was quite short in clubs. In this bidding sequence, South almost surely has exactly five spades, and North has two. West has almost as many spades as South, and if he could make South trump just once, he would have as many trumps as South. So our hero in the West seat leads clubs, his long suit. Dummy plays low, East wins the trick with the ten and leads back a second club. South's natural instinct is to trump, but whether he trumps it or not he is going to be set. Let's assume he does trump. You can wiggle and squirm all you want to with the South hand, but no matter what you do, the defense can find a counter and keep you from taking ten tricks. Probably in real life the declarer would trump the second club and then lay down three spades and find that West has as many spades as he does. If he goes ahead and takes West's last trump away from him, South will also be out of trumps. When he finesses the jack of diamonds, the defenders will cash quite a few club tricks. If declarer stops after pulling three rounds of trumps to take the diamond finesse, West will lead clubs once more, and if declarer trumps this trick, he will now have fewer trumps than West. One of those little trumps in the West hand will have become as big as an ace.

Four small trumps can create havoc with declarer's plans too often to have them designated as worthless trumps. Trumps which are worthless unless they are used to trump something will usually be in a hand which has not more than three trumps.

2. YOU CONTROL THE TRUMP SUIT. If you hold only three small trumps, it is not at all unlikely that when you surrender the lead to the declarer, he will take them away from you and you will never be able to use them to trump anything. The holding of A-4-2 is ideal for having small trumps to use for ruffing. A-2 is not too bad, and K-3-2 is often very good.

3. YOU THINK THAT WHEN YOU REGAIN THE LEAD WITH YOUR HIGH TRUMP, PARTNER WILL HAVE SOME CARDS WHICH WILL ENABLE YOU TO GIVE HIM THE LEAD. That raises the question which is worthy of closer examination. What would lead you to place your bet on partner's ability to gain the lead to give you a ruff?

If he has done any bidding, there is a good chance he will

have an entry, but suppose he has done nothing except pass. In that event, you have nothing to guide you except the mathematical odds. This is not the greatest guide in the world, but under the circumstances is the best available. What you need is an ace in your partner's hand. If you hold eight HCPs or fewer, and the opponents are in a game contract of hearts or spades, there is a pretty good chance your partner has an ace. With your side holding usually about 16 HCPs when the opponents are in a major suit game, and you have eight or fewer, your partner will probably hold eight or more. Let me show you a table of probabilities, not that anyone should remember the numbers, but just to show how it seems to work out.

PROBABILITY THAT A GIVEN NUMBER OF HIGH CARD POINTS WILL INCLUDE AN ACE			
HCP	Probability	HCP	Probability
4	20.5%	9	71.3%
5	29.2%	10	79.9%
6	37.8%	11	85.3%
7	53.7%	12	90.2%
8	62.2%	13	93.6%

If we extended this table, it would not reach 100% until you hold 25 HCPs. It is possible to hold 24 HCPs and not have an ace in your hand. Your hand then would consist of all four kings, four queens, and four jacks, with one smaller card. I suggest you don't worry about that too much. If your partner holds that hand, you are not likely to be defending anyway, and that hand only occurs one time out of 17,639,265,530.

Our table is called an A-Priori Table, meaning that these are the chances before the deal. The odds after you see your own hand may be changed somewhat, depending on the exact cards which you have in your hand. For example, if you are holding two aces in the eight HCPs that you have, chances that your partner will hold an ace have been greatly reduced. Contrariwise, if you have eight HCPs and no aces at all, the chances your partner will have an ace if he has also eight HCPs have been somewhat increased. However, that increase does not change the proposition that when you hold eight or fewer HCPs your partner is quite likely to hold an ace. The only holding which you can have which significantly changes the probabilities of the number of aces in his hand from those shown in the table is your holding in aces. Otherwise, this table is going to represent approximately the chance your partner will have an ace, depending on the number of high-card points he has.

Unfortunately, there is nothing guaranteed about this. Even when the bidding tells you that there is nothing to lead you to believe that your side has anything other than 16 HCPs, you still may hold either more or fewer HCPs than this. And even if your estimate as to the total number of HCPs that you hold is correct, there is still that chance that your partner will not have an ace. The fact that he will have an ace about 62% of the time also means that 38% of the time he will not have the ace. Still, this estimate of probabilities will tell you when the odds favor your partner having an ace.

Of course, when your opponents are obviously sacrificing and it seems like your side has more HCPs than the other side has, chances that your side will also have more aces have been increased.

Let's see how the championship players put these theories to practical use.

The first hand is one of those where declarer obviously made his bid as a sacrifice, and the opening leader had every reason to believe that there would not be a shortage of entries into his partner's hand. This is a hand from the 1965 World Championship.

E-W vul., dealer South.

```
                        NORTH
                        ♠ J 9
                        ♡ J
                        ◇ K J 10 7 3
                        ♣ K Q J 9 5
        WEST                        EAST
        ♠ K 10 8 5 3 2              ♠ A 7 6
        ♡ K 10 9                   ♡ Q 7 4 3
        ◇ 5                        ◇ A 9 8 4 2
        ♣ A 10 4                   ♣ 2
                        SOUTH
                        ♠ Q 4
                        ♡ A 8 6 5 2
                        ◇ Q 6
                        ♣ 8 7 6 3
```

The bidding:

SOUTH	WEST	NORTH	EAST
Leventritt	Belladonna	Schenken	Avarelli
Pass	1 ♠	2 NT	Double
3 ♣	3 ♠	5 ♣	5 ♠
6 ♣	Double	Pass	Pass
Pass			

The 2NT bid by Schenken in the North seat was the Unusual
Notrump, showing length in both minor suits. The Italian pair
bid the limit of their hands when they bid five spades. When
Peter Leventritt, representing the United States, refused to let
them play that contract, the defenders were faced with the job
of defeating the six-club contract by four tricks if they wanted
to show a profit on the hand. Let's take a look at Belladonna's
hand to see what we think about his lead of the singleton diamond.

He has the trump control. Does he have a worthless trump?
Small trump honors like the ten and jack sometimes need small
cards with them to be able to take tricks under their own power.
For instance, if East held the jack, there would be two trump

137

tricks available without trumping anything and getting the ruff would represent no gain. After getting the ruff, only one additional trump trick would be available. Even if only one of those honors was in the South hand and the other in North, the spot cards might be so distributed that getting in a ruff would be no gain. However, the bidding sequence suggested that this was not the situation on this hand. The club honors would appear to be with North behind the ace. If so, Belladonna had some worthless trumps.

As to entries in the East hand, Belladonna had no doubt that they were ample. East had been very active in the bidding.

Under the circumstances, the lead of the singleton has everything to gain. Belladonna led his diamond. Avarelli won the ace and returned the nine of diamonds for Belladonna to trump. Had Belladonna known that Leventritt had a doubleton spade, he could have led the king and a small spade to the ace and trumped another diamond with the club ten. In this case, the set would have come to 900 points. However, on the bidding, Avarelli well could have had four spades, leaving Leventritt with only one, so Belladonna tried to make sure of a score of at least 700 points by leading a small spade to Avarelli's ace. This limited the penalty to 700 points because on the diamond return Leventritt discarded his second spade.

In the replay of the hand with Forquet and Garozzo against B. J. Becker and Dorothy Hayden Truscott, Dorothy was on lead against a five-club contract with the East hand. Because he didn't play the Unusual Notrump convention, Garozzo, North, simply bid both of his suits. It happened that this worked out better in two ways. First, Garozzo got to play five clubs doubled rather than six clubs. Second, having no singleton, Hayden opened the ace of spades. Nonetheless, the defenders found their ruff. When Becker got in, he led the five of diamonds to Dorothy's ace and still got his ruff. By doing so he limited the net loss to 300 points.

In the semi-finals of the 1974 World Championship, with two matches going on simultaneously, the hands were duplicated so the same hands were played in both matches. This adds interest to the study of these particular hands. Here is one of them:

NORTH
- ♠ J 9 2
- ♡ 10 8 5 4
- ◇ Q 7
- ♣ A Q J 4

WEST
- ♠ 10 7 6 5 4
- ♡ A 3 2
- ◇ K J 6 5
- ♣ 9

EAST
- ♠ A K 3
- ♡ 7
- ◇ 10 9 8 3
- ♣ 10 7 5 3 2

SOUTH
- ♠ Q 8
- ♡ K Q J 9 6
- ◇ A 4 2
- ♣ K 8 6

The hand was played four times. All four of the North-Souths reached a contract of four hearts played by South. West had all of those components which make the odds favor the singleton lead: trump control, otherwise worthless trumps, and only eight HCPs, which makes it likely that his partner has approximately eight HCPs and will have an ace for an entry to give him a ruff. Three of the four defenders got off to an opening lead of the nine of clubs.

Two of them got their ruff; one did not. When I make a play like that made by Pietro Forquet of Italy, my wife tells me that I "got caught thinking". Let's see what happened to him.

The opening lead of the nine of clubs was won in the North hand with the ace, and the Indonesian declarer promptly led a trump. Forquet won that with his ace and it would seem that he tried to figure out which ace his partner held. If his partner held the ace of spades, he could get the ruff all right, but that would give the defenders exactly three tricks—one with the ace of spades, one with the ace of trumps, and one with a small trump. On the other hand, if East held the ace of diamonds, the defenders could take two top diamonds, the ace of trumps and a small trump, and would have four tricks to defeat the contract. Forquet led the king of diamonds. Had he led a small spade, he could have made tricks with both of his small trumps to add to the ace and king of spades and the ace of hearts to set the hand two tricks. The lead of the king of diamonds was not a great success. Instead of going set two tricks, the declarer made an overtrick.

Bobby Wolff, of the U.S.A., and Pedro Branco, of Brazil, did not find the way to set the hand two tricks, but they did settle for the way to set it one trick. They also led the nine of clubs. In both instances declarer won in the dummy and promptly led a heart. Wolff and Branco simply let him win that trick, planning to take the second heart and get a signal from partner. On the second heart it was up to East to tell his partner what to lead. Not having a high enough spade for a signal, both Easts played the three of diamonds. East had played a small club and now a small diamond, so it was not difficult for the defenders to lead a spade. This gave the defense only one small trump trick, but in addition, they took two spade tricks and the ace of trumps.

A great many years ago, one of my mentors told me that when I was on opening lead with an extremely weak hand I should lead any singleton that I had as a "desperation" lead. That is still good advice, and today we have discovered why. When we are on opening lead and have a very weak hand, the corollary is that our partner has a very good hand. If he has ten points or more, the chance is good that he will have either the ace of the suit we lead or control of trumps, so that if we just held some small trumps, there was a good chance we could make a trick with one of them.

Here is a hand from the 1953 World Championship which illustrates the point:

None vul., dealer East.

```
                    NORTH
                    ♠ Q 5 2
                    ♥ A Q 10 6 3
                    ◊ K 6
                    ♣ K 7 4
        WEST                        EAST
        ♠ J 6 4                     ♠ K 10
        ♥ 5                         ♥ K 9 8 7 2
        ◊ Q J 10 9 7 2              ◊ 8 5 4 3
        ♣ J 10 9                    ♣ A 6
                    SOUTH
                    ♠ A 9 8 7 3
                    ♥ J 4
                    ◊ A
                    ♣ Q 8 5 3 2
```

The bidding:

OPEN ROOM

SOUTH	WEST	NORTH	EAST
Anulf	Rapee	Lilliehook	Stayman
			Pass
1 ♣	Pass	1 ♥	Pass
1 ♠	Pass	3 ◊	Pass
3 ♠	Pass	4 ♠	Pass
Pass	Pass		

In the closed room, Howard Schenken played the hand in four spades and got the lead of the queen of diamonds. He conjured up some old Schenken magic and took ten tricks. He won the first trick with the diamond ace and led the ace and one spade, ducking that trick to the doubleton king in the East hand. East returned a diamond. Schenken discarded a club and won dummy's king. He then led the queen of spades, taking West's last trump away from him and led a small heart towards his jack. East won with the king and led yet another diamond, which Schenken trumped. He overtook his jack of hearts with dummy's ace and discarded two more clubs on dummy's good hearts. Now, he conceded a trick to the club and and ended up losing just three tricks in all.

George Rapee, West in the open room, had different ideas. Holding only five HCPs himself, he had heard nothing in the bidding to suggest that his side did not hold the normal 16 or so HCPs. This meant that his partner had approximately an average hand in high cards. He made that old-fashioned "desperation" lead of his singleton heart, betting that this partner had what was necessary to defeat this hand if only he could take a trick with one if his small trumps. He won the wager. From that point on, Anulf, South, was destined to lose at least a heart, a club, and two trump tricks no matter what he did. At the table, he took the heart finesse at once. Stayman won the king and led the deuce of hearts for Rapee to ruff.

On the next hand, Norman Kay, on opening lead with the West hand, thought that he had trump control plus a small useless trump. On the other hand, he had ten HCPs, and his partner had done nothing during the auction except pass. This indicated that his partner had approximately six HCPs. Therefore, the chance he held an ace was probably less than 50%. Was Kay simply lucky that his lead of a singleton enabled him to defeat the contract? The hand is from the finals of the 1967 World Championship, North America versus Italy.

N-S vul., dealer North.

NORTH
- ♠ J 9
- ♡ Q 10 7
- ◇ K 10 9 7 5
- ♣ A K J

WEST
- ♠ K 7 3
- ♡ J 6 5 3
- ◇ A
- ♣ Q 10 5 3 2

EAST
- ♠ 5 4
- ♡ A 9 4 2
- ◇ Q 6 3
- ♣ 9 7 6 4

SOUTH
- ♠ A Q 10 8 6 2
- ♡ K 8
- ◇ J 8 4 2
- ♣ 8

The bidding:

SOUTH	WEST	NORTH	EAST
Belladonna	Kay	Avarelli	Kaplan
		1 ♣	Pass
2 ♠	Pass	3 ◇	Pass
4 ♠	Pass	Pass	Pass

Analysis shows that Kay's lead was correct and not just lucky. Before we see just why this is so, let's take a brief look at the bidding. The Italians were playing the Roman system. The sequence of bids that Avarelli had made indicated that he had a balanced hand with no singleton or void and from 12-16 HCPs, but without particularly good support for spades. Belladonna knew, nonetheless, that Avarelli had at least two spades in his hand and put the contract where he thought it should be. There was nothing in the bidding to indicate to the defenders that they had anything other than their normal quota of about sixteen HCPs.

The thing that made the odds favor the opening lead of the ace of diamonds was the fact that this was a different sort of a singleton. It was a singleton ace. When you lead a small singleton, you rather expect that the declarer will win the trick. If you have trump control, you are going to have exactly one shot at giving your partner the lead. That will be when you gain the lead with your trump. If, however, you lead a singleton ace, and have trump control, you will have two chances to give your partner the lead. Even if your partner does not have an ace, your lead can be successful if you can find him with a second round control and can work out where it is. That can be either a king and queen or a king sitting in back of an ace in the dummy. The dummy told Kay that Kaplan had no points at all in clubs and that the best chance to give him the lead was to lead a heart. He did that. When Kaplan sacrificed his queen of diamonds by returning the suit, Kay trumped it. That made the third trick for the defenders and Kay still had a sure trick with his king of spades.

Had Kaplan been unwilling to sacrifice his queen of diamonds for the good of the cause, Belladonna could have found ample discards from the dummy to get rid of his losing diamonds and the defenders would have won only their two aces plus the king of trumps.

In the room where the North American team held the North-South seats, Sammy Kehela of Canada, sitting North, played three notrump, taking ten tricks against the opening lead of the four of clubs.

Let's look at another hand from one of those famous matches of the Italian Blue Team versus the United States. This one is from the finals of the 1972 Olympiad Games.

Both vul., dealer West.

                    NORTH
                    ♠ K 10 2
                    ♡ 10 7 6
                    ◇ K 7 6 3
                    ♣ A Q 6
        WEST   EAST
        ♠ 7 5   ♠ A 8 3
        ♡ A K J 9 4 2   ♡ Q 8 5
        ◇ A   ◇ J 8 5
        ♣ K 9 8 5   ♣ 7 4 3 2
                    SOUTH
                    ♠ Q J 9 6 4
                    ♡ 3
                    ◇ Q 10 9 4 2
                    ♣ J 10

The bidding:

                    CLOSED ROOM
SOUTH   WEST   NORTH   EAST
Belladonna   Lawrence   Avarelli   Goldman
                1 ♡   Double   2 ♡
2 ♠   4 ♡   4 ♠   Pass
Pass   Double   Pass   Pass
Pass

Here Mike Lawrence led a singleton against a four-spade contract although he was holding 15 HCPs and had no semblance of a trump control. What justified that lead?

He had two things going for him: first, the singleton that he had was an ace, allowing him to retain the lead after his singleton had been played; the other was that, in spite of his 15 HCPs, he expected to find some cards in his partner's hand. The Italians had obviously bid four spades as a sacrifice and didn't have the 24 or 25 HCPS your opponents usually have when they have bid game. Goldman had gotten into the bidding with the East hand. Lawrence not only thought Goldman had some high cards, but he also thought he knew where Goldman had an entry. So he led the ace of diamonds and then a small heart. Goldman won and led a diamond for Lawrence to trump. They beat the contract with one diamond, one heart, one spade, and one ruff.

While the Italians obviously had bid four spades as a sacrifice, you will notice that the routine play of leading the ace and king of hearts would have let them make their contract. The defenders would have won tricks with their three aces, but it is hard to see where they would have come to any additional tricks.

Take another look and you will see that if the Italians had simply passed, Lawrence would not have taken ten tricks. The clubs were poorly placed for him, and he would have had to lose one spade trick and three clubs. That is exactly what happened in the open room where the Americans held the North and South hands. They passed throughout and duly collected 100 points. This added to the 200 points gained by the pair of Lawrence and Goldman gave the Americans 300 points on the hand.

Leading doubletons can occasionally let you take a trick with one of those small trumps. Here is an example from the 1962 World Championship, with North America pitted against Great Britain.

N-S vul., dealer East.

```
                      NORTH
                    ♠ K Q 8 3
                    ♡ K Q 10
                    ◊ K 9 6 2
                    ♣ 5 3
        WEST                        EAST
      ♠ A 4                       ♠ J 7
      ♡ A 7 6 4 2                 ♡ J 9 8 3
      ◊ 7 3                       ◊ A Q 5
      ♣ 9 8 6 2                   ♣ Q J 10 7
                      SOUTH
                    ♠ 10 9 6 5 2
                    ♡ 5
                    ◊ J 10 8 4
                    ♣ A K 4
```

The bidding:

SOUTH Von Der Porten	WEST Rose	NORTH Mathe	EAST Gardener
			Pass
Pass	1 ♡	Double	2 NT
4 ♠	Pass	Pass	Pass

In the open room, the bidding was passed around to Kenneth Konstam, of Britain, in the North seat. He opened the bidding with one spade and ended up playing four spades. Against an opening lead of the queen of clubs, he lost a total of four tricks when the diamonds proved to be badly placed for him. This gave the Americans their 100 points.

The bidding in the closed room was quite different. It is shown above. Albert Rose, West, had trump control all right, but when you yourself are holding two aces, you do not normally count on finding an ace in your partner's hand. That is, you do not unless the bidding has told you otherwise. The bidding takes precedence over those mathematical odds.

The 2NT bid by Nico Gardener after Lew Mathe's takeout double was a limit jump raise showing that Gardener had around 11 or 12 points in support of hearts. That made it likely that he had an entry. Rose opened the seven of diamonds and Gardener won the queen. He could not be sure whether Rose had led a two-card or three-card suit, so he switched to the queen of clubs. Von Der Porten won in his hand with the ace and led a spade. Rose went right up with the ace and clarified the diamond situation by leading the three. Gardener had seen the deuce in the dummy, and he knew that Rose had signalled him that he had started with only two diamonds. He led his last diamond back for Rose to trump and the defenders still had the ace of hearts coming. That gave them 200 points, compared to 100 gained by the Americans in the open room, making a net of 100 points for Great Britain.

In the 1955 World Championship, Europe versus the United States, Lew Mathe had very few points, but made a highly aggressive lead with a doubleton. It worked.

None vul., dealer South.

```
                        NORTH
                        ♠ A K 3
                        ♡ A 9 8 2
                        ◇ J 5
                        ♣ J 10 9 5
        WEST                            EAST
        ♠ J 9 6 5 4                     ♠ Q 10 8 7 2
        ♡ 6 5                           ♡ K Q
        ◇ 8 7 6 3                       ◇ Q 9 2
        ♣ K 7                           ♣ A 6 3
                        SOUTH
                        ♠ None
                        ♡ J 10 7 4 3
                        ◇ A K 10 4
                        ♣ Q 8 4 2
```

The bidding:

CLOSED ROOM

SOUTH	WEST	NORTH	EAST
Roth	Dodds	Ellenby	Meredith
Pass	Pass	1 ♣	1 ♠
2 ♡	2 ♠	3 ♡	3 ♠
4 ♣	Pass	4 ♡	Pass
Pass	Pass		

OPEN ROOM

Reese	Mathe	Schapiro	Rosen
1 ♡	Pass	4 ♡	Pass
Pass	Pass		

In the closed room, all the British got out of all that bidding
was the feeling that they had not surrendered without a struggle.
Dodds duly opened spades, his partner's suit, but that got him
nowhere. Alvin Roth won with dummy's ace and led the ace and
a heart. When the suit split, he conceded two club tricks and got
on to the next hand.

The matter was quite different in the open room. Terrence Reese, on behalf of Great Britain, chose to bid one heart with the South hand, where Alvin Roth had passed. Boris Shapiro, sitting North, elected to go straight to four hearts. This effectively cut Rosen out of the bidding with the East hand, and left Lew Mathe, West, with nothing to guide him in choosing his opening lead. It turned out that this worked to his advantage. Let's see what conclusion we can come to. With only four HCPs in his hand, he had every reason to believe that his partner has about 12 HCPs. A desperation lead of a short suit is made when your partner is so strong that he may have control of your short suit so he can give you an immediate ruff. Lacking that, he may have control of trumps and an entry so that you can still get your ruff. In this case, Mathe's short suit was headed by the king. He went ahead and chose that suit anyway. With his ace, Rosen was delighted with this development, and played the six to encourage the continuation of the suit. Mathe led the seven of clubs and got his ruff with a small heart. That made three tricks for the defenders, and Rosen still had a heart trick.

Basic textbooks tell us that sometimes we can lead our partner's singleton. They know about that in the big leagues, too. Take a look at this hand from the 1957 World Championship match, United States versus Italy.

N-S vul., dealer South.

NORTH
♠ Q J 9 6
♡ 7 5 2
◇ K J 6 3
♣ 6 2

WEST
♠ K 5 4 3
♡ A K
◇ A 10 9 5 4
♣ J 8

EAST
♠ 10 8 7 2
♡ Q J 10 8 4 3
◇ 7
♣ 7 5

SOUTH
♠ A
♡ 9 6
◇ Q 8 6
♣ A K Q 10 9 4 3

The bidding:

OPEN ROOM

SOUTH	WEST	NORTH	EAST
Avarelli	Ogust	Belladonna	Koytchou
1 ◇	Pass	2 ◇	Pass
3 ♣	Pass	Pass	3 ♡
4 ♣	Double	Pass	Pass
Pass			

CLOSED ROOM

Goren	D'Alelio	Leventritt	Chiaradia
1 ♣	Double	Pass	1 ♡
3 ♣	Pass	3 ◇	3 ♡
Pass	Pass	4 ♣	Pass
Pass	Pass		

Both the Italians and the Americans were pushed to four clubs on a hand where they probably would have set the three-heart contract. The difference was that the Americans doubled the contract because Harold Ogust thought the bidding told him how to go about setting it. D'Alelio had no such information to guide him and did not double. This gave the Americans 500 points on the hand, compared to the 200 points which the Italians got.

What was the information that convinced Ogust he could set the hand? The Italians were using an artificial opening club bid, so Avarelli opened one diamond. This promised at least three diamonds. Belladonna's raise promised at least four diamonds. So, Ogust figured that Koytchou had one diamond at the most. It was a matter of simple arithmetic—3 + 4 + 5 = 12. He felt sure he had an entry back to his hand. He led the ace and four of diamonds for Koytchou to trump. Koytchou returned a heart and Ogust led another diamond, which was trumped. A heart back represented the last trick for the defenders, but two hearts, one diamond and two trump tricks came to a total of five tricks for down two doubled.

Sometimes the experts find their partner's singleton even though there is nothing in the bidding to indicate the singleton is there. Take a look at this hand from the U.S.A. versus Argentina match in the 1958 World Championship.

N-S vul., dealer North.

```
                        NORTH
                        ♠ 2
                        ♡ 6 4 3 2
                        ◇ K 9 8
                        ♣ A 8 6 5 2
        WEST                            EAST
        ♠ Q 9 6                         ♠ 10 8 5 4 3
        ♡ A                             ♡ Q 9 8
        ◇ J 10 6 5 4 3                  ◇ 2
        ♣ Q 10 9                        ♣ K 7 4 3
                        SOUTH
                        ♠ A K J 7
                        ♡ K J 10 7 5
                        ◇ A Q 7
                        ♣ J
```

The bidding:

SOUTH	WEST	NORTH	EAST
Cabanne	Rapee	Lerner	Silodor
		Pass	Pass
1 ♡	Pass	3 ♡	Pass
4 NT	Pass	5 ◊	Pass
6 ♡	Pass	Pass	Pass

Do you think six hearts is a bad contract with North and South holding only 26 HCPs and a far-from-solid trump suit? Don't laugh too quickly. In the closed room, Johnny Crawford and B. J. Becker bid and made six hearts against an opening lead of the ace of trumps.

In the open room, George Rapee had different ideas about opening leads. With nine HCPs in his hand, he surely did not expect to find very much in his partner's hand, and probably would have been surprised to know that Silodor held a king and a queen. With his six diamonds, Rapee decided somebody ought to be short in diamonds, and he hoped it was Silodor. He led the five of diamonds.

Declarer put up dummy's king and there was nothing about the play of the deuce from Silodor to indicate he was entranced with this lead. After winning in the dummy with the king, Cabanne led a small heart and put in his ten. Rapee won, and led another diamond which was trumped by Silodor. This scuttled the slam contract.

The singleton lead against a small slam contract seems to work out well more often than anywhere else. If you gain "one more" trick, you have defeated the contract. Furthermore, you don't have to worry about your singleton lead giving them two or three extra tricks. Here is an example of North America versus Indonesia match in the 1973 World Championship.

E-W vul., dealer East.

NORTH
- ♠ K J 8 7 2
- ♡ K 9
- ◇ A Q 9 6 5
- ♣ 10

WEST
- ♠ 9 4
- ♡ 10 8 7 6 5 3 2
- ◇ 2
- ♣ J 4 3

EAST
- ♠ A 6 3
- ♡ Q 4
- ◇ 8 7 4 3
- ♣ K 8 7 5

SOUTH
- ♠ Q 10 5
- ♡ A J
- ◇ K J 10
- ♣ A Q 9 6 2

The bidding:

OPEN ROOM

SOUTH	WEST	NORTH	EAST
Becker	Lasut	Rubens	Aguw
			Pass
1 NT	2 ◇	3 ♠	Pass
4 ♠	Pass	Pass	Pass

CLOSED ROOM

Walujan	Soloway	Sacul	Swanson
			Pass
1 NT	Pass	2 ♡	Pass
2 ♠	Pass	3 ◇	Pass
4 ♠	Pass	4 NT	Pass
5 ♡	Pass	6 ♠	Pass
Pass	Pass		

The singleton lead against a small slam should not be made when you hold your side's quota of high-card points yourself, and particularly it should not be made when you hold an ace. Assuming that your opponents are competent, they probably

153

have at least three aces to get into a slam contract, and when you have an ace the chance of giving your partner the lead is slight indeed. However, if your hand is weak and if you don't have an ace, there is a good chance that your partner does, as small slams are often bid missing one ace. If his ace happens to be in the suit you lead, you immediately set the hand. If his ace happens to be in trumps, your chances to set the hand are excellent. That gives you two extra chances to pick up that "one more trick".

The Indonesian players seemed to be gung-ho on transfer bids. The two-diamond bid by West in the open room is not a typographical error. It was used by the Indonesian players to transfer to two hearts. Likewise, North's bid in the closed room was a transfer to spades.

The overcall may or may not have had something to do with keeping B. J. Becker and Jeff Rubens from reaching a slam. Six notrump seems to be unbeatable and would have been more comfortable with South playing the contract. However, the Americans stopped in four spades and took 12 tricks.

In the closed room, the Indonesians did an awful lot of bidding. However, they did not wind up in the unbeatable 6NT contract, but rather in the six-spade contract which could be, and was, defeated. Paul Soloway, West, had that desperation hand with a singleton diamond. That was his opening lead and now the hand was sure to go set. His partner didn't have the ace of diamonds, but he did have the ace of trumps, and when he won the spade ace, he led back a diamond for Soloway to trump.

Here is a hand with a different angle. It is from a United States against France match in the World Championships of 1960.

N-S vul., dealer West.

                    NORTH
                    ♠ A 6 2
                    ♡ Q 4 3
                    ◇ A K 5 2
                    ♣ 10 6 5
WEST   **EAST**
♠ J 10 9 7 4 3   ♠ 5
♡ J 5 2   ♡ K 9 7 6
◇ 6   ◇ Q 9 8 7 4 3
♣ 9 8 4   ♣ J 2
                    SOUTH
                    ♠ K Q 8
                    ♡ A 10 8
                    ◇ J 10
                    ♣ A K Q 7 3

The bidding:

CLOSED ROOM

SOUTH	WEST	NORTH	EAST
Trezel	Rubin	Jais	Jacoby
	3 ♠	Pass	Pass
3 NT	Pass	4 NT	Pass
6 ♣	Pass	6 NT	Pass
Pass	Pass		

OPEN ROOM

Rubinow	Delmouly	Mitchell	Bourchtoff
	Pass	1 ◇	Pass
2 ♣	Pass	2 NT	Pass
4 ♣	Pass	4 ♠	Pass
5 ♡	Pass	6 ♣	Pass
Pass	Pass		

Down through the years, Ira Rubin has gotten some fantastic results with some bizarre opening three-bids. On this hand, his luck seems to have left him. The French pair reached a 6NT contract which couldn't be defeated. Rubin led the jack of spades, and Trezel won. He led two clubs to be sure that suit was going to break, and then led the jack of diamonds. No matter who had the queen of diamonds, he was going to take twelve tricks. Jacoby won with the queen, but Trezel had three diamond tricks to add to his five clubs, three spades, and the ace of hearts, for a total of twelve tricks.

In the open room, the French seemed to have done better by simply passing. Rubinow ended up in six clubs instead of 6NT. Delmouly, West, had one of those very bad hands with a singleton, and so he led the singleton. Rubinow could not get three diamond tricks if he won in the dummy. Hoping that the six was not a singleton, Rubinow let the diamond ride to Bourchtoff's queen. Bourchtoff led back a diamond and the defenders took the first two tricks.

Suppose you were to say to me, "Easley, leading a doubleton under the right circumstances has a good chance to work out, and leading a singleton has a good chance to succeed. Under what circumstances do you lead a void suit?" I would say it's a good idea if you can get by with it. That's not exactly what Edgar Kaplan did on my next hand, but comes about as close to it as you can get.

Dealer West.

```
                    NORTH
                    ♠ A K Q J
                    ♡ K J 9
                    ◇ 8 2
                    ♣ K J 10 8
        WEST                        EAST
        ♠ 9 5 4 2                   ♠ 10 8 6 3
        ♡ 8 6 3                     ♡ 4
        ◇ A K Q 10 9 3              ◇ J 6 5 4
        ♣ None                      ♣ 7 6 5 3
                    SOUTH
                    ♠ 7
                    ♡ A Q 10 7 5 2
                    ◇ 7
                    ♣ A Q 9 4 2
```

The bidding:

SOUTH	WEST	NORTH	EAST
	Kaplan		Sheinwold
	3 ◇	Double	Pass
4 NT	Pass	5 ◇	Pass
6 ♡	Pass	Pass	Pass

The record does not say who was vulnerable, but it does say that Kaplan led the three of diamonds. When Sheinwold's jack held that trick, he knew what he had to do. He led back a club for Edgar to trump.

Let's review briefly the way the big-league players gain by leading short suits. They lead them when they have control of the trump suit, when they have an otherwise worthless trump, and when they think they can give their partner the lead. Normally, when defending against a major suit game contract, they think they can give their partner the lead when they have eight HCPs or fewer. They take special liberties when the singleton is an ace, and also when they have five or six HCPs or less. With hands this weak, there is a good chance their partner can furnish the trump control and the entry to give them a ruff.

Even then, opening a short suit carries with it an element of risk. Of course, almost any opening lead carries an element of risk, but opening short suits seems to carry more than most. Sometimes the short suit lead allows declarer to keep control of the hand while getting his long suits established. Here is such a hand.

Both vul., dealer North.

```
                        NORTH
                        ♠ 8 4 3 2
                        ♡ 5 2
                        ◇ A Q 9 3 2
                        ♣ 9 4
          WEST                        EAST
          ♠ A 10 6                    ♠ Q 5
          ♡ K J 10 7 6                ♡ Q 9 3
          ◇ 6                         ◇ J 10 8 5
          ♣ J 6 5 3                   ♣ A 10 7 2
                        SOUTH
                        ♠ K J 9 7
                        ♡ A 8 4
                        ◇ K 7 4
                        ♣ K Q 8
```

The bidding:

SOUTH	WEST	NORTH	EAST
		Pass	Pass
1 NT	2 ♣	2 ◇	2 ♡
2 ♠	Pass	3 ♠	Pass
3 NT	Pass	4 ♠	Pass
Pass	Pass		

This hand was played in the 1978 Grand Nationals in the final round, with Florida versus Chicago. The bidding needs some explanation. The two-club bid by West was the Brozel Convention, showing length in hearts and clubs. North showed his diamond suit. East had a fit in both of his partner's suits and decided to compete in hearts, feeling confident that his side had a 5-3 heart fit. The level of the bidding allowed Bud Reinhold, of the Florida team, to show his spade suit at the two-level. With four-card trump support, North bid three spades. South still thought 3NT might be the best spot and bid it, but North carried the bidding back to four spades.

Had West chosen to lead a heart, the defenders would have taken one heart trick, one club trick, and two trump tricks.

West led his singleton diamond. In the course of play, he got to trump a diamond, but he still had only two trump tricks. In other words, he had two trump tricks if he got a ruff, and he also had two if he didn't get a ruff. The six of spades turned out not to be a worthless trump. It had value as a guard to the ten. And, in maneuvering to get this ruff, the defenders got no heart tricks at all.

We must sympathize with West in his case. It is not at all clear that the six of trumps was a useful trump. On the other hand, the bidding did suggest that the spade suit held by North and South was far from sturdy, and that East may well have held the queen or jack doubleton, either of which would have promoted West's ten-spot.

Here is how the play went. Reinhold won the opening lead with dummy's ace and led a small spade, finessing his jack. West won with the ace. East had played the five of diamonds on the first trick, which West took as a suit preference signal. He dutifully returned a club. East won the ace and gave West his ruff. Now the king and queen of clubs had been promoted into winners and declarer still had the heart suit under control. West shifted to a heart, but it was too late. Reinhold won with his ace. The king of trumps cleared up the trump suit. He sluffed dummy's heart on the clubs. He now had two trumps in each hand and was in full control. He had no heart losers. As a matter of fact, he had no other losers at all.

If leading a short suit except under specific circumstances is a high-risk lead, what are the alternatives? One possibility is to lead long suits, and so this hand serves nicely as a transition to my next subject.

CHAPTER 4:
WHEN TO LEAD LONG SUITS

AGAINST NOTRUMP CONTRACTS

When defending against a notrump contract, the small cards in your long suits are not at the mercy of declarer's trumps, as declarer doesn't have any trumps. He has given up that source of winning tricks. Experience has taught us that leading long suits is likely to be the best defense against a notrump contract, as long as there is a reasonable chance that we can establish this suit and then regain the lead. So, early in our learning career, we are told that the best lead against a notrump contract is the fourth-best from our longest and strongest suit. That means the fourth-best down from the top. That is usually the best defense...but not always.

Suppose the bidding has gone

1 NT - 2 NT - 3 NT

and you are on lead with this collection of cards:

♠ J 10 5
♡ Q 4
♢ 10 8 5 4 3
♣ 8 4 2

The chances that you can get that diamond suit established and regain the lead are remote. By examining your hand and the auction, you know your partner has ten to twelve HCPs. So you try to find the suit your partner is long in and would lead if he could, and hope you will have supporting cards for him. We know from experience that leading from a queen doubleton in an unbid suit doesn't work out well too often, and most players will start off by leading the jack of spades. In that suit you have two cards which can help your partner to get his suit established.

The next question to ask is, "What is a long suit?" Is a four-card suit a long suit? Many authorities say that you should not lead small from a suit which is A-K-3-2. Why is that?

Let's see if a little table I have prepared will help us to understand this matter.

CARDS HELD	CHANCES FOR A LONG CARD TRICK						TOTAL LONG CARD TRICKS
	Trick						
	2	3	4	5	6	7	
4	0.15%	5.6%	36.7%				0.4
5	0.6	12.3	53.2	87.2			1.5
6	1.7	23.8	69.8	94.0	99.4		2.9
7	4.8	40.5	83.6	97.8	99.9	100	4.3

Let's take a look at this table, not for the purpose of memorizing it, but for a clearer understanding of the principles involved. A trick which is taken by a card because the opponents have no cards left in this suit is sometimes called a low card trick and sometimes a long card trick. This table indicates how many long card tricks you can expect on the average, from suits of four, five, six and seven cards in length. Take a look under the top line where it refers to trick four. That means when you lead the fourth time from a four-card suit, your opponents will be out of cards in that suit 36.7% of the time. However, it is theoretically possible for them to have been exhausted of the suit before the fourth lead, and you will see that they will have been exhausted by the third lead 5.6% of the time. The chances they will be exhausted on the second lead are well below 1%. For neither of them to have more than one card in the suit, it is necessary that your partner have at least seven. Actually, it is even possible that they would be out the first time the suit is led because your partner happened to hold the other nine cards. I have not taken this chance into account, as it will only happen one time in 296,385.

When I add these possibilities together, I come to a total of 42.45. That means that forty-two times out of a hundred there will be a long card trick. So let's say that a four-card suit is worth four-tenths of a long card trick.

By the same process, you can see that when you hold five cards in a suit, the chances are that both opponents will be out on the fourth lead—that is, after the suit has been led three times—a little more than half the time. Adding together all the possibilities, we can say that a five-card suit is worth 1.5 long card tricks. In *Contract Bridge Complete,* published by Ely Culbertson in 1949, he said, "If I have A-K-4-3-2, I expect that the other eight cards of the suit will be divided 3-3-2 in the other hands." Of course, he knew better than that. That exact distribution will occur only slightly more than 31% of the time.

The preceding table is known as an "A Priori Table", and, in reality, is applicable only when you have heard no bidding, but it is certainly more useful than Culbertson's crude figures. By the time you make an opening lead, you will have heard some bidding and if your long suits have not been bid by the opponents, the probable long card tricks are slightly more than indicated in this table. However, that difference is really not significant, the only really significant difference being that when the opponents have bid your long suit, the probable long card tricks are much less than shown in the table. In all other circumstances, you can go along with it and not be very far wrong.

Now let's get back to that lead of a small card against a notrump contract with the A-K-3-2. In that suit, you already have two tricks. You would lead the deuce, either in hopes of finding your partner with the queen, or in the hope that you can develop a long card trick. Before making that play, it is wise to compare the probable loss with the probable gain.

If your opponents have reached a three notrump contract, the chances that your partner has the missing queen are very small, and so you had better consider the probabilities of gaining a long card trick. Against this, weigh the possibility of giving your opponent a trick with his queen that he could not have taken had you not led the suit. Such a trick is sometimes referred to as a "free" trick. Now you will see that, what the experts have learned from playing many thousands of hands, you can learn immediately. The possibility of loss is much greater than the possibility of gain, and that is why experienced players are cautious about leading the fourth-best from their longest and strongest suit when it happens to be A-K-3-2.

It is not too easy to find a hand played by the experts where an opening lead was made from such a suit. I did find one in the 1962 World Championship with North America versus Great Britain.

E-W vul., dealer East.

```
                    NORTH
                    ♠ Q 4 3 2
                    ♡ 10 6 2
                    ◇ A 4
                    ♣ J 4 3 2
      WEST                          EAST
      ♠ A 6 5                       ♠ K J 10 7
      ♡ A K 9 5                     ♡ J 7 3
      ◇ 10 5 2                      ◇ Q 9 6
      ♣ 9 7 6                       ♣ Q 8 5
                    SOUTH
                    ♠ 9 8
                    ♡ Q 8 4
                    ◇ K J 8 7 3
                    ♣ A K 10
```

The bidding:

CLOSED ROOM

SOUTH	WEST	NORTH	EAST
Gardener	Coon	Rose	Murray
			Pass
1 NT	Pass	Pass	Pass

OPEN ROOM

Nail	Priday	Mathe	Truscott
			Pass
1 ◇	Pass	1 ♠	Pass
1 NT	Pass	Pass	Pass

In the closed room, the British were opening with a weak
notrump, and Gardener's opening bid of 1NT closed the bidding. Charlie Coon led his five of spades. Eric Murray won the
ten and led back the seven to the ace for another lead through
dummy's queen. The defenders cashed four spade tricks.
Gardener had to make two discards. It didn't look like he could
spare one of his guards for the queen of hearts, so he discarded
the ten of clubs and a small diamond. Murray got off lead with
a diamond which Gardener won with the jack. Declarer cashed

the other three diamonds and the ace-king of clubs. At this point, he had nothing left but his three hearts and had to lead them himself. The defenders took the last three tricks.

In the open room, The Americans were playing the strong notrump, so Bobby Nail opened the South hand with one diamond. Priday opened a high heart. Alan Truscott played the three-spot, and Bobby Nail, South, did the best he could by playing the eight. In spite of Truscott's play of a small heart, Priday continued the suit by leading a small heart. This gave Nail one heart trick in the bank. When the diamond finesse worked and the suit broke, he took five diamonds plus the ace and king of clubs, making an extra trick.

Of course, one hand proves exactly nothing, but let's consider the implications of this particular hand. Although each of his opponents held precisely three cards in the heart suit and the long card trick was there, getting that trick established proved to be fatal for the defense. The timing was lost. Bobby Nail not only got that free trick with his queen of hearts, but he also got the lead at trick two. He was able to develop his tricks before the defenders could cash their long card trick.

Our sympathies must go to Priday of the British team. After Lew Mathe bid one spade, all leads looked miserable. Usually you don't get rich leading dummy's suit, and we can understand his reluctance to lead spades.

How about leading small from A-Q-3-2 in an unbid suit? Against a suit contract, this would be considered a no-no. It doesn't stand out as anything great against a notrump contract, but it is not as bad as leading low from A-K-3-2. The lead of a small card from A-Q-3-2 should only be made, if at all, when your partner has enough high-card points to make it likely that he is going to be able to gain the lead before declarer has succeeded in taking enough tricks to make his contract. If the opposing contract is three notrump, the chances your partner has the king are slim. You make this lead only to guide your partner into returning the suit when he gains the lead, in the belief that your ace and queen are behind declarer's king. You are willing to give the declarer a free trick, hoping it is not his ninth trick, in return for the possibility that you will get two tricks when your partner returns the suit, plus the four-tenths of a trick represented by the four-card suit length. Of course, if you have better spot cards than the three and deuce, the lead of the suit becomes a better proposition. Eights, nines, and tens will sometimes get promoted pretty fast to cards of the first rank.

Do not fall in love with this lead unless you have reason to believe the king is to your right rather than to your left. On bad days you might run into this situation:

```
                K 7 6 5
      A Q 3 2              10 9 4
                J 8
```

Your lead of a small card here will give the declarer two tricks in the suit instead of only one.

How about leading from K-J-x-x? Now we've entered a new world. There are two cards (the ace and queen) your partner could hold which would be likely to make this lead successful. Your partner needs nine HCPs to make the raw odds better than even money that he will hold one of these two cards.

I said "raw odds" because these odds usually change after you have heard the bidding. Of course, if the opponents have bid the suit, it's usually better to stay away from this lead. On the other hand, if you are sitting South and the bidding has gone

West	East
1 ♡	1 ♠
3 ♡	3 ♠
4 ♠	Pass

It sounds like you had better get your high cards established and cashed before declarer gets around to discarding his losers on dummy's heart suit. Even when your partner has only seven or eight HCPs, the lead of this suit will have more to gain than it has to lose.

If you hold Q-10-3-2, your partner can hold any one of three cards (the ace, king or jack) which will make this a profitable lead. Here, the raw odds that he will hold one card out of three are better than even, provided that he holds seven or more HCPs. Actually, if he holds as many a nine, the chances he will hold one of these three useful cards get to be pretty close to two times out of three.

In deciding whether to lead small from a four-card suit with some honor cards, there are several things to be considered.

You have a better chance to promote your intermediate cards and any long card tricks against notrump, than you have against a suit contract. The most important single aid you have in deciding whether or not to lead this suit is the bidding. There are times when you have to get your tricks established and cashed before they get their long suits established. And lastly, do not overlook the importance of those high spot cards.

Leading low against notrump from a five-card suit is a different thing entirely. Instead of going into combat with a BB-gun, you enter the foray with a cannon. The raw odds are that 53% of the time both of your opponents will be looking for discards after three leads, and your five-card suit would be worth two long card tricks. Looking at the entire picture, your five-card suit is worth at least one-and-one-half long card tricks in addition to its high card tricks, and slightly more if your opponents have not bid the suit. About all you need to justify the lead of the suit is something that looks like it is a probable entry so you can cash your long card tricks after they are established.

Before I show you some real-life hands, let me show you some teaching hands to illustrate what can be accomplished by leading from five-card suits when the distribution of the outstanding cards is favorable for you. Of course, this lead from a five-card suit will not always succeed, but neither will any other lead. It is just that leading from five-card suits against a notrump contract has an excellent batting average. On these hands, let us assume that North has opened the bidding with one diamond, that South has jumped to 2NT and North has rebid 3NT. Let's make a pre-lead estimate on the next hand just as though we could not see any of the other three hands. That is the situation we really have to face when we are making an opening lead.

```
              NORTH
              ♠ A 6
              ♡ 7 6
              ◊ K Q J 7 3
              ♣ K 6 5 4
   WEST                    EAST
   ♠ 8 7 5 3              ♠ J 10 4 2
   ♡ A Q 9 3 2            ♡ 10 5 4
   ◊ 6 5                  ◊ A 8
   ♣ 10 8                 ♣ Q J 9 3
              SOUTH
              ♠ K Q 9
              ♡ K J 8
              ◊ 10 9 4 2
              ♣ A 7 2
```

On this bidding sequence, the opponents will typically have 27 or more HCPs, divided about equally between the two hands. South has shown 13-15 HCPs. You may find a surprise when the dummy comes down with as few HCPs as 12, but he might have been satisfied to bid three notrump with as many as 16 or 17 HCPs. Your best preliminary estimate is that North and South have about 27 HCPs. Holding six in your hand, count on your partner for about seven, and be thankful if he has anything more. There are several things in your favor. It is unlikely that either opponent has as many as four hearts. Unless North is a confirmed five-card major addict, he is unlikely to bid one diamond when he had four hearts of any consequence. Likewise, if South has four good hearts, he probably would respond one heart rather than 2NT. If your partner has the seven HCPs you are crediting him with, it is quite likely he will have an entry. So you lead the three of hearts.

This gives declarer a heart trick he could never have developed under his own power, but it defeats him. Outside of the heart trick, he has only three spade tricks and two clubs. Your partner will play the ten. If declarer refuses to take the trick, he is going to lose the first five tricks. His only chance is to win the heart and lead a diamond, hoping that you hold the ace and not your partner. When your partner gets in with his ace of diamonds, he will return the five of hearts. You will take four heart tricks to defeat the contract.

When you don't think it is possible for your partner to have an entry, the lead from the heart suit is not nearly so good, but if it doesn't work, nothing else is likely to work either.

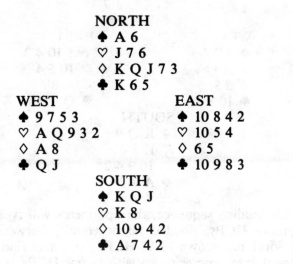

NORTH
♠ A 6
♡ J 7 6
♢ K Q J 7 3
♣ K 6 5

WEST
♠ 9 7 5 3
♡ A Q 9 3 2
♢ A 8
♣ Q J

EAST
♠ 10 8 4 2
♡ 10 5 4
♢ 6 5
♣ 10 9 8 3

SOUTH
♠ K Q J
♡ K 8
♢ 10 9 4 2
♣ A 7 4 2

Here we have the same bidding, but this time you have 13 HCPs, so you just about know your partner is entryless. Your best chance is that declarer holds the king doubleton. So you might as well go ahead and lead your small heart, for if that doesn't work, nothing else is likely to either. You just happen to have too good a hand this time.

Your heart suit can be weaker and still you should lead from your long suit where there is a possibility you have an entry.

Even a five-card suit headed by the king is worth a try. You still may be able to bring in those long card tricks if the cards turn out to be distributed like this:

```
                    NORTH
                    ♠ A 6
                    ♡ J 7 6
                    ◊ K Q J 7 3
                    ♣ K 6 5
   WEST                              EAST
   ♠ 8 7 5 3                        ♠ J 10 4 2
   ♡ K 9 5 3 2                      ♡ Q 10 4
   ◊ 6 5                            ◊ A 8
   ♣ 10 8                           ♣ Q J 9 3
                    SOUTH
                    ♠ K Q 9
                    ♡ A 8
                    ◊ 10 9 4 2
                    ♣ A 7 4 2
```

If the dummy plays a little heart, your partner will simply play the ten, while if dummy plays the jack, partner will play the queen. Either way, those long card tricks are going to come in. Your partner has the HCPs you hoped for, and just the right ones to serve your purpose.

That's the way things work out when hands are constructed to illustrate a point. It is entirely proper that such hands should contain only one problem and that the selected solution should always work. That is the way to teach the principles involved.

Of course, in real life, the chosen solution does not always work, and the particular problem being considered may be hidden away among some other problems in the same hand. So let's stop looking at these teaching hands and look at some hands dealt in actual competition.

My first hand is from the 1960 Olympiad Games, with the United States Team pitted against the Italian Blue Team.

E-W vul., dealer West.

NORTH
♠ A Q J 9 5
♡ 3
♢ K J 9 2
♣ A 8 4

WEST
♠ 10 7 3
♡ A J 10 9 4
♢ Q 6
♣ 10 7 6

EAST
♠ 6
♡ 8 6 5
♢ A 10 8 7 5
♣ K 9 3 2

SOUTH
♠ K 8 4 2
♡ K Q 7 2
♢ 4 3
♣ Q J 5

The bidding:

SOUTH Belladonna	WEST Grieve	NORTH Avarelli	EAST Rubin
	Pass	1 ◇	Pass
1 NT	Pass	2 ♠	Pass
2 NT	Pass	3 ♣	Pass
3 NT	Pass	Pass	Pass

When Sam Stayman and Victor Mitchell, representing the United States, held the North and South hands, they got to a four-spade contract without breathing hard. In the play of the hand, Mitchell, North, led a small diamond from the dummy, and played his jack. He won ten tricks, losing only one trick in each of the side suits.

It was a different ballgame when the Italians sat North-South. Avarelli's bidding showed that he had long spades and, it seems to me, he did everything he could to avoid playing notrump. Belladonna prevailed and they ended up playing 3NT. I presume he figured that his holding in hearts and his square hand justified going for the nine-trick game. He went set two tricks.

Bill Grieve, West, had the near-perfect setup for leading the top of an interior sequence. The bidding sounded like any stoppers in the heart suit were held in the South hand. Grieve would need for his partner to get the lead once to lead hearts. With seven HCPs himself, he could credit his partner with about the same number, making it probable that his partner had an entry. Furthermore, his sequence was buttressed by the nine, a card which, when held by the opponents, can sometimes be most annoying. So he led his jack of hearts.

Belladonna concluded that holding up would get him nowhere. He took the first heart trick with his queen. He led a spade to dummy's queen and then led a club from the dummy. Ira Rubin stepped up with his king to lead the eight of hearts, which held the trick. He played another heart, and the defenders ended up taking four hearts, a club, and the ace of diamonds.

The hand is such a classic example of leading from an interior sequence that I once tried to use it to illustrate the point in a beginner's class. This turned out to be a bad idea. In the first place, I had one heck of a time justifying Belladonna's bidding, and the bidding sequence became so intriguing that my pupils wanted to learn the Roman system of bidding rather than learn about opening leads. Furthermore, I got myself into a bit of trouble, as when I did get their attention back to the opening lead problem, they wanted to know what happened when one of the honors was to their left and the other to their right. I gave them the following example to indicate how even with that holding the lead could be successful.

```
                    Dummy
                    Q x
You                            Partner
A J 10 9 x                     x x x
                    Declarer
                    K x x
```

I pointed out that with this holding, declarer would almost certainly play the queen from the dummy and then, when partner got in to return the suit, I would have my four tricks. One of my bright pupils was not satisfied with this explanation and wanted to know what would happen if the doubleton were in the declarer's hand while there were three in the dummy. After some thought, I came up with the following hand:

171

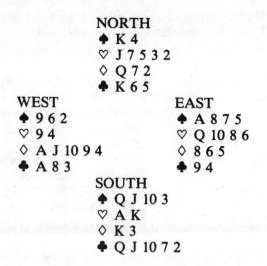

NORTH
♠ K 4
♡ J 7 5 3 2
♦ Q 7 2
♣ K 6 5

WEST
♠ 9 6 2
♡ 9 4
♦ A J 10 9 4
♣ A 8 3

EAST
♠ A 8 7 5
♡ Q 10 8 6
♦ 8 6 5
♣ 9 4

SOUTH
♠ Q J 10 3
♡ A K
♦ K 3
♣ Q J 10 7 2

When you lead the jack of diamonds, declarer will win with the king and your side will win whichever black suit he leads. You will promptly give him a second diamond trick. He cannot take nine tricks without establishing both black suits. When he gives up the lead again, West will take his ace plus two long card diamond tricks. That way, the defense will get three diamond tricks plus the two black aces.

The next week, my star pupil brought me this hand:

NORTH
♠ J 10 4
♡ A 5 2
♦ A 8 6 3
♣ Q 8 3

WEST
♠ 9 7 5
♡ Q 10 8 4
♦ 5
♣ A J 10 9 5

EAST
♠ K 8 6 2
♡ J 9 7
♦ Q J 10 9
♣ 7 4

SOUTH
♠ A Q 3
♡ K 6 3
♦ K 7 4 2
♣ K 6 2

He said that, holding the West hand, he opened the jack of clubs against 3NT. With the spade finesse working, the declarer had seven tricks off the top and, by taking two club tricks, he managed to take nine. He won the first club trick in his hand and, when he found that he would be unable to develop a trick in diamonds, he led a club towards dummy to develop the second club trick. My pupil said that he could not find any way that declarer could have made the hand had he not led the club.

I don't know what my pupil learned from this, but I know that I learned something. Be honest with your pupils, whether they are beginners or not. Your beginners are seeking formulas to solve their problems at bridge and they are hoping to find plays and bids which are guaranteed to win. I learned to tell my pupils that there are very few sure things in bridge and fewest of all in opening leads. Playing bridge gives us a valuable lesson in living. Justice is not always done. The best-laid plans of mice and men, etc. All we can do is choose to do those things which have the best chance to succeed, whether it is in living or in playing cards.

On my student's hand, declarer had to give up the lead only once to get his ninth trick. That did not give us time to establish our club suit and to cash our long card tricks as well. After the declarer led towards his queen of clubs, we had three club tricks all right, but declarer had nine tricks. After he took his nine, we had more winners than there were tricks left. It is necessary in bridge not only to develop your tricks, but also to develop them before the declarer gets his suit established.

I thought the next hand had several points of interest. It is from the 1965 World Championship, in the match between Great Britain and Italy.

NORTH
♠ A J 6
♡ A K Q 10 8
◇ A J 8
♣ 10 2

WEST
♠ K Q 8 7 5
♡ 3
◇ Q 9
♣ A 9 7 5 4

EAST
♠ 10 9
♡ J 9 7 6 5
◇ 10 6 5 3
♣ K 3

SOUTH
♠ 4 3 2
♡ 4 2
◇ K 7 4 2
♣ Q J 8 6

In both rooms, the final contract was 3NT played by South. The only suit mentioned was hearts, bid by North. With a holding like the West hand, it is tempting to lead the king of spades to get that one high-card trick established as quickly as possible. That is exactly what should be done when defending against a suit contract, but when defending a notrump contract, a good case can be made for leading a small spade. The idea is that the high-card trick will not get lost and that by starting this way, you increase your chances to promote your long card tricks. The Italian leader led high. The British leader led the seven. Let's see what happened.

The Italians lead second-best from a sequence, so Avarelli led the queen. Jeremy Flint, playing South for Great Britain, let the queen hold the trick. Avarelli continued with a small spade and Flint won dummy's jack. He led the ace and king of hearts and found no nourishment there when Avarelli discarded a club. With hearts behaving so badly, Flint now needed some club tricks to make his contract. He led the ten from the dummy. Belladonna, East, could have won with his king, but he had no more spades to lead. Instead, he played low and Avarelli won with the ace. He led another spade. That was won with dummy's ace and Belladonna had a discard coming. He discarded the king of clubs! You can see that Belladonna had no good discard. Not only would a discard from either red suit help Flint to establish that suit, but also, if Belladonna kept the club in his hand, he would be thrown in and have to lead one of those red suits himself. Discarding the king of clubs wasn't so great, either. Flint promptly cashed his two club tricks, letting Belladonna find two more discards. This time he discarded one heart and one diamond. Flint now took the diamond finesse and brought in four tricks in that suit. He ended up losing one trick to the queen of spades and another to the ace of clubs, taking eleven tricks.

It was quite a different story when Terence Reese was on opening lead with the West hand. He led the seven of spades. Benito Garozzo, South, won the jack, and he also tested the heart suit by cashing the ace-king. Finding out the story there, he switched to a small club. Boris Schapiro, East, flew up with his king to return his remaining spade. Reese overtook his partner's spade so that when Garozzo let the queen hold, Reese could continue a small spade to knock out dummy's ace. Garozzo led the ten of clubs. Reese won the ace and cashed two spade tricks for down one.

On the next hand, the opening leader followed the old maxim, "If they are good enough to bid, they are good enough to lead". The hand is from the 1958 World Championship, with Argentina pitted against the United States.

Both vul., dealer East.

```
                    NORTH
                    ♠ K 7 4
                    ♡ 3
                    ◇ K J 10 7
                    ♣ A K Q 4 2
        WEST                    EAST
        ♠ A Q 5                 ♠ 10 9 3 2
        ♡ A Q 10 6 5            ♡ 9 7 4 2
        ◇ A 6 2                 ◇ Q 9
        ♣ 5 3                   ♣ 9 7 6
                    SOUTH
                    ♠ J 8 6
                    ♡ K J 8
                    ◇ 8 5 4 3
                    ♣ J 10 8
```

The bidding:

SOUTH	WEST	NORTH	EAST
Rapee	Lerner	Silidor	Cabanne
			Pass
Pass	1 ♡	Double	Pass
1 NT	Pass	2 NT	Pass
3 NT	Pass	Pass	Pass

Cabanne had sixteen HCPs and couldn't expect anything much from his partner when his opponents reached 3NT. He knew when he led a small heart that he was leading right into Rapee's hand and that Rapee had hearts protected. But if he doesn't lead a heart, what do you suggest?

He had exactly one heart trick for sure if he had to lead the suit himself. If he could get two low card tricks in the suit, giving him three heart tricks, he could add those to his two aces and declarer would be defeated. Even if he had to give the declarer two tricks to develop his heart suit, he still might get three tricks in the suit. There were the additional chances that the king was doubleton in Rapee's hand or that the Americans had gone overboard in their bidding and that his partner had an entry after all with a heart or two to lead. So, Lerner led the six of hearts, as you and I would have done.

After winning with the jack of hearts, Rapee was looking at five additional tricks off the top. A lot of good things had to happen to him to bring in nine tricks. They did not happen. At trick two, he led a small diamond and when Lerner played small, he put in dummy's ten. Already Cabanne, East, had gained the lead. The Americans were overboard, reaching 3NT with only 22 HCPs. Cabanne led back a heart and the roof fell in. Before they turned the declarer loose, the defenders had taken four heart tricks, two diamond tricks, and the ace of spades, for a three-trick set. The return in the heart suit must have exceeded Lerner's fondest expectations, as he got not three tricks from the suit, but four tricks. Such is the advantage of having a good partner who will manage to get the lead when the only picture card he has in his hand is a queen.

In the replay of the hand, when the Argentine team held the North-South hands, they let the Americans play in two hearts, making exactly eight tricks.

One more comment on this hand. Do you ever find that you

have bid too much? Don't let it discourage you. They sometimes do that in the big leagues, too.

Just how weak a five-card suit do you use for an opening lead against a notrump contract? My next illustration is from the 1962 World Championship, with North America again playing against the Italian Blue Team.

Both vul., dealer West.

```
                    NORTH
                    ♠ 10 9 3
                    ♡ Q 10 5 3 2
                    ◇ K Q
                    ♣ Q 6 3
   WEST                          EAST
   ♠ Q 2                         ♠ K 7 6 5
   ♡ K 7 6                       ♡ 9 8 4
   ◇ A 6 5                       ◇ J 7 4 3
   ♣ 10 9 7 5 4                  ♣ A 2
                    SOUTH
                    ♠ A J 8 4
                    ♡ A J
                    ◇ 10 9 8 2
                    ♣ K J 8
```

The bidding:

SOUTH	WEST	NORTH	EAST
Coon	Forquet	Murray	Garozzo
	Pass	Pass	Pass
1 ♠	Pass	2 ♣	Pass
2 NT	Pass	3 NT	Pass
Pass	Pass		

That two-club bid by Eric Murray was the Drury Convention. It is generally used after a third or fourth hand opening in one of the major suits and asks the opening bidder whether he has opened the bidding with full or shaded values. If his bid has been shaded, he rebids two diamonds. If he has a full opening bid, he bids anything else. Charlie Coon surely had a full opening bid and he described his distribution by bidding two notrump. This seemed to be all the information Eric Murray,

North, needed to get him to bid 3NT with his nine HCPs. So the North American team was trying to take nine tricks at notrump with 23 HCPs and no substantial suit to run. Surely there must be a better way to use the Drury Convention.

Forquet, West, led a small club, even though the highest card he held in this suit was the ten. Garozzo won the ace and returned a club. Coon laid down the ace and jack of hearts. Forquet won the king and led a third club. Coon won and tried to reach the dummy by leading a diamond. Forquet rose with the ace and cashed his two club tricks. The defense took the ace of clubs, the ace of diamonds, the king of hearts and two long card tricks in clubs.

On the replay of the hand, the Italian pair managed to stop at one notrump, played by North, and went home with eight tricks against an opening lead of the nine of hearts.

On the next hand, the lead from a weak five-card suit brought an even more startling result, although this time the declarer's side had their 26 HCPs.

NORTH
♠ J 8
♡ Q J 4
◇ Q 9 4
♣ A 7 6 5 2

WEST
♠ 9 7 6 5 3
♡ K 6 5
◇ J 6
♣ K 10 8

EAST
♠ A K 4 2
♡ 10 9 3 2
◇ 10 8 7 5
♣ 9

SOUTH
♠ Q 10
♡ A 8 7
◇ A K 3 2
♣ Q J 4 3

This hand is from the match between Great Britain and America, played in the 1960 Olympiad Game. In the closed room, George Rapee, South for the United States, bid one notrump with his 16 HCPs. Sidney Silodor, North, holding ten HCPS and a five-card suit, went straight to 3NT. Jeremy Flint, West, led a small spade, and the defenders took the first five spade tricks. Eventually, they got a club trick as well to set the hand two tricks.

When the British held the North-South hands, Terence Reese and Boris Schapiro managed to stop at one notrump, played by Schapiro in the North seat. That left Norman Kay, East, on opening lead. This was the time the lead of a high card from a four-card suit headed by the ace-king would work out well, but, of course, the odds are against such an opening lead. Kay led the five of diamonds. Too often, when you lead low from a four-card suit headed by the ace-king, you give the opponent tricks he could not otherwise get. Even if you regain that one trick, you have merely given up one to get one and that is not a good enough return. Schapiro ended up taking eight tricks.

All of the authorities say that when you hold K-Q-J-10 of one suit and a mediocre five-card suit, that the preferred lead is the king of the four-card suit. We can't argue with that. You immediately establish three of the five tricks your side needs to defeat a three notrump contract. Some experts tell us that a suit like K-Q-J-2 should also be preferred. This one is not nearly so sure, but it is pretty good. All sorts of good things could happen. You get two of your tricks promptly established, and there is always a slight chance that your partner has the ace with some small cards. There is a better chance that he has either the ten or that your two-spot will become a long card trick. It is also possible that he has something like the 9-8-7 and will have an entry to lead the suit through the declarer's ten. The lead of the king from K-Q-10-2 is frequently recommended in preference to a mediocre five-card suit, but I rate this one as close. Too often, the jack with a couple of small cards turns up in the dummy. I think when the occasion arises where I have to make this decision, I am going to lead the five-card suit, provided it is headed by an ace or king.

The Q-J-10-9 is also a strong favorite over a mediocre five-card suit. At the worst, your opponents will hold both the ace and king, but even then you aren't giving them anything they couldn't take under their own power. After giving them two tricks, you also will have two, and, with an assist or so from your partner, will be able to bring them in. The Q-J-10-2 is slightly ahead of a mediocre five-card suit, but for my money, if it is a Q-J-9-2, I am going to go with the five-card suit.

None of the authorities discuss the problem of the J-10-9-8 as compared to a five-card suit. Of course, the dummy could hold the queen, your partner have the king, and declarer the ace, and you could immediately establish three tricks in the suit. What is more likely is that you are going to have to lead the suit three times to get one trick established. I have always thought that other things being equal, you should opt for a five-card suit headed by the king or better in preference to such a four-card suit. I have searched the records to see if I could find such a hand in real life, and I found exactly one. It occurred in the 1966 World Championship in the match between North America and Italy.

<pre>
                        NORTH
                        ♠ 8 6
                        ♡ A K 9 7 4 3
                        ◊ 10 4
                        ♣ A 5 4
         WEST   EAST
         ♠ A 9 7 5 3   ♠ J 10 4
         ♡ 8 2   ♡ J 10
         ◊ A 6   ◊ Q J 9 8 5
         ♣ J 10 9 8   ♣ K 7 6
                        SOUTH
                        ♠ K Q 2
                        ♡ Q 6 5
                        ◊ K 7 3 2
                        ♣ Q 3 2
</pre>

Both the Italians and the North Americans played 3NT from the South hand after North opened the bidding with one heart. Benito Garozzo, for the Italians, led the jack of clubs. Sammy Kehela, representing North America, led the five of spades. In this instance, the Americans proved to be right and the Italians wrong.

Where Garozzo led the jack of clubs, the contract was played for North America by Ira Rubin. He ducked the club lead in dummy. East won the king. He switched to the queen of diamonds, which Rubin let hold the trick. East continued the jack of diamonds. This time, Rubin covered. West won the ace. Garozzo had no more diamonds to lead so he led a club. Rubin won dummy's ace and established a spade trick. He ended up taking one spade, six hearts, and two clubs.

On the replay, Kehela led the five of spades. The Italian declarer, Avarelli, let East win the first trick with the ten of spades. Eric Murray, East, continued spades. Kehela won the second trick with the ace and led the nine of spades. Avarelli had his first trick. He took his six hearts and the ace of clubs, but that was all. When he tried for a diamond trick, Kehela won his ace and took the rest of the tricks with his spades.

Once more, I must repeat that a single hand proves nothing. However, until my experience tells me I am wrong, I will continue to lead from a mediocre five-card suit rather than a solid four-card sequence headed by the jack.

When an ace is led against a notrump contract, it is ususlly from a solid or nearly solid suit in the hopes that the suit will run. The lead of the ace asks partner to clarify his holding in the suit. One way is to play that the ace asks partner for the highest card he has in the suit. A better way is to ask him to play any jack or higher card and, lacking that, to signal how many cards he has in the suit. He does this by playing a small card with an odd number of cards and his highest card with an even number of cards. Lew Mathe made this lead for the United States in the World Championship against Great Britain back in 1955. It worked out all right, but Mathe was kept busy bringing home the setting trick.

E-W vul., dealer North.

```
                    NORTH
                    ♠ A 9 5
                    ♡ A K 10 6 2
                    ♢ Q 6 4 2
                    ♣ 10
        WEST                    EAST
        ♠ K 7                   ♠ Q 8 3
        ♡ 8 4                   ♡ Q J 7 5 3
        ♢ A 8 3                 ♢ J 9 7
        ♣ A K Q 9 8 3           ♣ 7 5
                    SOUTH
                    ♠ J 10 6 4 2
                    ♡ 9
                    ♢ K 10 5
                    ♣ J 6 4 2
```

The bidding:

SOUTH	WEST	NORTH	EAST
Meredith	Mathe	Dodds	Moran
		1 ♡	Pass
1 NT	Double	Pass	Pass
Pass			

The record states that Mathe led the ace of clubs, that his partner, Johnny Moran, played the seven, and that Meredith, South, played the four. Whichever method of signalling they were using, it was sufficient to convince Mathe that the suit was not going to run and that he needed a club lead from his partner's hand. The bidding indicated that Moran had some high cards in hearts. Therefore, Mathe switched to a heart. Meredith won dummy's ace and led a small diamond, playing the ten from his hand. Mathe won the ace and led a second heart. Declarer got to his hand with the king of diamonds and led the jack of spades. Mathe played low and Meredith put up dummy's ace. He cashed the queen of diamonds and, when the suit broke, the six. At this point, Mathe had nothing left but the king of spades and five clubs. He was about to get thrown in and forced to lead a second club. He had no intention of doing this. On the six of diamonds, he discarded his king of spades.

When declarer led a spade, Moran won his queen. On this, Mathe had nothing to discard except clubs. He still didn't get to run his club suit, as Moran cashed the queen and jack of hearts before leading a club. This gave the defenders seven tricks and a one-trick set.

LONG SUIT LEADS AGAINST SUIT CONTRACTS

Sometimes you can damage declarer by leading your long suit, forcing him to trump and shortening his trump suit. We will take a look at the so-called "forcing game" later on. Right now, we are more concerned with being sure we get all our high card tricks before declarer can discard his losers. Generally, when we lead a long suit, we hope to cash the top cards in our or partner's hand, or, if we don't have the top cards, to promote our high cards so that they become winners. We may lead a high card in our long suit, knowing full well declarer can trump it, because such leads are safe and avoid giving declarer anything he could not otherwise get.

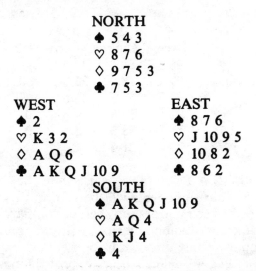

NORTH
♠ 5 4 3
♡ 8 7 6
◊ 9 7 5 3
♣ 7 5 3

WEST
♠ 2
♡ K 3 2
◊ A Q 6
♣ A K Q J 10 9

EAST
♠ 8 7 6
♡ J 10 9 5
◊ 10 8 2
♣ 8 6 2

SOUTH
♠ A K Q J 10 9
♡ A Q 4
◊ K J 4
♣ 4

For instance, on this hand the best defense against a spade contract by South is for West to lead clubs and to continue to lead clubs every time he gets the lead. Although he will get only one club trick, he avoids giving South a trick he could not otherwise get. Any trick South gets by trumping clubs is a trick he could have gotten just as easily by leading trumps, so club leads aren't giving up anything. We all know that long solid suits are wonderful when they are trumps, but not worth a great deal defending against a trump contract by the opponents. To dramatize the difference, here is another one of my tables:

DEFENSIVE VALUES OF HIGH CARDS					
Round	1	2	3	4	Defensive Tricks
	Ace	King	Queen	Jack	
A K Q	98.3	85.6	49.5	—	2.33
A K Q J	97.1	78.0	35.1	4.0	2.14
A K Q J x	94.9	67.7	21.0	0.8	1.84
A K Q J x x	91.5	54.3	9.6	0	1.55
A K Q J x x x	85.9	38.3	2.5	0	1.27
A K Q J x x x x	77.4	21.5	0	0	0.99

These are strictly A-Priori tables which show the probabilities that neither of your opponents will be void in the suit by the time you lead the card in question, before you have heard any bidding or looked at dummy. Obviously, if your partner bids a suit where you have only three cards, or if the dummy shows up with a long holding in such a suit, these probabilities are going to be altered. However, the tables are still significant and should guide us in deciding whether to be active or passive on defense.

Again, the tables indicate when one of your opponents will be void in the suit by the time you lead the round in question. They do not take into consideration that when dummy is void your partner will sometimes also be void and be able to overruff the dummy. But, no knowledge you have of the deal before you have seen the dummy is going to be the straight road to heaven anyway, so instead of concentrating on what is wrong with the table, let's see what is good about it.

In the first place, we might notice that even with only a three-card holding, the ace is not a sure thing to take a trick. More than one percent of the time even that card will be trumped by an opponent. But the impressive thing about the table is that the third round is a very doubtful value whenever you hold four cards or more in the suit. Defensively, the fourth round has no defensive value whenever you have six cards or more and is virtually valueless when you have four or five cards in the suit. One thing more. Whenever you have an eight-card holding, the total defensive value of the whole ten HCPs is, on the average, less than one full trick, although if the suit were trumps, the suit would be worth eight tricks.

Why is it that everyone tells us that an opening lead from a three- or four-card sequence headed by a queen or a jack is generally a good lead? First, it is probably not giving anything away, i.e., it is "safe". Second, at times you will get a quick promotion so that you will have the highest card in the suit after only one round. Even a sequence headed by the jack can give you an immediate promotion to the winning card for the second round when the cards are distributed just right for you. For example:

```
                    Dummy
                    Q 4
     You                        Partner
     J 10 9 5                   K 8 6 3
                    Declarer
                    A 7 2
```

When you lead the jack, declarer will probably play the queen in the hope that you have led from the K-J-10. The ten-spot has been promoted to top dog after only one trick has been played. By looking back at the table on page 184, under the column headed "2", you will see that the second lead of the suit is likely to give you a trick unless you started with seven or more.

Leading from a sequence headed by the queen can be effective more often. Of course, the cards can be distributed in such a way that these leads are not winning leads, but they will be winning leads much more often than they will be losing leads, and that is the best we can hope for.

But suppose we are trying to get our high cards established where we hold K-J-6-4-2. A lead from this suit will be great if partner has the ace or queen. The best layout is if partner has the ace, and the right-hand opponent has the queen. It is even possible, though unlikely, that we can cash three tricks in the suit. It is also pretty good if our partner holds the queen, because now we have a quick promotion. But, of course, a lead from this holding is dangerous. If partner holds neither the ace nor the queen, it well may give the declarer a trick he could not have gained otherwise. And, it is not like defending against a notrump contract when we may gain several tricks with our small cards by giving up a free trick to the declarer. So, it comes down to this: How good are the chances that our partner will hold either the ace or the queen in this suit when it has not been bid by either side?

You will remember that the raw odds say that when the opponents are in a game contract, your partner will have to hold about nine HCPs for the odds to be even or better that he has one of two cards. In the absence of information from the bidding that a lead from this suit is called for, the lead against a four-spade or four-heart contract may win, but it is a bad gamble.

However, against a notrump contract, a lead from the K-J-6-4-2 is a good bet. Why is there this difference? Let's say that your opponents hold both the ace and the queen. Among the several distributions they have, let's say that it is your right-hand opponent who holds both of these cards. You still might come out ahead leading against notrump. Your partner may get the lead and return the suit. You can end up with three tricks from the suit. If declarer had to play the queen to win the first trick, you yourself might be able to force out the ace and still gain three tricks at the cost of two. Playing against a suit contract, it is a different proposition. The declarer will win the first trick with the queen and the second one with the ace. That means your king is reduced to being a third round winner. As we know by now, the third round of a five-card suit will find your opponents both holding cards in that suit about one time out of five. Even where the suit is only four cards long, the third lead of the suit will find both opponents with cards in the suit only slightly more than one time out of three.

All I can say about a suit headed by the king, but without the jack, is that it is even more risky. Among other things, you may establish the jack for the declarer.

As for underleading a queen, the queen with the ten is not all that bad. However, don't regard it too highly as an attacking lead against a suit contract. Unless your partner happens to hold precisely the king, you must think of it only in terms of winning only the third round of the suit. However, when other leads look bad, it might turn out to be a successful, neutral lead. There are no fewer than three cards which your partner could hold which would make it possible that this lead would not cost anything. If he holds the jack, you have not given anything away. If he holds the ace or the king, it is probable that you have given nothing away. However, the queen without the ten tends to work out poorly against a suit contract. All of these leads are slightly better from a four-card suit than from a longer suit.

As for leading from the A-Q-x(x) against a suit contract, only an auction that shouted for the suit to be led would persuade me to lead from this combination. The only card my partner can hold which would help would be the king. If some day the bidding screams so loudly for the lead of this suit that I decide to lead it, I am going to lead the ace. Of course, if I hold A-Q-x in the trump suit, I have found that the lead of the ace has much to gain and little to lose.

The Forcing Defense

I have already introduced you to the forcing defense. Now it is time to become better acquainted.

Both vul., dealer North.

```
                    NORTH
                    ♠ K 10
                    ♡ Q 10 5
                    ◊ A Q J 8 4
                    ♣ J 7 4
    WEST                            EAST
    ♠ 6 4 3 2                       ♠ 8 5
    ♡ A 7                           ♡ 9 8 6 4
    ◊ 6 3                           ◊ K 5 2
    ♣ A K Q 9 3                     ♣ 10 8 6 5
                    SOUTH
                    ♠ A Q J 9 7
                    ♡ K J 3 2
                    ◊ 10 9 7
                    ♣ 2
```

187

The bidding:

SOUTH	WEST	NORTH	EAST
		1 ◇	Pass
1 ♠	2 ♣	2 ◇	Pass
3 ♠	Pass	4 ♠	Pass
Pass	Pass		

At first glance, the declarer might think he has only three losers, even if the diamond finesse is wrong, and therefore he will have ten winners left. Little does he know that he is going to lose a trump trick in addition to the three losers in the side suits.

West, holding four trumps, is aware of that possibility. He holds two, or possibly three, side trick winners himself. Holding thirteen HCPs, there is a chance his partner holds approximately three or four points, which might also bring in a winner. In any event, he is going to lead the king of clubs.

Dummy is just about what is expected. Dummy is not likely to be trumping anything for a while, if ever. The only opponent who can trump clubs is the declarer. If declarer has only five trumps, he is going to be reduced to the same length as West after trumping just once. So West continues with a club and, sure enough, declarer trumps. Declarer leads three rounds of trumps. East discards a heart on the third one. Declarer and West each have one trump left. If he takes West's last trump away from him, then nobody will have any trumps. Long card tricks come into their own when there are no opposing trumps against them. Whether declarer tries to finesse diamonds or to establish hearts first, the opponents will take at least three more club tricks plus their ace of hearts. Declarer probably will leave one trump outstanding and try a diamond finesse. When that fails, East will lead clubs. When declarer trumps the club, his side will be the one out of trumps, while the defenders still have one. As soon as the defenders win a trick with the trump, they can take all of their long card tricks in clubs with no interference.

The club suit in this hand is what is known as the "forcing suit" or, in those instances where more vulgar language is appropriate, the "pumping suit". If we examine these hands, we see that there are four factors which tend to make the forcing game successful:

1. One of the defenders has four or more trumps.

2. The defenders have an established or quickly establishable suit.

3. Declarer has a long trump suit in one hand and a short trump suit in the other. It is the long trump suit which has to be forced.

4. The defenders have stoppers in those suits which declarer has to establish to fulfill his contract.

When a defender has a stopper in the trump suit itself, a new dimension is added to the defense. The fact that you can delay taking your high trump until you want to take it may enable you to exhaust the dummy of trumps before you win your trump trick. Here is an example:

```
                       NORTH
                       ♠ Q 10 9
                       ♡ K Q
                       ◊ 5 4 2
                       ♣ K Q 8 7 2
        WEST                          EAST
        ♠ A 6 5 2                     ♠ 3
        ♡ J 9 2                       ♡ 10 8 7 6 5 4
        ◊ K Q 6 3                     ◊ A J 9 7
        ♣ 6 4                         ♣ 10 3
                       SOUTH
                       ♠ K J 8 7 4
                       ♡ A 3
                       ◊ 10 8
                       ♣ A J 9 5
```

It looks like declarer has one loser in spades and two in diamonds, but the possession of four trumps in the West hand can enable the defenders to secure another trick. By forcing declarer, they can either win a trick with one of those small trumps, or they can win a long card trick in diamonds. Let's see how it would go.

The defense starts leading diamonds and declarer has to trump the third diamond because the ace of trumps is yet to be lost. At this point he doesn't know it, but he and West now have the same number of trumps. He starts leading trumps, hoping they are divided 3-2. West should refuse to take the first and second trump trick. After he does this, the declarer must go set. If he leads a third trump, West will win and lead another diamond, forcing South to either let it win or trump with his last trump. Now the only player left with a trump will be West.

Even when the declarer has control of your long suit, the forcing game can be effective if you counter with control of his long suit.

NORTH
♠ 9 6 2
♡ A K 7
◇ 5 3
♣ K Q J 9 4

WEST
♠ A 5 4 3
♡ J 8 4
◇ K Q 10 2
♣ 8 7

EAST
♠ 7
♡ 10 6 5 2
◇ J 9 8 6 4
♣ A 5 3

SOUTH
♠ K Q J 10 8
♡ Q 9 3
◇ A 7
♣ 10 6 2

At a four-spade contract, West could get a ruff by leading the eight of clubs, if his partner ducks the first club lead. When West regains the lead with the ace of trumps, he could lead a small club to his partner's ace and then trump a club return. That would give the defenders three tricks, and the declarer his contract. The defenders would never come to a diamond trick, as declarer would discard his losing diamond on the established club suit.

If, instead, West takes the farsighted view that it is better to lead his own suit when he has four trumps in his own hand, he will lead the king of diamonds. Now the defenders can always come to their diamond trick in addition to their two black aces and, sooner or later, will either get a ruff with a small trump or exhaust South of trumps and have a lot of low card tricks in diamonds. South will win the diamond trick and lead trumps. West will let him hold the first two trump tricks. If he leads a third trump, exhausting dummy of trumps, West will win his ace and lead diamonds. When South trumps a diamond, he and West will each have one trump left and his club suit is not yet established. When East gets in with the ace of clubs, he will lead a diamond, forcing South to go set immediately or give up his last trump. That will leave West with a small trump which will take a trick.

After declarer sees East discard a heart on the second trump, he will stop leading trumps and establish the club suit. This will limit his losses to down one. West will signal that he has an even number of clubs, so East will take the second club with his ace and then West will still get his club ruff. The diamond trick will come home. The defenders will have taken one diamond trick, one club, the ace of spades, and a small spade.

Under the right conditions, you can force the declarer to give you a trick with one of your small trumps even though he has four trumps in each hand. Take a look at this one:

None vul., dealer South.

```
                    NORTH
                    ♠ Q J 9 6
                    ♡ K Q 8 2
                    ◇ 6 3
                    ♣ J 10 7
        WEST                        EAST
        ♠ A 5 4 2                   ♠ 8
        ♡ 9 6 4                     ♡ J 10 7 3
        ◇ K J 9 5                   ◇ A Q 7 4
        ♣ 4 2                       ♣ 9 8 6 3
                    SOUTH
                    ♠ K 10 7 3
                    ♡ A 5
                    ◇ 10 8 2
                    ♣ A K Q 5
```

The bidding:

SOUTH	WEST	NORTH	EAST
1 NT	Pass	2 ♣	Pass
2 ♦	Pass	4 ♠	Pass
Pass	Pass		

There is an old saying that when the opening leader has four trumps, he should lead his longest side suit. That is an over-simplification, but it does have some element of truth. West thought a diamond lead the best chance to build up tricks. He had no other suit which looked promising, and not only did he have four spades, he also had control of the spade suit. His partner should hold about six or seven HCPs, and West hoped he would find East with one of the diamond honors.

He was luckier than he expected to be. East had both of the diamond honors. East won the first trick with the ace and returned the four. This was covered by the eight and West won with the nine. West decided that, in spite of the fact that both declarer and dummy had four trumps, there was a chance he could shorten both and develop a small trump trick for himself. This ploy is not usually successful against a 4-4 trump fit, because declarer can crossruff the hand. To be able to crossruff a hand, however, the declarer needs length in a suit in one hand opposite shortness in the other. West did not see any great length in the North hand, and the fact that South had opened the bidding with one notrump indicated that he had neither great length nor shortage in any suit in his own hand. So West continued diamonds and let dummy trump. West had two diamond tricks, a sure trick with the ace of trumps, and was now on his way to establishing a second trump trick. Declarer trumped the diamond in the dummy and led trumps. West let him hold two trump tricks. Now if declarer led a third trump, dummy would be out of trumps, West could win and lead yet another diamond, exhausting the trumps from South as well. The only remaining trump would be in the West hand, and he would be sure to take a trick with it sooner or later. Should declarer quit leading trumps after two leads and try to cash his winners, West would trump a club with his small trump and would still have the ace of trumps for the setting trick.

Where you have control of three suits, you may be able to make one of your small trumps with the forcing game, even though you have only three trumps and the declarer has five. Your first control will cut him down to one trump more than you have. The next time you gain the lead, you can cut him down to the same number of trumps you have, and the third time you get the lead cut him down to one fewer trumps than you have. If you exhaust him of trumps while you still have a trump left, you can take tricks with all the small cards in your long suit. The only defense he has is to go ahead and let you win one small trump along with your high card winners:

```
                    NORTH
                    ♠ 6 4 3
                    ♡ Q 10 9
                    ◇ K Q 2
                    ♣ 8 7 6 5
WEST                            EAST
♠ A 8 5                         ♠ 7 2
♡ A 6                           ♡ 7 5 4 3 2
◇ 6 3                           ◇ 10 9 8 5
♣ A K J 9 4 2                   ♣ Q 10
                    SOUTH
                    ♠ K Q J 10 9
                    ♡ K J 8
                    ◇ A J 7 4
                    ♣ 3
```

Against a four-spade contract, West leads clubs. West has three aces and is going to win tricks with all of them. By continuing clubs, he is either going to win a lot of club tricks or a trick with one of his small trumps. Declarer will trump the second club lead and probably lead the king of spades. West will refuse the first spade lead, but win the second and lead a third club. When declarer trumps, he will have exactly one trump left and so will West. If declarer draws West's last trump, he can cash his diamonds, but that will give him only a total of eight tricks. Declarer's best play is to leave the one trump outstanding and lead diamonds. West can trump a third diamond with his small trump and, to everybody's surprise, it will be the North

193

hand which has one trump left when everybody else is out. His six of trumps will stand guard to keep West from cashing even more clubs. The defenders will end up with only their three aces and one small trump trick.

When the declarer holds five trumps and a defender has three, he has exactly two more trumps than that defender. If having three suits under control by the defenders makes it possible for a forcing game to work with that trump distribution, can it work when the trump distribution is six for the declarer and four for one of the defenders? The answer is that it can, provided the other necessary conditions exist.

```
                  NORTH
                  ♠ 6 5 3
                  ♡ A 9 5 2
                  ◇ 9 6 4
                  ♣ K Q 10
     WEST                        EAST
     ♠ A 8 4 2                   ♠ None
     ♡ 7 4 3                     ♡ K 8
     ◇ K Q J 5                   ◇ 10 8 7 3 2
     ♣ 7 5                       ♣ A J 6 4 3 2
                  SOUTH
                  ♠ K Q J 10 9 7
                  ♡ Q J 10 6
                  ◇ A
                  ♣ 9 8
```

At a four-spade contract, it looks like the declarer has a magnificent trump suit. The forcing game can demolish it.

West leads the king of diamonds and, so far, no harm is done. Declarer simply wins the ace. He has five assured tricks in trumps. If the heart finesse loses, he has only three heart tricks. The diamond ace is his ninth trick. He is going to have to get a club trick as well. The trouble is that for him to take these tricks, the opponents are going to gain the lead three times.

Let's say he starts by leading the king of trumps. To keep a trump control from developing in the dummy, West lets South hold both the first and second spade tricks. If trumps are continued, he wins the third trick, as the dummy is now out. West leads a second diamond for South to trump. At this point, declarer has two trumps left and West has one trump left. If declarer takes West's last trump away from him, declarer has just one trump, and as yet he has not established his clubs or hearts. Whichever one he tries to establish, East wins and leads another diamond. That takes declarer's last trump. When East gets the lead in the other suit, his diamonds are all good.

Probably, the declarer will not lead the third trump. He takes the heart finesse. East wins the king and leads a diamond for declarer to trump. When declarer leads a club, East wins and leads another diamond for South to trump. Declarer is down to two trumps, the same number as West, and West still has the ace. Declarer has to lead hearts and let West make his small trump. That limits the defenders to their three high-card tricks and one trick with a small trump.

It is not necessary that the trump control be the ace. The king of trumps can be just as deadly.

```
                    NORTH
                    ♠ 10 7
                    ♡ A 10 5
                    ♢ K Q J 10 4
                    ♣ K J 9
        WEST                    EAST
        ♠ K 5 3 2               ♠ 6 4
        ♡ K Q J 7 6 4           ♡ 3 2
        ♢ A 8                   ♢ 7 6 3 2
        ♣ 6                     ♣ 7 5 4 3 2
                    SOUTH
                    ♠ A Q J 9 8
                    ♡ 9 8
                    ♢ 9 5
                    ♣ A Q 10 8
```

Against a four-spade contract, West makes the obvious lead of the king of hearts. Declarer wins in the dummy and probably leads the ten of spades for a finesse. To be sure dummy doesn't have a trump left to control hearts, West lets the ten hold the trick. He wins the second spade finesse and continues hearts. After cashing a heart trick, West forces declarer with another heart. At this point, South has two trumps left, as does West. His diamonds are not established. His best play is to pull the two trumps and cash his four clubs for down one. If he monkeys around, he may well end up down more.

These hands I have been showing you are all nice teaching hands. In each case, the contract has been precisely game in a major suit. Each hand has been defeated by exactly one trick. In each hand, there has been exactly one problem. That is the way it should be in teaching hands. It is by seeing the hands this simply that we learn the basic principles involved. In real life, the forcing game is used against part score contracts as well as game contracts and, at times, even against slam contracts. The play is not always so clear in real life. Often, the problem of the forcing game is mixed in with other problems for the defense. Let's look at some hands from real life and see how we can apply these principles we have learned.

First, let me broaden my vocabulary. The declarer is sometimes forced, he is tapped, he is punched, or he is pumped. All of these terms mean the same thing. They mean that you shorten one of your opponent's trump suits by forcing him to either trump or lose the trick.

Now let's take a look. Here is the first example.

N-S vul., dealer East.

```
                    NORTH
                    ♠ J 9 8 3
                    ♡ Q 5
                    ◇ 9 7
                    ♣ Q J 8 4 2
        WEST                        EAST
        ♠ A 10 4 2                  ♠ K Q 6 5
        ♡ 9                         ♡ 8 6 4 3 2
        ◇ 10 8 6 3 2                ◇ 4
        ♣ K 7 5                     ♣ 10 9 6
                    SOUTH
                    ♠ 7
                    ♡ A K J 10 7
                    ◇ A K Q J 5
                    ♣ A 3
```

The bidding:

CLOSED ROOM

SOUTH	WEST	NORTH	EAST
Santamarina	Jacoby	Attaguile	Nail
			Pass
2 ♡	Pass	2 NT	Pass
3 ♢	Pass	3 ♡	Pass
4 ♢	Pass	4 ♡	Pass
Pass	Pass		

OPEN ROOM

Robinson	Calvente	Jordan	Rocchi
			Pass
2 ♣	Pass	2 ♢	Pass
2 ♡	Pass	3 ♣	Pass
3 ♢	Pass	3 ♡	Pass
4 ♣	Pass	4 ♡	Pass
Pass	Pass		

This hand was played in the 1963 World Championship, with North America pitted against Argentina. In the closed room, the natural bidding sequence used by the Argentine players did not allow them to get in those club bids. The situation was not too clear to West, Jim Jacoby. He led the nine of hearts. This did not turn out to be the best lead in the world. Santamarina won that with dummy's queen and had no difficulty taking five hearts, four diamonds, and the ace of clubs.

In the open room, the American bidders did manage to bid clubs—both of them. Calvente, in the West seat, was warned away from the club lead, diamond lead, and heart lead, so he led the ace of spades. It turned out that this initiated a forcing game. The opening leader didn't have trump length, but his partner did. As a matter of fact, he started with as many as the declarer held. He followed suit with the six, and Calvente continued with a small spade. Arthur Robinson, South, trumped and led the ace and jack of hearts, which he overtook with dummy's queen. He found out that Rocchi, East, now had more trumps than he did. Robinson led a diamond to his ace and king. Rocchi trumped and led the king of spades. When Robinson trumped that, he again had fewer trumps than East. Robinson cashed his heart and led the diamond queen. Rocchi trumped and shifted to the club six. Robinson ducked and West won the king. Robinson had now lost two trump tricks plus the king of clubs and ace of spades. Somewhere in the proceedings, West had discarded a diamond, so the balance of Robinson's hand was good and he was set only one.

The next hand is more complicated. It involves pumps in two different suits and a refusal by a defender to overruff. It is from the 1965 World Championship, with the United States playing Italy.

None vul., dealer North.

```
                    NORTH
                    ♠ 10 8 2
                    ♡ A K 7
                    ◇ K 10 9 5
                    ♣ 9 8 4
        WEST                        EAST
        ♠ J 9 6 3                   ♠ K
        ♡ Q 8 6 4                   ♡ 2
        ◇ 8 4 2                     ◇ A Q 6 3
        ♣ K 2                       ♣ A J 10 7 6 5 3
                    SOUTH
                    ♠ A Q 7 5 4
                    ♡ J 10 9 5 3
                    ◇ J 7
                    ♣ Q
```

The bidding:

OPEN ROOM			
SOUTH	WEST	NORTH	EAST
Avarelli	Leventritt	Belladonna	Schenken
		Pass	2 ♣
2 ♡	Pass	4 ♡	Pass
Pass	Pass		

In the closed room, Ivan Erdos and Kelsey Petterson,

representing the U.S.A., passed throughout. Garozzo, East, got to four clubs under his own power. Erdos, South, led the jack of hearts. When it held the trick, he switched to the queen of clubs. Garozzo used dummy's only entry to finesse diamonds. That worked, but he still had to lose two diamond tricks plus a trick in each major for down one. That was 50 points for the U.S.A.

The bidding in the open room is shown above.

Before I show you just how the defense went, let me tell you just what tricks the defenders won. In the minor suits, they won one club and two diamonds, which is about what you would expect. They won a trick with the jack of spades. The queen of hearts did not win a trick, but they won two trump tricks with their small trumps. Now let me show you how all of this happened.

Peter Leventritt led the king of clubs and continued the suit. South trumped. At this point, West had as many trumps as South did. Avarelli led a small trump to dummy's ace and then led a small spade. When the king came up, he had another spade trick for sure, but he was certainly a long way from finding ten tricks. He won the ace of spades and cashed the queen. He led the jack of diamonds and let it ride to Schenken's queen. Schenken led a high club and Avarelli trumped with the jack of hearts, trying to tempt Leventritt to overruff. Leventritt would have none of it. He discarded the four of diamonds. At this point, he had more trumps than Avarelli.

Avarelli led another diamond, and this time East won with the ace. He could no longer punch declarer by leading a club, as the dummy was out of clubs, but he could punch declarer by leading a diamond. He did that and Avarelli tried once more to tempt Leventritt into overruffing by playing the ten. Leventritt discarded his nine of spades. We have now reached the stage where declarer had one trump left, dummy had two, and West had three. Here is the way it looked:

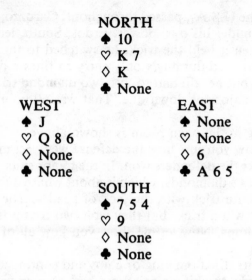

NORTH
♠ 10
♡ K 7
♢ K
♣ None

WEST
♠ J
♡ Q 8 6
♢ None
♣ None

EAST
♠ None
♡ None
♢ 6
♣ A 6 5

SOUTH
♠ 7 5 4
♡ 9
♢ None
♣ None

The defenders already had their book. They had won one
club and two diamonds. They were destined to win three of the
last four tricks to set declarer three tricks. Avarelli led a small
spade which Leventritt won with the jack. He led the queen of
trumps, smothering the singleton nine in declarer's hand. Dummy's king won the trick, but the last two tricks belonged to
Leventritt, West, with his two small trumps.

I promised you some hands which were not game hands,
didn't I? Will a hand at four diamonds do? This one is also
U.S.A. versus Italy, but it is from the Olympiad Games of 1968.

E-W vul., dealer East.

```
                        NORTH
                        ♠ A 8 4
                        ♡ 10 6 3 2
                        ◇ A K
                        ♣ K 9 6 3
         WEST                        EAST
         ♠ K 10 3                    ♠ Q J 7 6 5 2
         ♡ J 4                       ♡ A 9 7 5
         ◇ 10 8 7 3                  ◇ 6 5
         ♣ A J 7 5                   ♣ Q
                        SOUTH
                        ♠ 9
                        ♡ K Q 8
                        ◇ Q J 9 4 2
                        ♣ 10 8 4 2
```

The bidding:

CLOSED ROOM

SOUTH	WEST	NORTH	EAST
Avarelli	Kay	Belladonna	Kaplan
			Pass
Pass	Pass	1 ♣	1 ♠
Pass	2 ♣	Double	3 ♠
4 ◇	Pass	Pass	Pass

In the open room, the Americans, Jordan and Robinson, let Garozzo, East play three spades. Robinson led his king of hearts. Garozzo played well to go down only one trick.

In the closed room, the Italians were not willing to let Edgar Kaplan play three spades, as you can see from the bidding given. They tried four diamonds. They went down two tricks not vulnerable for 100 points, making a total of 200 points to the American team on the hand. When Avarelli's trumps got shortened, he pulled trumps anyway. The defenders ended up taking three tricks with small spades. Here is how the play went.

West opened the three of spades. Declarer played the ace. He led a heart to his king, a diamond to the ace and king, and then he led another heart. This time, Kaplan rose with his ace, and Norman Kay had to play his jack. Kaplan could have given his partner a ruff right now, but instead he made a better play. He gave declarer a ruff. He led a high spade. Avarelli ruffed while Kay cooperated by unblocking his king. At this point, South had two trumps, as did West. Avarelli cashed his two trumps and the queen of hearts. When he led a club towards dummy's king, Kay went up with the ace and led the ten of spades. Kaplan overtook and won the last three tricks with three small spades.

The last hand at the four level may have been a little high to illustrate the forcing defense against a part score. Let's try one at the two level. The hand is from the World Championship of 1963 with North America versus France.

None vul., dealer East.

```
                    NORTH
                    ♠ K 10 8
                    ♡ A 7 5 4 2
                    ◇ J
                    ♣ K 10 5 3
      WEST                        EAST
      ♠ 7 3 2                     ♠ A 4
      ♡ J 10 8 3                  ♡ K 9 6
      ◇ A K                       ◇ Q 9 5 3
      ♣ A Q 9 7                   ♣ J 8 6 4
                    SOUTH
                    ♠ Q J 9 6 5
                    ♡ Q
                    ◇ 10 8 7 6 4 2
                    ♣ 2
```

The bidding:

CLOSED ROOM

SOUTH	WEST	NORTH	EAST
Desrousseau	Nail	Theron	Jacoby
			Pass
Pass	1 ♣	1 ♡	1 NT
2 ◊	Pass	Pas	Double
Pass	Pass	Pass	

When the hand was played in the open room, the Americans, Leventritt and Schenken, North-South, doubled the Italians at three clubs and set them one trick. The bidding in the closed room is shown.

The way it worked out, Jim Jacoby, East, ended up pulling trumps. The defenders took a total of seven tricks to set the contract two, doubled, for 300 points. Adding this to the 100 points from the open room, North America won a total of 400 points, which equals nine international match points (IMPs).

Jacoby's bid of 1NT after the heart overcall showed heart strength, so Bobby Nail opened the jack of hearts. South won dummy's ace and led the jack of diamonds, won by West. West continued with a second heart and South trumped. South led the ten of diamonds. Apparently he was trying to smother a singleton nine, but it didn't work out that way. Nail won the ace. He led another heart, which South trumped. After South trumped two hearts and led trumps twice, he had two diamonds left, as did Jim Jacoby, East. The difference is that Jacoby's trumps were high. Desrousseau led a spade toward dummy's king. Jacoby won the ace and cashed the queen and nine of diamonds. Now nobody had any trumps. Jacoby led a small club to the ace and Nail took the seventh trick for the defenders with his eight of hearts.

To go to the other extreme, let's try the forcing game against a slam contract. Of course, the slam contract was bid for a sacrifice. The teachers tell us that we should not make sacrifice bids when we are vulnerable against non-vulnerable opponents. This hand seems to suggest that the teachers are right.

N-S vul., dealer East.

```
                      NORTH
                      ♠ J 10 9 8
                      ♡ 10 9 7
                      ◇ Q 10 4
                      ♣ Q 7 2
       WEST                        EAST
       ♠ A 7 3                     ♠ 5
       ♡ J 6 3                     ♡ A K Q 8 5 4 2
       ◇ K J 7 5 2                 ◇ A 9 8
       ♣ 8 6                       ♣ A 4
                      SOUTH
                      ♠ K Q 6 4 2
                      ♡ None
                      ◇ 6 3
                      ♣ K J 10 9 5 3
```

The bidding:

OPEN ROOM

SOUTH	WEST	NORTH	EAST
Sheehan	Besse	Dixon	Fenwick
			2 ♣
3 ♣	3 ◇	Pass	3 ♡
3 ♠	4 ♡	4 ♠	5 ♣
Pass	5 ♠	Pass	6 ♡
Pass	Pass	6 ♠	Double
Pass	Pass	Pass	

This hand is from the 1972 Olympiad Games when
Switzerland played Great Britain. In the closed room, the Swiss
players let the British play six diamonds without bothering them
too much, and the opening lead was a small club. Double dummy, the hand could have been made, but when the British player
took the normal play of a diamond finesse, the Swiss cashed a
club trick for a one-trick set. This was 50 points to Switzerland.

The bidding in the open room is given. The British refused to
let the Swiss play a contract of six hearts, which could have been
defeated on a club lead. The Swiss players, not knowing that the

slam failed in the other room, set out to defeat the British by a larger score than they would have received if they had been allowed to bid and make the slam. This meant they had to defeat the British by four tricks, or take five tricks in all. I want you to watch that little seven of spades in the West hand. Believe it or not, that is the card that is going to provide the *coup de grace* after the forcing game has taken all of South's trumps away from him.

Jean Besse, West, chose the jack of hearts for his opening lead. East went up with the queen and South trumped. Sheehan led a small spade towards dummy. West ducked, letting dummy's eight win the trick. A small club was led from dummy. East ducked, letting Sheehan win the king. When South led a second spade, Besse went up with the ace and led another heart. Sheehan trumped. Having trumped twice, he now had the same number of trumps as Besse. Not only had he trumped two times, but he had also led trumps twice, so both South and West had only one trump, but North still had two. Clubs were still not established. South led a club which East won with the ace. Fenwick cashed the ace of diamonds and led a diamond to his partner's king. West led a third heart. The defenders had won tricks with the ace of spades, the ace of clubs, and the ace and king of diamonds, and very badly wanted to get at least one more trick. They were going to get it. Here are the cards which were left when West led the heart:

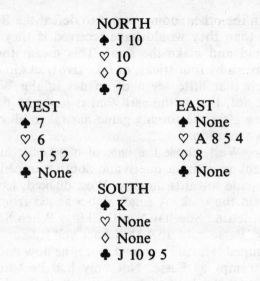

NORTH
- ♠ J 10
- ♡ 10
- ◇ Q
- ♣ 7

WEST
- ♠ 7
- ♡ 6
- ◇ J 5 2
- ♣ None

EAST
- ♠ None
- ♡ A 8 5 4
- ◇ 8
- ♣ None

SOUTH
- ♠ K
- ♡ None
- ◇ None
- ♣ J 10 9 5

South trumped the heart with his last trump. Now the dummy could have pulled trumps, but the lead was on the wrong side of the river. South had the lead and he had nothing left but clubs. When he led a club, Besse trumped it with the little seven of spades and brought the penalty up to 1100 points, giving Switzerland a net total of 1150, worth 15 IMPs.

As the final hand in this series, I have chosen a hand from my files which is a curiosity in two respects. Instead of having stoppers in two suits, the defender had two stoppers in the trump suit. In addition, he had to solicit some help from the declarer to get the pumping suit going.

206

E-W vul., dealer South.

NORTH
♠ 7 5 2
♡ 6 4
◊ K 6 5 4 3
♣ A K 9

WEST
♠ 10 8
♡ A Q 5 2
◊ Q J 10 9 7
♣ 7 5

EAST
♠ J 9 6 3
♡ 7 3
◊ 8 2
♣ Q J 10 6 4

SOUTH
♠ A K Q 4
♡ K J 10 9 8
◊ A
♣ 8 3 2

The bidding:

SOUTH	WEST	NORTH	EAST
1 ♡	Pass	2 ◊	Pass
2 ♠	Pass	2 NT	Pass
3 ♡	Pass	4 ♡	Pass
Pass	Pass		

West led the queen of diamonds. South won his ace and went to dummy with the king of clubs to lead a trump. He played the jack from his hand; West played the deuce with no hesitation. If West had taken the trick, declarer would have conceded another trump trick and still been in control of the hand with enough trumps to pull West's trumps. Declarer would then win three trump tricks, three spade tricks, and two tricks in each of the minor suits. But when his jack of trumps held, declarer thought East had the queen. He returned to dummy with the other high club, cashed the king of diamonds to discard his losing club, led another trump to his hand, and was surprised when West won with the queen. West played a diamond, which South trumped. At this point, South and West each had two trumps, and West had the ace. If South led another trump, West would win and lead another diamond, forcing South to ruff with his last trump. West would then have the only trump left in the game. West would win a trump trick and two diamond tricks in addition to the two trump tricks already taken. Nor could declarer take ten tricks if he left two trumps outstanding and started leading spades. West would trump the third spade, cash the ace of trumps, and lead a diamond. The jack of spades in the East hand would take the setting trick.

CHAPTER 5:
WHEN TO LEAD TRUMPS

I will have to go along with all the other writers and say that "doubt" is not a sufficient reason for leading trumps. There are five good reasons for leading trumps:

1. To keep declarer from cross-ruffing.
2. To stop declarer from making extra trump tricks by ruffing in dummy.
3. To make a safe, passive lead; i.e., avoid giving declarer a trick he could not otherwise take.
4. To get two trumps for one.
5. Your partner has passed your takeout double.

When declarer has bid two suits, you have strength in one of his suits, and dummy has supported the other, there is a good chance that he plans to win a lot of tricks by cross-ruffing. Here are some hands that illustrate the point. Suppose you are West, defending against a four-heart contract with the following hand:

♠ A Q 10 8
♡ 10 9
◇ K Q 10 9
♣ Q 10 2

The king of diamonds would seem to be the best opening lead against any contract. But if the bidding is:

SOUTH	WEST	NORTH	EAST
1 ♠	Pass	1 NT	Pass
2 ♡	Pass	3 ♡	Pass
4 ♡	Pass	Pass	Pass

Try to visualize the North and South hands. North has shown

six to nine HCPs, no more than two spades, and at least four hearts. Only after hearts are bid does he show any interest in a game. South sounds like he has at least nine, and possibly ten, cards in the major suits. That means that he is short in the minor suits, and is likely to be trumping them early in the game. In other words, there is a good chance that declarer will be trumping spades in the dummy and one of the minor suits in his own hand. You know he is not likely to grab many first-round spade tricks with your holding in that suit. So it looks like he is going to depend on a cross-ruff to bring him in ten tricks. What is the best way to stop a cross-ruff? Lead trumps. So you lead a trump and this turns out to be the entire deal:

```
                    NORTH
                    ♠ 3
                    ♡ Q 8 7 4
                    ◊ A 8 6 3
                    ♣ K 5 4 3
        WEST                    EAST
        ♠ A Q 10 8              ♠ 7 6 2
        ♡ 10 9                  ♡ 6 2
        ◊ K Q 10 9             ◊ J 7 5 2
        ♣ Q 10 2               ♣ A 9 8 6
                    SOUTH
                    ♠ K J 9 5 4
                    ♡ A K J 5 3
                    ◊ 4
                    ♣ J 7
```

Had you opened the king of diamonds, declarer would have won the ace and led a spade. You would win, and now you would lead a heart, but it would be too late. Declarer would trump three spades in the dummy and three diamonds in his own hand. Then he would draw the last trump and cash the fifth spade. He wouldn't make a club trick; however he would take eight trump tricks, one spade trick, and the ace of diamonds. But since you have opened a trump and can lead a second trump when you get in with the first spade, he can trump only two spades in the dummy and you will win two spade tricks. Your side will also win two club tricks and down he will go.

In the next hand, you hold the ace of trumps. You lead a small trump so that you can get the trumps led three times.

NORTH
♠ 3
♡ Q J 7 5
♢ A Q 10 8 2
♣ 7 6 5

WEST
♠ Q 10 8 7
♡ A 8 2
♢ 6 4
♣ J 10 9 8

EAST
♠ A 6 4
♡ 4 3
♢ K J 9 5
♣ Q 4 3 2

SOUTH
♠ K J 9 5 2
♡ K 10 9 6
♢ 7 3
♣ A K

SOUTH	WEST	NORTH	EAST
1 ♠	Pass	2 ♢	Pass
2 ♡	Pass	3 ♡	Pass
4 ♡	Pass	Pass	Pass

Here your spade suit is not quite as strong as on the first hand, but it is good enough. The bidding indicates a cross-ruff in the offing. However, if you lead the ace and a trump, declarer can get home with ten tricks. He can win the second trump in the dummy and lead a spade. If East does not play the ace of spades, declarer can play the king, trump two spades, concede a spade trick to West, and end up losing one spade, one trump, and one diamond. However, if you open the deuce of hearts, you get to lead hearts three times and declarer can trump only one spade. On the opening lead of the small trump. declarer will win the jack in dummy and lead a spade. East will fly up with the ace to return a trump, which you win and return a third trump. Declarer will lose a spade and a diamond in addition to the trump and spade tricks he has already lost and down he will go.

Let's see how some of these principles work in real life. The

211

first hand is from the 1963 World Championship with North America playing Argentina.

E-W vul., dealer West.

```
                        NORTH
                        ♠ Q J 8 3 2
                        ♡ A Q 6 5
                        ◇ Q 9 8
                        ♣ 2
        WEST                        EAST
        ♠ A 7                       ♠ K 10 9 6 5 4
        ♡ 9 4 3 2                   ♡ 8
        ◇ A 10 3                    ◇ 6 5 4
        ♣ K J 10 9                  ♣ 8 6 3
                        SOUTH
                        ♠ None
                        ♡ K J 10 7
                        ◇ K J 7 2
                        ♣ A Q 7 5 4
```

The bidding:

CLOSED ROOM

SOUTH	WEST	NORTH	EAST
Jordan	Schenone	Robinson	Saravia
	1 ♣	Double	1 ♠
2 ♠	Pass	3 ♡	Pass
4 ♡	Pass	Pass	Pass

OPEN ROOM

Santamarina	Leventritt	Attaguile	Schenken
	Pass	Pass	Pass
1 ♣	Pass	1 ♠	Pass
2 ♡	Pass	4 ♡	Pass
Pass	Pass		

In the closed room, where Arthur Robinson, North, played four hearts, Saravia, East, heard nothing to indicate a trump lead. He dutifully led his partner's suit. The bidding left no doubt in Robinson's mind about who had the king of clubs, so he played dummy's ace and led a small club and trumped it. Next he led the nine of diamonds to dummy's king, which West won with his ace. A look at dummy told West to lead a heart. It was too late. Robinson won in the dummy with the ten and cross-ruffed spades and clubs. When diamonds broke, he won two diamonds, one club, and seven trumps, for ten tricks.

In the open room it was a different story. Leventritt passed the hand which Schenone had opened. The result was that Santamarina, South, opened one club, and the Argentina team duly reached four hearts, but this time played by South. This sequence of bidding clearly called for a trump lead. Leventritt's right-hand opponent had bid two suits, was playing in the second suit, and Leventritt had control of the first suit. South's bidding indicated shortness in spades, while North's bidding indicated length in both major suits and shortage in at least one of the minors. All of the symptoms were there that the declarer needed to cross-ruff the hand. Leventritt's opening heart lead frustrated this plan. Santamarina won his ten and led the king of diamonds. West won the ace and led a second heart. Santamarina won dummy's queen and counted his tricks: two diamonds, six hearts (on a cross-ruff), and no spades. Therefore, he needed two club tricks, so he led a club to his queen. Leventritt won and led a third heart. That left Santamarina with one trump and the dummy with one trump. He won the third trump lead with his jack, trumped a club with dummy's ace of hearts, cashed dummy's queen of diamonds, led a diamond to his jack, and pulled Leventritt's last heart. When diamonds broke, Santamarina was able to take three diamond tricks, compared to only two which Robinson had taken in the closed room. But the big difference was that Santamarina won only five trump tricks. It is interesting to compare the number of tricks won in each suit in the two rooms. Here is a countdown.

TRICKS WON BY DECLARER

	Closed Room	Open Room
Spades	0	0
Hearts (Trumps)	7	5
Diamonds	2	3
Clubs	1	1
	10	9

You will see that in the closed room, the bidding by the Argentines kept them from getting the information they needed to lead trumps. In the open room, the Americans followed the principle of talking less and listening more. Sometimes you wonder whether the information given by a defending pair who take part in the bidding is more helpful to the declarer's side than to their own.

On the next hand, the bidding methods of the Roman Club System were too explicit and guided Charlie Goren to the killing trump lead. This deal is from the 1957 World Championship, with the United States against Italy.

E-W vul., dealer North.

```
                    NORTH
                    ♠ K 8 3 2
                    ♡ A Q 10 9 6
                    ◇ A J 7 4
                    ♣ None
    WEST                            EAST
    ♠ A Q J                         ♠ 9 6 5 4
    ♡ K 4 2                         ♡ J 8 5 3
    ◇ 5 3 2                         ◇ 10
    ♣ A K 8 6                       ♣ 10 9 7 2
                    SOUTH
                    ♠ 10 7
                    ♡ 7
                    ◇ K Q 9 8 6
                    ♣ Q J 5 4 3
```

The bidding:

CLOSED ROOM

SOUTH	WEST	NORTH	EAST
Sobel	Chiaradia	Seamon	D'Alelio
		1 ♡	Pass
2 ◊	Double	Redouble	Pass
Pass	2 ♠	3 ◊	Pass
4 ◊	Pass	5 ♣	Pass
5 ◊	Pass	Pass	Pass

OPEN ROOM

Belladonna	Goren	Avarelli	Leventritt
		2 ♣	Pass
2 NT	Pass	3 ♣	Pass
5 ◊	Pass	Pass	Pass

In the closed room, West led a high club. Helen Sobel trumped in the dummy. Because of the take-out double by Chiaradia, she played West for the ace of spades, so she led the ace of hearts, trumped a heart, and led the ten of spades. West won the ace, and played the spade queen. With that, Helen cross-ruffed the next seven tricks, trumping hearts and spades in her hand and clubs in the dummy. In the meantime, Helen had won a trick with each trump in both hands, for nine tricks. The spade king and heart ace were her tenth and eleventh tricks.

In the open room, Avarelli opened two clubs, an artificial bid showing a three-suited hand, either 4-4-4-1 or 5-4-4-0, with 11 to 16 HCPs. Belladonna, South, held two five-card suits and knew that Avarelli had at least four-card support for one of them. His two notrump bid was artificial and asked Avarelli to tell him where his short suit was. Avarelli's three-club bid said that he had a singleton or void in clubs. Given this information, Belladonna went straight to five diamonds.

Maybe he would have done better to find a crooked road.

Charlie Goren, on opening lead with the West hand, had been listening to the auction. Having seventeen HCPs, he knew that the opponents' bidding must be based on distribution. Avarelli had said that he had length in spades, hearts and diamonds. It was obvious that South was short in the majors. It was as clear to Goren as it was to Belladonna that the hand would be played in a cross-ruff. To stop that, Goren led a trump. After the trump lead, Belladonna knew he was going to have to scramble for tricks somewhere other than with a cross-ruff. He won the first trick in his hand and led a heart to the queen. That gave him an extra heart trick which Helen Sobel had not gotten in the other room, but it didn't solve his problem. Belladonna cashed the ace of hearts, discarding a spade, ruffed a heart, and led the ten of spades. Goren went up with his ace and led another diamond. The net result was that Belladonna got seven trump tricks instead of the nine which Helen Sobel got in the closed room. With the three tricks from the majors, he had a total of ten, along with a score of minus fifty. The lesson of this hand is that when one opponent shows a three-suited hand, you should almost always lead a trump. This is true even if you have a trump honor.

Some few years ago there was quite a bit of cheering when the Italian method of showing three suits with one opening bid got them into a four-spade contract, making, while the Americans never got beyond the one level. Explicit systems can sometimes do wonderful things for you. However, there is another side to this story. The help they give to the defense is not so dramatic. Good defense doesn't get the attention or the cheers that bidding gets when it succeeds.

I think it's about time we take a good look at just what the defenders are able to do when they are offered a road map by these explicit systems. Could it be that sometimes it is better to be more vague about your bidding? There is an old theory that instead of it being wise to tell your partner everything about your hand, it is wiser to tell him only those things which will help him make a good decision. Smart opponents have a way of tuning in when you give a complete description.

Now let's look at a part score. The hand features the Swedish version of the two-club opening bid with a three-suited hand. Based on the Marmic System, the bid was supposed to show 13 to 15 HCPs, so when Larsen, North, opened two clubs, he was fudging a bit. This hand was played in the 1953 World Championships, with the Swedes against the United States.

E-W vul., dealer North.

```
                        NORTH
                        ♠ A K 10 9
                        ♡ J 7 6 4
                        ◇ 10 7 6 5
                        ♣ K
        WEST                            EAST
        ♠ J 7 4 2                       ♠ Q 8 3
        ♡ Q 9                           ♡ A K 8
        ◇ K 9 4                         ◇ Q J 8
        ♣ J 9 8 3                       ♣ A 10 7 5
                        SOUTH
                        ♠ 6 5
                        ♡ 10 5 3 2
                        ◇ A 3 2
                        ♣ Q 6 4 2
```

The bidding:

OPEN ROOM

SOUTH	WEST	NORTH	EAST
Wohlin	Becker	Larsen	Crawford
		2 ♣	Pass
2 ◇	Pass	3 ♣	Pass
3 ♡	Pass	Pass	Pass

CLOSED ROOM

Schenken	Lilliehook	Rapee	Anulf
		Pass	1 ♣
Pass	1 ◇	Double	Redouble
1 ♡	1 ♠	2 ♡	Pass
Pass	Pass		

Let's put ourselves in B. J. Becker's place and consider our opening lead. Usually a queen doubleton is a bad lead, and it is even worse when it is in trumps. However, the knowledge that North had a short suit and no establishable side suit suggested a trump lead. B. J. also knew that Crawford had a pretty good hand. Becker had only seven HCPs and the opponents had not bid to game. He expected about 11-13 HCPs from Crawford and was probably surprised when he discovered that Crawford actually had 16 HCPs. In any case, the Swedes would ruff clubs in the North hand and spades and diamonds in South. This called for a trump lead, so B. J. led the queen of hearts. When that held, he continued hearts. After the smoke cleared away, the unfortunate Swedish declarer had only one trump in each hand. He went down two.

In the closed room, Rapee, North, passed. In spite of the fact that the Swedes opened the bidding, the Americans found their fit and bought the hand for two hearts. Lilliehook, West, had good reasons to choose a club for his opening lead. His partner had bid clubs. Anulf won the ace, and switched to trumps. His play was not nearly so effective as Becker's had been, as he laid down the ace, king, dropping his partner's queen, and a third heart, which Howard Schenken won with the ten. He led a spade to dummy's nine. East won the queen and led the queen of diamonds, which Schenken ducked. East switched to a club. Schenken won the queen, and he took a second spade finesse. When that won, he had three spades, a club, a diamond, and a heart. There was a heart left in each hand, and by winning those separately on a cross-ruff, he got home with eight tricks.

Don't get the idea that it is only three-suit opening bids which can inspire a defender to open a trump, hoping to stop a cross-ruff. There are a lot of bidding sequences which will do this no matter what bidding method is used. We have looked at game hands, we have looked at part-score hands; now let's look at a slam hand where natural bidding methods were used.

This hand is from the 1972 Olympiad Games, in the ladies' series, the United States versus the Netherlands. Both declarers managed to avoid playing three notrump, but both of them got too high in clubs. In one room, Dorothy Truscott, for the United States, led trumps three times and set the Dutch two tricks. In the other room, the Dutch ladies did not lead trumps, and Mary Jane Farrell made her slam. Here is the hand.

E-W vul., dealer North.

NORTH
- ♠ 10 5
- ♡ K J 10 8 7
- ♢ 10 8
- ♣ A K 8 2

WEST
- ♠ Q 7
- ♡ A Q 6 3
- ♢ Q 6 4 3
- ♣ 10 9 6

EAST
- ♠ K J 9 3 2
- ♡ 9 5 4 2
- ♢ J 9 5
- ♣ 4

SOUTH
- ♠ A 8 6 4
- ♡ None
- ♢ A K 7 2
- ♣ Q J 7 5 3

The bidding:

CLOSED ROOM

SOUTH	WEST	NORTH	EAST
Hoving	Truscott	Niji	Mitchell
		Pass	Pass
1 ♢	Pass	1 ♡	Pass
1 ♠	Pass	3 NT	Pass
4 ♣	Pass	5 ♣	Pass
6 ♣	Pass	Pass	Pass

OPEN ROOM

Farrell	Hoogenkamp	Johnson	Van Dam
		1 ♡	Pass
2 ♣	Pass	2 ♡	Pass
2 ♠	Pass	3 ♣	Pass
3 ♢	Pass	3 NT	Pass
5 ♣	Pass	6 ♣	Pass
Pass	Pass		

First, let's look at the play in the closed room. South refused to play three notrump, and Dorothy Truscott properly decided this indicated declarer was going to try to take tricks with a cross-ruff. She opened the six of clubs. Mrs. Hoving, the Dutch declarer, saw only three immediate tricks outside of clubs. With trumps being led, there was no way to take nine trump tricks. That would require that each club take a trick separately. Mrs. Hoving saw one faint chance. She won the opening lead in the dummy and led the king of hearts on which she discarded a spade. Mrs. Truscott won and led a second trump, won in dummy. Mrs. Hoving led the jack of hearts, discarding another spade. Dorothy won and led a third trump. Mrs. Hoving had to win in her hand. She cashed two diamonds, trumped a diamond, and led the ten of hearts, discarding her last diamond. The heart distribution was cruel. Not only were the ace and queen both in the West hand, but the nine of hearts didn't even fall out. Mrs. Hoving had to lose a spade trick in addition to the two heart tricks she had already lost.

Now let's see how Mary Jane Farrell made out in the open room. Mrs. Hoogenkamp had not gotten the message about the distribution. She opened the three of diamonds. The ten was played from the dummy, and jack was won by Mary Jane with her ace. Preparing for a cross-ruff, she led ace and another spade. This was the last chance the defenders had to lead a trump. Whether Mrs. Hoogenkamp would have led a trump had she been allowed to win that trick with the queen, we will never know, as Mrs. Van Dam overtook the trick with the king to return another diamond. This is just what Mrs. Farrell needed. She took a trick with each of her nine clubs. Nine clubs, ace and king of diamonds, and the ace of spades came to a total of twelve tricks. She won the king of diamonds and trumped diamonds and spades in dummy and hearts in her hand.

The conditions which call for an opening lead of a trump when dummy has fewer than four trumps are the same as the conditions which call for a trump lead to stop a cross-ruff. If the bidding indicates that the declarer has losers in a suit in which the dummy is short, chances are declarer is going to use dummy's trumps to ruff those losers. The way to stop that is to lead trumps.

Suppose you are sitting West with the following hand:

♠ 6
♡ A J 8 3
♢ K 10 9 8 6
♣ 9 8 4

and hear the following auction:

SOUTH	WEST	NORTH	EAST
1 ♣	Pass	1 ♡	Pass
2 ♢	Pass	2 ♠	Pass
3 ♢	Pass	4 ♣	Pass
5 ♣	Pass	Pass	Pass

This bidding screams for a trump lead almost without looking at your hand. South holds five diamonds and at least six clubs. North has length in both major suits, and support for clubs. It would be surprising if dummy held more than one diamond. A look at your hand tells you that South has several diamond losers, even though he has bid them twice. These must have been the thoughts that went through Mike Lawrence's mind, for his opening lead was a trump.

Here is the hand.

NORTH
♠ K J 9 8
♡ Q 10 9 7 5
♢ A
♣ 10 7 3

WEST
♠ 6
♡ A J 8 3
♢ K 10 9 8 6
♣ 9 8 4

EAST
♠ Q 10 7 5 4 3 2
♡ K 6 4
♢ J 7
♣ Q

SOUTH
♠ A
♡ 2
♢ Q 5 4 3 2
♣ A K J 6 5 2

This hand is from the finals of the 1971 World Championship, with the Aces defending their World Championship against the French.

Stoppa, South, the French declarer, was probably destined to go down a trick no matter what Lawrence led. Lawrence's club lead set him two tricks. Stoppa won the club king, cashed the ace of spades, and went to the dummy with the ace of diamonds to lead the king of spades, discarding a heart from his hand. He must have been surprised when Lawrence trumped the king of spades. Lawrence led a second club and the dummy was reduced to one trump. Stoppa trumped a diamond. He got six clubs in his own hand, one ruff in dummy, and his two aces, for a total of only nine tricks.

When the Aces held the North-South hands, Jim Jacoby and Bobby Wolff played three notrump. The distribution was just right for that contract when the queen of clubs fell on the first round. The declarer now had six clubs, two spades, the ace of diamonds, and no further problems.

A trump lead is often best when you fear that any other lead may give up a trick. One good reason for such a fear is that you hold practically all the high-card strength your side has, and have no solid three-card or longer sequence. Under these circumstances, it is unlikely that your partner is going to have much support for your holdings. On the next hand, the French defender chose the passive lead of a trump, while the American defender led from a two-card sequence. It turned out that the French player was right. The hand was played in the 1960 Olympiads.

N-S vul., dealer South.

```
                        NORTH
                        ♠ 10 9 8 7
                        ♡ K Q 9
                        ◇ J 2
                        ♣ A 8 6 3
        WEST                         EAST
        ♠ K Q 4                      ♠ 6 5 3 2
        ♡ A 10 5                     ♡ 8 3
        ◇ 10 3                       ◇ Q 9 8 7 4
        ♣ K J 10 9 5                 ♣ 4 2
                        SOUTH
                        ♠ A J
                        ♡ J 7 6 4 2
                        ◇ A K 6 5
                        ♣ Q 7
```

The bidding:

OPEN ROOM

SOUTH	WEST	NORTH	EAST
Crawford	Bourchtoff	Stone	Delmouly
1 ♡	2 ♣	2 ♡	Pass
3 ♡	Pass	4 ♡	Pass
Pass	Pass		

CLOSED ROOM

Trezel	Silidor	Jais	Rapee
1 ◇	Double	Redouble	Pass
1 ♡	Pass	2 ♡	Pass
3 ♡	Pass	4 ♡	Pass
Pass	Pass		

In the open room, Bourchtoff led the five of hearts. From the auction, it was likely the Americans had around 24 HCPs and a few distribution features. Bourchtoff held 13 HCPs, so it was unlikely that his partner would be of much help in the defense. As both his opponents had bid hearts, he hoped he wouldn't be giving anything away by leading from his heart holding. Johnny

Crawford won in the dummy and led a spade to his jack. West won and led the ace and another heart. He not only was able to get off lead twice without giving anything away, but he also had kept Crawford from using any of dummy's trumps for ruffing purposes. Crawford now led a spade to his hand and a small diamond toward dummy's jack. The one high card in the East hand was the queen of diamonds, so the indirect finesse failed. After winning the queen of diamonds, East returned a club. This limited Crawford to four hearts, two diamonds, one club, and one spade, for a total of eight tricks, down two.

In the closed room, Silidor attacked with the lead of the spade king. Trezel, South, for France, won the ace and returned the jack. Silidor led a third spade which Trezel won in dummy, discarding a club. Trezel was setting up a cross-ruff for himself. He led the ace of clubs, trumped a club, cashed the ace and king of diamonds, and trumped a diamond in the dummy. He led dummy's last spade, but instead of trumping it, he discarded his last diamond as Silidor won a trick with his small trump. Silidor now led the ace and another heart, but the balance of the tricks belonged to South. He lost two trump tricks and one spade trick, but lost no tricks in either minor suit.

There are times when the bidding tells you that a trump lead is called for. Look at this hand from the 1968 World Bridge Olympiad, with Canada playing against the United States.

None vul., dealer South.

```
                        NORTH
                        ♠ A 4 2
                        ♡ 9 8
                        ◊ A K 6 5
                        ♣ K Q J 7
        WEST                            EAST
        ♠ 10 9 5                        ♠ Q 3
        ♡ A Q 5 3                       ♡ J 10 7
        ◊ Q 2                           ◊ J 10 7 4
        ♣ 10 9 5 2                      ♣ A 8 6 3
                        SOUTH
                        ♠ K J 8 7 6
                        ♡ K 6 4 2
                        ◊ 9 8 3
                        ♣ 4
```

The bidding:

OPEN ROOM

SOUTH	WEST	NORTH	EAST
Kaplan	Elliott	Kay	Sheardown
Pass	Pass	1 ♣	Pass
1 ♠	Pass	2 ◊	Pas
2 ♠	Pass	3 ♣	Pass
4 ♠	Pass	Pass	Pass

CLOSED ROOM

Murray	Jordan	Kehela	Robinson
Pass	Pass	1 NT	Pass
2 ♣	Pass	2 ◊	Pass
2 ♠	Pass	4 ♠	Pass
Pass	Pass		

In the open room, Norman Kay, North, showed length in
clubs and diamonds and secondary spade support. When a
player has clubs, diamonds and spades, he is short in hearts.
Bruce Elliott, West, had some heart strength, and it sounded to
him like Edgar Kaplan would trump a heart or two in dummy,

so he led a trump.

A look at the combined North and South hands shows how right he was. With the spade suit behaving nicely, declarer had five spades, two diamonds, and two clubs. That was nine tricks. The best chance for a tenth trick was to trump a heart in dummy. But the opening lead made it unlikely that Edgar Kaplan was going to be able to get that ruff. There were several other possibilities for a tenth trick. He did the best he could by trying all of them.

He won the first trick in his hand and led a small club to dummy's king. Percy Sheardown, East, won his ace and led a second trump. Kaplan won the jack and led a diamond to dummy's ace. On dummy's two high clubs, he discarded two diamonds and ruffed a diamond in his hand. He led a spade to the ace and cashed the king of diamonds. If the diamonds had been three-three, he would have picked up his tenth trick with the long diamond. When that didn't work, he led a heart to his king. If East had the heart ace, then the heart king would be his tenth trick. When that, too, failed, he ended up with the nine tricks he had started with.

In the closed room, the bidding did not reveal so much about the distribution. All Robert Jordan knew was that North had a notrump bid and three spades, and that South had a five-card spade suit and enough to make a game try. He opened a club, won by Arthur Robinson, East, with the ace. Robinson switched to hearts and the defenders got their two heart tricks. Now Eric Murray was going to get to trump a heart. As a matter of fact, the defense led a third heart, which Murray trumped. That turned out to be his tenth trick when the queen of spades showed up on the second spade lead.

When the opponents are playing in a four-four fit, and the opening leader has the remaining five cards in the trump suit, he can always get two trumps for one simply by leading trumps. That situation arose in the 1973 World Championship, when Indonesia played the World Champion Aces from Dallas, Texas.

None vul., dealer South.

                        NORTH
                        ♠ A 9 6 3
                        ♡ A 10 8 4 2
                        ◇ 8 2
                        ♣ K 7
        WEST   EAST
        ♠ K 10 7 5 2   ♠ None
        ♡ 9 5   ♡ K 7 3
        ◇ A J 3   ◇ Q 10 9 7 4
        ♣ Q J 6   ♣ A 9 8 5 2
                        SOUTH
                        ♠ Q J 8 4
                        ♡ Q J 6
                        ◇ K 6 5
                        ♣ 10 4 3

The bidding:

                    OPEN ROOM
        SOUTH   WEST   NORTH   EAST
        Jacoby   Lasut   Wolff   Aguw
        Pass   Pass   2 ♡   Pass
        3 ♠   Pass   Pass   Double
        Pass   Pass   Pass

Bobby Wolff's third-hand opening bid of two hearts was
Flannery, promising four spades and five hearts, with 11 to 15
HCPs. Jim Jacoby's three-spade bid was invitational. Jacoby's
fitting cards in the major suits encouraged him to make this invitation, but, of course, Wolff, with his complete minimum,
declined. When the bidding got back to Aguw, East, he made
what he intended to be a takeout double, asking his partner to
bid a minor suit. As Wolff's opening bid guaranteed four
spades, Lasut felt confident that he was playing against a four-
four fit. He converted what was intended to be a takeout double
into a penalty double.
  On the lie of the cards, East-West can take eleven tricks in
either minor suit. However, the defenders got an even better

score against three spades doubled. Against the 5-0 trump break, and with every card in every other suit badly located for the declarer, Jacoby was bound to take a beating.

Looking at all four hands, you can see that the defenders were automatically entitled to one heart, two diamonds, two clubs, and at least two trump tricks for a three-trick set. Their only job was to be sure they took their tricks. Lasut led a trump every time he was in and the defenders got them all.

An old adage in bridge states: If partner passes a takeout double, you must lead a trump. The premise is that partner will convert the takeout double to a penalty double only when his trumps are long enough and strong enough to pull the enemy trumps. The idea is to prevent the declarer from scoring his small trumps by ruffing. In effect, when partner passes your takeout double, he is saying that he wants to play the contract in that suit even though he knows that you are short in the suit and that an opponent has four or five trumps. Ideally, he should have at least five cards in the suit and a four- or five-card honor sequence. Let's look at two teaching hands first—one from the 1940s, the other from the 1970s—and then we'll examine some hands from real competition and see how real life differs from the ideal.

First, the early teaching hand.

N-S vul., dealer South.

NORTH
♠ 10 8 7 6 5
♡ 7 6 2
◇ 6
♣ K 8 4 2

WEST
♠ A K J 9 4
♡ 3
◇ Q J 10 4
♣ A Q J

EAST
♠ Q 2
♡ Q J 10 9 4
◇ K 9 3 2
♣ 5 3

SOUTH
♠ 3
♡ A K 8 5
◇ A 8 7 5
♣ 10 9 7 6

The bidding:

SOUTH	WEST	NORTH	EAST
1 ♡	Double	Pass	Pass
Pass			

The author states that West opened the king of spades, and with only the queen outstanding, led a low spade. South ruffed, cashed the diamond ace, ruffed a diamond, and led another spade. East ruffed with the heart nine as South discarded a club. At long last the defenders led trumps. East played the queen of hearts which South won. He ruffed another diamond and led another spade. At this point, East could not prevent declarer from winning two heart tricks with his king and eight. If he ruffed high, declarer would discard a diamond, so East did the best he could and discarded a club. South ruffed again, and although he never made dummy's king of clubs, he did make seven tricks.

The writer goes on to point out that if West had opened a small trump, declarer will go down.

The trouble with this picture is that in the 1970s, I don't think there is any way South would play one heart doubled. So, let's look at the 1970 model.

```
                    NORTH
                    ♠ 8 7 4 3 2
                    ♡ 7 6 3
                    ◊ K 2
                    ♣ 7 4 3
    WEST                        EAST
    ♠ A K 10 6                  ♠ Q J 5
    ♡ 2                         ♡ K Q J 10 9
    ◊ Q J 10 8                  ◊ 9 5 3
    ♣ K Q 8 5                   ♣ 6 2
                    SOUTH
                    ♠ 9
                    ♡ A 8 5 4
                    ◊ A 7 6 4
                    ♣ A J 10 9
```

The bidding sequence is the same. South is supposed to open one heart, West to double, and everybody pass. A heart lead defeats the hand two tricks, as declarer wins nothing except his four high-card tricks and a diamond ruff. With any other lead, declarer will win seven tricks.

This one looks unrealistic to me. Maybe there are players who make a vulnerable opening bid of one heart with the South hand, and sit there when a penalty double is slapped on them, but if there are, I don't know them.

Certainly in the version from the 1970s, East's trump suit is one with which he would like to pull trumps, and the idea of passing a takeout double with either of these hands is excellent. The trouble is that you don't get these absolutely solid trump suits often enough, and it is more likely that you are going to have to make do with something less.

In *Bridge World* magazine, a panel of experts was asked what they would do with the following hand if their left-hand opponent opened one diamond, their partner doubled, and their right-hand opponent passed. We are told that both sides were vulnerable.

♠ 6 5 4 2
♡ K Q
◊ K Q 10 6 4
♣ Q 5

The diamond suit is not solid, and if your left-hand opponent is sitting there with something like five or six diamonds to the ace, jack, nine, eight, your chances of pulling trumps are not all that good. Nonetheless, 15 out of 33 panelists voted for a penalty pass. That was more than voted for any other action. The next most popular choice was a bid of two notrump, with nine votes.

In real life, the experts sometimes make do with considerably less than a solid trump suit. Witness this exhibit from the Ladies' Pairs Championship from the 1978 Olympiad Game.

E-W vul., dealer West.

```
                 NORTH
                 ♠ 3
                 ♡ 9 7
                 ◊ K 10 6 4 3
                 ♣ J 9 8 7 4
     WEST                      EAST
     ♠ A                       ♠ Q 9 7 6 4 2
     ♡ Q J 10                  ♡ K 6 5 4
     ◊ A Q 9 8                 ◊ 7 5 2
     ♣ A Q 10 6 5              ♣ None
                 SOUTH
                 ♠ K J 10 8 5
                 ♡ A 8 3 2
                 ◊ J
                 ♣ K 3 2
```

The bidding:

SOUTH	WEST	NORTH	EAST
Moss	Wei	Mitchell	Radin
	1 ♣	Pass	1 ◊
1 ♠	Double	Pass	Pass
Pass			

Kathy Wei, West, opened the bidding with one club, showing 16 or more HCPs, and Judy Radin, East, responded one diamond, showing fewer than eight HCPs. Gail Moss, South, bid one spade. Kathy doubled for a takeout, but Judy decided that she would just as soon play one spade doubled as anything else, in spite of her broken spade suit.

Kathy led the ace of spades, and switched to the queen of hearts. Gail managed to get only four tricks, suffering a penalty of 500 points.

On the next hand, Allen Walsh, of Australia, was able to select his own opening lead against a contract doubled at the one level. His partner doubled for a takeout, but Walsh converted it into a penalty double. The hand is from the World Championship Pair Event held in the 1978 Olympiad Game in New Orleans.

E-W vul., dealer East.

```
                    NORTH
                    ♠ J 9 5 4
                    ♡ 3
                    ◊ 9 8 7 5
                    ♣ 10 8 5 2
        WEST                    EAST
        ♠ A 3                   ♠ K Q 10 8 2
        ♡ K Q 10 9 2            ♡ J 4
        ◊ A 10 4                ◊ Q 6 2
        ♣ K 7 4                 ♣ Q J 3
                    SOUTH
                    ♠ 7 6
                    ♡ A 8 7 6 5
                    ◊ K J 3
                    ♣ A 9 6
```

The bidding:

SOUTH	WEST	NORTH	EAST
	Walsh		Havas
			Pass
1 ♡	Pass	Pass	Double
Pass	Pass	Pass	

At most of the tables, East-West played three notrump vulnerable, making either ten or eleven tricks. When Walsh and George Havas sat East-West, there was a different story. South opened the hand with one heart and West passed. Havas, East, made a takeout double. Although his opponents were not vulnerable, and Havas had passed in first seat, Walsh decided to defend one heart doubled. He led the king of hearts. South let that hold the trick. Not knowing who had the jack of hearts, Walsh shifted to the ace of spades and, responding to his partner's signal with the eight, continued with a small spade. Havas won and led the queen of spades. South trumped and West overtrumped.

Walsh treated his partner's lead of the queen, rather than the king, as a suit preference signal, so he led the king of clubs. Declarer let that hold, and Walsh continued with a club to the jack. South took his ace before it got trumped, as it looked like Walsh might have led from a king doubleton of clubs. He laid down the ace and a little heart. This let Walsh pull trumps, and he still had a club to lead to Havas. East now cashed his two good spades. The ace of diamonds took the last trick. Down five. The declarer took only his two aces. Plus 900 points gave the Australian pair 76 out of 77 of the match points.

The last hand in this section on opening trump leads is reported to be from the First Interplanetary Bridge Tournament, where the people from Earth played the people from Mars. Personally, I am not too sure that this is the actual truth, but I can only give it to you as it has been reported to me.

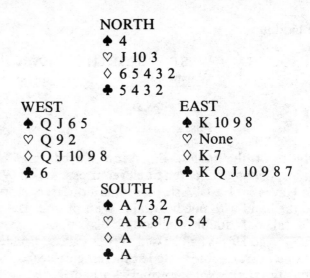

NORTH
♠ 4
♡ J 10 3
◇ 6 5 4 3 2
♣ 5 4 3 2

WEST
♠ Q J 6 5
♡ Q 9 2
◇ Q J 10 9 8
♣ 6

EAST
♠ K 10 9 8
♡ None
◇ K 7
♣ K Q J 10 9 8 7

SOUTH
♠ A 7 3 2
♡ A K 8 7 6 5 4
◇ A
♣ A

Both the Earthlings and the Martians reached six hearts, played by South. When the Earth people were defending, West led the queen of diamonds. The Martian South won the ace, cashed the ace of clubs and the ace of spades, and cross-ruffed spades and diamonds. Eventually, he gave up a trump trick to West's queen, taking an easy twelve tricks. The Earthlings had estimated that this was a tie board. They were surprised when they found that their teammate had gone set. They couldn't imagine how that had happened. Their teammates informed them that it all depended on the opening lead, but this only perplexed the unsuccessful defenders even more. True, West might have opened a trump, and kept South from trumping one spade; but then declarer would not have lost a trump trick. Finally, their teammates told them what the opening lead had been. The Martian had led the queen of hearts!

Now when declarer ruffed two spades in dummy, West's nine of hearts was promoted to a winner. Declarer had to lose a spade also to go down one.

Unfortunately, the tournament was cut short because the Martians had to return home, so we did not find out some of the other tricks of the trade they claimed to have. But they promised to show us more at the next Interplanetary Tournament.

CHAPTER 6:
WHEN TO LEAD
PARTNER'S SUIT

We had better clarify what we call "partner's suit". We refer to a bid by him in a suit which suggests he is likely to have high cards and some length in the suit bid. Of course, not all bids he makes indicate this. When using the Stayman Convention, a two-club response says nothing about the club suit, nor does an opening bid of one or two clubs by a player who uses such bids as strong and artificial. Most of us will respond at the one level with a weaker suit than we are likely to use for either opening bids or overcalls. Responses at the one level to opening bids are suspect, unless later bidding clarifies the situation. A good partner might bid one heart with J-6-3-2, in response to an opening bid of one club, and some of us will respond with an even weaker suit. Suits bid in response to takeout doubles are also doubtful.

Many of the hands used as illustrations in the text have been drawn from International Matches. Many European players, and some American champions, use the Canape bidding method, where the second suit bid is the better suit. The first suit can be a weak four-card suit, or—on occasion—a three-card suit. So the second suit bid is considered the real suit by those players who use the Canape approach.

Now let us change the opening question a bit and ask, "When do you not lead your partner's suit?" The answer is, "When you want to see what a mad partner looks like." If your lead of a suit other than the one he bid works, he probably will give you little credit, but if it does not work—and leading his suit would have—you might have him so upset he is going to misplay two or three hands in a row.

In my classes I frequently give my pupils the following hand:

N-S vul., dealer North.

NORTH
♠ 6 5 3
♡ A 8 4
♢ K 9
♣ A Q J 8 7

WEST
♠ 7 2
♡ Q J 10 9 5
♢ 7 3 2
♣ 4 3 2

EAST
♠ Q J 10 8 4
♡ 3 2
♢ A 6 5 4
♣ K 5

SOUTH
♠ A K 9
♡ K 7 6
♢ Q J 10 8
♣ 10 9 6

The bidding:

SOUTH	WEST	NORTH	EAST
		1 ♣	1 ♠
2 NT	Pass	3 NT	Pass
Pass	Pass		

I regret to tell you that far too many of my pupils start the proceedings by leading the queen of hearts from the West hand. This will cause the declarer no pain. He can win the first heart in his hand and finesse the ten of clubs. When it loses, if East returns a heart, he can win it or duck it. In either event, when East gets in with the ace of diamonds, East will have no hearts left. No switch by East, after he wins the king of clubs or the ace of diamonds, is going to do him any good. The timing has been lost.

Of course, should West lead the seven of spades, the suit his partner bid, there would have been a different story. The timing has been gained. After the club finesse loses, declarer cannot bring in nine tricks unless he gets a diamond trick. So he will have to lose the lead to East two times in the minor suits, and East will finally win two minor suit tricks plus three spade tricks.

West will explain that he had such a good heart suit. In a kind way, the teacher must tell him that he had no entries to his hand, and that when he holds only three HCPs himself, he should expect his partner to hold somewhere between 10 and 12, making it likely that his partner does have entries for his suit. If West complains that he should not lead a spade because South bid 2NT, right over his partner's spade overcall, West might be told that it is better bridge to trust your partner than it is to trust your opponent. Of course, if he says that his partner is not worthy of trust, the only answer is that he might look around and see if he can find a partner who is trustworthy. However, usually it is not wise for the teacher to say that, especially if the partner is a paying customer.

I must tell you that I have checked a lot of hands from World Championships and by other high-ranking players, and I find that they do not always agree with me. However, in keeping with my belief that the results should determine the theory rather than vice versa, I have watched for hands where players failed to lead suits their partners had bid, and I am still of the opinion that it is good business to lead your partner's suit. If he bid a minor suit, I tend to lead it. His suit will be long more often than it will be short. A major suit is a better bet, and an overcall indicates even a better suit (a vulnerable overcall at the two level practically demands the lead of that suit). I must say that I have found about five times as many hands where failure to lead partner's suit resulted in a disaster as I have found where such a lead turned out better. Let's look at some of those hands.

The first exhibit is in the match of Argentina versus North America in the 1962 World Championships.

N-S vul., dealer East.

```
                    NORTH
                    ♠ 5
                    ♡ 10 6 2
                    ◇ A K J 10 6
                    ♣ A K 9 5
WEST                                EAST
♠ K J 9 8 4                         ♠ 6 3
♡ 9 5                               ♡ A K J 7 3
◇ 7 2                               ◇ Q 9 3
♣ 10 6 4 2                          ♣ Q 8 3
                    SOUTH
                    ♠ A Q 10 7 2
                    ♡ Q 8 4
                    ◇ 8 5 4
                    ♣ J 7
```

The bidding:

SOUTH	WEST	NORTH	EAST
		Von Der	
Key	Attaguile	Porten	Jaques
			1 ♡
Pass	Pass	3 ◇	Pass
3 NT	Pass	Pass	Pass

If Attaguile had led the nine of hearts, Jaques could have simply let Key win the first heart trick, and from there on there was no way the declarer could take nine tricks before the opponents could take five. But Attaguile chose to lead the four of spades.

There are some similarities between this hand and the one I show my pupils. Unless East had some high spades, just what did Attaguile intend to use as entries once he got his spade suit established? And as his partner had shown opening bid values, was not his partner more likely to have entries for his own suit than Attaguile was to be likely to run the spade suit? Once Key has two spade tricks in his pocket, plus the timing, he was pretty well in the clear. After losing the diamond finesse, he had eight

238

tricks and time to develop one in hearts if he needed to. Actually, the defenders got too busy in clubs, and his jack of clubs took the ninth trick.

In the other room, Eric Murray, for North America, responded one spade with the West hand. North doubled for takeout, but South decided to convert it to a penalty double. Murray got out for down one. With the Americans being plus 600 in one room and minus 100 in the other room, North America had a net plus score of 500 points.

On several hands in a row, Robert Jordan and Arthur Robinson were involved in the problem of whether or not to lead their partner's suit. The first hand was played in 1963 with North America playing against the Italian Blue Team.

E-W vul., dealer West.

```
                      NORTH
                      ♠ J 7
                      ♡ A J 10 7 6 4
                      ◇ 3
                      ♣ J 8 6 2
        WEST                        EAST
        ♠ A 6 5 3                   ♠ K 10 8 4 2
        ♡ K Q 9 5 2                 ♡ 8 3
        ◇ 10 8 6 4                  ◇ A J 2
        ♣ None                      ♣ K 10 5
                      SOUTH
                      ♠ Q 9
                      ♡ None
                      ◇ K Q 9 7 5
                      ♣ A Q 9 7 4 3
```

The bidding:

SOUTH	WEST	NORTH	EAST
Belladonna	Robinson	Pabis Ticci	Jordan
	Pass	Pass	1 ♠
2 NT	4 ♠	Pass	Pass
5 ♣	Pass	Pass	Double
Pass	Pass	Pass	

Belladonna's 2NT bid was the Unusual Notrump, asking for partner to bid a minor suit. When Pabis Ticci declined this invitation, after Robinson's jump to four spades, Belladonna chose his own minor suit.

You can see that had Robinson started leading spades, the defense would have taken the first two tricks, and no way has yet been discovered to keep them from also taking a diamond. However, as my wife would say of Robinson, he "got caught thinking" when he decided that Belladonna was probably short in spades rather than hearts. He chose to lead the king of hearts. Well, that was the suit in which Belladonna was void. He won with dummy's ace and discarded one of his losing spades. Now he led a diamond and the defenders got their two tricks, but that was all. Belladonna got to dummy by trumping diamonds. When he tackled clubs, he carefully led the jack. This is correct when there are exactly three cards in the suit missing and they are precisely the king, ten, and a small one. It went jack, king, ace, and when Robinson showed out, it became a simple matter to go back to the dummy by trumping another diamond and finesse against Jordan's ten of clubs.

In the open room, where the Americans sat North-South, Jim Jacoby opened the North hand with three hearts and everybody passed. He took six tricks, for a minus score of 150. When you add this to the minus score of 550, which North America got when Belladonna made his five-club bid doubled, you can see that the Italians won a total of 700 points, which converted into 12 International Match Points (IMPs).

Later in that same 1963 World Championship, Robinson and Jordan were the beneficiaries of their opponent's refusal to lead the suit bid by partner, rather than the victims of their own decision not to do so.

N-S vul., dealer East.

<pre>
                        NORTH
                        ♠ A Q
                        ♡ K 9
                        ◇ K 3
                        ♣ Q 10 9 7 5 4 2
        WEST   EAST
        ♠ 10 6 2   ♠ K 5 3
        ♡ Q 10 7 4 3 2   ♡ 6 5
        ◇ 10 9   ◇ A J 8 6 4 2
        ♣ 8 3   ♣ A 6
                        SOUTH
                        ♠ J 9 8 7 4
                        ♡ A J 8
                        ◇ Q 7 5
                        ♣ K J
</pre>

The bidding:

CLOSED ROOM

SOUTH	WEST	NORTH	EAST
Robinson	Calvente	Jordan	Rocchi
			1 ◇
1 ♠	Pass	3 ♣	Pass
3 NT	Pass	Pass	Pass

Maybe Calvente's decision not to lead his partner's suit was
based on the fact that, in the system they were playing, his partner could have opened a three-card diamond suit. As a matter
of fact, he had opened a six-card diamond suit. Had Calvente
led the ten of diamonds, Robinson would not have had a
chance. Instead, Calvente decided to lead his own suit, even
though he had no entry. He led the four of hearts. Robinson
was able to get six club tricks established almost immediately,
and the way the play actually went, he ended up taking eleven
tricks by end-playing Rocchi.

With the ten of diamonds opening lead, the defenders would

have established their suit before Robinson knocked out the ace of clubs. If the king was not played from dummy, Rocchi could simply let South win with the queen, and then when he got the lead in one of the black suits, he could take five diamond tricks. In the more likely event that dummy played the king of diamonds at trick one, Rocchi would win the ace and simply continue with the diamond jack. If Robinson took the second diamond lead with the queen, he would have to give up the lead in clubs, at which point the defenders would take five diamonds and a club.

A year later, Robinson and Jordan were back in the World Championship, and this time we find them carefully opening their partner's suit in a deal against the United Arab Republic. This time, the partner's bid was an overcall. It is interesting to note that Robinson overcalled on a four-card suit, while Mrs. Awad, of the Egyptian team, declined to do so. Let's look at the results.

N-S vul., dealer West.

```
                    NORTH
                    ♠ 9 7 5
                    ♡ A K Q 9 7 6
                    ◇ 5 3
                    ♣ K 3
    WEST                          EAST
    ♠ 8 2                         ♠ A K Q 4
    ♡ 10 4 3                      ♡ J 8 5 2
    ◇ 8 6                         ◇ J 9 2
    ♣ J 9 7 6 5 4                 ♣ 8 2
                    SOUTH
                    ♠ J 10 6 3
                    ♡ None
                    ◇ A K Q 10 7 4
                    ♣ A Q 10
```

The bidding:

CLOSED ROOM

SOUTH	WEST	NORTH	EAST
Krauss	Awad	Hamman	Mrs. Awad
	Pass	1 ♡	Pass
3 ◇	Pass	3 ♡	Pass
3 NT	Pass	4 NT	Pass
6 ◇	Pass	Pass	Pass

OPEN ROOM

Zananiri	Jordan	Sharif	Robinson
	Pass	1 ♡	1 ♠
2 ◇	Pass	2 ♡	Pass
3 ♣	Pass	4 ♡	Pass
5 ◇	Pass	Pass	Pass

In the closed room, the Egyptian couple did not enter the bidding at all, and Bob Hamman and Don Krauss somehow managed to get to a six-diamond contract. Mr. Awad, West, had nothing to guide him for his opening lead, and he chose a club. Krauss won in his own hand, pulled trumps, went to the dummy with the king of clubs, and quickly threw away three losing spades on dummy's three good hearts. He ended up losing just one spade trick.

In the open room, we find Omar Sharif taking a leave-of-absence from moviemaking to represent his country in the World Championship. Arthur Robinson overcalled one spade on his excellent four-card suit at favorable vulnerability. Jordan opened the eight of spades and Robinson took the first three tricks. He then led a fourth spade, on which Zananiri had to follow suit, and Jordan was able to take a trick with his six of diamonds. So, where the overcall was not made to suggest a lead, the declarer was able to make a small slam, while in the other room where an overcall was made, the declarer was set two tricks in a game contract.

The next exhibit is taken from the Vanderbilt Team Game of 1974.

None vul., dealer East.

```
                    NORTH
                    ♠ A K 10
                    ♡ Q 10 6
                    ◇ A 8 7
                    ♣ A 9 8 2
        WEST                    EAST
        ♠ Q 7 6 4 3 2           ♠ J 9 8 5
        ♡ 3 2                   ♡ A
        ◇ 5                     ◇ K J 10 6 4 3
        ♣ J 7 4 3              ♣ Q 10
                    SOUTH
                    ♠ None
                    ♡ K J 9 8 7 5 4
                    ◇ Q 9 2
                    ♣ K 6 5
```

The bidding:

SOUTH	WEST	NORTH	EAST
Feldman	Kokish	Goldstein	Silver
			1 ◇
1 ♡	Pass	2 ◇	Pass
4 ♡	Pass	6 ♡	Pass
Pass	Pass		

Eric Kokish, of Montreal, apparently figured that his opponents were well prepared for a diamond lead, and so decided to lead a spade. The spade lead didn't work out so well. Lest those of you who are not acquainted with the sharp young players of today don't know about Eric Kokish, let me tell you that his team won the event, in spite of this hand.

With the opening spade lead, Mark Feldman saw some chance for developing the twelfth trick. Preparing for a throw-in against East, he did not win the opening lead in the dummy, but instead trumped it in his hand. Next he led the king of clubs and then a club to the ace. Now he took the ace and king of spades, and on these two cards he discarded one club and one diamond. Having no clubs left in his hand, he now led a club

244

from the dummy. Joe Silver could not profit by trumping that with his singleton ace, so just discarded as Feldman trumped it. At long last, declarer led a trump. Silver won this, but he was end-played. If he led a spade, Feldman would discard a second diamond from his hand while trumping in the dummy. Therefore, Silver led a diamond, but Feldman won the queen in his hand, pulled the last trump, and all the cards in his hand were good. He lost only one trick to the ace of trumps.

In each section, I try to find something special for the last hand. I hope you find it amusing.

None vul., dealer North.

```
                    NORTH
                    ♠ J 4 3
                    ♡ J 9 3
                    ◇ 10 9 8
                    ♣ K Q 8 6
        WEST                        EAST
        ♠ K 6 2                     ♠ A Q 8 7
        ♡ K 10 8 7 4                ♡ 2
        ◇ 7                         ◇ J 5 3 2
        ♣ J 5 3 2                   ♣ 10 9 7 4
                    SOUTH
                    ♠ 10 9 5
                    ♡ A Q 6 5
                    ◇ A K Q 6 4
                    ♣ A
```

The bidding:

OPEN ROOM			
SOUTH	WEST	NORTH	EAST
Tai	Flint	P. Huang	Cansino
		Pass	Pass
1 ♣	2 ◇	Double	Pass
Pass	Redouble	Pass	2 ♠
3 ◇	Pass	3 ♠	Pass
3 NT	Pass	Pass	Pass

This hand was played in the 1972 World Championships, with Great Britain versus the Republic of China players from Formosa.

Jeremy Flint, West, found a way which I am not going to recommend to discover what his partner's suit was. The Chinese players were playing the Precision Club System. South opened with one club to show a strong hand. Flint made a strange jump overcall of two diamonds. Huang's double said that he had from five to eight HCPs. Tai, South, passed, thinking that two diamonds doubled was just a lovely place to play the hand. Flint redoubled, saying, "Partner, will you please pick the suit", and Jonathan Cansino picked spades. From there on, the Chinese went on helter-skelter to a 3NT contract.

Flint led the two of the suit he had requested his partner to bid. The defense promptly took four spade tricks. On the last spade trick, South discarded a heart and Flint discarded the eight of hearts. Cansino then led the two of hearts. Tai believed what they said about hearts, and won his ace. Unless the jack of diamonds was a singleton, he was going to have some transportation troubles getting back and forth. He laid down the ace of diamonds and nothing good happened. He tried another diamond. When the suit didn't split, he led the ace of clubs and a small heart towards the dummy. That left him with the singleton queen of hearts. Flint went up with his king and promptly led back a heart, putting Tai right back in his own hand. Tai finally had to concede a diamond trick for down two.

Of course, there are hands where leading something other than the suit your partner has bid is the winning opening lead. I can make up dozens of them. The trouble is that they don't appear too often in real life, and they are hard for the opening leader to find. No one should ever play bridge by formula. When you are convinced that another lead is called for, it is not necessary for me to tell you to go ahead and make that other lead. You are going to do it anyway. I can only tell you that players who are good enough to compete for the world championship don't do very well when they lead suits other than those their partners have bid.

CHAPTER 7:
SPECIAL ATTACKING
OPENING LEADS

We have already talked about some attacking opening leads. Leading a short suit in hopes of taking tricks with small trumps is certainly an attacking lead. Leading a long suit, to shorten declarer's trumps can be the most vicious attack of all. But in this section, I am talking about a different kind of attacking leads.

I am talking about leading from tenace combinations, such as A-Q, K-J, and leading from suits which have unsupported high honors. Leads from such suits when they contain five or more cards are frequently made against notrump contracts in the belief that the chance to take tricks with the small cards justifies the risk involved in leading such a suit. Against suit contracts, such leads are not made as often as they should be. Risky as such leads are, there are times when the bidding suggests that if you don't get your high cards established at once, declarer may be able to discard his losers in those suits on a long side suit.

You always have to measure the potential risk against the potential gain. Let's look at a couple of examples.

Hand #1	Hand #2
♠ A Q 4 2	♠ 7 4 3
♡ 7 5	♡ 8 6 5
◇ Q 6 4 3	◇ 6 4
♣ K J 4	♣ K J 9 5 4

Let us say that there has been nothing in the bidding which gives us any guidance, so that our choice of a lead is based solely on the cards we hold. One example would be where the bidding goes

1 NT - 2 NT - 3 NT

and you are on lead.

With Hand #1, there is every reason to lead the seven of hearts. Your long suits are only four cards in length, so the chances you can take long-suit tricks are not too good. Your partner would have to have specific high cards in his hand to promote the high cards in your hand, and he is not likely to have them. You have twelve HCPs, and that leaves your partner something in the neighborhood of two or three HCPs, making it unlikely he has any specific cards you might want him to have.

With Hand #2, the five of clubs, a genuinely attacking lead, is a standout. Here your partner has nine or ten HCPs, increasing the likelihood that he holds either the ace or the queen of clubs. Either card gives you a good chance to get your suit established. If partner has some length in clubs in addition to the entries implied by his nine or ten HCPs, you might take several tricks even though you have only four HCPs.

Suppose the bidding has gone

1 ♡ - 3 ♡ - 4 ♡

and you are on lead with these two hands. With Hand #1, you still should go passive. With Hand #2, I would recommend that you attack just as you did when the contract was in notrump. Here your partner's strength is not as clearly defined as in the first sequence as your right-hand opponent might have some extra values. The chances are good that your partner has from an average hand in high cards to an opening bid . It may be essential to get your high cards established as quickly as possible. With this hand, I would lead the suit where I have some high cards which have a chance to get established.

Before I show you some attacking leads made in high-level competition, I really should show you a passive lead or two for comparison. The trouble is that, from the viewpoint of opening leads, the passive lead is not interesting. It is not intended to gain anything and it seldom does. It is just an attempt to get the play started without giving up anything. Any interest in the hand usually comes up later in the play and not with the opening lead. But I have picked out one to illustrate the point. The Polish team has created a lot of attention, as they are the first bridge players from behind the Iron Curtain to win a World's

Championship. They won the Olympiad Team Game in New Orleans in 1978. I think this hand illustrates my point, and it will give me a chance to introduce these Polish players. I hope you will find the play interesting as it develops.

Both vul., dealer South.

NORTH
♠ K 10 3
♡ 7 2
♦ A K Q J 10 7
♣ 10 5

WEST
♠ None
♡ A 10 8 5 3
♦ 8 4
♣ A J 7 6 4 3

EAST
♠ J 8 6 2
♡ Q J 9 4
♦ 9 3
♣ Q 9 2

SOUTH
♠ A Q 9 7 5 4
♡ K 6
♦ 6 5 2
♣ K 8

The bidding:

SOUTH	WEST	NORTH	EAST
1 ♠	2 ♣	4 ♠	Pass
Pass	Pass		

This hand was played in the Caransa-Phillip Morris International Swiss Team Game in Amsterdam, Holland, in 1978. South was Janusz Polec, of Warsaw, a member of the Polish team that won the New Orleans Olympiad. I must say that the bidding as reported was very much to the point.

If West leads from either of his long suits, he obviously gives Polec a trick which he could not earn otherwise. Of course, leading either ace would have been a bad play, and underleading would have been worse. West held nine HCPs in his hand and had no reason to believe his partner had the king to go with either of his suits, as East probably had fewer HCPs than West.

From West's viewpoint, South could be bothered by a bad break in the trump suit, and he thought it best to wait and have his aces led up to. In both rooms, the final contract was four spades by South, and in both rooms the opening lead was the eight of diamonds.

The hand looks like a cinch. There are six diamond tricks and at least five trump tricks even if a trump trick has to be lost. In addition, there should be no problem in keeping East from getting the lead. A careful declarer will concede a trick to West if he happens to hold the spade jack, to be sure he makes his contract. However, it didn't turn out to be that simple in either room.

First, let's go to the room where the Polish team were defending with the East and West hands. Declarer saw a book safety play to avoid losing a spade trick no matter which player had four to the jack, except he overlooked the little matter of entries. He won the diamond lead in the dummy and led a small spade to his ace. Now, no matter who showed out, he could finesse against the other player for the jack. West did show out, so South went back to the dummy with the king of spades and led the ten. Here he got stabbed. East refused to cover. Declarer was stuck in the dummy with no good way to get out.

He struggled mightily. First, he cashed a second diamond, and when both players followed suit, he knew that he had stripped West of any cards in that suit. Now he led a small club, intending to put in his eight if East played low. West could go ahead and cash a couple of club tricks, but then he would be endplayed. Andrew Wilkosz was playing East, and here showed that he was qualified to be playing with the world's champions, because he put in the nine. Now if declarer let that hold the trick, the queen of hearts would come through and declarer would lose two heart tricks and two club tricks. Declarer played the king, but West won and returned a club to his partner's queen and the heart came through after all.

Where Polec had the South hand, he forgot about a safety play which would be sure to trap the jack of trumps. He won the first diamond in the dummy and led the ten of spades. He came home with six diamond tricks and six spade tricks.

Leading or underleading a king or queen, with no supporting honors, must be called an attacking lead. How about leading unsupported aces? Well, sometimes they are, and sometimes they are not. If they are made in hopes of finding a singleton in partner's hand, so a ruffing trick will come home, they must be classified as attacking leads. When they are made just because any other lead looks worse, they come more under the head of passive leads. The following hand must be called an attacking hand.

Both vul., dealer South.

```
                    NORTH
                    ♠ K 9 7 3
                    ♡ 7 3
                    ◊ 9 8
                    ♣ 10 9 6 5 2
    WEST                            EAST
    ♠ A Q J 10 5 2                  ♠ 8
    ♡ Q 6 2                         ♡ K J 10 9 8 5 4
    ◊ 6                             ◊ 7 4 2
    ♣ K 7 3                         ♣ 8 4
                    SOUTH
                    ♠ 6 4
                    ♡ A
                    ◊ A K Q J 10 5 3
                    ♣ A Q J
```

The bidding:

SOUTH	WEST	NORTH	EAST
2 ◊	2 ♠	Double	3 ♡
5 ◊	Pass	Pass	Pass

This deal is from a Regional Open Pair game in the 1940s. West decided that East should be short in spades. To rescue a partner's overcall by going to a higher level would be unforgivable if the player happened to hold two trumps, unless he was making his bid in the hopes of fulfilling his contract. So West decided his best defense was to let East trump a spade. He led the ace and then another spade and was proven correct as West always had a club trick coming.

In the match against Great Britain in the 1965 World Championships, Kelsey Petterson, playing for the United States, thought his hand justified an attacking lead from a king. Let's take a careful look and see what brought him to this conclusion.

Both vul., dealer East.

NORTH
♠ K 7 4
♡ J 8 7
♢ Q
♣ A J 10 8 6 5

WEST
♠ A 2
♡ K 10 2
♢ 10 9 8 7 5 4
♣ 9 3

EAST
♠ J 8
♡ A Q 4 3
♢ J 6 2
♣ K 7 4 2

SOUTH
♠ Q 10 9 6 5 3
♡ 9 6 5
♢ A K 3
♣ Q

The bidding:

OPEN ROOM

SOUTH	WEST	NORTH	EAST
Konstam	Petterson	Schapiro	Erdos
			Pass
1 ♠	Pass	2 ♣	Pass
2 ♠	Pass	4 ♠	Pass
Pass	Pass		

CLOSED ROOM

Schenken	Reese	Leventritt	Flint
			Pass
2 ♠*	Pass	3 ♠	Pass
4 ♠	Pass	Pass	Pass

*Weak two bid

252

Kelsey had only seven HCPs. Therefore, he expected his partner to have about seven to eleven HCPs. The opponents had bid the black suits, which increased the chance that Erdos' hand held some honors in hearts. The two-club response by Boris Schapiro suggested a possible suit for discards. Kelsey led the two of hearts and the defense took the first three heart tricks plus the ace of trumps for down one.

In the closed room, Terence Reese, West, took a different view. He did not have the advantage of the two-club bid from North to warn him against that suit, so he guessed that his partner's high-card strength would be in clubs and, holding control of the trump suit, he went for a ruff by leading the doubleton club. Declarer won the club ace, cashed the diamond queen, came to his hand by trumping a club, and discarded two of dummy's hearts on the ace and king of diamonds. He then led a heart. Reese won and led a seond heart which was trumped in the dummy. Schenken led a club back to his hand and trumped with the queen of spades. Reese declined to overruff, so Schenken led his last heart and trumped that with dummy's seven. Next he led the king of spades. Reese got his ace of trumps, and Flint made a trick with the jack of trumps, but Schenken had his ten tricks.

You will notice that the weaker the hand, the more attractive an attacking opening lead becomes. Leading players have a fantastic record of successfully opening the king from king doubletons. It is difficult to find a hand where this lead by an expert was disastrous, but hands where the lead brought down an otherwise impregnable contract are plentiful. Usually the opening leader will have a few bits of evidence other than the weakness of his own hand. Here is a deal where Bill Root found the lead against a slam contract.

Both vul., dealer South:

                    NORTH
                    ♠ J 2
                    ♡ K 6
                    ◇ K J 7 5
                    ♣ A K Q 8 5
    WEST   EAST
    ♠ K 7   ♠ A 10 8 6 5 4 3
    ♡ 8 7 3 2   ♡ 10 5
    ◇ 9 6   ◇ 4 2
    ♣ J 7 4 3 2   ♣ 10 9
                    SOUTH
                    ♠ Q 9
                    ♡ A Q J 9 4
                    ◇ A Q 10 8 3
                    ♣ 6

The bidding:

SOUTH	WEST	NORTH	EAST
	Root		
1 ♡	Pass	2 ♣	Pass
2 ◇	Pass	4 NT	Pass
5 ♡	Pass	6 ◇	Pass
Pass	Pass		

It was evident from the bidding that North had a powerful hand and that he had a lot of cards in the minor suits. It was equally evident that South had length in the two red suits. Bill Root couldn't actually see the opponents' hand, as you and I can, but in his mind's eye he could see declarer finding whatever discards he needed on North's club suit. With whatever spade losers South had likely to go off on dummy's club suit, Bill had nothing to lose by leading the king of spades. The way it turned out he had everything to gain. East held with that magic ace, and the defenders took the first two tricks.

On the next hand, the weakness of his own holding, plus action taken by his partner, convinced Phil Feldesman that the time had come to lead the king from the king doubleton. The hand is from the World Championship Match of 1966, played in St. Vincent, Italy,.

None vul., dealer South.

```
                    NORTH
                    ♠ K 7 2
                    ♡ A J 8 4
                    ◇ 9 8 4 3
                    ♣ J 9
        WEST                    EAST
        ♠ 8 3                   ♠ A 9
        ♡ 9 7 5                 ♡ K Q 3 2
        ◇ K 2                   ◇ Q 10 6 5
        ♣ Q 10 7 6 4 2          ♣ K 5 3
                    SOUTH
                    ♠ Q J 10 6 5 4
                    ♡ 10 6
                    ◇ A J 7
                    ♣ A 8
```

The bidding:

SOUTH	WEST	NORTH	EAST
Avarelli	Feldesman	Belladonna	Rubin
1 ♠	Pass	1 NT	Double
2 ♠	3 ♣	3 ♠	Pass
Pass	Pass		

The Italian pair stopped at three spades. It looked like they would have preferred to stop at two spades. This, plus the takeout double by Ira Rubin, East, suggested that the defenders had just about as many HCPs as the Italians. With only five HCPs in his own hand, with the Italians trying to play as cheaply as possible, and with Rubin's takeout double, Feldesman had a pretty good idea about how many HCPs were in the East hand.

If those points included the ace of diamonds, the lead of the king would be an immediate success. If Rubin had the queen and jack of diamonds, the lead could turn out well. Or, if Rubin

255

had the queen of diamonds plus the ace of trumps, again the lead of the king of diamonds could be the killer. That is what Rubin had. When Rubin captured the first spade lead and led the queen of diamonds and then another for Feldesman to trump, the defenders raked in a heart, a diamond, a club, and two trump tricks.

On examining the hand, it can be seen that Feldesman found the only lead to defeat the three-spade contract. With any other lead, Avarelli would either have two entries to the dummy after trumps are drawn so that he could finesse diamonds twice, or Rubin would eventually be end-played in the red suits. Work it out.

In the other room, Forquet and Garozzo refused to let the Americans play three spades. The Italians played four clubs and went set themselves. This gave North America a plus score when they played North-South, and another plus when they played East-West.

World champion players seem to lead a charmed life with that lead of the king from the king doubleton. Could it be that is because they know when to make it? It is most often led when they hold not more than two of the honor cards and not more then seven HCPs.

Even though his partner held neither the ace nor the queen, look at the devastating effect of this lead when made by Benito Garozzo, of Italy, against the Chinese team in the 1969 World Championship.

None vul., dealer South.

```
                    NORTH
                    ♠ Q J 9
                    ♡ A 10
                    ◇ K Q 9 6 3
                    ♣ A Q 9
        WEST                    EAST
        ♠ A 10 8 3 2            ♠ K 6 5
        ♡ 7 3 2                 ♡ 9 4
        ◇ 10 5 4                ◇ A J 7
        ♣ K 3                   ♣ J 8 6 4 2
                    SOUTH
                    ♠ 7 4
                    ♡ K Q J 8 6 5
                    ◇ 8 2
                    ♣ 10 7 5
```

The bidding:

SOUTH	WEST	NORTH	EAST
Kovit	Garozzo	K. W. Shen	Forquet
Pass	Pass	1 ◇	Pass
1 ♡	1 ♠	2 NT	Pass
3 ♡	Pass	4 ♡	Pass
Pass	Pass		

Garozzo led the king of clubs. With any other lead, Kovit would have had no problem establishing the diamond suit for a discard using dummy's clubs as entries. That king of clubs began the attack on dummy's entries a little too early for Kovit to carry out this plan.

He pulled trumps in three leads and then led a diamond from his hand toward dummy. Forquet, East, let the queen hold the trick, and there declarer was—stranded in the dummy. Hoping that Garozzo might have started with the ace and a small diamond, he now led a small diamond from the dummy. But Forquet won the jack and then led a spade to Garozzo's ace. Garozzo returned a second club. Now declarer was doomed to lose two spades, a diamond, and a club.

The last hand in this section is taken from the 1978 South American Championships. It had a dramatic setting. The Brazilian team, which had won the Olympiad Games in 1976, was having the fight of its life. All other countries had been eliminated, and Brazil was playing an eight-board final against Venezuela. Everything had gone wrong for the Brazilians, and the dark-horse Venezuelans had been in the lead through most of the match. There were three twenty-deal segments to be played on Saturday, with the final twenty boards to played on Sunday, leaving time for the victory banquet. The third session on Saturday was played quite late at night, and when it was just about over, an announcement was made that the boards had been played in the wrong direction, and that both Brazilian pairs had played the same hands. That segment had to be played over beginning at three o'clock in the morning. In addition, Gabriel Chagas, the Brazilian captain, and his partner, Pedro-Paulo Assumpcao, felt they had had a fantastic game during the boards which were thrown out, and Chagas said that he really wanted to cry. It was finally decided that they would play only ten boards beginning at 3:00 A.M., and change the Sunday session into a thirty-board final. At the end of that ten-board segment, Venezuela was ahead by ten IMPs.

The hand I am showing is the last of the eighty hands played in this match. At this point, Brazil was still behind by seven IMPs. Of course, the players did not know that, but they usually have a pretty good feel about the game, and Chagas felt that it was very close. He was on lead against 3NT with the West hand shown.

Both vul., dealer North.

```
                    NORTH
                    ♠ 5
                    ♡ J 3
                    ◇ A Q 5
                    ♣ A Q J 8 7 4 2
        WEST                    EAST
        ♠ Q J 8 6 2             ♠ A 10 4
        ♡ A Q 6                 ♡ K 10 7 2
        ◇ 10 9 2                ◇ 8 7 6 3
        ♣ 9 5                   ♣ 6 3
                    SOUTH
                    ♠ K 9 7 3
                    ♡ 9 8 5 4
                    ◇ K J 4
                    ♣ K 10
```

The bidding:

SOUTH	WEST	NORTH	EAST
		1 ♣	Pass
1 ♠	Pass	3 ♣	Pass
3 NT	Pass	Pass	Pass

This time it is not necessary for me to tell you what I think Chagas was thinking. It's better to let him speak for himself. Here is his explanation:

"I wasn't sure what to lead. A spade looked all right, but I thought there was a good chance we needed a swing. Neither opponent had bid hearts. So, finally I led the heart ace, and when I got an encouraging card from my partner, it was child's play to take the first five tricks.

We were South American Champions by just four IMPs! We had gone from despair to jubilation in about sixteen hours!"

In a replay of the hand, when Venezuela had to make a lead

259

from the West hand, the Brazilian South had not bid spades, and West made the normal lead of a spade. East went up with the ace and continued the suit, and that let the Brazilian team take eleven tricks. The 460 points they won added to the 50 points won by Chagas with his lead of the ace of hearts gave them a total of 510 points, which translated into eleven IMPs on this final hand in the match.

CHAPTER 8:
DANGEROUS OPENING LEADS

In my book, *Play of the Hand,* I give a list of the six leads which I call "dangerous leads". I am going to repeat those leads here, but this time I am going to give illustrations for some of them from championship play. There are times when you will have these dangerous holdings in each of the four suits, and you are just going to have to choose the one which you consider the least dangerous. They tell a story of a famous player who told a pupil of his never to lead from a suit headed by a jack. One day, the pupil looked at his hand, and quit the game forever. All four of his suits were headed by jacks.

Better he should have reviewed the bidding to determine which suit would be the least dangerous, or possibly to get a clue that one of them was not likely to be dangerous at all.

I am going to start with those leads which seem least bad, and work up to the ones which I consider the worst of all.

1. The lead of the ace in an unbid suit.
There are two old sayings about this one. One of them is "Lead the ace so you can see the dummy". The other one is "Aces were meant to catch kings and queens, not deuces and treys". I go along with the second of these sayings. The rules require that you get to see the dummy no matter what you lead, so it is not necessary to lead an ace for that purpose. Later on, we will talk about leading aces against slam contracts and leading them against pre-emptive bids, but for the present we are talking about leading them against a less-than-slam contract, where there is nothing unusual about the bidding.

What do you lead from the West hand against a four-spade contract when South had opened the bidding with one spade and North has gone straight to four?

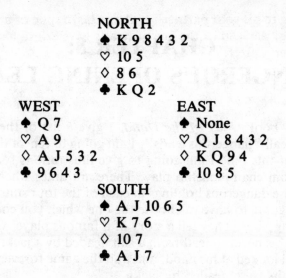

NORTH
- ♠ K 9 8 4 3 2
- ♡ 10 5
- ◇ 8 6
- ♣ K Q 2

WEST
- ♠ Q 7
- ♡ A 9
- ◇ A J 5 3 2
- ♣ 9 6 4 3

EAST
- ♠ None
- ♡ Q J 8 4 3 2
- ◇ K Q 9 4
- ♣ 10 8 5

SOUTH
- ♠ A J 10 6 5
- ♡ K 7 6
- ◇ 10 7
- ♣ A J 7

The hand is from the Great Britain vs. North America match from the 1962 World Championship. The bidding was the same in both rooms. Terence Reese, West for Great Britain, led the ace of hearts. Robert Nail, for North America, led the three of clubs. In this instance, Nail turned out to be right, and Reese turned out to be wrong.

Let's see what can be said in favor of both leads. From Reese's viewpoint, if he was going to lead either ace, he would do so in hopes of finding his partner with a king to go with it. If his partner happened to have the king of hearts, he might be lucky enough to win the first three tricks. The ace of diamonds would not be so good a lead. If, indeed, his partner had the king of that suit, it was not very likely it would take a trick. Although North did not have a singleton, his bidding sounded as though he did; and from Reese's hand, that singleton would more likely be a diamond than anything else. And, as a purely mathematical proposition, what the Europeans call an "accident", is nearly four times as likely in a suit where you have five cards as it is in a suit where you are holding only two cards. The Europeans describe a singleton or a void as "accident". When deciding which suit to lead when you have two suits headed by the ace, you should tend to lead from the longer suit only when you suspect that your partner is more likely to be short in the suit than either of your opponents. You lead the short suit when you are trying to hit your partner's high cards. In spite of all this fine reasoning, the lead of the ace of hearts gave South his contract on a silver platter.

Now let's see what merit we can find in the lead of a club. From Nail's viewpoint, why lead either ace? He held eleven HCPs himself, and this made it almost a certainty that South held more HCPs than did East. There was nothing in the bidding to indicate that anybody had any long side suits on which losers could be discarded. It seemed better to make a passive lead and just lie back and let declarer lead those red suits up to his hand.

Against the passive club lead, Claude Rodrigue, South for Great Britain, didn't have a chance. He won his ace, drew trumps, cashed dummy's two clubs, and led a diamond. East rose with the queen, and led the queen of hearts. The defense now took two heart tricks and another diamond trick for down one.

Of course, almost any opening lead could either succeed or fail. But it seems to me there was more merit in the Nail argument than there was in the Reese argument.

On the next hand, Bob Hamman found himself on opening lead with the trump queen and the three outside aces. The hand was played in the 1970 World Championship against the Chinese team.

None vul., dealer North.

```
                    NORTH
                    ♠ 9 8 3
                    ♡ A 8 5
                    ◊ 9 8 6 2
                    ♣ Q 8 2
        WEST                    EAST
        ♠ A Q J 7               ♠ K 10 2
        ♡ Q                     ♡ 10 9 7
        ◊ A Q 4                 ◊ K 10 7 5 3
        ♣ A 10 5 4 3            ♣ K 6
                    SOUTH
                    ♠ 6 5 4
                    ♡ K J 6 4 3 2
                    ◊ J
                    ♣ J 9 7
```

The bidding:

SOUTH	WEST	NORTH	EAST
Tai	Hamman	Huang	Lawrence
		Pass	Pass
3 ♡	Double	4 ♡	Double
Pass	Pass	Pass	

Hamman doubled the three-heart opening bid for takeout, but North persisted to four hearts. Mike Lawrence, East, decided to double for penalties. Bob Hamman seldom gets his hand on a wrong card. He chose the club ace as his opening lead. Note that he chose the suit which did not have a tenace holding. It turned out that he also found his partner's short suit, which simplified the matter of extracting the maximum penalty.

At trick two, Hamman led a second club won by Lawrence's king. Lawrence returned the two of spades, indicating that he had a high card in the suit. Hamman won the jack and gave his partner the club ruff. The defenders took two more spades and a diamond for a 700-point penalty. When the Chinese team sat East-West, they bid five diamonds, making six when the minor suits broke nicely for them. That gave them only 420 points, so the American team had a net gain of 280 points.

I have described the lead of an ace as the least bad of those dangerous leads. There are times when all other leads look worse and, under these circumstances, the lead of an ace may be chosen by process of elimination.

None vul., dealer North.

NORTH
♠ K J 8 5
♡ 4
◇ 7 5 3
♣ J 10 9 4 3

WEST
♠ 10 2
♡ Q 8 5 2
◇ A 9 6 2
♣ A 8 7

EAST
♠ Q 9 7 4 3
♡ 10 9 6
◇ K 8 4
♣ K 2

SOUTH
♠ A 6
♡ A K J 7 3
◇ Q J 10
♣ Q 6 5

The bidding:

SOUTH	WEST	NORTH	EAST
Lerner	Belladonna	Cabanne	Avarelli
		Pass	Pass
1 ♡	Pass	1 ♠	Pass
3 ♡	Pass	Pass	Pass

This hand is from the 1958 World Championships, with Argentina holding the North-South hands, while Italy was defending with the East-West hands. Belladonna considered his spade holding to be too dangerous to lead after his left-hand opponent bid the suit. The lead of a trump from his holding was, of course, the last thing he wanted to do. That left the two minor suits. He led the ace of diamonds. The dummy came down and each of the defenders had a pretty good idea of how strong his partner's hand was in high cards. A jump rebid such as South had made is usually made with about the high-card equivalent of a strong notrump bid, and a strong six- or seven-card suit. When dummy appeared with only five HCPs, it was easy to add these to the 16 or 17 which South had shown, and to see that the total defensive values came to about 18 or 19 HCPs. It didn't take long for the defenders to find out where these cards were.

Belladonna continued with a second diamond. Avarelli won his king and led a third diamond. Declarer won his queen, went to dummy with the king of spades, and led a heart to his jack. Belladonna won the queen and led the thirteenth diamond. Avarelli trumped with the nine. South didn't like this development. He discarded a club. This encouraged Avarelli to lead the king of clubs and a second club to Belladonna's ace. Belladonna played a third club which Avarelli trumped with the ten. South had run out of cards to discard and so he finally over-ruffed. Declarer managed to win only two spades, two hearts, and a diamond to go down four tricks.

In the replay of the hand, the Italians stopped at three clubs with the North-South hands. They lost two clubs and two diamonds to bring home their contract. This gave them a total net score of 310 points, which translated into four IMPs.

There are times when the clues you have from the bidding, added to the evidence you have from the cards in your hand, cause you to lead an ace against a suit contract, when the decision is not wholly based on the process of elimination.

E-W vul., dealer North.

NORTH
♠ Q 8 2
♡ 9 8 5
◇ K 4
♣ A Q J 10 4

WEST
♠ A 6 5 3
♡ Q
◇ A Q 8 6 3
♣ 8 7 6

EAST
♠ K J 9
♡ 7 6 3
◇ J 10 7 5 2
♣ 5 3

SOUTH
♠ 10 7 4
♡ A K J 10 4 2
◇ 9
♣ K 9 2

The bidding:

OPEN ROOM

SOUTH	WEST	NORTH	EAST
Erdos	Attaguile	Petterson	Rocchi
		1 NT	Pass
4 ♣	Pass	4 ♡	Pass
Pass	Pass		

CLOSED ROOM

Berisso	Becker	Lerner	Hayden
		1 ♣	Pass
1 ♡	Pass	2 ♣	Pass
4 ♡	Pass	Pass	Pass

In the open room, Kelsey Petterson and Ivan Erdos were playing that a notrump opening bid showed a balanced 12 to 14 HCPs when not vulnerable. Thus, Kelsey, North, bid 1NT. Erdos' four-club bid was a transfer bid commanding Petterson to bid four hearts. This put East on opening lead. Nothing in the bidding was helpful for choosing a lead. He finally decided on a short suit lead, and led the five of clubs. It didn't take Kelsey Petterson long to take eleven tricks in hearts and clubs, and give the last two tricks to the opponents.

In the closed room, the bidding was more revealing. North had bid and rebid clubs. Mr. Becker did not want to lead the opponents' long suit. A heart lead would give up the timing on the hand, as it was expected that declarer would get discards on dummy's club suit. That left diamonds and spades. Again notice that the expert opening leader did not choose the suit where he had a tenace situation, but chose instead the ace of spades. After taking a look at dummy, Becker cashed the ace of diamonds and continued spades. The defenders took the first four tricks.

Leading unsupported aces does not constitute a good opening lead, but at times when all other leads are worse, that may be the lead you will choose.

2. The blind lead of a short suit—a singleton or doubleton. In a previous chapter, I discussed at some length the opening lead of a singleton. One of the objections to this lead is that it often helps the declarer establish his secondary suit. I spent some time looking for the worst example of this I could find from actual play, and while I had to go all the way to Perth, Australia, I found one which will do. It was played in the fall of 1977, in the National Australian Championship.

E-W vul., dealer North.

NORTH
♠ A 10 6
♡ 8 7 5 4
◊ J 6 3
♣ J 3 2

WEST
♠ K Q J 9 5 4
♡ Q 9 6
◊ 10
♣ Q 8 5

EAST
♠ 7 3 2
♡ 10
◊ K 9 7 4 2
♣ A 10 6 4

SOUTH
♠ 8
♡ A K J 3 2
◊ A Q 8 5
♣ K 9 7

The bidding:

SOUTH	WEST	NORTH	EAST
		Pass	Pass
1 ♡	1 ♠	2 ♡	2 ♠
4 ♡	Pass	Pass	Pass

The opening lead in one room was the ten of diamonds. West's hand is an excellent example of when not to lead a singleton: he had a natural trump trick, but no useless trumps; thus, even if he does get his ruff, it is likely to cost him a trump trick; it is likely that the diamond suit is the opponent's second suit; and the ten is a valuable enough card on its own—that wasting it on the opening lead may enable the declarer to play the suit in such a way that he would be unlikely to find if left to his own devices.

When a defender has bid a suit, has been supported, and leads a different suit, the lead is likely to be a singleton. They know about that south of the equator just as well as we do up here in the Northern Hemisphere. South played the ten of diamonds to be a singleton. The ten was covered by the jack, king and ace. Declarer cashed the ace and king of trumps, played a spade to dummy's ace, and led a small diamond to the eight in his hand. West chose to discard a spade. Declarer led the queen of diamonds and West discarded a second spade, again refusing to trump. Declarer trumped his last diamond in dummy, ruffed a spade in his hand, and put West on lead by playing a heart. Now he was going to make his king of clubs no matter who had the ace. West was down to the singleton king of spades and three clubs. South discarded a club when West cashed the spade king. West had nothing left but clubs. A club to East's ace and a club return gave South his tenth trick. Altogether he lost one trick each in hearts, spades and clubs.

Try taking ten tricks with South hand against the lead of the king of spades. In the other room, the declarer was pushed to five hearts. Against the lead of the king of spades, he took nine tricks.

3. The lead of a suit bid by the dummy.

When inexperienced players don't have a short suit to lead, they frequently lead the suit bid by the dummy, on the theory that they are "leading through strength". This maxim would be better if it read "lead through strength except when it is also length". Better still, there might be another maxim which says, "Stay away from long suits held by either declarer or dummy". This admonition applies particularly when the suits are five cards long or longer, as they well may be when the dummy has bid them. Unless there is something in the bidding to suggest otherwise, it is better to lead your suits than it is to lead declarer's suits. When you lead his suits, too often you are helping him get those suits established.

The evidence in choosing an opening lead is based not only on what you see, but also on what you hear. In other words, it depends on the auction as well as the combination of cards in your own hand. Look at this hand reported by Dr. Sidney Lee of England, which was played in a high-stakes game at the Hamilton Club in London.

N-S vul., dealer South.

NORTH
♠ K 9 7 3
♡ Q 9
◇ 3 2
♣ A J 10 9 4

WEST
♠ 4 2
♡ 8 7 6 4
◇ A Q 10 9
♣ K Q 7

EAST
♠ 6 5
♡ 5 3 2
◇ 8 7 6 5 4
♣ 5 3 2

SOUTH
♠ A Q J 10 8
♡ A K J 10
◇ K J
♣ 8 6

The bidding:

SOUTH	WEST	NORTH	EAST
1 ♠	Pass	2 ♣	Pass
3 ♡	Pass	5 ♠	Pass
6 ♠	Pass	Pass	Pass

Dr. Lee accuses West of being one who bases his opening lead solely on what he sees, without giving due consideration to what he hears. The normal lead against a six-spade contract would be the king of clubs to establish the queen while you still had the ace of diamonds for an entry. This is what West did lead, and it proved to be an error. You can see the declarer simply takes the trick, draws trumps, discards dummy's diamonds on hearts, and concedes the club trick.

Dr. Lee points out that, had West paid more attention to the bidding, he would have led the ace of diamonds. He suggests that the bidding indicates that if declarer had a losing club he has no place to discard it. However, if dummy has a losing diamond, the three-heart rebid by South strongly hints that declarer does indeed have a place to discard any losing diamonds. So Dr. Lee says that this time West should avoid the

271

"normal" lead and lead the ace of diamonds, even though it appears that South probably has the king doubleton in that suit. As you can see, had West done so, South had no way to get rid of that losing club in his hand, and West would still have come to a club trick.

The next hand was played in the 1970 World Championship, in the match between North America and Norway.

N-S vul., dealer South:

```
                    NORTH
                    ♠ J 5
                    ♡ A 5
                    ◇ A Q 6 3
                    ♣ Q J 8 4 3
      WEST                          EAST
      ♠ 4                           ♠ Q 10 9 8 7
      ♡ J 10 7 6                    ♡ Q 8 4 3
      ◇ J 9 8 5 4                   ◇ 7
      ♣ A 7 5                       ♣ K 10 6
                    SOUTH
                    ♠ A K 6 3 2
                    ♡ K 9 2
                    ◇ K 10 2
                    ♣ 9 2
```

The bidding:

SOUTH	WEST	NORTH	EAST
1 ♠	Pass	2 ♣	Pass
2 ♠	Pass	3 ◇	Pass
3 NT	Pass	Pass	Pass

The bidding was identical in both rooms. In the open room, Willy Varnaas, of Norway, led his long suit in spite of the fact that that suit had been bid naturally by Bob Hamman on his left. Mike Lawrence was the declarer. He won the small diamond lead with the ten. He could now count four diamond tricks, the ace-king of hearts, and the ace-king of spades. He needed only one more trick. Varnaas had led a suit where

Lawrence now had four stoppers. That gave him plenty of time to go for the better than 2-to-1 chance that he would be able to establish one more trick with one of his high clubs. He led up to dummy's club suit twice. When the suit broke 3-3 with one of the two honors on his left, he took three clubs and took eleven tricks in all.

In the closed room, Jim Jacoby simply led his fourth-best card in the unbid suit. This posed an entirely different problem for Louis Strom of Norway. A count of sure tricks showed that he had only seven. Jacoby had led a suit where he had only two stoppers. There was no guarantee a quick club trick could be established, and even if it could, doing so would require giving up the lead twice. In the meantime, the defenders might be able to establish three heart tricks. Strom took the best percentage play when he led small toward the jack of spades. If West had the queen, either two, three or four long, or if the suit split 3-3, he would now pick up the two additional tricks he needed, while losing the lead only one time; hence, before the defenders could get their hearts established. That was not a success. Declarer ended up taking only seven tricks, four fewer than Mike Lawrence had won in the open room. Still, as the commentators pointed out, Strom took the percentage play for winning nine tricks once he received a heart lead.

Let's look at the opening lead problem which faced Mike Passell, of Dallas, Texas, in the World Championship of 1977. He had to find an opening lead from

♠ 10 9 6
♡ K J 9 5 4
◇ J 6 5 3
♣ 2

when he had heard the following bidding from Billy Eisenberg and Eddie Kantar:

SOUTH	WEST	NORTH	EAST
Eisenberg	Passell	Kantar	Hamilton
			Pass
1 ♣	Pass	1 ♦	Pass
3 ♣	Pass	3 ♡	Pass
3 NT	Pass	4 ♠	Pass
6 ♣	Pass	Pass	Pass

When we are talking about Mike Passell, we are not talking about any minor league player. In 1976, he won the McKenney Trophy as the leading player in North America, with a total of 1,815 Master Points, which at that time was more than any player had ever earned in a single year. He had been chosen to fill a vacancy on the North American team, which was defending the World Championship.

You will find the champion players usually attack against a small slam in a suit contract. The attacking lead was a small heart. However, champion players frequently avoid leading the suit the dummy had bid. If Passell adopted that principle, he would not lead a heart. What would you do?

Bear in mind that the heart suit had been bid secondarily and was almost certainly no more than four cards long, and the declarer had shown no direct interest in the suit. The only alternative seemed to be a spade lead. The four-spade bid by Kantar was not a suit bid, but a cue bid showing a feature in spades. However, a spade lead certainly would not be an attacking lead, and it is worth noting that after Eisenberg heard that bid he went directly to a slam.

Passell led a heart.

None vul., dealer East.

NORTH
♠ K 2
♡ A 10 3 2
♢ A 10 9 4 2
♣ 10 7

WEST
♠ 10 9 6
♡ K J 9 5 4
♢ J 6 5 3
♣ 2

EAST
♠ Q 8 7 4 3
♡ 7 6
♢ K Q
♣ J 6 5 3

SOUTH
♠ A J 5
♡ Q 8
♢ 8 7
♣ A K Q 9 8 4

The heart lead turned out to be a disaster. Eisenberg won the eight, cashed the spade king-ace, and trumped a spade. When he took two top trumps, he discovered that East had started with four clubs to the jack. That didn't bother him. He went to the dummy with the ace of hearts, trumped a heart, returned to the dummy with the ace of diamonds, and led the last heart from the board. Hamilton could not gain by trumping, so he discarded, but Eisenberg trumped the heart, and got off lead with his remaining diamond. Whoever won that trick, he was going to win the last two tricks with his queen and nine of clubs.

The sad part of this story, from the viewpoint of the defending champions, was that with the lead of any of the other three suits it was probable that Eisenberg would have gone set.

Of course, there are exceptions when the suit bid by the dummy should be led, but these are hard to find before you have seen the dummy. One exception would be when the opponents have bid all four suits. Unless there is something in your hand that tells you otherwise, it is probably better to lead the dummy's long suit than the declarer's long suit.

You will also find that leading players are not so reluctant to lead the first suit bid by those players who use a Canape approach. Some of these modern bidding methods have a lot going for them, but often they give the defenders the information needed to find the right defense. In Canape, the second suit bid is the long suit and first suit bid will often be not more than four cards long and might even be a weak four-card suit. Earlier, I showed you a hand where Jim Jacoby led the first suit bid by dummy, and it is so apt that I am going to repeat it here.

N-S vul., dealer North.

```
                    NORTH
                    ♠ Q 9 8 7
                    ♡ 2
                    ◇ A 5 4
                    ♣ A K J 6 5
        WEST                        EAST
        ♠ A 4 2                     ♠ K J 10 5 3
        ♡ J 7 6 3                   ♡ K 8
        ◇ 6 3 2                     ◇ J 10 9 8
        ♣ 10 8 3                    ♣ Q 4
                    SOUTH
                    ♠ 6
                    ♡ A Q 10 9 5 4
                    ◇ K Q 7
                    ♣ 9 7 2
```

The bidding:

SOUTH	WEST	NORTH	EAST
		1 ♠	Pass
2 ♡	Pass	3 ♣	Pass
3 NT	Pass	Pass	Pass

Let's take a look at the clues which Jacoby had that caused him to make that devastating lead of a small spade, which enabled the defenders to take the first five tricks.

Jacoby himself had only five HCPs. Therefore, it was likely his partner held somewhere in the neighborhood of nine. Where were they?

North-South were playing Canape. Therefore, his long suit was clubs, not spades. South's bid of two hearts was natural and indicated he had length there. South's 3NT rebid showed diamond strength. With both hearts and diamonds in his hand, it sounded as though South was short in the black suits. Aware that North's opening bid of one spade might be on such a suit as it was, Jacoby led the two of spades. After the defenders took the first five tricks, Bobby Wolff, East, talked declarer into going for the club finesse, rather than the heart finesse, by leading the eight of hearts. Declarer went for it, and so Wolff took two more tricks, one with his queen of clubs and another with his king of hearts, for a three-trick set.

4. The lead of a doubleton queen or jack in a suit your partner has not bid.
Many years ago, I said that unless the bidding clearly called for the lead of a suit with this holding, the lead would cost about three tricks every time it gained one. That well may have been a prejudice of mine, or even a superstition, so I have been watching championship hands for some time, trying to see what evidence there is one way or the other. The lead simply isn't made too often, and the few hands I have found are not conclusive.

The first exhibit illustrates a hand where a jack was led from J-x in the trump suit. In the 1964 World Championship, Hans Goethe, of Sweden, led the jack of spades against a four-spade contract by Benito Garozzo, of Italy, on this hand.

N-S vul., dealer South.

NORTH
♠ Q 9 6 5 4
♡ None
◇ Q 10 9 2
♣ 10 6 4 3

WEST
♠ J 3
♡ Q 10 8 6 2
◇ K J 6
♣ A 7 2

EAST
♠ K 7
♡ A K J 7 5
◇ 8 4 3
♣ Q 9 8

SOUTH
♠ A 10 8 2
♡ 9 4 3
◇ A 7 5
♣ K J 5

The bidding had been short and to the point. Garozzo had dealt and bid one spade with the South hand. His partner bid four spades, and everybody passed. When Goethe led the jack of spades, it was covered by the queen, king and ace. What had been a sure spade loser was no longer a loser. The spade suit was now solid.

Garozzo went to the dummy with the nine of spades and led a small club to his jack. Goethe won the ace and led back a second club. Garozzo won and exited with his five of clubs. East won and led a small diamond. It appeared the defenders were determined that they would not lead hearts. Garozzo played small and the king of diamonds was the last defensive trick. The defenders had taken two clubs and one diamond. Just what would have happened had Goethe chosen the normal lead of the six of hearts we will never know, as in the other room East and West bought the contract for four hearts, going set one trick. One thing is clear. The lead of the jack of spades simplified life for Garozzo. Maybe Garozzo would have guessed the minor suits just right to avoid losing more than two tricks in those suits, but he certainly did not limit his minor suit losers to two tricks the way the hand was actually played.

The next hand is from the qualifying round in the World

Championships of 1977. Six teams were playing, and as hands had been duplicated for all the teams, this hand was played six times.

Both vul., dealer South.

```
                    NORTH
                    ♠ K 9 6 4 3 2
                    ♡ J 7 2
                    ◇ 7 5 2
                    ♣ Q
        WEST                    EAST
        ♠ J 10                  ♠ 8 7 5
        ♡ Q 10                  ♡ A 9 8 4
        ◇ 10 4 3                ◇ Q 9 8 6
        ♣ 10 9 8 4 3 2          ♣ A 6
                    SOUTH
                    ♠ A Q
                    ♡ K 6 5 3
                    ◇ A K J
                    ♣ K J 7 5
```

The final contract in all six matches was four spades, but in only one of the matches did North become the declarer. In the other five matches, either the Jacoby Transfer or the Texas Transfer bid was used, and South became the declarer.

In the hand where North was the declarer and South was exposed as dummy, Fred Hamilton led the ace of clubs. After looking the dummy over, he switched to the nine of hearts. Declarer played low from dummy. Mike Passell won the queen, returned a heart to Hamilton's ace, and trumped a heart, sending declarer down one.

In one of the hands where South was the declarer, the opening lead was the ten of clubs. East won with the ace and switched to a small diamond. Eddie Kantar was the declarer at this table. He rose with the king of diamonds and pulled trumps. He had no trouble fulfilling his contract. At three of the tables where South was the declarer, the opening lead was a club won by East who led back a heart. At two tables, South played a small heart. West won the queen, played a heart to his partner's ace, and got a heart ruff. East-West took the first four tricks.

Jim Borin, of Australia, was the exception. In his case, it was Bob Hamman who switched to the heart at trick two. The record shows that Borin took a long time before playing to this trick, but finally decided to play the king from his hand. He had come to the conclusion that Hamman was less likely to lead a heart if he held the queen than if he held the ace. His decision let him make his game contract.

At the fifth table, Augustin Santamarina, of Argentina, chose as his opening lead that horror, the queen of hearts. That made it easy for Hugh Roth, sitting South. East won the opening lead with the ace and, hoping the queen was a singleton, returned a small heart. Roth rose with the king and took eleven tricks, losing only to the two opposing aces.

I mentioned to one of my advanced classes that in championship play, leads from queen doubleton and jack doubleton, unless the bidding simply screamed for the lead of that suit, were hard to find. I explained that times when this lead defeated a hand which otherwise would have been made were practically nonexistent so far as I could discover. The next week, one of my pupils brought me this hand.

None vul., dealer North.

```
                    NORTH
                    ♠ 10 6 2
                    ♡ Q 7 6
                    ◊ Q J 9
                    ♣ K Q 8 7
      WEST                        EAST
      ♠ K 9 3                     ♠ J 4
      ♡ J 5                       ♡ K 10 8 3 2
      ◊ 10 4 2                    ◊ K 7 5 3
      ♣ A 10 9 6 3                ♣ 5 4
                    SOUTH
                    ♠ A Q 8 7 5
                    ♡ A 9 4
                    ◊ A 8 6
                    ♣ J 2
```

The bidding:

SOUTH	WEST	NORTH	EAST
Shapiro	Ellenby	Reese	Roth
		Pass	Pass
1 ♠	Pass	2 ♣	Pass
2 NT	Pass	3 NT	Pass
Pass	Pass		

This student must have a pretty good bridge library himself, as the hand was from the World Championship of 1955, with Europe, represented by Britain, against the United States. It is true that on this hand, Milton Ellenby chose the jack of hearts as his opening lead against 3NT and that Boris Shapiro, South, took only eight tricks. It is also true that in the other room, North was the declarer at 3NT. On the lead of the three of hearts by East, John Moran, of the U.S.A., took ten tricks. At first it looked like my student had found what I had been unable to find. But let's take another look.

My first question is, did the bidding invite the lead of a heart? North had bid clubs and South had bid spades, so the bidding certainly suggested that neither black suit be led. While the jack-doubleton is usually a rotten lead, three to the ten-spot is just about as bad. With a miserable hand to lead from, the lead of the major suit jack-doubleton in preference to the minor suit three-to-the-ten-spot doesn't seem to be all that bad.

Leaving aside the question of the opening lead, let us look at the play of the hand. The question is not did Shapiro go set, but rather should he have gone set.

Of course, if he had played the queen of hearts at trick one, he would have had two stoppers in the suit. That would have been a double dummy play, as once the jack was led by West the ten was more likely to be in the West hand than the East hand. Against the lead of the jack, the better play was to hope the lead was from the J-10-(x-x-x). So I think we will all have to agree that Shapiro had no reason to rise with dummy's queen. East played the three and Ellenby continued the suit. When Roth came up with the ten, Shapiro saw that he had misjudged the hearts. It seemed likely it was from a doubleton, for if West had held the jack three- or four-long, he certainly would have led a

281

small card. So Shapiro won the second trick with the ace of hearts and led the jack of clubs and hoped for the best. His wish was granted, as it was West, instead of East, who won the trick. After Ellenby won the ace of clubs he came on with the three. Shapiro was not about to let East gain the lead if he could help it, so he rose with dummy's king and led a spade and finessed the queen. Ellenby won the king and led the ten of clubs. Shapiro won the queen and led a small spade to his ace. Now he got another break. The jack of spades fell out from East and he now had a total of four spade tricks for the taking. He won the ace and then went to the dummy with the ten of spades. He needed a third break, which he got when he led the queen of diamonds and found the king onside. With four spade tricks plus two club tricks and a heart trick, all he needed was two diamond tricks to bring home his game. For some reason he didn't do that, but instead led the nine of diamonds to his ace and cashed his good spades. Now the opponents, who in the meantime had won three tricks, won the last two tricks.

Why didn't Shapiro lead the queen of diamonds at trick nine? I am sure I don't know, but I would guess that he simply had miscounted his tricks.

I have suggested before that I am a great believer in looking at what has happened down through the years in trying to decide which theories are correct and which ones are incorrect. Nothing I have seen has caused me to change my opinion that, unless the bidding calls for the lead of a suit holding the queen-doubleton or jack-doubleton, that lead will lose much more than it will ever gain.

5. The lead of a suit (not trumps) bid on your right.

It is not often that you will choose to lead the suit which your right-hand has bid. Frequently, when you lead the suit bid to your right, it will be because you think your partner can get a ruff. Here is a hand used to illustrate that point to a class of new players. Suppose you're sitting West with

♠ A   ♥ J 10 9   ♦ 8 7 6 3 2   ♣ A 7 4 3

and you hear the following bidding:

SOUTH	WEST	NORTH	EAST
1 ◊	Pass	2 ◊	Pass
2 ♠	Pass	3 ♠	Pass
4 ♠	Double	Pass	Pass
Pass			

If you are a teacher, you would be justified in telling your pupils to double the opponents on this bidding sequence. You expect your partner to be void in diamonds and, as you hold the ace of trumps, you think your partner is going to get to trump diamonds twice. His two ruffs plus your two aces automatically set the hand one trick, and if he turns up with another trick in his hand you can get a larger set.

This hand illustrates the point beautifully. It separates the problem of leading the suit bid to your right from all other problems, and well establishes the principle that you do this when you think you can give your partner a ruff. The trouble is that the bidding seems unlikely. However, if you should hear this bidding and you should hold this hand, you definitely should lead a diamond whether you double or not.

Here is a deal from real life, where the need for the lead of the right-hand opponent's suit is not so easy to see. But, Alan Hudson saw it. The hand was played in a team of four game in England in February, 1979.

Both vul., dealer South.

NORTH
- ♠ J 5 4
- ♡ Q 7 3
- ◇ K Q 10 3
- ♣ K 6 2

WEST
- ♠ A K 7 3
- ♡ A 4
- ◇ J 6
- ♣ J 9 8 5 3

EAST
- ♠ Q 10 9 8 6 2
- ♡ 9 2
- ◇ A 9 7 2
- ♣ 4

SOUTH
- ♠ None
- ♡ K J 10 8 6 5
- ◇ 8 5 4
- ♣ A Q 10 7

The bidding:

SOUTH	WEST	NORTH	EAST
Goldberg	Hudson	Shenkin	McGloughlin
1 ♡	Double	Redouble	2 ♠
3 ♣	4 ♠	Pass	Pass
5 ♡	Double	Pass	Pass
Pass			

Hudson, West, struck gold when he led a club. He was soon in the lead with the ace of trumps, and he led another club for his partner to trump. East had the ace of diamonds for the set-ting trick. In the replay of the hand, the West player, on the same bidding, led the king of spades, and declarer made his con-tract, losing only one heart trick and one diamond trick.

Let's review the bidding and see why Hudson chose to lead a club instead of a spade. Holding the ace of trumps, he didn't think there was much chance spade tricks were going to disap-pear. In this he was right, as the defenders had no spade tricks anyway. But why lead a club? South had bid clubs, but North had never supported them.

On reviewing the bidding, you will see that the clues were

there. With the North hand, Shenkin redoubled the first time around. When it came his time to bid again, he passed. He referred the decision back to his partner. That indicated that he had a balanced hand. Had his redouble been based on great heart length, or length in any other suit, he would have taken action himself instead of passing the decision back to Goldberg. He had some hopes of successfully fulfilling a contract in either of Goldberg's suits. All of this implied some sort of a fit in clubs. Hudson did hold five of them. He based his defense on a bet that the action by North showed a balanced hand that chances his partner could trump a second round of clubs was a good risk. In this case, it was definitely the right decision.

This deal is an exception to the rule. Aside from unusual circumstances like these, it is highly dangerous to lead the suit bid to your right. Not only are you leading the opponents' length, but you are probably leading into his strength as well.

6. The underlead of an ace against a suit contract.

The late Joe Cain, of Indianapolis, was the sort of player who enjoyed getting sensational results even more than he enjoyed winning. For years, he tried, unsuccessfully, to score by underleading aces against suit contracts, in rubber bridge games. Just how much this cost him I do not know, but finally he struck gold. One day, he found the king in the dummy, the jack in the declarer's hand, and the queen doubleton in his partner's hand, and he was on lead against a slam contract. He underled his ace and declarer played low from the dummy, and Joe's partner actually played the queen and returned the suit to Joe's ace and trumped the third round. Joe let out a whoop like an Apache Indian and got up and danced around the room three times. Finally, all of the money he had spent and all of the time he had waited came to this supreme moment. If you, too, enjoy the thrill of a spectacular result more than you enjoy winning, I recommend you make it a habit to underlead your aces against suit contracts. It will cost you a lot of match points, or IMPs, or Victory Points, or coin of the realm, or whatever you play for, but finally it will work for you, provided only you don't lose all of your partners before that happy moment.

Let me emphasize the fact that I am not talking about opening lead against notrump contract. Let me further state that there are times when, in suit contracts, after looking at the dummy, you can judge that underleading an ace is more likely to win than to lose. The point I am making is that underleading aces against suit contracts before you have seen the dummy is, on balance, a losing proposition.

Nonetheless, that potential thrill attracts all sorts of players, like the call of the sirens attracted Odysseus. Experts of world championship caliber are not immune. They should be better able to find those occasions when the lead is a winning lead than lesser mortals, so let's take a look at the record.

As it happens, the most famous of these hands is indeed a success story. It was made in 1935 by Mrs. Culbertson, in a famous match with Mr. and Mrs. Ely Culbertson playing Mr. and Mrs. P. Hal Sims.

N-S vul., dealer West.

```
                    NORTH
                    ♠ K J 3
                    ♡ 7
                    ◇ A Q 7 4
                    ♣ K Q 9 4 2
    WEST                            EAST
    ♠ A 5 4                         ♠ Q 10 7 6
    ♡ 8 4 3 2                       ♡ 10 5
    ◇ K 9 6                         ◇ J 10 5 3 2
    ♣ A 10 7                        ♣ 6 3
                    SOUTH
                    ♠ 9 8 2
                    ♡ A K Q J 9 6
                    ◇ 8
                    ♣ J 8 5
```

The bidding:

SOUTH	WEST	NORTH	EAST
Sims	Mrs. Culbertson	Mrs. Sims	Culbertson
	Pass	1 ♣	Pass
1 ♡	Pass	2 ◇	Pass
3 ♡	Pass	3 NT	Pass
4 ♡	Pass	Pass	Pass

Sims' reluctance to play notrump suggested that he was weak in spades, while Mrs. Sims' willingness to play notrump suggested she was strong in spades. One thing that makes the underlead of an ace successful is for the king to be in dummy. So Mrs. Culbertson decided to lead the four of spades. Sims played low from the dummy and Mr. Culbertson won the trick with his ten. He led back a club which Mrs. Culbertson won with the ace, and now she led the second small spade. It has been recorded that it took Sims quite some time to make his play to this second spade trick. Finally, he decided that surely Mrs. Culbertson would not underlead an ace two times and he played the jack. Ely won with his queen and now led back a spade to his wife's ace. The defenders won the first four tricks.

Possibly this hand has led other players to attempt the same coup, but not all of them have been so successful. I shall show them—the failures and the successes—in chronological order.

On the next hand, I do not know who the North and South players were, but East was David Bruce (formerly Burnstine), and West was Oswald Jacoby.

N-S vul., dealer South.

NORTH
♠ J 10
♡ A J 9 8
◇ K Q J
♣ K J 7 6

WEST
♠ 9 6 5 3
♡ 6 2
◇ 10 5 4 2
♣ A 5 2

EAST
♠ 7 2
♡ 7 4 3
◇ 9 8 6 3
♣ Q 9 4 3

SOUTH
♠ A K Q 8 4
♡ K Q 10 5
◇ A 7
♣ 10 8

The bidding:

SOUTH	WEST	NORTH	EAST
1 ♠	Pass	2 NT	Pass
3 ♡	Pass	4 ♡	Pass
5 ◇	Pass	6 ◇	Pass
6 ♡	Pass	Pass	Pass

Jacoby has the fastest mind in bridge, and I am confident he lost no time making the only lead which had a chance to beat the contract. It might take you and me a little longer to come to his conclusion. It was clear that both North and South were strong in the red suits. It also sounded as if South was strong in spades. Hence, a club lead was called for, but North's jump to 2NT sounded like he was strong in clubs as well as in the other suits. Because the dummy might have the K-J of clubs, Jacoby led the two.

Declarer couldn't imagine Jacoby was underleading an ace against a slam contract and played dummy's six. Now the fate of the deal was in the hands of David Bruce. Who was this David Bruce? He was an all-round star, and his teammates were inclined to rate him the best bidder in the game. All-round star he was. He was a member of the team known as the Four Horsemen, who swept the boards clean. In 1933, he formed his own team known as the Four Aces. That team took complete leadership of the field. When the American Contract Bridge League started its Master Point plan, David Burnstine was chosen to be Life Master No. 1. Well, he didn't believe Jacoby would underlead an ace either. He decided that Jacoby must have a four-card holding and that South had the singleton ace. So why waste his queen? Burnstine played low and the declarer won the first trick with his eight. Declarer had twelve tricks off the top, and that club trick made number thirteen. That extra trick can be mighty important at match point duplicate.

Let's move on up to 1952.

None vul., dealer South:

```
                    NORTH
                    ♠ A 9 4
                    ♡ Q J
                    ◇ A Q J 7 6 4
                    ♣ A 5
      WEST                      EAST
      ♠ 10 6 5                  ♠ Q 7
      ♡ A 10 9 3                ♡ 8 7 5
      ◇ 9 5 3                   ◇ K 8 2
      ♣ J 4 3                   ♣ Q 9 8 6 2
                    SOUTH
                    ♠ K J 8 3 2
                    ♡ K 6 4 2
                    ◇ 10
                    ♣ K 10 7
```

The bidding:

SOUTH	WEST	NORTH	EAST
Pavlides	Reese	Kempson	Schapiro
Pass	Pass	2 NT	Pass
6 ♠	Pass	Pass	Pass

This hand was played in a Pairs contest at the Hamilton Club in London. Such games are scored by match points, where overtricks are important.

Ewart Kempson reports that after two passes he made a bold attempt to play the hand himself by bidding 2NT. His partner, Col. Jordanis Pavlides, had other ideas and went straight to six spades. This left Terrence Reese on lead. He chose the three of hearts.

With every suit behaving beautifully, Pavlides took all thirteen tricks. He pulled trumps and then took a ruffing finesse in diamonds and ended up with five spades, five diamonds, two clubs, and a heart. Some people would say that Reese "had to go to bed with his ace." Pavlides got that overtrick, and Reese—for his opening lead—got what is known in the vernacular as "a cold bottom."

The match in which the next hand was played is from the World Championship of 1954, with Europe; represented by France, playing against the United States.

E-W vul., dealer South:

```
                NORTH
                ♠ 7 4
                ♡ Q 10 8 3
                ◊ A K 6
                ♣ 10 9 6 3
  WEST                      EAST
  ♠ 5                       ♠ K J 9 8
  ♡ A 5 4                   ♡ K 9 7 6 2
  ◊ 8 7 5 4 2               ◊ None
  ♣ K J 8 7                 ♣ A Q 4 2
                SOUTH
                ♠ A Q 10 6 3 2
                ♡ J
                ◊ Q J 10 9 3
                ♣ 5
```

290

The bidding:

SOUTH	WEST	NORTH	EAST
Steen	Bacherich	Oakie	Ghestem
1 ♠	Pass	1 NT	2 ♡
2 ♠	3 ♡	Double	Pass
3 ♠	Pass	Pass	Pass

After Doug Steen won the opening trick with the jack of hearts, he simply laid down the ace of spades and started leading diamonds. After winning a cheap trick with the jack of hearts, he wasn't about to take any chances on his contract. He was perfectly willing to lose three spades and a club.

You may be wondering how in the world he won the first trick with the jack of hearts. That was easy. Bacherich, for France, underled his ace, and Ghestem refused to put up his king. Ghestem simply didn't believe Bacherich would underlead the ace, and credited Steen with having the singleton ace. This turned out quite well for the United States, for in the other room the French pair got to four spades, got doubled, and went set two tricks with the North and South hands. Milton Ellenby, for the U.S.A., led a diamond. Bill Rosen, East, took three trump tricks, a heart trick, and the ace of clubs.

Let's jump to 1959, where we find the United States, Italy and Argentina playing for the World Championship. This hand is from the match with the United States opposing Argentina.

Both vul., dealer East:

```
                    NORTH
                    ♠ K Q 7
                    ♡ 8 6
                    ◇ 6 5 4
                    ♣ Q J 10 8 3
       WEST                     EAST
       ♠ 8                      ♠ J 9 5 3
       ♡ K 9 5 4                ♡ 7 3
       ◇ A 7 3 2                ◇ Q J 10
       ♣ K 6 5 2                ♣ A 9 7 4
                    SOUTH
                    ♠ A 10 6 4 2
                    ♡ A Q J 10 2
                    ◇ K 9 8
                    ♣ None
```

The bidding:

SOUTH	WEST	NORTH	EAST
Stakgold	Calventi	Harmon	Rocchi
			Pass
1 ♠	Pass	2 ♣	Pass
3 ♣	Pass	4 ♠	Pass
Pass	Pass		

Calventi, West for Argentina, led the two of diamonds. Stakgold won the trick and didn't have too much trouble limiting his losses to two diamonds and one heart. He went to the dummy with the king of spades and finessed a heart. The defense cashed two diamond tricks, Stakgold won the heart return, led a spade to dummy's queen, revealing the 4-1 trump break, and finessed the ten of spades. He took his ten tricks.

Where the team for the Argentine had the North-South hands, clubs were never bid. Sam Fry, Jr., West, led the two of clubs. Alejandro Castro, for Argentina, lost four tricks, for a one-trick set.

Next, we move along to the World Championship of 1962, in a match with North America versus Italy.

N-S vul., dealer West.

```
                        NORTH
                        ♠ K 9 5
                        ♡ A 6
                        ◇ K Q J 5 2
                        ♣ Q J 7
        WEST                            EAST
        ♠ 8 7 4 2                       ♠ 10 6
        ♡ Q 9 7 3                       ♡ 2
        ◇ A 8                           ◇ 10 9 7 6 3
        ♣ 9 4 3                         ♣ A K 8 5 2
                        SOUTH
                        ♠ A Q J 3
                        ♡ K J 10 8 5 4
                        ◇ 4
                        ♣ 10 6
```

The bidding:

CLOSED ROOM

SOUTH	WEST	NORTH	EAST
Mathe	Garozzo	Nail	Forquet
	Pass	1 NT	Pass
2 ♣	Pass	2 ◇	Pass
3 ♡	Pass	4 ◇	Pass
4 ♠	Pass	5 ♡	Pass
Pass	Pass		

OPEN ROOM

Belladonna	Murray	Avarelli	Coon
	Pass	1 NT	Pass
2 ◇	Pass	2 NT	Pass
4 ♡	Pass	Pass	Pass

Lew Mathe and Bobby Nail reached an impossible contract of five hearts. Benito Garozzo made a neutral opening lead of a club. They immediately cashed their three top tricks. As the hearts lay badly, they also had a heart trick, for a two-trick set. In the open room, Eric Murray picked this moment to underlead an ace. He opened the eight of diamonds. The official report says that Belladonna won the jack and took the ace and king of hearts. Learning the heart situation, he went to the dummy with the king of spades and led the king of diamonds, on which he discarded a club. It was not too late for the defense to recover. If, after he won with the ace of diamonds, Murray had led a club to his partner's hand, and Coon had returned a diamond, Murray would have taken two trump tricks. If Belladonna had trumped low, Murray would simply overtrump with the nine. If Belladonna had trumped high, Murray would discard and still have two trump tricks coming. Obviously, that is not the way the defense went. The official report gives no more detail of the play after Murray won with the ace of diamonds, but simply says the defense made one club, the heart queen, and the ace of diamonds.

Let's move along to 1966, where we find North America playing The Netherlands in the World Championship. Again, we find Eric Murray underleading an ace against a suit contract. One of the troubles with making this lead is that, even when the dummy holds the king and your partner the queen, your partner will not play his queen in the belief that you could not possibly have underled an ace. In this 1966 hand, Murray's partner did play his queen. Let me show you why.

Both vul., dealer South.

```
                        NORTH
                        ♠ K J 9 7
                        ♡ Q 6 5
                        ◇ 2
                        ♣ A K J 10 7
        WEST                            EAST
        ♠ A 8 5 3                       ♠ Q
        ♡ K 9 8                         ♡ 10 4 2
        ◇ 10 6 3                        ◇ Q 9 8 7 4
        ♣ 9 3 2                         ♣ Q 8 5 4
                        SOUTH
                        ♠ 10 6 4 2
                        ♡ A J 7 3
                        ◇ A K J 5
                        ♣ 6
```

The bidding:

OPEN ROOM

SOUTH	WEST	NORTH	EAST
Kreyns	Murray	Slavenburg	Kehela
1 ♡	Pass	2 ♣	Pass
2 ◇	Pass	2 ♠	Pass
3 ♠	Pass	4 ♡	Pass
Pass	Pass		

CLOSED ROOM

Feldesman	Boender	Rubin	Oudshoorn
1 ♡	Pass	2 ♣	2 ◇
3 ◇	Pass	3 ♡	Pass
4 ♡	Pass	Pass	Pass

One interesting thing about this hand is the fact that both the Hollanders and the North Americans missed the four-spade contract, with a 4-4 fit. The four-spade contract probably would have been successful, but it would have been a bit touchy with that 4-1 break. But we should not worry about that too much, as our interest right now is in seeing how underleading an ace against a suit contract works out. Murray led the three of spades.

Kreyns, in the open room, was convinced that Murray would not underlead an ace, and so he failed to play his king. It didn't make any difference what Kehela thought with the East hand. His only option was either to play his queen or revoke. I do not know whether he was or was not surprised when his queen held the trick. He led back a diamond. Declarer won the ace and went to the dummy with the ace of clubs to finesse the jack of hearts. Murray won with his king and then laid down the ace of spades and gave Kehela a spade ruff for the setting trick.

In the closed room, the opening lead was a club. Declarer won in the dummy with the king and finessed hearts. Boender, for Holland, won the king, laid down the ace of spades and gave his partner a ruff, but that came to only three tricks for the defense as the queen of spades never took a trick.

How about underleading an ace, not in a side suit, but in a suit your partner has bid? Can that possibly deceive your partner?

On the next hand, it could be that underleading the ace only cost an extra trick. Vernon, of Venezuela, might have made four spades, regardless of the opening lead. He would have been walking on eggs all the way, and might not have taken ten tricks. Against the opening lead he got, he took eleven tricks. We have no way of comparing the play in the other room, because when the Americans had the North-South hands, they played 1NT and, with the help of careless defense, took nine tricks. Here is the hand.

Both vul., dealer East.

```
                    NORTH
                    ♠ A K 10 3
                    ♡ Q 10 9 8 4
                    ◊ K 4
                    ♣ 8 5
        WEST                    EAST
        ♠ J 4                   ♠ Q 5 2
        ♡ A 7 3                 ♡ K 6 5 2
        ◊ J 6 5 2               ◊ Q 3
        ♣ A J 10 2              ♣ 9 6 4 3
                    SOUTH
                    ♠ 9 8 7 6
                    ♡ J
                    ◊ A 10 9 8 7
                    ♣ K Q 7
```

The bidding:

SOUTH	WEST	NORTH	EAST
Vernon	Root	Benaim	Roth
			Pass
Pass	1 ♣	Double	1 ♡
1 ♠	Pass	2 ♠	Pass
4 ♠	Pass	Pass	Pass

The hand is from the 1967 World Championship, with the North American team playing the team from Venezuela. Al Roth, East, had responded one heart, and Bill Root, West, chose to lead the three of hearts. Believe it or not, the official report says that the first trick went three of hearts, four of hearts, six of hearts, and jack of hearts. So, with the ace and king of the suit both missing, Vernon took the first trick with the singleton jack. He cashed the king and ace of diamonds, his two high trumps, and led a club to his king. Root won the ace and returned a club. Declarer won and led the nine of diamonds, letting it ride when West did not cover. Roth trumped with the queen and returned a heart. Vernon trumped in his hand and then forced out Root's jack of diamonds, trumping it in the dummy. He returned to his hand with a heart ruff and had eleven tricks.

It is not recorded what Alvin Roth said to Bill Root about his opening lead after the hand.

Whether the play by the defenders gave the declarer one extra trick or an even larger bonus, the result certainly did nothing to enhance the opinion we have of this opening lead.

N-S vul., dealer North.

```
                        NORTH
                        ♠ 7 4
                        ♡ J 10 9
                        ◇ K 3
                        ♣ K Q 7 6 5 2
        WEST                        EAST
        ♠ 9 8 2                     ♠ K J
        ♡ A 8 7 5 3                 ♡ 6
        ◇ A 10 7 5 4                ◇ J 9 8 6 2
        ♣ None                      ♣ 10 9 8 4 3
                        SOUTH
                        ♠ A Q 10 6 5 3
                        ♡ K Q 4 2
                        ◇ Q
                        ♣ A J
```

The bidding:

SOUTH	WEST	NORTH	EAST
Katz	Soloway	Cohen	Swanson
		Pass	Pass
2 ♠	Pass	3 ♣	Pass
3 ♡	Pass	3 ♠	Pass
4 ♠	Pass	Pass	Pass

In the 1974 trials, Paul Soloway made his try at underleading an ace against a suit contract. Over the Labor Day weekend, the winners of the four major national team championships gathered in Washington to play off for the privilege of representing North America in the 1974 World Championship.

Soloway's team went on to win the event. On this deal, he could have done better.

The bidding methods used by Katz and Cohen called for an opening bid of two spades with a South hand. They arrived at a four-spade contract after bidding spades, clubs, and hearts. The bidding called for the opening lead of a diamond, and Paul Soloway, with the West hand, led a diamond. But the diamond he led was not the ace, it was the four. He hoped his partner would win the king and return a club for him to ruff. Dr. Katz was happy to win the trick with his singleton queen. Katz apparently decided to avoid any unnecessary risks, so he laid down the ace and then another spade. Paul Soloway won his king and then returned a diamond. Dr. Katz trumped, pulled the last trump, and, after giving up a trick to the ace of hearts, claimed eleven tricks.

It is true that the bidding called for a diamond lead, but the standard lead from a suit headed by the ace is to lead the ace, unless you are defending against a notrump contract. Let's see what would have been likely to happen if Soloway had followed the normal procedure and led the ace of diamonds.

What he saw there would have made my Aunt Susie happy. My Aunt Susie believed that you always led an ace so that you could look at the dummy. I am suggesting that the ace might have been led because it was in the diamond suit, but whatever the reason was for leading the ace of diamonds, Soloway would have seen something that would have told him how to proceed. Three hearts would show up in the dummy, South had bid hearts, and Soloway had five of them. That meant that Swanson had not more than one. He would have switched to the ace of hearts, and then would have led the smallest heart he had to ask Swanson to return clubs. On this line of defense, the defenders would have taken six tricks before Katz even got to lead, consisting of four trump trumps and the two red aces.

If Paul Soloway has tried this opening since then, I can find no record of it.

We will leave World Championship matches now and pick up a hand played in 1977 in the Blue Ribbon Pairs. This is an event run by the American Contract Bridge League each fall for its leading players, and it must be as prestigious as any event held anywhere in the world. It is a match point contest where extra tricks are extremely important. It was won by Thomas Sanders, of Nashville, Tennessee, and Louis Bluhm, of Atlanta, Georgia.

On the last hand of the match, Tommy Sanders managed to win two heart tricks while losing none. Here is the hand.

Both vul., dealer West.

```
                    NORTH
                    ♠ A K 8 7
                    ♡ K J 7 3
                    ◇ K 6
                    ♣ A Q 2
     WEST                          EAST
     ♠ None                        ♠ J 9 4
     ♡ A 10 2                      ♡ Q 8 6 5 4
     ◇ A J 5 3                     ◇ Q 7 4 2
     ♣ K J 10 9 8 3                ♣ 6
                    SOUTH
                    ♠ Q 10 6 5 3 2
                    ♡ 9
                    ◇ 10 9 8
                    ♣ 7 5 4
```

The bidding:

SOUTH	WEST	NORTH	EAST
Sanders	Janitschke	Bluhm	Hughes
	1 ♣	Double	1 ♡
3 ♠	4 ♣	4 ♠	Pass
Pass	Pass		

We have here yet another hand where the opening leader underled an ace of a suit bid by partner, but where the partner refused to believe it. The play to the first trick was: Jan Janitschke led the two of hearts; dummy played low; Robert Hughes, East, played the four; and Tommy Sanders won his singleton nine! By going to the dummy with trumps and ruffing two more hearts, he was able to establish dummy's king of hearts. He then pulled trumps, and when the king of clubs and ace of diamonds both turned out to be in the West hand, he

300

took twelve tricks by the simple expedient of discarding one of his clubs on dummy's good heart.

When you underlead an ace, and your partner has the king doubleton, so that you can win the first two tricks in the suit and sometimes can get a third trick by ruffing the lead of the suit, you may say you have made a "power" play. When you find the king in the dummy, the queen in your partner's hand, and the jack in either the dummy or the closed hand, you may say that your play has been a "deceptive" lead. Gabriel Chagas, of Brazil, found one of these deceptive leads in the qualifying round of the World Olympiad Pairs game in 1978. This hand demonstrates that the lead does sometimes work.

Dealer North.

```
                    NORTH
                    ♠ A K J 2
                    ♡ J 10 8
                    ◇ K J 6
                    ♣ A Q 8
        WEST                      EAST
        ♠ None                    ♠ 10 8 7 5 3
        ♡ 9 5 2                   ♡ Q 7
        ◇ A 10 7 5 4              ◇ Q 3 2
        ♣ J 10 7 6 5             ♣ 9 3 2
                    SOUTH
                    ♠ Q 9 6 4
                    ♡ A K 6 4 3
                    ◇ 9 8
                    ♣ K 4
```

The bidding:

SOUTH	WEST	NORTH	EAST
		1 ♣	Pass
1 ♡	Pass	3 NT	Pass
4 ♠	Pass	5 ♠	Pass
Pass	Pass		

Chagas, West, chose a small diamond as his opening lead.

The declarer played dummy's jack and East won the queen. East returned a small diamond to the ace and the defense later came to a trump trick, setting the contract one trick. Twenty-seven of the thirty-two pairs who played this hand were in a contract of six spades, most of them going down only one trick, so Chagas had to find this opening lead just to hold his own. However, for this lead to succeed as a "deceptive" lead, there are no fewer than three cards which must be properly placed. It is necessary that dummy have the king, that your partner have the queen, and that the jack is either in the dummy or in the declarer's hand. It is also necessary that declarer does not somehow figure to go up with the king, and that partner does not somehow figure that he should not play the queen.

Look at this hand from the 1979 London Sunday Times Pairs. This is a prestigious event in which sixteen of the leading pairs from all over the world are invited to participate.

None vul., dealer South.

```
                    NORTH
                  ♠ K J 9 6 5 2
                  ♡ 10 9
                  ◇ 10 8
                  ♣ A 9 7
      WEST                      EAST
    ♠ 10                      ♠ Q 8 7 3
    ♡ K 7 6 5 2               ♡ Q
    ◇ A 6 2                   ◇ Q 9 7 4 3
    ♣ Q 10 8 2                ♣ J 4 3
                    SOUTH
                  ♠ A 4
                  ♡ A J 8 4 3
                  ◇ K J 5
                  ♣ K 6 5
```

The bidding:

SOUTH	WEST	NORTH	EAST
1 NT	Pass	2 ♡	Pass
2 ♠	Pass	4 ♠	Pass
Pass	Pass		

With sixteen pairs playing, the hand was played eight times. Once it was played in 3NT, making nine tricks, the other seven times it was played in four spades. Four spades was found to be a difficult contract—only three of the seven declarers were successful. One of the declarers had an easy time. The above auction was the bidding at that table. The two-heart bid by North was a transfer to spades, and so South, rather than North, ended up playing four spades.

The thing that saved this declarer a lot of trouble was that West led the two of diamonds. His partner had the queen all right, but from the viewpoint of West, the king was in the wrong hand. You would think on the bidding that it rated to be in South, but apparently the West player did not think so. Not only did East have the queen, but this time he played it. Declarer won the king and promptly cashed the ace and king of spades. Next he led the jack of spades, giving East his trick. Whatever East returned, declarer was able to go to the dummy with the ace of clubs, finish drawing trumps, and lead the ten of diamonds to establish a diamond trick on which he could discard one of dummy's clubs. His losses were limited to three tricks—a spade, a heart, and a diamond.

The last deal in this series shows a hand where the bidding told the opening leader that the king of the suit was where the opening leader wanted it to be, and the opening leader was lucky enough to find the queen and jack of the suit stationed to suit him. This is a success story.

None vul., dealer South:

                    NORTH
                    ♠ Q 5
                    ♡ K 8 3
                    ◇ A J 10 9 4
                    ♣ A 8 4
    WEST   EAST
    ♠ J 4   ♠ 9 8
    ♡ A 10 7 2   ♡ Q 6 4
    ◇ 8 7 6 2   ◇ Q 5 3
    ♣ Q 9 5   ♣ K 10 6 3 2
                    SOUTH
                    ♠ A K 10 7 6 3 2
                    ♡ J 9 5
                    ◇ K
                    ♣ J 7

The bidding:

SOUTH	WEST	NORTH	EAST
1 ♠	Pass	2 ◇	Pass
2 ♠	Pass	2 NT	Pass
3 ♠	Pass	4 ♣	Pass
4 ◇	Pass	4 ♡	Pass
4 ♠	Pass	5 ◇	Pass
6 ♠	Pass	Pass	Pass

This hand is reported in the syndicated bridge column written by Charles Goren and Omar Sharif. It was played in the Pan-American Championships held in Venezuela. The East and West players are not identified. The North and South players are two of our brightest young stars, Ronnie Rubin and Neil Silverman.

The bidding was long and highly descriptive. South's repeated bid of spades indicated he had a good seven-card spade suit and not much else. Four clubs was a cue bid showing a good card in clubs for a slam contract. This started a series of control-showing bids, and when controls were finally described in every suit, South bid six spades. As Goren and Sharif say, the trouble is that the West defender was listening to the bidding. That four-heart bid by North indicated a control in hearts. The control had to be the king and not a singleton, in view of the previous bid of 2NT, which promised a balanced hand. So West knew that the king of hearts was where he wanted it. The rest might be called "positive thinking". He wanted his partner to hold the queen, but not the jack. If his partner held both, South might play the king from dummy on an opening lead of a small heart as a desperation play. West wanted South to have an option, so he wanted him to have the jack of hearts; or, as an alternative, the jack could be in the North hand. So it turned out to be. On the opening lead of the two of hearts, a small card was played from the dummy. As Goren and Sharif say in their bridge column, "After all, who underleads an ace against a slam?" In this case, East had no reason not to play the queen. When it won the trick, he led back to his partner's ace to defeat the slam before South even had a chance to establish the diamond suit and bring home all the goodies.

In this section, there have been four hands where underleading the ace against a suit contract gained tricks, and eight where this lead lost tricks. This is just about the ratio you would expect from the world's greatest bridge players. If you like that sort of odds, or if you think you can do better than the world's greatest bridge players, go ahead and underlead your ace. If winning is more important than the thrill of bringing off a coup, I recommend you avoid making this opening lead.

Emile Borel takes a look at this lead in his classic book, *The Mathematical Theory of Bridge*. He points out that the chances of success depend upon the number of cards in the suit led. Assuming all of the cards except the ace are small cards, he gives twelve situations where the defense would have won one more trick than they did had they not underled an ace. He does not attempt to give the number of cases where the underlead of the ace gained a trick. This would probably be impossible, from the viewpoint of mathematics, as the results depend not just on what cards are held, but on what action is taken by the partner of the opening leader, who may have refused to believe his partner has underled an ace.

Borel does give the following table which might be of some interest.

TRICKS LOST PER 100 LEADS BY UNDERLEADING AN ACE, AND BY LEADING THE ACE		
Holding	Underleading the Ace	Leading the Ace
A x x	10.8	5.6
A x x x	13.3	4.6
A x x x x	17.3	4.0

Where the suit is five cards long, Borel says the highest of the small cards must be no larger than a nine for his table to be correct, and that where the suit is three cards or four cards long, the highest of the small cards must be a seven or lower. Borel goes on to say that there are limits within which his calculations are precise, and that they are based on certain assumptions. This table applies only to opening leads against suit contracts.

If there is any lesson to be learned from Borel's table, it is that when you have a choice between underleading an ace and leading one, it is much more dangerous to underlead it than to lead it. Or you might say that it might be better yet to look for another suit to lead.

On the last hand, the bidders had pinpointed the location of the king of hearts, and that helped the defender choose his opening lead. This leads right up to the next subject, which is concerned with those opening leads which are dictated more by the bidding than by the holding in the suit led.

CHAPTER 9:
OPENING LEADS BASED
ON THE BIDDING

Choosing the suit to lead sometimes depends on your holding in the suit, sometimes on the bidding you have heard, but more often on a combination of the two. Let's look at some hands where the bidding itself is of prime importance.

There are times when the bidding indicates that you should make a lead in a suit in one of those categories which in the last section were labeled as "Dangerous Opening Leads". If the bidding strongly indicates that the suit holding such a combination of cards is the one to lead, then the lead should be made in spite of the fact that it otherwise would have been a dangerous lead. The one exception would be Number 6. If the bidding calls for the lead of a suit which is headed by the ace, and you are leading against a suit contract, take the opening lead I labeled Number 1 in preference to the one I labeled Number 6.

In other words, lead the ace itself; do not underlead it.

In the first example, the bidding stated that a diamond had to be led no matter what the leader's holding in the diamond suit was. It was played in the 1974 World Championship, in the match between North America and New Zealand.

N-S vul., dealer West.

```
                        NORTH
                        ♠ 6
                        ♡ 9 8 7 6 5
                        ◇ J 10 6 4
                        ♣ A K J
        WEST                            EAST
        ♠ Q 8 4 3                       ♠ J 10 9 2
        ♡ Q                             ♡ 10 3 2
        ◇ K 7                           ◇ A 3 2
        ♣ Q 9 8 7 5 2                   ♣ 10 4 3
                        SOUTH
                        ♠ A K 7 5
                        ♡ A K J 4
                        ◇ Q 9 8 5
                        ♣ 6
```

The bidding:

SOUTH	WEST	NORTH	EAST
Brightling	Goldman	Marston	Blumenthal
	Pass	Pass	Pass
1 ♡	Pass	4 ♡	Pass
4 ♠	Pass	5 ♣	Pass
5 ♡	Pass	Pass	Pass

Among a considerable number of expert players, once a forcing situation has been set up, and a suit agreed upon, they start cue bidding controls, searching for those elusive slams which can be made with only 24 or 25 HCPs, because there are first and second round controls in all the suits. Whether instituting that search was justified on this particular hand was doubtful. Marston, North, had already passed. He was not likely to hold just the cards which would bring in a slam, and the search had to be instituted at the high level of five. However, you will see that had North's clubs and diamonds been switched, the slam would have been a reasonable contract. The way it turned out, these cue bids told Bobby Goldman, for North America, just how to go about setting the final contract.

South indicated he had spades under control, and North indicated he had clubs under control. Each player indicated he did not have a slam holding in diamonds. The official record of the event says that Goldman led the king of diamonds without even looking around for applause, and that the defenders took the first three tricks, setting the contract.

On the next hand, with North America playing Italy in 1975 World Championship, both opening leaders found the killing lead of a king doubleton. One of the fairly modern devices, called a "splinter" bid, aided one of the opening leaders, and the other may have been guided to the lead by a pre-emptive opening bid. In the open room, Garozzo simply opened four spades, and that was the end of the bidding. In the closed room, the bidding was as shown below.

None vul., dealer South.

```
                    NORTH
                    ♠ K Q 2
                    ♡ 9
                    ◇ A K Q 4 2
                    ♣ Q J 8 4
    WEST                            EAST
    ♠ 4                             ♠ 8 7
    ♡ Q J 10 7 6 5                  ♡ A 4 2
    ◇ 10 8 6 5                      ◇ J 9 7 3
    ♣ K 2                           ♣ A 10 9 7
                    SOUTH
                    ♠ A J 10 9 6 5 3
                    ♡ K 8 3
                    ◇ None
                    ♣ 6 5 3
```

The bidding:

SOUTH	WEST	NORTH	EAST
Wolff	Pittala	Hamman	Franco
1 ♠	Pass	2 ◇	Pass
2 ♠	Pass	4 ♡	Pass
4 ♠	Pass	Pass	Pass

Bob Hamman's four-heart bid on the second round showed that he had good spade support and either a singleton or a void in hearts. The fact that Hamman bid diamonds, where Bobby Wolff was short, and that Hamman had a control in hearts, where Wolff also had a control in hearts, did not fascinate Wolff at all, and he simply rebid four spades. Apparently the bidding did fascinate Pittala, West for Italy. With Hamman short in hearts, there was little hope for tricks in that suit. Hamman had indicated some interest in a slam by making his splinter bid of four hearts. As he had bid diamonds, he probably had considerable strength in that suit. The lead of singleton trumps doesn't usually get you anywhere, so what was left? It sounded from the bidding like a club lead was called for. That is what Pittala led, and when Franco indicated he liked the suit, Pittala continued it. Franco returned the highest club he could to let Pittala get in his trump and at the same time to ask him to lead back a heart. Pittala obliged, and Franco tried one more club, but, of course, there was no way Pittala could overtrump Wolff, as he didn't have any trumps left at all. Nonetheless, the defenders had taken the first four tricks and the hand had gone set.

Billy Eisenberg saved the day in the open room by making the same lead against the opening bid of four spades by Benito Garozzo. Some leading players claim that the best action to take against the big pre-emptive bid is to cash your aces if you have them, otherwise to lead the highest card you have in your hand.

The successful opening leader considers not only his own 13 cards, but he also gives a lot of thought to the other 39. It is always a help to him if his opponents have done a lot of bidding to describe the strength and distribution of their 26 cards. On the next hand, one pair had told very little about their hands in their bidding process, while the other had described theirs in considerable detail.

The hand is from the 1969 World Championship, with North America playing against Nationalist China.

E-W vul., dealer East.

NORTH
- ♠ J 6
- ♡ K 8
- ◇ A 10 6 4 3
- ♣ K 10 7 5

WEST
- ♠ K 10 8 3
- ♡ 10 6 4
- ◇ K J 8 2
- ♣ 8 4

EAST
- ♠ A Q 9 4 2
- ♡ J 7 5 2
- ◇ Q 9
- ♣ 9 2

SOUTH
- ♠ 7 5
- ♡ A Q 9 3
- ◇ 7 5
- ♣ A Q J 6 3

The bidding:

CLOSED ROOM

SOUTH	WEST	NORTH	EAST
C. S. Shen	Goldman	F. Huang	Eisenberg
			Pass
2 ♣	Pass	2 ◇	Pass
2 ♡	Pass	4 ♣	Pass
5 ♣	Pass	Pass	Pass

OPEN ROOM

Kantar	Rai	Hamman	P. Huang
			Pass
1 ♣	Pass	1 ◇	Pass
1 ♡	Pass	3 ♣	Pass
3 ♡	Pass	4 ◇	Pass
5 ♣	Pass	Pass	Pass

The Chinese players were playing the Precision Club System. In the closed room, the opening bid of two clubs showed a five-card club suit with 11 to 15 HCPs. The two-diamond bid by F. Huang, North, showed nothing whatsoever about diamonds, but said he had 11 or more points and asked the opening bidder to describe his hand further. C. S. Shen, South, showed his four-card heart suit. North bid four clubs and South bid five clubs. Bobby Goldman, on lead, knew that declarer had four hearts in his hand, but he had no information about the spade or diamond suits in view of the artificial nature of Huang's two-diamond response. Against five clubs he decided to attack, and chose the suit where he had the king and the jack, instead of the one where he had the king and ten. Shen won the diamond opening lead with dummy's ace and pulled trumps in two rounds. He then cashed three rounds of hearts and discarded one of dummy's spades. He conceded a diamond trick and a spade trick, and claimed eleven tricks.

In the open room, Eddie Kantar and Bob Hamman, for North America, gave each other a lot of information about their hands, and Tai, for China, received the same information. The opening club bid and diamond response were both natural, as was the heart rebid. Once Hamman established the trump suit by his jump to three clubs, the three-heart bid verified a control in that suit and left room for 3NT, if Hamman wished to bid it. Without a spade stopper, Hamman did not wish to try notrump, and verified his holding of the ace of diamonds in case that information should prove valuable. It was valuable to Tai. He knew that the opponents had hearts, diamonds, and clubs stopped, and he also knew they did not have spades. He led the three of spades and the defenders took the first two tricks in that suit. They always had a diamond coming to set the contract one trick.

Now look at the beautiful way Billy Eisenberg heard the Italian players describe their hands to each other in the 1976 World Championship.

N-S vul., dealer South.

NORTH
- ♠ A K Q 9 3
- ♡ A Q
- ◇ A 5
- ♣ 10 5 4 2

WEST
- ♠ 10 7 2
- ♡ K 9 4 3
- ◇ K 10 7
- ♣ A 6 3

EAST
- ♠ J 8 6 5 4
- ♡ J 8
- ◇ 6 3
- ♣ K 9 8 7

SOUTH
- ♠ None
- ♡ 10 7 6 5 2
- ◇ Q J 9 8 4 2
- ♣ Q J

The bidding:

SOUTH	WEST	NORTH	EAST
Vivaldi	Eisenberg	Pittala	Hamilton
Pass	Pass	1 ♣	Pass
1 ◇	Pass	1 ♠	Pass
2 ◇	Pass	2 NT	Pass
3 ♡	Pass	3 ♠	Pass
4 ◇	Pass	5 ◇	Pass
Pass	Pass		

The Italians were playing what they call the "Precision Ultra" System. The opening bid by Pittala was artificial, and said only that he had 16 or more HCPs. In their system, they use step responses. The one-diamond response showed nothing about the diamond suit, but only said that he had very few high card points. From there on, the bidding was natural for a few rounds, with each of the players showing his suit or suits. In the process, Pittala said that he had a spade suit and a big hand, while Vivaldi, South, said that he had diamonds and hearts, a lot of distribution, few high cards, and no control of the club suit. Well, if the Italians hold spades and hearts and diamonds, it sounds like the Americans ought to start leading clubs. That's exactly what Billy Eisenberg did with the West hand. He led the ace of clubs. The defenders took the first two tricks with the ace and king of clubs. Chances that Vivaldi would get home with eleven tricks had been reduced from slight to zero, as Eisenberg always had a diamond trick coming to him.

When the hand was replayed with the United States holding the North and South hands, the Americans did not get involved in the problem of trying to unravel the hand for eleven tricks in diamonds. In their room, West actually opened the bidding. Ira Rubin held the North hand. Ira believes that with certain strong hands you make a simple overcall. He bid one spade. That is probably the strongest simple overcall made in some time, but it had the virtue of bringing the Americans a plus score. With his misfit and his weak hand, Paul Soloway was not tempted to find any bid except "Pass", and Rubin managed to take eight tricks for a score of 110.

You may have trouble believing the next hand, but it is recorded in the history books as having been played in the Italy vs. France match in the World Championship of 1972.

Both vul., dealer North.

```
                    NORTH
                    ♠ J 4
                    ♡ A K Q 7 6 5 2
                    ◇ A
                    ♣ J 6 3
        WEST                      EAST
        ♠ 10 9 5 2                ♠ None
        ♡ 9 4                     ♡ J 3
        ◇ Q J 10 3 2              ◇ K 9 8 7 6 5 4
        ♣ 10 5                    ♣ A K Q 9
                    SOUTH
                    ♠ A K Q 8 7 6 3
                    ♡ 10 8
                    ◇ None
                    ♣ 8 7 4 2
```

The bidding:

OPEN ROOM

SOUTH	WEST	NORTH	EAST
Delmouly	Belladonna	Bourchtoff	Avarelli
		2 ♣	2 ◇
2 ♠	Pass	3 ♡	Pass
3 ♠	Pass	4 ◇	Pass
5 ◇	Pass	5 ♡	Pass
5 ♠	Pass	6 ♠	Pass
Pass	Pass		

CLOSED ROOM

D'Alelio	Chemla	Pabis Ticci	Leclery
		1 ♣	1 ◇
1 ♠	2 ◇	2 ♡	4 ◇
5 ◇	Pass	5 ♡	Pass
6 ♠	Pass	Pass	Pass

I don't want to disillusion you about the world's greatest bridge players, but I must tell the truth. The truth is that two of the world's great pairs got into a contract of six spades on these North-South hands. This only goes to show that world championship players are human after all.

Some explanation of the bidding may be in order. Bourchtoff and Delmouly, of France, state that their general approach to bidding is "Natural Bidding". Maybe so, but the opening bid of two clubs by North was artificial and forcing for one round. The two-spade response by South showed that he held the ace of one of the major suits. From here on they went into their act. The four-diamond bid by North showed that he had a diamond control, and the five-diamond bid by South said that he also had a diamond control. They forgot to say anything about club controls, and arrived at a six-spade contract.

In the closed room, the Italians announced that they were playing a Modified Precision Club System. An opening bid of one club showed 16 or more HCPs. Pabis Ticci evaluated his hand to be worth a normal 16 HCP hand because of his playing strength. The one-spade response showed eight or more HCPs and a five-card or longer suit. On their way to the spade slam, only one of the players in the closed room showed that he had diamonds under control.

In the open room, Belladonna was convinced. When both of his opponents told him they had diamonds under control he decided to believe them, but as they had been so anxious to bid hearts and spades, he decided to test the club situation. The test was successful, the defenders took the first three tricks.

Where the French were defending the hand, Chemla seemed not to be convinced. Maybe two people have to say they have control of diamonds to be completely convincing, but anyway Chemla led the queen of diamonds. Needless to say, with hearts breaking 2-2, that gave the declarer 15 tricks if he needed them.

The next hand shows how bidding styles, and therefore opening leads, can affect the final results of a deal.

Both vul., dealer South.

```
                        NORTH
                        ♠ K Q 8 4
                        ♡ 2
                        ◊ 10 8 7
                        ♣ A K Q 10 9
        WEST                            EAST
        ♠ 10 7 6 5                      ♠ 9 3
        ♡ A K 3                         ♡ Q J 7 5 4
        ◊ Q J 6 5                       ◊ 4 3
        ♣ 3 2                           ♣ J 8 5 4
                        SOUTH
                        ♠ A J 2
                        ♡ 10 9 8 6
                        ◊ A K 9 2
                        ♣ 7 6
```

The bidding:

SOUTH	WEST	NORTH	EAST
Cabanne	Goethe	Scanavino	Morath
1 ◇	Pass	2 ♣	Pass
2 NT	Pass	3 ♠	Pass
3 NT	Pass	Pass	Pass

OPEN ROOM

Flodquist	Attaguile	Sundelin	Santamarina
1 ♡	Pass	2 ♣	Pass
2 NT	Pass	3 ♠	Pass
3 NT	Pass	Pass	Pass

This deal is from the Sweden vs. Argentina match in the 1977 World Championship.

In the closed room, North had described a black-suit hand. Goethe, West for Sweden, had heard his opponents bid three suits, so he decided to lead the one they had not bid. He led the king of hearts, and the defense promptly took the first five tricks.

The Swedish pair, playing in the open room, were playing that almost any four-card major suit is biddable for an opening bid. Flodquist started the bidding with one heart. One result was that diamonds were never bid. Another was that Attaguile, West, was convinced that South held a stopper in hearts, and, quite naturally, he led a small diamond. That enabled the North-South pair to take the first ten tricks, and if clubs had not broken so badly, they would have taken twelve.

All of which goes to show that all bidding methods have both their good points and their bad points.

There are times when the evidence from the bidding does not give so clearcut a message. It is then that the opening leader has more of a problem in determining the correct lead. In the next deal, the evidence was sufficiently strong to enable the opening leader to pick out the winning lead in one room, while in the other room there was insufficient evidence. Once again, this hand demonstrates how the bidding procedure influences the defense. The hand is from the 1970 World Championship, with

North America playing against Nationalist China.

E-W vul., dealer South.

```
                        NORTH
                        ♠ A 10 6 3 2
                        ♡ 6 2
                        ◇ Q J 5 4 2
                        ♣ 5
        WEST                            EAST
        ♠ J 9                           ♠ Q 8 7 5
        ♡ A Q 5 4                       ♡ 10 9 8 3
        ◇ A 10 7 6                      ◇ 3
        ♣ 10 9 2                        ♣ K J 8 3
                        SOUTH
                        ♠ K 4
                        ♡ K J 7
                        ◇ K 9 8
                        ♣ A Q 7 6 4
```

The bidding:

CLOSED ROOM

SOUTH	WEST	NORTH	EAST
Hsaio	Wolff	Cheng	Jacoby
1 ♣	Pass	1 ♠	Pass
2 ♣	Pass	2 ◇	Pass
2 NT	Pass	3 ◇	Pass
3 NT	Pass	Pass	Pass

OPEN ROOM

Lawrence	Tai	Hamman	Huang
1 NT	Pass	2 ♡	Pass
2 ♠	Pass	3 ◇	Pass
3 NT	Pass	Pass	Pass

In the closed room, it was the job of Bobby Wolff, West, to pick out the best opening lead. On the face of it, it looks like leading any of the four suits would be a mistake. Let's do what Bobby had to do, and, by a process of elimination, decide just which of the four suits stands the best chance to succeed.

First, let's see what message was conveyed by the bidding. The one-club opening bid by Hsaio was the Precision Club bid and said that Hsaio held 16 or more HCPs, but said nothing about the distribution of his hand. The one-spade response by Cheng showed five or more spades and eight or more HCPs. He evaluated his hand to be worth a normal eight-count because of his two five-card suits and because all his strength was concentrated in his long suits. The two-club bid by Hsaio showed a club suit, and the two-diamond bid by Cheng showed a diamond suit. Two notrump by South showed a balanced hand without four hearts or three-card spade support. Three diamonds by Cheng showed that in addition to a five-card spade suit, he had a five-card diamond suit. The 3NT by Hsaio completed the bidding, and now it was up to Wolff to choose a lead.

Let's start with clubs. South had indicated a genuine club suit, and it is not often correct to lead right into his suit. How about diamonds? North had indicated a five-card or longer diamond suit, and Wolff's holding in that suit certainly is not the sort to encourage the lead of the suit bid to your left. How about hearts? Leading small from four to the ace-queen is not the way to garner a lot of tricks against notrump, and in this case, South's repeated notrump bids suggested that he had a strong heart holding. How about spades? Leading the jack-doubleton is not a lead you go out of your way to make. But let's think a little more about that spade suit. North's bid had showed five, and South's failure to support the suit indicated he had fewer than three. His 2NT bid indicated that his hand was square, so probably he held two spades. This meant that Jacoby had four spades. They at least were positioned behind the five-card spade suit. Have you or I, by process of elimination, come to the conclusion that the lead of the jack of spades stands the best chance, in spite of the fact it is not a holding we like to lead from? Wolff led the jack of spades.

South won with the king and led a diamond toward the dummy. Wolff ducked and dummy's jack won the trick. Declarer then led a diamond back towards his king, and Wolff won the ace as Jacoby discarded a heart. Wolff returned the nine of spades. Declarer won dummy's ace and took a winning club finesse. Next, he laid down the ace of clubs. He had taken five of the first six tricks, but he was just about to run out of good leads. He was also just about to quit taking tricks. For lack of anything better to do, he led a small club. Jacoby won the jack. He led back the ten of hearts, which declarer covered with the jack, and Wolff won the queen. Wolff's ten of diamonds smothered South's nine as dummy won the jack. Declarer led a heart to his king. Wolff won the ace. Everybody had three cards left. Jacoby had the good queen of spades, the good ten of hearts, and the good king of clubs. Wolff wasn't about to let Jacoby take all three of those tricks. He cashed the good seven of diamonds and Jacoby had to discard one of his high cards. His partner had no clubs or spades left, so Jacoby had to hold onto the ten of hearts to gain the lead to cash his two good tricks. He threw away his good queen of spades and took the last two tricks with the high heart and high club. Declarer had managed to take two tricks in spades, two in diamonds, and two in clubs, for a total of six tricks. The defenders had taken more tricks than he had.

There was a different story as far as the bidding was concerned in the open room. Mike Lawrence's opening bid of 1NT showed 15 to 18 HCPS and a balanced hand. Bob Hammond's two-heart bid, in the North seat, guaranteed five or more spades and asked Lawrence to bid two spades. Lawrence duly bid two spades. Hammond's three-diamond bid showed that he also had a diamond suit and suggested to Lawrence that, unless he could take care of the other two suits, he might be wise to play the hand in one of North's two suits. Lawrence bid 3NT. This sequence did not disclose the long club suit.

Now let's put ourselves in the position of M. F. Tai and see what information he had to go on in choosing his opening lead. He knew that North had a spade suit and a diamond suit, and that in spite of that, Lawrence preferred to play notrump. It seemed that he had to guess whether to lead hearts or clubs. The heart lead was unappetizing, and having no idea whether Lawrence had length in clubs or not, he chose the ten of clubs. That got the defenders off to a bad start from which they never recovered. Mike Lawrence took full advantage of every bobble they made. East played his king, and Lawrence won the ace. He also attacked diamonds by leading towards the dummy. The queen was permitted to win, and he returned a diamond to his king and West's ace. Tai had second thoughts about leading hearts, and led the four. Lawrence won with the jack, and led his last diamond. Tai covered and dummy's jack won. Lawrence led a fourth diamond, won by West with the seven. East had been having trouble discarding, and had let go a club. Tai led the nine of clubs, and Lawrence let it hold the trick. He won the club continuation, and now had nine tricks, consisting of two spades, one heart, three diamonds, and three clubs. He had taken three more tricks than his Chinese counterpart in the closed room.

On the next deal, the reason given for choosing the killing opening lead is even more subtle. To make matters worse, they tell me that it really is my fault.

None vul., dealer South.

```
                    NORTH
                    ♠ None
                    ♡ A J 8 5 2
                    ◊ K 10 8 4
                    ♣ K 7 6 3
        WEST                        EAST
        ♠ Q 8 6 2                   ♠ 9 7 5 4 3
        ♡ 10 9 7                    ♡ K Q 4
        ◊ Q J 7 5 2                 ◊ A 6 3
        ♣ J                         ♣ 8 2
                    SOUTH
                    ♠ A K J 10
                    ♡ 6 3
                    ◊ 9
                    ♣ A Q 10 9 5 4
```

The bidding:

CLOSED ROOM

SOUTH	WEST	NORTH	EAST
Chemla	Charney	Leclery	Crissy
1 ♣	Pass	1 ♡	Pass
1 ♠	Pass	3 ♣	Pass
4 NT	Pass	6 ♣	Pass
Pass	Pass		

OPEN ROOM

Kehela	Delmouly	Murray	Bourchtoff
1 ♣	Pass	1 ♡	Pass
1 ♠	Pass	2 ♢	Pass
3 ♣	Pass	5 ♣	Pass
6 ♣	Pass	Pass	Pass

This hand is from the 1972 World Championship, with Canada playing France. In the closed room, the Canadian West, Gerry Charney, led the ten of hearts. Paul Chemla, the French South, didn't have a chance. There was no way to get rid of that losing heart, and he always had to lose to the ace of diamonds. The official record of the World Championship says that Charney chose the heart lead rather than the more normal-looking queen of diamonds because the 4NT bid by Chemla in this sequence had suggested that he had a diamond control. On this inference, he chose to lead through dummy's suit, which had not been supported. It worked like a charm.

In the open room, Sammy Kehela and Eric Murray, of Canada, reached six clubs without the benefit of the Blackwood Convention, and Claude Delmouly, from France, had no such inference that South had a diamond control. He led the queen of diamonds. Sammy Kehela let it hold the trick. West shifted to a trump, but Kehela won dummy's king, trumped a diamond, drew the outstanding trumps, and led the ace and king of spades. Next he ruffed a spade in dummy and ruffed another diamond in his hand. This felled the ace from the East hand, and the king of diamonds was now established for a heart discard.

Why am I supposed to be the guilty party in this transaction?

It seems that had I never originated that Blackwood Convention, Charney, in the closed room, would never have had the inference that South had a diamond control. In that case, he, too, would have chosen to open the queen of diamonds.

However, let's don't be too harsh on the Blackwood Convention. It would have served the Chinese players well on the next hand. This deal is from the World Championship of 1977, with the Chinese playing North America.

N-S vul., dealer East.

```
                    NORTH
                    ♠ K Q 10 4 3
                    ♡ Q 2
                    ◇ A Q 7
                    ♣ J 5 4
     WEST                           EAST
     ♠ 8 6                          ♠ J 7 2
     ♡ J 8 7 6 5                    ♡ A 9 4 3
     ◇ K 10 9 4 3                   ◇ 8 5 2
     ♣ 6                            ♣ 10 8 3
                    SOUTH
                    ♠ A 9 5
                    ♡ K 10
                    ◇ J 6
                    ♣ A K Q 9 7 2
```

The bidding:

CLOSED ROOM

SOUTH Hsiao	WEST Soloway	NORTH Cheng	EAST Swanson
			Pass
1 ♣	Pass	1 ♠	Pass
2 ♠	Pass	3 ♦	Pass
4 ♦	Pass	5 ♦	Pass
5 NT	Pass	6 ♦	Pass
6 NT	Pass	7 NT	Double
Pass	Pass	Pass	

OPEN ROOM

Kantar	Lin	Eisenberg	Tai
			Pass
1 ♣	Pass	1 ♠	Pass
3 ♣	Pass	3 ♦	Pass
3 NT	Pass	4 ♣	Pass
4 ♠	Pass	4 NT	Pass
5 ♣	Pass	Pass	Pass

The Chinese report that they were playing the Precision System with variations. Hsaio's one-club opening bid showed 16 or more HCPs. Cheng's one-spade response showed 8 or more HCPs and a five-card or longer spade suit. South's two-spade rebid asked North about the quality of his spade suit. The three-diamond bid told him it was five cards long and had two of the top three honors. The four-diamond rebid by South was an asking bid, asking his partner how well he could control the diamond suit. The five-diamond bid showed the ace. From here on, you're on your own. I'm not quite sure just what the subsequent rounds of bidding meant. I do know that by the time Cheng bid five diamonds, it was too late to use the Blackwood Convention. Many players using the Precision System use the D.I. 4NT Convention. That means declarative-interrogative 4NT. The idea is that a 4NT bid is the Blackwood Convention only when used during the first two rounds of bidding or when used as a jump bid. Other 4NT bids simply ask their partners to show an undisclosed feature which might be helpful in deciding whether to bid slam or not.

Maybe they didn't declare enough, or maybe they didn't inquire about the right things. Whatever the reason, they got to 7NT missing an ace.

The thing we are interested in is the fact that Soloway decided that Paul Swanson's double asked him to lead a heart. The ACBL World Championship book reports it this way. The bidding had said that the Chinese had five solid spade tricks and the ace of diamonds. With only six known tricks, South had to have a solid running suit to justify his aggressive bidding. It was not diamonds, because he had inquired about the diamond suit. Was it hearts, or was it clubs? Neither opponent had bid hearts, and Soloway had five to the jack himself, so it just didn't seem likely that South had a solid heart suit. Presto—he had clubs. Therefore, the only ace not accounted for in the North and South hands must be the ace of hearts.

This took some careful thinking, but Paul Soloway led a heart and the defense took the first trick against the grand slam bid.

In the open room, the Americans were using Key-Card Blackwood, Roman style. Eddie Kantar's five-club response to Billy Eisenberg's 4NT bid stated that he had three controls. I see nothing about the results on this hand to justify any affection for that particular convention, as the Americans stopped at five clubs on a deal which has such good chances for a slam.

WHO HAS THE SHORTAGE?

Suppose you hold:

♠ A 4
♡ 6 2
♢ 7 3
♣ 9 8 6 5 4 3 2

and are on lead against a four-spade contract. You have one sure trick. Your partner easily could have as many as 13 HCPs. If they are well-placed, he might be able to get as many as three tricks out of them. On the other hand, he might take only one or two tricks. Should he hold a singleton club or a void in the suit, you probably can give him a ruff by simply leading a club. If he can't trump the first one, you should be in the lead very soon with the ace of trumps, and he will be able to trump the second. A ruff plus the two tricks he ought to be able to take should defeat the hand. What are the chances your partner will have a shortage—that is, either a singleton or a void—in clubs?

From what I have told you, they are not all that good. If the bidding has told you nothing significant about the hand, you have to go back to the so-called A-Priori odds, which say that when you hold a seven-card suit, your partner will hold a shortage in that suit 33.27% of the time. That is very close to one time out of three and is not very good odds. In addition to that, the declarer might also hold a shortage and might be able to over-ruff your partner.

But suppose the opponents have each told you that they don't have a shortage anywhere in their hands? Of course, they wouldn't deliberately tell you, but with many modern bidding devices, they can tell each other precisely that, and you can listen in. Let's look at a couple of these bidding devices which put out that nice information for anyone who cares to pay attention.

Suppose the bidding has gone:

SOUTH	NORTH
1 NT	2 ◊
2 ♡	3 NT
4 ♡	

Now let's say that our opponents were playing transfer bids. When South bid 1NT, he told you he did not have a shortage. The two-diamond bid by North transferred to hearts, and South dutifully bid two hearts. The 3NT bid by North said he did not have a shortage. If he had had a second suit, he would have bid it. North simply said he had enough HCPs to bid 3NT, but offered an alternative of four hearts in case South preferred that bid. South's four-heart bid stated his preference, even though he had no shortage.

Or, suppose the bidding has gone this way:

SOUTH	NORTH
1 ♠	2 NT
3 NT	4 ♠

The opponents are playing the Jacoby 2NT Convention. They are also playing splinter bids. North's 2NT bid said he had a hand strong enough to force to game with spades as trumps. It also suggested he did not have a singleton or void in any suit, for if he had that he would have used a splinter bid rather than the Jacoby 2NT bid. The 3NT rebid by South said that he had about 14 or 15 HCPs with no distributional feature. North's four-spade bid said that in spite of the fact that he had no singleton or void, he thought from his hand that four spades would be a better contract than 3NT. Again, neither opponent has a shortage and you are on opening lead with the hand as shown above, with seven clubs and the ace of trumps.

Now the odds your partner does have a club shortage have gone up to 61.97%. About two times out of three, you can get him a trump trick by simply leading clubs, and there is no chance the declarer can overruff him. Let me give you a little table which shows both the A-Priori chances your partner will have a singleton, and also the chances after you know that neither of your opponents has a shortage anywhere.

PROBABILITY OF SUIT SHORTNESS IN PARTNER'S HAND		
I	II	III
5	16.44%	22.68%
6	23.74%	37.43%
7	33.27%	61.97%

Column I shows the number of cards in your long suit. Column II shows the chances your partner has a shortage in your long suit before you know anything else about the hand. Column III shows the chances your partner has that shortage when you are persuaded that neither of your opponents has a shortage in his hand.

You should also be on the lookout for those situations where you have length in a side suit which has been bid by one opponent and supported by the other. A lead of that suit can be devastating when you have trump control, and at times may be effective when you do not. Here is a book example.

Both vul., dealer South.

```
                          NORTH
                          ♠ Q 5
                          ♡ J 10 3
                          ◇ K Q 6
                          ♣ K 10 9 7 3
            WEST                          EAST
            ♠ 10 9 7 6 3                  ♠ J 8 2
            ♡ K 4                         ♡ 8 6 5
            ◇ 10 7 5                      ◇ A J 9 4 3
            ♣ A 8 4                       ♣ 6 2
                          SOUTH
                          ♠ A K 4
                          ♡ A Q 9 7 2
                          ◇ 8 2
                          ♣ Q J 5
```

The bidding:

SOUTH	WEST	NORTH	EAST
1 ♡	Pass	2 ♣	Pass
3 ♣	Pass	3 ♡	Pass
4 ♡	Pass	Pass	Pass

The argument is that the two-club response by North, plus the raise by South, indicate to West that the opponents have at least eight clubs. Hence, East has at most two clubs. West expects to gain the lead with the trump king before declarer can extract trumps. With only seven HCPs in his hand, West rather expects his partner will be able to take at least one trick with high cards. If he can give his partner a club ruff, the hand will be set.

Therefore, West leads the ace and a club. Shortly he will regain the lead in trumps and lead a third club. East will win a trick with the small trump, and cash the ace of diamonds to complete the set.

This line of reasoning is quite sound, but let's not have implicit faith in the opening club lead. I have seen North players make a two-club response with only a four-card suit. Of course, even then it would be possible for South to have four. I think the odds greatly favor the opening club lead.

The hands we use to illustrate points to our pupils are effective in that they illustrate their point clearly and usually will be uncomplicated by other problems. The hands we find in real life are not often as clear as the ones we use in our constructions. Here is a hand to illustrate my point. It was played in the play-off to determine the American team to compete for the 1976 World Championship.

E-W vul., dealer West.

```
                    NORTH
                    ♠ 10 8 7
                    ♡ K Q 6 3
                    ◇ 6
                    ♣ A K Q 5 4
    WEST                            EAST
    ♠ 4 3                           ♠ A K 6
    ♡ A 7 5                         ♡ 10 9 8 4 2
    ◇ K Q 10 3                      ◇ 9 8 7 4
    ♣ 10 9 8 2                      ♣ 7
                    SOUTH
                    ♠ Q J 9 5 2
                    ♡ J
                    ◇ A J 5 2
                    ♣ J 6 3
```

The bidding:

TABLE ONE

SOUTH	WEST	NORTH	EAST
	Von Der		
Paulsen	Porten	Ross	Stansby
	Pass	1 ♡	Pass
1 ♠	Pass	2 ♣	Pass
Pass	2 ◊	2 ♠	3 ◊
4 ♠	Pass	Pass	Double
Pass	Pass	Pass	

TABLE TWO

Pender	Eisenberg	Baze	Hamilton
	Pass	2 ♣	Pass
2 ♠	Pass	4 ♠	Pass
Pass	Pass		

At Table One, North and South were using the Canape method, where the second suit bid is longer than the first-bid suit. When Hugh Ross rebid two clubs, he implied that his club suit was probably longer than his heart suit. Erik Paulsen passed two clubs, indicating he was prepared to play in that suit and also stating that, at this point, he thought he had no hopes for making game. After Von der Porten reopened with his two-diamond bid, Ross supported spades. Paulsen now pretty well knew Ross had five clubs, four hearts, three spades, and one diamond. He now reconsidered the matter of getting to game and decided that, with his partner holding that distribution, his chances were pretty good.

Having disturbed opponents who wanted to play in two clubs and giving them a chance to get to four spades, Ron Von der Porten felt that he had better find the killing opening lead. He found it.

The two-club bid by North showed five or more clubs. South's pass indicated he was satisfied with that suit. Simple addition showed that East probably held no more than one club. Von der Porten had only nine HCPs. Therefore, it sounded as though Stansby had somewhere in the neighborhood of seven HCPs. Von der Porten planned to get in with his ace of hearts to give his partner a club ruff. He led a club and you can see what happened. The defenders got the ace and king of trumps, the ace of hearts, and Stansby took a trick with his six of spades. Stansby had the two top spades, so even if he tried to get his partner in by leading diamonds, he would still regain the lead in trumps and have time to lead a heart to get his ruff.

At Table Two, the bidding was not nearly so revealing. Grant Baze and Peter Pender used an opening two-club bid to show a good five-card or longer club suit, which might or might not be accompanied by a four-card major suit. Pender bid two spades, showing a five-card or longer suit and a mild interest in game. Baze put the contract in four spades. Not having all of the information that Von der Porten had, Billy Eisenberg made the normal lead of a king of diamonds. Pender won with the ace and led the jack of hearts. That took the entry out of the West hand before East had played his only club, and the defense never had a second chance. Pender lost only two trump tricks and one heart trick.

There are times when the bidding by expert opponents might convince you that you have no tricks in aces and kings. At these times, you may decide that your only chance to get a trick is to give your partner a ruff. That is the line of reasoning that Boris Shapiro used on the next hand.

Both vul., dealer East.

NORTH
- ♠ A 10 3
- ♡ 2
- ♢ K 3
- ♣ K Q J 9 8 6 5

WEST
- ♠ K 9 8 6 5 4 2
- ♡ K Q 5
- ♢ 5 4
- ♣ 2

EAST
- ♠ None
- ♡ 10 9 8 6 4 3
- ♢ 10 9 8
- ♣ 10 7 4 3

SOUTH
- ♠ Q J 7
- ♡ A J 7
- ♢ A Q J 7 6 2
- ♣ A

The bidding:

OPEN ROOM

SOUTH	WEST	NORTH	EAST
Belladonna	Shapiro	Avarelli	Reese
			Pass
1 ♢	1 ♠	3 ♣	Pass
4 ♢	Pass	4 NT	Pass
5 NT	Pass	6 ♢	Pass
7 ♢	Pass	Pass	Pass

CLOSED ROOM

Flint	Garozzo	Gray	Forquet
			Pass
2 NT	Pass	4 ♣	Pass
4 NT	Pass	7 NT	Pass
Pass	Pass		

The hand was played in the 1964 World Championship, the Italians against Great Britain.

The three-club response by Avarelli, in the open room,

showed at least a five-card suit and a good hand. The jump to four diamonds, by Belladonna, said that he also had a good suit plus a good hand. The 4NT bid by Avarelli was more of that declarative-interrogative business, and did not specifically ask for aces. The 5NT bid by Belladonna showed a maximum for the holding he had already shown. So the Italians ended up in seven diamonds.

Against a grand slam, finding one trick on defense is adequate. The bidding and the quality of the opposition convinced Shapiro that his side was not going to take any tricks with aces and kings. The only chance was to give his partner a ruff. For that to work, even a singleton in his partner's hand would not be enough. Reese had to be void in spades. The chances for that were only about 7%, but Shapiro figured that was the best chance he had. He led a spade, Reese trumped it, and the bidding sequence by the Italians turned out to be disastrous. Critics have speculated as to the reason the Italians failed to get to 7NT instead of seven diamonds. It is possible that Avarelli feared that his partner was void in clubs instead of having the ace. In that event, it might be necessary to ruff out the ace of clubs.

In the closed room, the British had an easier time of it. In four bids, they reached the winning contract which the Italians had been unable to find with seven bids. Jeremy Flint's opening 2NT bid may not be right out of the textbooks, but it was effective. In this sequence, most leading players use the Gerber Convention, rather than the Blackwood Convention. Harrison-Gray's four-club bid was the old-fashioned Gerber Convention asking Flint how many aces he had. When Flint showed three aces, Gray had no doubt who held the ace of clubs, and went straight to 7NT. With any kind of a decent break in the minor suits, Flint was looking at fifteen tricks when the dummy came down.

On the next hand, the opening lead of a long suit found partner with a void... and gained five tricks! This time the lead was from a nine-card suit. The chances partner would be void were only about one in six, but if that is the best chance you have, take it. The hand was played in the Women's series of the 1968 Olympiad Games, the United States against Canada. The heroine of the hand is Hermine Baron.

None vul., dealer North.

NORTH
- ♠ 5 3
- ♡ A 6
- ◇ K J 10 7
- ♣ Q 9 6 3 2

WEST
- ♠ 10 9
- ♡ Q J 10 8 7 5 4 3 2
- ◇ 5 4
- ♣ None

EAST
- ♠ 8 6 2
- ♡ None
- ◇ 9 8 6 3 2
- ♣ K J 10 7 4

SOUTH
- ♠ A K Q J 7 4
- ♡ K 9
- ◇ A Q
- ♣ A 8 5

The bidding:

CLOSED ROOM

SOUTH	WEST	NORTH	EAST
Mrs. Truscott	Mrs. Begin	Mrs. Hawes	Mrs. Paul
		Pass	Pass
2 ♣	5 ♡	6 ♡	Pass
7 ♠	Pass	Pass	Pass

OPEN ROOM

Mrs. Mark	Mrs. Baron	Mrs. O'Brien	Mrs. Walsh
		Pass	Pass
2 ♣	6 ♡	Pass	Pass
6 ♠	Pass	Pass	Pass

In the closed room, Mrs. Begin, for Canada, led the five of diamonds against the seven-spade contract by Mrs. Truscott, for the U.S.A. There were thirteen tricks without a finesse. In the open room, Mrs. Baron, for the U.S., made it tougher on the Canadian players by going all the way to six hearts for her first bid, and the Canadians got only to six spades. Mrs. Baron led a heart. She chose to lead the two to suggest the club return. Mrs. Walsh trumped with her six of spades, planning to show that she had three trumps, and returned a small club. Mrs. Mark still could take twelve tricks if she could win the ace of clubs, so she played her ace. Mrs. Baron trumped and led another heart for Mrs. Walsh to trump. Mrs. Walsh then cashed her king of clubs and led a third club, which Mrs. Baron trumped. Finally, they had to let declarer get the lead, and after the defenders took the first five tricks, the declarer took the remaining eight.

Of course, you and I would have bid 7NT with the North-South hands. Wouldn't we? Well, maybe.

CHAPTER 10:
OPENING LEADS AGAINST SLAM CONTRACTS

The subject of opening leads against slam contracts is worthy of a section all its own. The approach will differ from that used against low-level contracts. Against a grand slam contract, one trick is all you need. Against a small slam contract, two tricks will make the difference between success and failure. If you already have one trick in your hand, all that's necessary is to build up an additional trick, while when defending against a lower-level contract, you obviously must look for opening leads likely to bring in a larger number of tricks.

You will find that most of the time, the experts seek passive leads when defending against a small slam at notrump, or when defending against any grand slam contract, whether it be at notrump or in a suit. Usually, when your opponents are in a 6NT, your side will have about eight or nine HCPs. That reduces the likelihood that your partner is going to be able to contribute any queen to go with a king of yours, or any king to go with a queen of yours. Your best bet is to seek a lead that will give nothing up, and let declarer break those suits where you have tenaces.

This is especially true when you happen to hold around eight or nine HCPs in your own hand. Take a look at this hand from the 1969 World Championship, with North America playing against Nationalist China.

None vul., dealer South.

NORTH
♠ 9 7 6 4
♡ 9
◊ 8 6 5 2
♣ A K J 10

WEST
♠ Q 10
♡ Q 10 7 6 5 2
◊ K J 9
♣ 3 2

EAST
♠ 8 5 3 2
♡ J 8
◊ 10 4 3
♣ 8 7 6 4

SOUTH
♠ A K J
♡ A K 4 3
◊ A Q 7
♣ Q 9 5

The bidding:

SOUTH	WEST	NORTH	EAST
C. S. Shen	Goldman	F. Huang	Eisenberg
2 NT	Pass	3 ♣	Pass
3 ♡	Pass	4 NT	Pass
5 ♠	Pass	6 NT	Pass
Pass	Pass		

Bobby Goldman, West, led a club. This is the lead most experts would choose against 6NT, with the bidding which the Chinese used to get there. A lead of any of the other three suits well might give up a trick. Shen went up with the dummy's king of clubs and finessed the spade. The defenders had their book when Goldman won with the queen. He returned a spade. Shen tried the diamond finesse, with no better luck. The defenders now had beaten the contract. Shen cashed his winners. He discarded his two losing hearts on the nine of spades and long club in the dummy. He still had to lose a diamond trick and ended up down two.

It just happened that, had Goldman led a heart, he would not have given up anything, but had he led a spade, Shen obviously would have taken eleven tricks instead of ten. Had he led a diamond, Shen could have taken twelve tricks. With two diamond tricks in the bag, he could lay down the ace and king of spades and, when the ten and queen fell out from West, he would have four spade tricks. These four spade tricks with two heart tricks, two diamond tricks, and four club tricks, make a total of twelve. Did I hear someone say that declarer would not be likely to lay down the ace and king of spades? You had better think that one over again.

In the other room, Eddie Kantar was playing South for North America. He and Bob Hamman had stopped at 3NT. Kantar did get an opening diamond lead. Actually, the lead was the king of diamonds, but the effect would be the same no matter which diamond was led. Declarer now had two diamond tricks. Kantar did, in fact, play the ace and king of spades and dropped the ten and queen from West. So he took twelve tricks against the diamond lead.

If you are on lead against a slam and hold a king-queen combination and a probable side entry, of course you should lead the top of your sequence. See how Norman Kay got into trouble back in 1961, in a World Championship match against Argentina.

Both vul., dealer East.

```
                    NORTH
                    ♠ Q 7 5
                    ♡ J 2
                    ◇ A K Q J 5
                    ♣ A Q 10
        WEST                        EAST
        ♠ K 9 2                     ♠ 3
        ♡ K Q 8 7                   ♡ 10 6 5 4 3
        ◇ 8 3 2                     ◇ 9 7 4
        ♣ 8 6 5                     ♣ 7 4 3 2
                    SOUTH
                    ♠ A J 10 8 6 4
                    ♡ A 9
                    ◇ 10 6
                    ♣ K J 9
```

The bidding:

SOUTH	WEST	NORTH	EAST
Silidor	Dibar	Kay	Bosco
			Pass
1 ♠	Pass	3 ◊	Pass
3 ♡	Pass	3 ♠	Pass
4 NT	Pass	5 ♡	Pass
5 NT	Pass	6 ◊	Pass
6 ♠	Pass	6 NT	Pass
Pass	Pass		

Norman Kay's correction from six spades to 6NT was influenced by Sidney Silidor's first rebid of three hearts. It did not turn out well.

Dibar had eight HCPs and couldn't count on his partner for much. However, that king of spades looked like it was probably an entry, and the king of hearts would establish a trick immediately. He led the king of hearts.

Silidor won the ace, and cashed five diamonds and three clubs, ending in the dummy. Finally, he led the queen of spades for a finesse. Dibar won that with his king and the rest of the tricks belonged to the defenders with their good hearts. The contract was down three tricks.

When the Argentine players had the North-South hands, they played six spades. Peter Leventritt, playing West for the U.S., also led the king of hearts. Ricardo Calvente, the Argentine declarer, won the ace of hearts and laid down the ace of spades. He then took three diamond tricks, discarding the nine of hearts from his hand. He now conceded a trick to the king of trumps and claimed twelve tricks.

The theory of leads against slams further states that an attacking lead is often best against a small slam in a suit contract. The world's leading players seem to follow that principle, with two exceptions. They will lead from unsupported kings or queens and from tenaces which are not headed with an ace, except when their holding is in a suit bid by one of the opponents, or when the opening leader himself holds practically all of the high cards that the bidding indicates are held by his partnership. More often than not, when the opponents have bid a small slam in a suit, the defenders between them will hold ten or eleven HCPs, and it is not at all unusual to see them holding thirteen or fourteen. The suit small slams are often based on tricks by ruffing and on letting long suits take tricks. If you have a king or queen which needs to be promoted into a winning trick, you will often find you need to do so before the declarer can get one of his long suits established on which he can discard his losers in your suit. To show you that this is not exactly a new idea, the next deal is from the 1952 European Championships.

Both vul., dealer South.

NORTH
♠ 10 9 7 3 2
♡ 7
♢ K Q J 8
♣ K 10 6

WEST
♠ K 5 4
♡ 10 9 4 3
♢ 6 4
♣ Q 9 3 2

EAST
♠ A J 6
♡ 8 6
♢ 10 9 7 5 2
♣ 7 5 4

SOUTH
♠ Q 8
♡ A K Q J 5 2
♢ A 3
♣ A J 8

The bidding:

SOUTH	WEST	NORTH	EAST
1 NT	Pass	2 ♠	Pass
4 ♣	Pass	4 ♠	Pass
6 ♡	Pass	Pass	Pass

The North and South players were from Austria. They were using the Vienna system, in which an opening 1NT bid showed a hand with nineteen or more HCPs and said nothing about distribution. The two-spade bid was natural and forcing to game. The rest of the auction was artificial and did not reveal

340

the spade weakness. You will notice that had West not been up to underleading his king of spades, declarer would have taken six hearts, four diamonds, and two clubs. He would have come home with twelve or thirteen tricks. That's not the way it turned out. Einar Werner, sitting West for Sweden, opened a small spade, and the defense took the first two tricks, disposing of that slam contract in an exemplary fashion.

Werner found his partner with an ace to go with his king, and it was not a matter of getting his tricks established quickly enough, but rather of being sure that he and his partner got the tricks which were already established. The underlead of a king or queen is often made, expecting that the defenders already have one trick but need to establish another before declarer can take discards. The opening leader is hoping that partner will have just the card to get a trick in his suit established.

The next hand was played in the 1978 Olympiad pairs. Of the twenty pairs who had the North and South hands, eleven reached a six-heart contract. Eight defenders chose to lead a small club.

N-S vul., dealer North.

```
                    NORTH
                    ♠ K Q 10 9 7 6
                    ♡ A 6 4
                    ◇ 8
                    ♣ A J 9
        WEST                    EAST
        ♠ J 8 2                 ♠ A 4 3
        ♡ 3                     ♡ J 5 2
        ◇ Q 6 5 3               ◇ J 10 9 7
        ♣ K 8 6 5 3             ♣ Q 4 2
                    SOUTH
                    ♠ 5
                    ♡ K Q 10 9 8 7
                    ◇ A K 4 2
                    ♣ 10 7
```

In the three cases where West chose something other than a club, the declarer brought home twelve tricks. These declarers were able to get a spade established for a club discard, and after that almost any line of play they took was bound to work. They could either establish spades for discards of the two bad diamonds, or they could trump two diamonds in the dummy.

In the eight cases where the opening lead was a club, declarer didn't have a chance. The defenders got their club trick established before the declarer got the spade trick established for a club discard.

The experts have a high batting average when it comes to deciding whether to attack or go passive against slam bids. Let's look at some more small slam bids with trumps and see whether we can determine factors they use which make them so successful. The first hand is from the 1960 World Championship, with North America playing against the Italian Blue Team.

E-W vul., dealer North:

```
                    NORTH
                    ♠ K J 6 3
                    ♡ Q 8
                    ◊ A K 10 8
                    ♣ Q 8 3
      WEST                        EAST
      ♠ 7 5                       ♠ Q 10 9
      ♡ 9 6 4 2                   ♡ 5
      ◊ Q 4                       ◊ 9 7 6 5 3 2
      ♣ K 7 6 5 4                 ♣ A 9 2
                    SOUTH
                    ♠ A 8 4 2
                    ♡ A K J 10 7 3
                    ◊ J
                    ♣ J 10
```

The bidding:

OPEN ROOM

SOUTH	WEST	NORTH	EAST
Belladonna	Allinger	Avarelli	Mathe
		1 ♣	Pass
1 ♠	Pass	2 ◇	Pass
3 ♡	Pass	3 ♠	Pass
5 ♠	Pass	6 ♠	Pass
Pass	Pass		

CLOSED ROOM

Ogust	Chiaradia	Schenken	Farqust
		1 NT	Pass
2 ♣	Pass	2 ♠	Pass
4 NT	Pass	5 ◇	Pass
6 ♡	Pass	Pass	Pass

Both the Americans and Italians got into slam contracts with South as declarer, the Italians with spades as trumps and the Americans with hearts as trumps. Paul Allinger, for the Americans, and Eugenio Chiaradia, playing for Italy, both chose small clubs for their opening leads. The club bids in both the open room and the closed room were artificial and did not show club suits. The defense promptly took the first two tricks. In the open room, where the Italians were playing six spades, Lew Mathe still had to get a spade trick, and so the Italians were down two tricks. In the closed room, Harold Ogust discarded one of his spades on dummy's established queen of clubs, and another on the king of diamonds. So he took the remainder of the tricks after losing the first two.

In the 1961 World Championship, the French team playing against North America got to six diamonds making five, while the Americans got to five diamonds making six. Let's look into that one.

None vul., dealer North.

NORTH
♠ A K Q J
♡ Q 10
◇ Q J 3 2
♣ 9 8 7

WEST
♠ 10 6 3 2
♡ K 8 5 4 3 2
◇ 6
♣ J 5

EAST
♠ 8 5 4
♡ A J 9
◇ 10
♣ K Q 6 4 3 2

SOUTH
♠ 9 7
♡ 7 6
◇ A K 9 8 7 5 4
♣ A 10

The bidding:

CLOSED ROOM

SOUTH	WEST	NORTH	EAST
Le Dentu	Kay	Trezel	Silidor
		1 NT	Pass
3 ◇	Pass	4 ◇	Pass
4 NT	Pass	5 ◇	Pass
6 ◇	Pass	Pass	Pass

OPEN ROOM

Leventritt	Bacherich	Schenken	Ghestem
		1 ♠	2 ♣
2 ◇	2 ♡	3 ◇	3 ♡
4 ♣	Pass	4 ◇	Pass
5 ◇	Pass	Pass	Pass

In the closed room, Le Dentu, South, tried the Blackwood
Convention after he learned that his partner fit his diamond
suit. That convention is not recommended for a player who
holds two worthless doubletons. When Le Dentu learned that

his partner had only one ace, his 4NT bid had given him no helpful information. In the meantime, while the French were having a lot of fun bidding, the Americans maintained silence. The result was that Norman Kay had to pick a lead with no help from his partner. He chose a heart lead, and the Americans cashed the first two tricks.

In the open room, the French were very busy in the bidding. As far as I can tell, the only good it did them was to give them the feeling that they had not given up without a fight. With his doubletons in the major suits, Peter Leventritt, South, tried the more sensible procedure of cue bidding clubs. When Schenken gave him no encouragement, he stopped at five diamonds.

Rene Bacherich courteously led his partner's suit, and that didn't help him a bit. Leventritt won the opening club lead with the ace, cashed seven diamonds and four spades, and ended up with twelve tricks.

The next exhibit is from the Olympiad Games of 1964, with a team from Mexico playing against a team from the U.S.A.

N-S vul., dealer South.

```
                    NORTH
                    ♠ K Q 8 3
                    ♡ A K 7 3
                    ◇ Q J 8 4
                    ♣ A
        WEST                    EAST
        ♠ J 2                   ♠ 6
        ♡ J 9 2                 ♡ Q 8 6 5 4
        ◇ K 3 2                 ◇ A 10 9 6
        ♣ 10 9 6 3 2            ♣ K Q 5
                    SOUTH
                    ♠ A 10 9 7 5 4
                    ♡ 10
                    ◇ 7 5
                    ♣ J 8 7 4
```

The bidding:

SOUTH	WEST	NORTH	EAST
Krauss	Fua	Hamman	Barroso
Pass	Pass	2 ◇	Pass
2 ♠	Pass	3 ♣	Pass
4 NT	Pass	5 ♡	Pass
6 ♠	Pass	Pass	Pass

Don Krauss and Bob Hamman were playing a version of the Roman two-diamond opening bid. Bob Hamman's two-diamond bid showed a 4-4-4-1 or 5-4-4-0 distribution with 17 or more HCPs. His three-club rebid showed his short suit. Constant Fua, for Mexico, knew that the dummy was going to show up with either a singleton club or none, four spades, four hearts, and four diamonds. It was likely the declarer could take discards in his hand if two tricks weren't established quickly. He opened the two of diamonds and the defenders promptly took the first two tricks. In the other room, the Mexican North-South stopped at four spades. The opening lead was the deuce of hearts. South discarded a diamond on his king of hearts and led the ace of clubs. He took twelve tricks by trumping all three of his losing clubs. That gave him nine trump tricks, two heart tricks, and a club trick.

Attacking a suit the opponents have bid when it shows a genuine suit is a hazardous proposition. Attacking a suit which the opponents have cue bid also his its own dangers, but the risk is often worth taking. To illustrate this point, look at the next hand from the finals of the 1968 Olympiad Games, with Italy playing the United States.

None vul., dealer South.

```
                        NORTH
                        ♠ Q J 5 4
                        ♡ 9 6
                        ◇ A 8 4
                        ♣ A J 10 2
        WEST                            EAST
        ♠ 10 9 3                        ♠ 6 2
        ♡ K 8 5 3 2                     ♡ Q J 10 4
        ◇ J 10                          ◇ K 6
        ♣ Q 8 5                         ♣ K 7 6 4 3
                        SOUTH
                        ♠ A K 8 7
                        ♡ A 7
                        ◇ Q 9 7 5 3 2
                        ♣ 9
```

The bidding:

SOUTH	WEST	NORTH	EAST
D'Alelio	Kay	Pabis Ticci	Kaplan
1 ♠	Pass	2 ♣	Pass
2 ◇	Pass	3 ♠	Pass
4 ♣	Pass	4 ◇	Pass
4 ♡	Pass	4 NT	Pass
5 ♡	Pass	6 ♠	Pass
Pass	Pass		

Playing the Roman Club, the Italian pair used the Canape approach. D'Alelio's bidding indicated that his suits were spades and diamonds, but that he had more diamonds than spades. North's jump in spades established that suit as trumps. Further bids by South were cue bids.

From Norman Kay's viewpoint, the heart bid did not show a suit, so it might be possible to set up a heart trick. Kay led a small heart and established a heart for the defense before the declarer could get his diamonds established. D'Alelio went quietly. After drawing three rounds of trumps, he played the ace of diamonds and a low diamond toward his queen. Edgar

Kaplan won the diamond king and cashed the queen of hearts for the setting trick.

Against any other lead, South could have pulled trumps and led the ace and a diamond. When the diamond suit became established with the loss of one trick, declarer would have had an easy twelve tricks.

Many years ago, I was told that when I was defending against a small slam in a suit, I should lead from the nearest thing to a trick I had. There are exceptions to this, of course, but generally it seems to be a pretty good idea. Jim Borin, of Australia, used this principle on the following hand.

Both vul., dealer North.

```
                    NORTH
                    ♠ 8 2
                    ♡ A Q 7 6 2
                    ◊ A J 7
                    ♣ A 9 8
        WEST                      EAST
        ♠ 6 3                     ♠ A 9 7 4
        ♡ 8 5 3                   ♡ 10
        ◊ Q 8 6 4                 ◊ K 10 3 2
        ♣ J 6 5 4                 ♣ Q 10 7 2
                    SOUTH
                    ♠ K Q J 10 5
                    ♡ K J 9 4
                    ◊ 9 5
                    ♣ K 3
```

The bidding:

SOUTH	WEST	NORTH	EAST
Jais	J. Borin	Trezel	N. Borin
		1 ♣	Pass
1 ♡	Pass	3 ♡	Pass
3 ♠	Pass	4 ◊	Pass
4 NT	Pass	5 ♠	Pass
6 ♡	Pass	Pass	Pass

This hand was played in the 1971 World Championship. Six teams from six different regions of the world were playing in the event. Hands were being duplicated so that the same hands would be played in all matches. On four occasions, the final contract was six hearts, and on two occasions the final contract was four hearts. Five times North was declarer. The French were using the Canape approach where, with good hands, they bid a short suit. Because of this procedure, South ended up as declarer in six hearts.

Jim Borin had a choice of leading a diamond or a club. The only suits in which length had been guaranteed were the major suits. You often figure that when the opponents stop at a small slam, your side has one trick in its pocket and needs to develop a second one as quickly as possible. Underleading a jack is not going to get you many second round tricks. Underleading a queen can do so if your partner happens to have the king. It was obvious that the diamond bid by North was a cue bid. So Jim Borin led the four of diamonds.

Jais went up with dummy's ace and pulled trumps. Then he led a spade towards his hand. Norma Borin, East, taking no chances on any sort of domestic discord, rose with the ace and cashed the king of diamonds to set the hand.

When the final contract was played by North, the winning opening lead must not have been so easy to find. Three times the final contract was six hearts played by North, and three times that contract was fulfilled. We must sympathize with East on those occasions where he had the opening lead. Holding 9 HCPs in his own hand, he did not expect to find much in his partner's hand. The chances were remote that the West hand contained the queen of diamonds, the one card needed to make a diamond lead successful.

Now let's leave the World Championships for a while, and go visit the 1976 Far East Championships held in Auckland, New Zealand. It is the 19th of 22 rounds to be played, and we find Taiwan leading, with India and Australia in a terrific battle for second place. India is slightly ahead, and the choice of the opening lead on this hand is going to decide which of these two teams is the runner-up.

None vul., dealer West.

NORTH
- ♠ 10 5
- ♡ A Q 9 8
- ◊ 7 6 3
- ♣ A Q J 10

WEST
- ♠ K 9 8
- ♡ 3
- ◊ K J 9 8 5
- ♣ 9 8 6 4

EAST
- ♠ 3
- ♡ J 10 6 4 2
- ◊ A Q 10 4
- ♣ 7 3 2

SOUTH
- ♠ A Q J 7 6 4 2
- ♡ K 7 5
- ◊ 2
- ♣ K 5

The bidding:

CLOSED ROOM

SOUTH	WEST	NORTH	EAST
			Unidentified
Lester	Panjabi	Lathbury	Indian
	Pass	1 ♣	Pass
2 ♠	Pass	2 NT	Pass
3 ♠	Pass	4 ♠	Pass
4 NT	Pass	5 NT	Pass
6 ♠	Pass	Pass	Pass

OPEN ROOM

Unidentified			
Indian	Cummings	Campos	Seres
	Pass	1 ♡	Pass
1 ♠	Pass	2 ♣	Pass
3 ♠	Pass	4 ♠	Pass
4 NT	Pass	5 ♡	Pass
6 ♠	Pass	Pass	Pass

In the closed room, it was the Indian West who had the opening lead problem. His name was Panjabi. A singleton is often a good lead against a suit small slam when the opening leader does not have an ace. Frequently, the declarer has reached this small slam with his side having only three aces, and the fourth ace will be in your partner's hand. If it happens to be the ace of the suit led, you have the hand set almost immediately. If he happens to have a quick entry in trumps, he can give you a ruff. On the other hand, if you're going to follow the old precept about leading the nearest thing you have to a trick outside of the trump suit, then a diamond lead is called for. Notice that in the closed room, the opponents had bid spades and clubs, leaving no inference about their holdings in the red suits. Panjabi chose the three of hearts as his lead. Lester, of Australia, won and led three rounds of clubs. He discarded his losing diamond before he surrendered the lead to Panjabi's king of spades, and got home with his twelve tricks.

In the open room, the bidding was different. There, the opponents had bid hearts, clubs, and spades. Dick Cummings, for Australia, led the eight of diamonds. That was the lead that scuttled the contract and Australia took over second place from India, and held it to become the runner-up to Taiwan.

Let us follow this Australian pair to Manila, in the Philippines, where the World Championship was being held in 1977. The Australians had come there, not as runners-up, but as current champions of the South Pacific zone. They were one of six teams in competition. They played the following hand against the Argentines, who were champions of South America. Both the Argentines and the Australians had arrived at a contract of six hearts, and West had the problem of choosing an opening lead.

E-W vul., dealer.

```
                        NORTH
                        ♠ A Q 10 7 6 2
                        ♡ A 9 2
                        ◇ J
                        ♣ J 9 6
        WEST                              EAST
        ♠ K J 9 4                         ♠ 8 5 3
        ♡ 8 5 4                           ♡ 10 6
        ◇ A                               ◇ 10 9 8 5 4 3
        ♣ K 10 5 4 3                      ♣ 7 2
                        SOUTH
                        ♠ None
                        ♡ K Q J 7 3
                        ◇ K Q 7 6 2
                        ♣ A Q 8
```

West's ace of diamonds looked good for the first trick needed by the defense. The problem was to take at least one more trick. If West wished to make an attacking lead, he would lead a spade or a club. Spades had been bid by North, which tended to discourage the lead of that suit. Clubs also had been bid, but they had been bid as a cue bid.

Neither defender led a black card. Both chose trumps as their opening lead, and they led a second trump when they got in with the ace of diamonds. Argentina went set one trick; Australia went set two tricks.

If you will look carefully, you will see that if West had led either a spade or a club, the contract could have been made. With a spade lead, the queen could be finessed in the dummy, and both of South's clubs could have been discarded. Nothing could have then stopped South from trumping two diamonds in the North hand. Declarer would have twelve tricks consisting of two spades, seven trumps, two diamonds, and a club. A club lead would have made it just as easy, as declarer would then have to discard only one club, and North's ace of spades would provide facilities for that. Again, one diamond could have been conceded, and two small ones ruffed in North's hand.

What is the difference between this hand, where expert

defenders chose a neutral lead, and those hands I have been showing you where the leading players chose attacking leads?

If you will look at the hands where the experts chose attacking leads, you will find that they tended to hold somewhere between 3 and 6 HCPs. Actually, in five of the eight hands, the opening leader had 5 HCPs or less. In only one deal did an opening leader have as many as 7 HCPs. On the current hand where the opening leaders chose to go passive, they were looking at 11 HCPs. This meant that East probably had a very weak hand, and made it most unlikely that East would be able to promote anything in West's hand. In addition, the existence of an ace in the opening leader's hand suggested that the declarer's side had the other three aces.

West did not feel he could promote a trick in the black suits by leading them. However, he had every reason to think the chances were good that, somewhere along the line, he would take a black suit trick if he just left it up to the declarer to lead the suit. So in this case, both opening leaders decided the best chance was to make a neutral lead. Actually, it did not turn out to be quite as passive in nature as anticipated. It kept the declarer from trumping diamonds in the dummy.

In spite of the excellent record experts have in making attacking opening leads against small slams in suit contracts, they can't always work. However, finding hands where attacking leads by experts led to disaster is not easy to do. In the section on attacking leads in general, there was an example where Mike Passell led a heart against six clubs, allowing declarer to make his contract, and where the lead of any other suit would have defeated the contract (page 274). That really was not a good example, as North had bid hearts, and attacking in a suit bid by opponents carries extra risks. Of all the World Championship hands for the five years 1973 through 1977, the following hand is the closest to being an example of a player coming to grief by making an attacking lead against a small slam in a suit.

E-W vul., dealer North.

NORTH
♠ Q 6
♡ A Q 10 6
♢ J 9 6 5
♣ A 9 3

WEST
♠ K J 5 3 2
♡ 7 4 2
♢ 4
♣ 7 6 5 4

EAST
♠ 9 8 4
♡ J 9 5 3
♢ Q 7 2
♣ Q 8 2

SOUTH
♠ A 10 7
♡ K 8
♢ A K 10 8 3
♣ K J 10

In the qualifying rounds of the 1974 World Championship, North America was playing New Zealand. Bobby Wolff and Bob Hamman, for North America, had arrived at six diamonds with Wolff, South, as declarer. North had bid hearts and South had bid diamonds; no other suits had been mentioned. Stanley Abrahams, of New Zealand, led the seven of clubs. It appears, on the surface, that this saved Wolff the problem of deciding which way to finesse clubs, but not so. One of the clubs could have been discarded on one of declarer's hearts. Wolff let the club ride around to his hand, winning the queen with his king. He now took the percentage play of laying down the ace and king of diamonds, and got the bad news that he was going to have a trump loser. Wolff tried every conceivable way to avoid losing a second trick. First, he cashed his two clubs, and then played three high hearts. On the queen of hearts, he discarded a spade. Had the jack fallen out, he would have been able to discard a second spade on the ten of hearts. But that didn't work, so he trumped dummy's last heart. Next, he put East in with a trump. Had East possessed the king of spades, he would have been beautifully end-played. No such luck. East led a spade with no cost at all, and when Wolff let that ride to his queen, he lost his second trick to the king of spades.

The official commentator on the play of the hand said that this was a well-played hand by Wolff for a loss.

In the other room, also a diamond contract, Bobby Goldman, from North America, was on lead. He led the three of spades. Declarer won the queen in the dummy, and he also played the ace and king of diamonds. When the queen failed to fall out, he claimed the balance of the tricks, pointing out that he would discard a losing club from his hand on the queen of hearts and ruff a spade in the dummy.

Now I've got to let you in on all of the facts. Goldman was not leading against six diamonds. The New Zealand players had stopped at five diamonds. So the player who bid six diamonds took eleven tricks against a passive lead, while the player who bid only five diamonds took twelve tricks against an attacking lead. I don't think I have been unfair in showing you this hand, for it does demonstrate what can happen when an attacking lead is made.

In spite of the fact that bad things can come from these attacking leads, you can see that our leading players gain much more by making attacking leads against small slams than they lose. To quote Benito Garozzo, "Heroic measures are rarely needed when leading against a game contract. The defenders can expect to get the lead again after dummy has been exposed, and the early play offers further clues to what they should do. Not so against slams. Unless two tricks can be cashed at once, the defense must strike a telling blow to develop the setting trick by the opening lead. Later is too late."

An examination of results achieved in high-level competition supports Garozzo's statement. Of course, attacking leads are dangerous. However, against small slams in a suit contract, they gain more often than they lose. An examination of these hands does suggest some modifications to Garozzo's statement:

1. The attacking lead becomes doubtful when it is in a suit which the opponents have bid to show a playable suit. When, however, the opponents have bid a suit as a cue bid, attacking leads in that suit are still called for.

2. When you hold as many as eight HCPs, attacking leads become much more dangerous, and should be avoided if you hold as many as nine or ten HCPs. The chances are too small

that your partner will have what it takes for you to build up a trick with your attacking lead.

3. Attacking leads from short suits have a better chance to succeed than attacking leads from long suits. Suppose your right-hand opponent has opened one spade, your left-hand opponent has bid three spades, and, after checking on aces, your right-hand opponent bids a small slam in spades. You hold:

♠ 6 4   ♡ K 10 7 4 2   ◇ K 10 4   ♣ 7 5 3

You can make a passive lead by leading a club, or you can make an attacking lead by leading one of the red suits. An attacking lead offers the best chance, and you should lead the four of diamonds in preference to the four of hearts.

You might look at some of the tables of probabilities, which you will find in many bridge books, and be able to calculate that the chances one of your opponents will have a void or singleton in either hearts or diamonds is sufficiently remote, and that it doesn't make much difference from that standpoint whether you lead hearts or diamonds. The trouble with all of those tables is that they are all 'A-Priori' tables, and that means the odds quoted are correct provided you know nothing whatsoever about the distribution of any of the other hands. As your opening lead is made after you have heard the bidding, it should never be true that you make a lead when you know nothing whatsoever about the distribution of the other hands. On the example given, if your opponents happen to open only five-card or longer major suits, you know that the declarer has at least five spades. That being true, the probabilities that he has a shortage in hearts (either void or a singleton) are almost 38%, while the chances he has a shortage in diamonds are only 24%. Give yourself six hearts, and let him rebid to indicate six spades, and the chances he has a shortage in hearts are better than 53%. These odds are quite different from those 'A-Priori' odds.

Just to illustrate the point, let me give you a table which shows the A-Priori odds, and then the odds when you know something about declarer's hand.

CHANCES SOUTH WILL HAVE A SHORTAGE
(VOID OR SINGLETON) IN HEARTS

When declarer's spade holding is:

You have	Unknown	At least 5	At least 6
3 hearts	7.2%	24.0%	29.4%
4 hearts	11.1	29.8	36.5
5 hearts	16.4	37.6	48.6
6 hearts	23.7	46.5	53.1

Suppose this is your holding.

♠ 6 4   ♡ K 10 7 4 2   ◊ Q 10 4   ♣ 7 5 3

Now the king of diamonds has been replaced by the queen. If you can build up the second round in either of the red suits, the second round is much more likely to hold up in diamonds than it is in hearts. On the other hand, when you lead a diamond, you're hoping to find the king in your partner's hand. Should you lead a heart, you would be happy to find either the king or the ace. Should your partner happen to hold the ace of hearts, the chances that you can take two tricks in hearts immediately are not all that bad.

While it is close, the chances still slightly favor the lead of a heart unless you are convinced that your partner does not have an ace. In that case, the lead of the diamond would be the preferred lead.

The longer the suit with the king and the shorter the suit with the queen, the more attractive the lead of the short suit becomes. Let's look at a hand where that problem faced Bob Hamman, playing in the trials for the right to represent North America in the 1979 World Championship.

Both vul., dealer East.

NORTH
♠ Q 10 9 2
♡ K Q J 8 7 4
♢ None
♣ A J 7

WEST
♠ K J
♡ 9 6 2
♢ K 10 8 6 4 3
♣ Q 2

EAST
♠ 6 3
♡ 10 3
♢ Q 9 7 2
♣ K 10 9 8 6

SOUTH
♠ A 8 7 5 4
♡ A 5
♢ A J 5
♣ 5 4 3

The bidding:

SOUTH	WEST	NORTH	EAST
Larsen	Hamman	Hamilton	Wolff
			Pass
1 ♠	Pass	2 ♡	Pass
2 ♠	Pass	3 ♠	Pass
4 ♡	Pass	5 NT	Pass
6 ♡	Pass	6 ♠	Pass
Pass	Pass		

Hamilton's three-spade bid on the second round agreed spades as trumps. Larsen's four-heart bid was a cue bid showing the ace of that suit. Hamilton's 5NT bid was the Grand Slam Force, asking Larsen to bid seven spades if he held two of the three top honors in that suit. His failure to do so indicated that he did not have both the ace and king.

Now Hamman had to choose a lead from the West hand. There were two inferences from the bidding. Hamman almost certainly had a trump trick. Hamilton should not have had both the ace and queen of spades and still bid 5NT. The other inference was that players seldom bid the Grand Slam Force unless they hold all four aces. So Hamman, holding one trick, was looking for a second trick to set the hand. Either the queen of diamonds or the king of clubs in his partner's hand would establish a second round winner. The chances declarer was short in diamonds were obviously much greater than the chances he was short in clubs. In spite of the fact that leading from the queen doubleton is generally considered a bad lead when leading against less than a slam contract, Hamman led the small club. You can see how right he was. Had he led hearts or diamonds, Larsen could simply have played the ace and another spade, giving Hamman his trump trick while he still retained the ace of each of the other suits. There were more than enough discards on dummy's heart suit to bring in the slam.

But why should I try to tell what Hamman thought? This is one of those exceptional cases where the player has told us himself. Let's hear what Bob Hamman had to say about the lead:

> "It was clear that there was a diamond short-
> ness somewhere, and it was clear from the bidding
> that we didn't have any aces. The only hope was that
> we could set up a trick before trumps were drawn. Our
> best chance had to be in clubs, so I led the deuce."

You can see that the East hand had just what it took to pro-mote a second round winner in either diamonds or clubs. You can also see that it was only the club second round winner which could take a trick.

4. How about leading from a sequence, as compared with underleading a king or queen? Suppose your opponents are in six spades and you are on lead with one of the following hands.

1. ♠ 6 3   ♡ K Q J 5   ◇ K 10 4 2   ♣ 7 5 2
2. ♠ 6 3   ♡ Q J 10 5   ◇ K 10 4 2   ♣ 7 5 2
3. ♠ 6 3   ♡ J 10 9 5   ◇ K 10 4 2   ♣ 7 5 2
4. ♠ 6 3   ♡ 10 9 8 5   ◇ K 10 4 2   ♣ 7 5 2

It would be difficult to think of any bidding sequence which would cause you to choose the lead of a low diamond rather than the king of hearts with Hand 1. In the first place, you have nine HCPs and you don't get rich underleading kings when your hand is that strong. More compelling is the simple fact that leading a diamond is a dangerous lead, while leading a heart is a safe lead, and certainly at least as good an attacking lead as the diamond.

Things are not quite so clear should you be on lead with Hand 2. The heart suit offers safety, but is not so aggressive as the diamond lead. Of course, it is always possible to find the king in the dummy and the ace in your partner's hand and set the contract immediately, but that's not too likely. I believe, however, that the element of safety would nearly always cause our leading players to lead the queen of hearts rather than a small diamond unless there was something quite unusual in the bidding.

With the J-10-9 combination, the lead of a small diamond becomes more attractive. Yes, I know if you lead the jack of hearts you might find the queen in the dummy, the king in your partner's hand, and the ace in declarer's hand and have an immediate second round establishment. However, I would not expect that to happen too often. It's really just about a toss-up whether you should go for the safety of the heart lead, or make the aggressive small diamond lead. You must look for clues in the bidding, and not in your holding.

With Hand 4, other things being equal, the small diamond becomes the preferred lead. With only three HCPs in your hand, chances have become quite good that you may find your partner with supporting cards and get an immediate promotion. Usually it would be better to forget about whatever safety there might be in the heart lead, and make the attacking lead of the diamond.

A two-card sequence headed by the king, queen, or jack, is not as safe as a three-card sequence, but is frequently chosen against a slam contract.

It goes without saying that even a three-card sequence headed by the queen or jack, when it is an exceptionally long suit, might be abandoned in favor of the underlead of a king in a shorter suit, in those cases where an attacking lead seems desirable.

ACE LEADS AGAINST SLAM CONTRACTS

Players who call themselves sophisticated seem to think it is amateurish to plunk down an ace on opening lead against a slam contract. Among more knowledgable players and theorists, there is no such unanimity of opinion. Some say do; some say don't. I'm going to go on record right now. Unless there are convincing clues, either from the bidding or from the holding in my own hand, I tend to lead aces against slam contracts. I lead them against small slam contracts at match point duplicate to keep my opponents from taking all thirteen tricks, which they often do if I don't lead my ace. I lead them against small slams in any form of total point bidding, in the hope that I can keep my opponents from taking twelve tricks.

First, let's take a look at what some authorities have said on this subject, and then let's take a look at the results which have been obtained in high-level competition.

In his *Red Book on Play,* published in 1934, Ely Culbertson straddled the fence. He said, "The lead of an ace, which is sometimes a good chance against a suit slam, is practically suicidal against notrump." Obviously, he is referring to small slam contracts, and not grand slam contracts.

Charlie Goren was most explicit in his *Better Bridge for Better Players,* published in 1942. He said, "Against slam bids, a very popular lead is an ace. This practice, however, does not have the approval of the experts."

In London, the bridge editor of the *Manchester Guardian,* writing under the pen name of Goulash in 1950, talking about opening leads against small slam contracts, said, "Not an ace, for the function of aces is to kill kings, not to smother deuces."

In their book, *How To Bid and What To Lead,* Charles Solomon and Bennet Disbrow said in 1953, "The lead of an ace (when not holding the king) may occasionally be a happy choice, but more often the opening will preface a sad ending."

In 1970, Alvin Roth and Jeff Rubens published *Bridge For Beginners.* In it they said, "It is usually a poor idea to lay down an unsupported ace against a small slam unless you have an excellent idea as to where your setting trick is coming from."

In that same year, Bob Ewen published a great book on opening leads, which takes a more careful look at the subject. He said that you will come out well ahead in the long run if you lead an ace against a small slam in a suit only when you have a probable second trick that needs no establishment. This could be the king of trumps, or where the bidding suggests that you may be able to take two quick tricks in the suit because partner has the king, a void, or a singleton. However, he says that, barring such exceptional circumstances, you should not lead an ace lacking a quick second trick, when the opponents have bid that suit (unless you're trying for a ruff), or when the bidding suggests one of the opponents is void in the suit.

In 1974, Eddie Kantar published the first modern book on complete defensive play in many years. His view was somewhat different. He says about leading aces: "Against slam contracts, it usually works out best, particularly at tournament bridge, where you might even lose your ace if you don't lead it. Also, if the opponents have bid three suits strongly, you might consider leading an ace in the unbid suit."

The Complete Book of Bridge, by Terence Reese and Albert Dormer, was published in 1973. Concerning the matter of leading aces against small slam contracts, they say, "Clearly, an ace should be led if the defender has another probable trick elsewhere, such as a trump trick, and also when the bidding offers no particular likelihood that the opponents have second round control of the suit. Equally clearly, one should not lead an ace in the suit that has been bid by the opponents if there is a reasonable prospect of establishing a second trick elsewhere. For the rest, our experience suggests that more slams are made because an ace was not led, than the other way around!"

As evidence in the matter accumulates, our writers and theorists are abandoning their ivory towers and are observing what is happening in the real world. The facts show that Reese and Dormer are right. It is easy to find deals where slams were made because an ace was not led, but hands which were made only because an ace was led are harder to come by. In this first hand, the lead of an ace would have scuttled the defense.

None vul., dealer West.

NORTH
- ♠ 4
- ♡ J 8 2
- ◇ A 10 9 6 2
- ♣ K 10 6 3

WEST
- ♠ J 5
- ♡ A 9 4
- ◇ Q J 7 5
- ♣ J 9 8 7

EAST
- ♠ 9 8 7 6
- ♡ Q 7 6 5
- ◇ 8 4
- ♣ Q 5 2

SOUTH
- ♠ A K Q 10 3 2
- ♡ K 10 3
- ◇ K 3
- ♣ A 4

The bidding:

SOUTH	WEST	NORTH	EAST
Mitchell	Garozzo	Stayman	Forquet
	Pass	Pass	Pass
2 ◇	Pass	3 ◇	Pass
3 ♠	Pass	4 ♣	Pass
4 ♠	Pass	5 ♠	Pass
6 ♠	Pass	Pass	Pass

This hand is from the finals of the 1964 Olympiad Games, with the United States playing Italy. Mitchell's two-diamond opening bid was an artificial game force. Had Garozzo chosen to lead the ace of hearts, declarer would have had a relatively easy time of it. With the jack of spades falling out for him and the queen of hearts finessable, he would have come home with six trump tricks and two in each of the other suits. However, Garozzo did not lead the ace of diamonds. His actual lead was the nine of clubs. From the way the hand was played, it appears that neither his partner, Forquet, nor Mitchell, had any idea that Garozzo had the jack of clubs. Forquet played the queen and Mitchell won with the ace. After drawing trumps, he tried for a 3-3 diamond split by taking the king and ace and trumping a diamond. When the suit didn't break, he went to the dummy with the king of clubs to lead the jack of hearts. Forquet did not cover, and Garozzo won his ace. He was able to lock Mitchell in his own hand by leading the jack of clubs. Mitchell trumped, but he had no entry to dummy, and finally had to lead the king of hearts from his own hand. East won the setting trick with his queen of hearts.

The next hand is from the 1963 Bermuda Bowl for the World Championship, with North America playing France.

Both vul., dealer East.

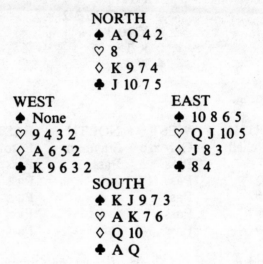

```
                    NORTH
                    ♠ A Q 4 2
                    ♡ 8
                    ◊ K 9 7 4
                    ♣ J 10 7 5
        WEST                    EAST
        ♠ None                  ♠ 10 8 6 5
        ♡ 9 4 3 2               ♡ Q J 10 5
        ◊ A 6 5 2               ◊ J 8 3
        ♣ K 9 6 3 2             ♣ 8 4
                    SOUTH
                    ♠ K J 9 7 3
                    ♡ A K 7 6
                    ◊ Q 10
                    ♣ A Q
```

The bidding:

CLOSED ROOM

SOUTH Desrousseaux	WEST Leventritt	NORTH Theron	EAST Schenken
			Pass
1 ♠	Pass	4 ♠	Pass
5 ♦	Pass	6 ♠	Pass
Pass	Pass		

OPEN ROOM

Robinson	Bacherich	Jordan	Ghestem
			Pass
1 ♠	Pass	1 NT	Pass
3 ♡	Pass	4 NT	Pass
5 ♡	Pass	6 ♠	Pass
Pass	Pass		

In the closed room, the French pair warned Peter Leventritt, by their bidding, not to lead the ace of diamonds. Desrousseaux, of France, had a choice of plays for his contract, and he guessed wrong. In the open room, the Americans gave the French no such information about the diamond suit, and Bacherich, of Franch, duly led the ace of diamonds. That took the guess out of it, and Robinson had a comparatively easy time of it.

In the closed room, the five-diamond bid by South is an asking bid, asking North to bid a slam if he has second round control of the diamond suit. North's king qualified as second round control, so he went to six spades. Warned about the diamond suit, Leventritt led the deuce of hearts. Desrousseaux won the king and trumped a heart. At trick three, he led a small diamond. Had he guessed to play the ten, he could have made his contract. Had the diamonds been reversed in the East and West hands, he would have been right to play the queen. However, Leventritt took the queen with his ace and led a second diamond to dummy's king. Declarer now took the losing club finesse, and it was all over.

In the open room, Arthur Jordan's 1NT response was forcing. When Robinson jumped to three hearts, Jordan took over and put the hand in six spades. Having no warning about the diamond suit, Bacherich helped solve Robinson's problem by leading the ace of diamonds. He led a second diamond to Robinson's queen. Declarer cashed the heart ace and ruffed a heart. He played the spade ace and found out about the trump suit. Next he led the diamond king and discarded the queen of clubs. Then he led the diamond nine. East could see no profit by trumping, so he discarded a club. Robinson discarded a heart and claimed the balance of the tricks, making his small slam contract.

It was Richard Miller, bridge editor of the *National Observer,* who said, "Sophisticated players tend to belittle the amateur when he plunks down an ace on opening lead." Let's look at some hands where the opening leader did not 'plunk down his ace on opening lead', and I will leave it up to you to decide what he looked like after the hand was over. I am afraid there are going to be some famous names in this section of my book, and so, if you are a bit squeamish about horror stories, I suggest you skip a few pages.

First, let's look at some cases where the opening leader had the contract set in his own hand, but declarer was successful in spite of this. Let's look at Claude Delmouly and Gerard Bourchtoff, of France, in action against the Chinese team from Taiwan in the Olympiad Games of 1972. Delmouly and Bourchtoff are former world champions and won the European championships on several occasions, so we are not talking about beginning players. But, enough of this prelude.

N-S vul., dealer East.

                        NORTH
                        ♠ J 10 6
                        ♡ K 9 4 2
                        ◇ 8
                        ♣ A J 10 5 4
        WEST   EAST
        ♠ A K 9 4   ♠ Q 3 2
        ♡ Q 10 8 7 3   ♡ J 6
        ◇ 9 5 3   ◇ J 10 6 4 2
        ♣ 8   ♣ 9 6 2
                        SOUTH
                        ♠ 8 7 5
                        ♡ A 5
                        ◇ A K Q 7
                        ♣ K Q 7 3

The bidding:

SOUTH	WEST	NORTH	EAST
P. Huang	Delmouly	Tai	Bourchtoff
			Pass
1 ♣	1 ♡	3 ♣	Pass
3 ♡	Pass	4 ♡	Pass
6 ♣	Pass	Pass	Pass

South's one-club opening bid was part of the Precision Club
System, showing 16 or more HCPs, but saying nothing about
the club suit. After the overcall, North jumped to three clubs
with his nine HCPs, showing his best suit and forcing to game.
From there on, something seems to have been out of control, as
the Chinese team ended up in a small slam contract with three
losers off the top—provided the French took them.

Delmouly led the king of spades, and Bourchtoff followed
with the deuce. The French don't use the high-low system of
signaling that we do, and the deuce from East simply said that
he had an odd number of spades. That could have been one,
three, or five. Delmouly thought that over and came to the conclusion that South would not have bid a slam with three spades

to the queen. He was right; South was not that strong. It occurred to him that South's heart bid may have shown a genuine heart suit, and that East's signal showed a five-card spade suit, leaving South with only one spade. The four hearts presumed to be in the South hand would also leave East void in that suit. So, Delmouly switched to a small heart to give his partner a ruff.

That play was something less than a sensational success. Huang won his ace and laid down the king of clubs, and led a small club to dummy's ace. He had to stop pulling trumps and hope the red suits broke favorably. On his three top diamonds, he discarded the remaining spades in dummy. The balance of the tricks were collected on a cross-ruff.

So, one of the reasons for cashing your tricks when you have them is that, if you don't do so, horrible accidents may happen. Another thing to remember is not to trust the enemy too much. They can get things loused up, too. For example, see this hand with a famous pair from North America playing against a famous pair from Brazil in the 1973 World Championship.

E-W vul., dealer West.

```
                    NORTH
                    ♠ K J 2
                    ♡ Q 7 4
                    ◇ K 6
                    ♣ A 8 7 6 3
      WEST                        EAST
      ♠ A Q 7 4 3                 ♠ 9 8 6 5
      ♡ 8                         ♡ None
      ◇ A Q 10 9                  ◇ 7 5 3 2
      ♣ J 10 5                    ♣ K Q 9 4 2
                    SOUTH
                    ♠ 10
                    ♡ A K J 10 9 6 5 3 2
                    ◇ J 8 4
                    ♣ None
```

The bidding:

SOUTH	WEST	NORTH	EAST
P. Branco	Becker	M. Branco	Rubens
	1 ♠	Double	4 ♠
6 ♡	Pass	Pass	Pass

Sometimes, it is a great help to be the sort of a player who knows nothing about the game and nothing about counting. Unfortunately for him, that is not the kind of a bridge player B. J. Becker is. My Aunt Emma would have set this six-heart contract, and probably would have doubled it as well. Mr. Becker did neither. He led his ace of diamonds, and then looked at those three spades to the king in the dummy. Players who don't count and don't remember the bidding might not have been impressed, but Becker was. Branco had bid like a man with a highly distributional hand and who probably had a singleton somewhere. Rubens had made a preemptive jump to four spades, and that bid is frequently made with a five-card holding. If, in fact, Rubens had five spades, you only had to be able to count to thirteen to see that Branco didn't have any. To lead the ace of spades would simply allow Branco to trump it and then have dummy's king of spades available for a discard.

Becker switched to the jack of clubs. He was right about one thing: Branco did have a void suit. However, it was not in spades, it was in clubs. Taking no chances, Branco trumped the club and went to the dummy with a trump. Now he led the ace of clubs and discarded his losing spade. The rest of the tricks were his.

Did you ever notice how often preemptive action hustles the opponents into a contract which they cannot make, but do make anyway?

Now let's leave World Championship events, and look in on the European Championship held in Torquay, England, in 1961. Here we find the British team playing the Italians. The Italian team that year was not the famous Blue Team, but a team of newcomers to international competition.

N-S vul., dealer West.

NORTH
♠ A K 10 5
♡ A 7 3
◇ A Q J 5 2
♣ K

WEST
♠ J
♡ K 9
◇ 8 4 3
♣ A J 10 8 6 5 3

EAST
♠ 6 3
♡ J 10 6 4 2
◇ 10 6
♣ Q 9 7 4

SOUTH
♠ Q 9 8 7 4 2
♡ Q 8 5
◇ K 9 7
♣ 2

The bidding:

SOUTH	WEST	NORTH	EAST
Cremoncini	Priday	Mascharoni	Truscott
	3 ♣	Double	Pass
4 ♠	Pass	5 ♣	Pass
7 ♠	Pass	Pass	Pass

Instead of leading his ace of clubs, Richard Priday, of England, made the neutral lead of jack of trumps. Obviously, he thought that North had guaranteed a void in clubs, and he did not wish to lead the ace, have it trumped in the dummy, and establish a king in the South hand for a discard. This gave Cremoncini a chance to show that though something went wrong with the bidding, there was nothing wrong with the way he played his hand. He led a second trump, exhausting the British players of trumps, and then cashed five diamond tricks. On these he discarded the deuce of clubs and a heart from his own hand. He then cashed the rest of his spades. Five diamond tricks plus six spade tricks comes to a total of eleven tricks, and left everybody with exactly two cards. Priday found himself in an impossible situation. Here is the way it looked when

Cremoncini led his last trump:

NORTH
♠ None
♡ A 7
♢ None
♣ K

WEST
♠ None
♡ K 9
♢ None
♣ A

EAST
Immaterial

SOUTH
♠ 2
♡ Q 8
♢ None
♣ None

Obviously, Priday could not discard his ace of clubs and make dummy's king good, so he discarded his nine of hearts. Cremoncini now discarded dummy's king of clubs, and the ace and queen of hearts won the last two tricks. Priday had to go to bed with his ace of clubs.

I had thought that South also believed that North's cue bid in clubs showed first round control. However, Alan Truscott, who was then playing on the British team, and has since moved to America and is now bridge editor of *The New York Times,* has set the matter straight. The truth of the matter is that the Italian players knew little or no English. English is the official language of international competition, and the Italians had learned enough English to bid and that was about all. However, this was a very exciting hand and Cremoncini thought he had said six spades, when in reality he had bid seven spades. Truscott points out, however, that there were two silver linings. One of them was that the British won this particular match against the Italians in spite of this hand, and the other is that they went on to win the entire championship of Europe.

In November, 1963, the sixteen leading pairs on the North American continent met in Miami Beach, Florida, to compete for the right to represent North America in the forthcoming

World Championship. Among these contestants were Victor Mitchell and Sam Stayman, who finished second, thereby qualifying for the international match, and B. J. Becker and Dorothy Hayden, who tied for fourth and fifth place. Becker and Hayden lost out on being the alternate pair to Lew Mathe and Edward Taylor, Mathe and Taylor having beaten them in their individual match. The next hand, where Stayman failed to lead an ace against a slam contract, is from this event.

Both vul., dealer South.

NORTH
♠ Q 8
♡ 10 6 3
♢ A Q J 9 6
♣ A Q 4

WEST
♠ 5 4 3
♡ A 8 5
♢ K 5 3 2
♣ 10 5 2

EAST
♠ J 10 7 2
♡ K Q 7 4
♢ 10 8 7
♣ 7 6

SOUTH
♠ A K 9 6
♡ J 9 2
♢ 4
♣ K J 9 8 3

The bidding:

SOUTH	WEST	NORTH	EAST
B. J. Becker	Stayman	Hayden	Mitchell
1 ♣	Pass	1 ♢	Pass
1 ♠	Pass	3 ♣	Pass
4 ♣	Pass	4 ♠	Pass
6 ♣	Pass	Pass	Pass

How did one of the world's finest pairs get to a six-club contract, with three losing hearts in each hand? Becker has told us how it happened. He and Dorothy had agreed that, in this particular sequence of bidding, any four-club bid would be the

Gerber Convention inquiring about aces, but B. J. Becker forgot and bid four clubs simply in an attempt to get to game. Dorothy had not forgotten, and made the bid which showed two aces—that is four spades. Becker took this to be a bid showing support for his second suit, and decided that, having bid three suits strongly, Dorothy was showing that she had a singleton heart. With that bit of misinformation to guide him, Becker bid the slam.

In reporting this hand, Sonny Moyse says, "With the usual aversion of experts to the opening of aces against small slams, Stayman led a low diamond." I might add that Becker and Hayden were an established partnership due every respect, and it is difficult to believe that they would have gotten into the slam with the opponents able to cash the first three tricks. Even with that lead, it is hard to see how Becker took twelve tricks, but it is dangerous to give B. J. Becker a second chance. He made his contract.

Dummy's jack was played on the opening lead and held the trick. On the ace of diamonds, Becker discarded one of his hearts. Now he trumped a diamond, and led a club to dummy's ace. Another diamond ruff felled the king from West and established dummy's queen. Becker now cashed his high club and then led a club to dummy. At this point, he was all out of trumps. Seven tricks had been played, and here are the six cards which each of the players had left:

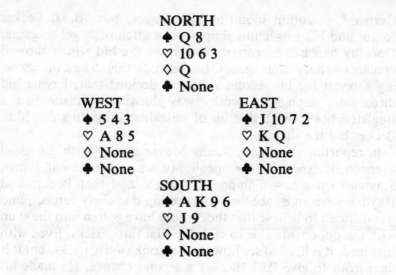

NORTH
- ♠ Q 8
- ♡ 10 6 3
- ◊ Q
- ♣ None

WEST
- ♠ 5 4 3
- ♡ A 8 5
- ◊ None
- ♣ None

EAST
- ♠ J 10 7 2
- ♡ K Q
- ◊ None
- ♣ None

SOUTH
- ♠ A K 9 6
- ♡ J 9
- ◊ None
- ♣ None

The lead was in the North hand as Becker led the queen of diamonds. Mitchell, East, knew he couldn't throw away a spade, so he had to discard the queen of hearts. Becker discarded the nine of hearts from his hand, and if you will examine the hand carefully, you'll see that now it doesn't make any difference what Stayman discarded. Actually, Stayman discarded a small spade.

Becker led the queen of spades, followed by the eight of spades. Whether Becker would have finessed the nine had Mitchell played low we will never know, for Mitchell split his honors by covering with the ten. It looks safe enough to do that, as the dummy had no entry to repeat the finesse. It looked safe, but it wasn't. Becker won the king and led the jack of hearts.

If Stayman won his ace, he would have nothing left but the eight and five of hearts, and whichever he led, dummy would take the last two tricks. Actually, Stayman ducked and let Mitchell win with his king. Now Mitchell had the jack and seven of spades and had to lead one of them to Becker's ace and nine.

It all goes to show that in spite of the brilliance Becker displayed in the play of the hand, it is not wise to trust the enemy's bidding too much when choosing your opening lead.

In the hands up until now, the lead of the ace would have worked because there was some sort of confusion or other on the part of the bidders. There are simpler reasons why aces succeed. One of them is that sometimes your partner happens to have the king which will never take a trick unless you lead the suit immediately. Look at this hand from the 1971 World Championship, with the World Champion Aces playing against the French.

Both vul. dealer West.

```
                    NORTH
                    ♠ A K 8 7 6 2
                    ♡ Q 8
                    ◊ 4
                    ♣ A Q 7 6
        WEST                        EAST
        ♠ 10 5                      ♠ J 9 4 3
        ♡ A 10 7 5 3                ♡ K 2
        ◊ 10 7 2                    ◊ J 9 8 6 3
        ♣ 10 3 2                    ♣ 9 5
                    SOUTH
                    ♠ Q
                    ♡ J 9 6 4
                    ◊ A K Q 5
                    ♣ K J 8 4
```

The bidding:

SOUTH	WEST	NORTH	EAST
J. Jacoby	Boulenger	Wolff	Svarc
	Pass	1 ♠	Pass
2 ♣	Pass	2 ♠	Pass
3 NT	Pass	4 ♣	Pass
4 ◊	Pass	4 ♠	Pass
6 ♣	Pass	Pass	Pass

The famous Aces Team defeated the French handily and retained the World Championship, but they did not do too well on this hand. If you will study the bidding by Jim Jacoby and Bobby Wolff, you will see that it simply screamed for a heart lead. That is what Boulenger, West, thought, so he led the ace of hearts. In spite of the fact that his partner could give no better signal than the two, he led a second heart and the hand was soon over. If you will examine the hand, you will see that Jacoby would have taken all thirteen tricks against any other lead. With the clubs breaking 3-2, he could establish the spades by ruffing and take five spades, three diamonds, and five clubs.

It seems to bring out the best in a great player when he is in a slam contract and the opponents fail to take the tricks they have right off the top.

NORTH
♠ Q 9 8 7 2
♡ K J 2
♢ A K 9 7 3
♣ None

WEST | EAST
♠ A 6 | ♠ K 5 3
♡ 6 5 | ♡ 10 9
♢ 6 4 2 | ♢ Q J 8 5
♣ K 9 8 7 6 3 | ♣ Q J 10 2

SOUTH
♠ J 10 4
♡ A Q 8 7 4 3
♢ 10
♣ A 5 4

Karl Schneider, the great Austrian player, played the hand in a six-heart contract against a German team, in the European Championship of 1954.

Had West led the ace and another spade, the defenders could have taken the first three tricks. However, he led a small club. That gave Schneider a chance to show his virtuosity.

When the dummy came down, Schneider saw nine tricks off the top. This could be raised to eleven if he could trump two clubs in the dummy, and manage to find entries back to his hand to pull trumps, but that still left him one trick short. The best chance seemed to be a squeeze play of some sort, but, generally, squeeze plays don't work out when you have two losers in your hand. You have to have only one loser. So, Schneider found himself in the position of very badly needing to lose a trick, and he had to be careful about which suit he chose to lose that trick.

He trumped the club in the dummy and led a small spade to his ten. He hoped that West would win that trick. West did win with the ace, but if West was not going to choose the ace of spades for his opening lead, he surely had no notion of continuing the suit, when it was the suit which Schneider was attacking at trick two. Instead, he led a second club. Schneider trumped in dummy. Now the problem was how to get back to his hand without establishing a trump trick for the opponents. He was rewarded for his valiant effort. When he overtook the king of hearts with the ace and led the queen of hearts, both opponents followed suit and he was not going to lose a trump trick. At this point, Schneider was pretty well convinced that East held the king of spades. If East also held both diamond honors, he was going to be in trouble. Schneider led the ace of clubs and all of his trumps. After he led his last trump, this was the situation.

<pre>
                    NORTH
                    ♠ None
                    ♡ None
                    ◊ A K 9
                    ♣ None
        WEST   EAST
        ♠ 6   ♠ K
        ♡ None   ♡ None
        ◊ 6   ◊ Q J 8
        ♣ K   ♣ None
                    SOUTH
                    ♠ J 4
                    ♡ None
                    ◊ 10
                    ♣ None
</pre>

You will notice that East has four cards, while each of the other hands has only three. This is because it took East a long time to decide what to discard. He could have waited until now and it would have done him no good. If he discarded his king of spades, Schneider's jack would be good. If he discarded the eight of diamonds, all of the dummy's diamonds would be good.

I would like to tell you that Karl Schneider was rewarded with a big win for his brilliance in playing this hand. However, when we are reporting history, we must report all of the facts, even where they are a big comedown. Schneider did not win points on the hand. It was a tie. In the replay of the hand, Judge Egmont von Bewitz, of Germany, played six spades with the North hand, and was successful in fulfilling that contract! Here is how it happened.

The opening lead was the queen of clubs. Von Bewitz won dummy's ace and led the jack of spades. The Austrian East had a king in a suit where declarer appeared to have just taken a finesse. Hoping that the "finesse" would be repeated, the Austrian East coyly played a small spade. He expected to win a second spade and then lead a third round of trumps so dummy would have no trumps for ruffing diamonds. That is not the way it worked out. The good judge was still alive. He couldn't afford to lead a second spade from the South hand, so he came to his hand with a diamond and led a small trump towards the dummy. Now East got nervous about his king of trumps. He was afraid he wasn't going to take a trick with it after all, so he played it. He didn't win a trick with it. West won the trick with the ace, and now there were twelve tricks for the taking.

In addition to those times when your partner will have a king opposite your ace, there are times when your partner will have a singleton or a void opposite your ace.

Both vul., dealer South.

                        NORTH
                        ♠ K J x x x x
                        ♡ K x
                        ◇ K Q x x x
                        ♣ None

        WEST   EAST
        ♠ A 9 x x   ♠ None
        ♡ 9 8 x x   ♡ Q 10 x
        ◇ x   ◇ J x x
        ♣ 9 x x x   ♣ K Q J x x x x

                        SOUTH
                        ♠ Q 10 x
                        ♡ A J x x
                        ◇ A 10 x x
                        ♣ A 10

The bidding:

SOUTH	WEST	NORTH	EAST
Crawford	Ricci	Becker	Chiaradia
1 ◇	Pass	1 ♠	1 NT
Pass	2 ♣	3 ♣	Pass
3 ♠	Pass	4 ◇	Pass
4 ♡	Pass	6 ◇	Pass
Pass	Pass		

Prior to 1958, a team from the United States played the champions of Europe for the Bermuda Bowl. This contest was generally accepted as determining the World Champions. In 1951, in Naples, an experienced team from the United States played an inexperienced team from Italy. The Italian players were experimenting with a number of new bidding methods. They didn't yet have the bugs out of them, and the Americans walloped them. That was the last time North Americans defeated the Italians for a long time. The Italians returned to international competition as European champions in 1957, and won the World Championship every year thereafter through 1969, when they temporarily retired from World Championship play. This hand, from that 1951 match, demonstrates that, even in the beginning, the Italians listened carefully to the bidding. Ricci heard B. J. Becker bid spades, which were eventually supported by Crawford. Ricci held four spades to the ace. If Becker held five and Crawford held three, then Ricci's partner held only one. A look at the hand tells you that if the defenders didn't take their tricks then, they were never going to get two tricks. Ricci led the ace of spades, and Chiaradia trumped the second spade to set the hand before Crawford got started.

The hands we teachers construct to illustrate a point seem to make that point more clearly than the hands which are dealt in real life. Even the Ricci lead does not illustrate the probability that you can give your partner a ruff so clearly as the hands I have used in some of my bridge classes. In the next hand, the evidence becomes more tenuous, but let's take a look to see if we can reason why Helen Sobel led the ace of clubs, hoping to find her partner with shortness in that suit, without being accused of discovering the evidence after we know the results.

E-W vul., dealer North.

```
                    NORTH
                    ♠ 9
                    ♡ A K 8 7 6
                    ◊ K 9 2
                    ♣ K J 7 2
      WEST                        EAST
      ♠ 6 5                       ♠ K J 10 8 7 4 2
      ♡ J 10 9 4 2                ♡ Q
      ◊ 4                         ◊ 8 6 5 3
      ♣ A 9 6 4 3                 ♣ 8
                    SOUTH
                    ♠ A Q 3
                    ♡ 5 3
                    ◊ A Q J 10 7
                    ♣ Q 10 5
```

380

The bidding:

SOUTH Chiaradia	WEST Sobel	NORTH D'Alelio	EAST Seamon
		1 ♡	2 ♠
2 NT	Pass	3 ♣	Pass
3 ◊	Pass	3 ♡	Pass
3 ♠	Pass	4 ◊	Pass
4 NT	Pass	5 ♡	Pass
6 ◊	Pass	Pass	Pass

If you had asked Helen why she made the killing opening lead of the club ace, she would likely have told you that she didn't exactly know, other than she just played a hunch. Whatever the reason, Helen was well-known for finding the killing opening lead. Not being possessed of her instinct in the matter, let's see if cold reason will give us any guidance on this hand.

How about leading spades? Her partner bid them. Usually it is better to trust your partner than it is to trust one of your opponents. But this time, Chiaradia not only bid 2NT over Bill Seamon's preemptive two-spade bid, but he also cue bid spades later on in the bidding. D'Alelio bid hearts, bid clubs, rebid hearts, and supported diamonds, so he had at most one spade.

As for Chiaradia, he showed absolutely no interest in the heart suit even after it was rebid. This would seem to indicate that, in spite of the fact that Helen held five hearts in the suit which North had rebid, her partner was not likely to be void in that suit.

Trumps were not to be considered, so let's think about clubs. Chiaradia showed strength in spades, shortness in hearts, and a good diamond suit. Let's try to get a tentative count of Chiaradia's distribution. He's unlikely to have more than three spades (he didn't double two spades); he's unlikely to have more than two hearts (he never supported a rebid suit); he's unlikely to have more than five diamonds (he might have bid them before trying notrump); ergo, he has at least three clubs. North has shown four clubs. Helen had five. Five plus four plus three equals twelve. Therefore, partner has only one club. The lead of the ace and another club will beat the slam. Helen would have scoffed at such reasoning, I know, but she did lead the ace and a club, and the defenders took the first two tricks.

For years, many of us have sneered at the old dictum that you should lead the ace so you can see the dummy, proving our cleverness by stating that you have to see the dummy no matter what you lead. We can still go along with the dictum that leads of aces against less-than-slam contracts are doubtful leads. The chances are too good that you are going to regain the lead after you have seen the dummy. When a few tricks have been played, with this added information, you can then know how to go about defending the hand. Maybe the first person who talked about leading aces to see the dummy was talking about leading them against small slam contracts in a suit. When your opponents are in a small slam, the chances are not too good you are going to have a second chance after you have seen the dummy. If you don't lead the ace, you probably are going to give the initiative to the declarer at trick one, and he may well be able to keep you from gaining the lead to cash your ace until he has disposed of his losers in the suit in which you have the ace. Leading the ace will sometimes give you some pleasant surprises when you see the dummy.

On the next hand, it is uncertain just what Bobby Goldman hoped to see, but after he led the ace of diamonds, he saw something that pleased him very much.

N-S vul., dealer West.

NORTH
♠ Q
♡ Q J 2
◊ K Q 5 4
♣ A Q 10 5 3

WEST
♠ 8 4 2
♡ 8 6 4
◊ A 10 7 6 2
♣ 8 4

EAST
♠ 10 7 6 5
♡ 5 3
◊ J
♣ K J 9 7 6 2

SOUTH
♠ A K J 9 3
♡ A K 10 9 7
◊ 9 8 3
♣ None

The bidding:

SOUTH	WEST	NORTH	EAST
Belladonna	Goldman	Garozzo	Lawrence
	Pass	2 ♣	Pass
2 ◊	Pass	2 NT	Pass
3 ♠	Pass	3 NT	Pass
4 ♡	Pass	6 ♡	Pass
Pass	Pass		

This hand was played in the 1973 World Championship, with the Italian team opposed by the then World Champion Aces from Dallas, Texas. The Italians were using what they call the Super Precision System of bidding. They retained many of their old Italian methods for overcalls, but had adopted the Precision idea of opening two clubs when they held 11-15 HCPs, with either a six-card club suit or a five-card club suit and a four-card suit. Garozzo must have discounted his singleton queen of spades when he opened two clubs. Had he given it full value, he would have had the requirements for opening the strong Precision one-club bid. Belladonna's two-diamond bid requested further information about Garozzo's distribution and, when

Garozzo rebid 2NT, he stated he did not have a six-card club suit. So he therefore had a side four-card suit. As he bid neither spades nor hearts, that four-card suit had to be diamonds. From there on, the Italian pair bid until they reached six hearts.

Let's look at the evidence that makes the lead of the ace of diamonds attractive. First, Bobby Goldman's partner might have the king. He had only four HCPs himself, and expected his partner had somewhere in the neighborhood of six. While Garozzo's bid had shown a four-card diamond suit, it did not specifically point out that his high cards were in diamonds. Second, Goldman knew that there were nine diamonds between his hand and North's hand. South had shown extreme shortness in clubs. Therefore, it was possible that he held three diamonds. If that was so, then Lawrence held a singleton diamond, and the lead of ace and another diamond would beat the contract. Third, the major suits looked well-placed for declarer, and he was unlikely to build up a spade trick by leading that suit. Fourth, the lead of the diamond ace would allow him to see the dummy, and then to decide which way to go.

When he saw four diamonds to the king-queen in dummy, and he saw Lawrence play the jack, that was all he needed to decide what to do next. He led another diamond and the hand was set.

In the replay of the hand where the Americans had the North-South hands, Bob Hamman, South, ended up playing only four hearts. The opening lead was the eight of clubs, and Hamman had no trouble taking twelve tricks.

Another good reason for leading an ace against a slam contract is that your partner may have an ace in his hand also, and a look at the dummy may tell you how to proceed. Usually, if your side holds somewhere around ten HCPs, and your opponents bid a suit slam, chances are better that your partner will have an ace when you don't have any high cards to go with your ace.

But, you will say to me, do the experts ever get to a small slam missing two cashable aces? The answer is simple. They do.

Look at this hand from the 1953 World Championship with Sweden, representing Europe, playing against the United States.

E-W vul., dealer South:

                        NORTH
                        ♠ K Q 10 7 4
                        ♡ 10 6 5 3
                        ◊ None
                        ♣ K Q J 2
    WEST   EAST
    ♠ 9 5   ♠ A 8 3 2
    ♡ 8 4 2   ♡ 9
    ◊ 8 5 4 2   ◊ 10 9 7 3
    ♣ A 9 7 3   ♣ 10 6 5 4
                        SOUTH
                        ♠ J 6
                        ♡ A K Q J 7
                        ◊ A K Q J 6
                        ♣ 8

The bidding:

CLOSED ROOM

SOUTH	WEST	NORTH	EAST
Schenken	Kock	Stayman	Werner
2 ♣	Pass	2 ♠	Pass
3 ♡	Pass	3 ♠	Pass
4 ◊	Pass	5 ♡	Pass
6 ♡	Pass	Pass	Pass

OPEN ROOM

Anulf	Crawford	Lilliehook	Rapee
2 ♡	Pass	3 ♡	Pass
3 ♠	Pass	4 ◊	Pass
6 ♡	Pass	Pass	Pass

Yes, the best of them sometimes get to a slam when the opponents have two cashable aces. There are some very famous names in the bidding box given below this hand. In the closed room, Kock, for Sweden, led the four of hearts. It didn't take Howard Schenken long to pull three rounds of trumps, and discard all of dummy's clubs on his diamond suit. He was then able to lead the jack of spades and claim twelve tricks.

In the open room, Anulf tried to muddy the water by bidding spades himself. Johnny Crawford was a great practical player, rather than a theorist, and as a practical player he led his ace of clubs and then examined the dummy carefully. His second play was a spade, and the Americans got their two tricks before they surrendered the lead.

You may tell me that 1953 was a long time ago, and that today people bid better. Well, maybe. Here is a hand from the 1973 World Championships where two teams got to the six level with the opponents holding two cashable aces.

Both vul., dealer West.

```
                    NORTH
                    ♠ 5 3
                    ♡ Q 5
                    ◇ K 10 8 6 5 4 3
                    ♣ Q 10
        WEST                    EAST
        ♠ Q J 8 2               ♠ 10 9 6
        ♡ 8 7 6                 ♡ A 10 2
        ◇ 2                     ◇ 9 7
        ♣ A K 9 7 2             ♣ J 6 5 4 3
                    SOUTH
                    ♠ A K 7 4
                    ♡ K J 9 4 3
                    ◇ A Q J
                    ♣ 8
```

The bidding:

OPEN ROOM

SOUTH	WEST	NORTH	EAST
Forquet	Goldman	Bianchi	Blumenthal
	Pass	Pass	Pass
1 ♣	Pass	1 ♢	Pass
1 ♡	Pass	3 ♢	Pass
3 ♠	Pass	4 ♡	Pass
6 ♡	Pass	Pass	Pass

CLOSED ROOM

Wolff	Belladonna	Jacoby	Garozzo
	Pass	Pass	Pass
1 ♣	Pass	1 ♡	Pass
2 ♡	Pass	3 ♢	Pass
3 ♠	Pass	4 ♡	Pass
5 ♢	Pass	6 ♢	Pass
Pass	Pass		

In the open room, the one-club opening bid and one-diamond response were artificial, but the balance of the bids were natural. That means the unbid suit was clubs. For some mysterious reason, Bobby Goldman, West, decided not to lead from the ace-king of the unbid suit, but instead led the eight of hearts. Mark Blumenthal won his ace and examined the dummy to see what clues he could get about his proper return. He also refused to lead the unbid suit, but led a spade. Forquet won the ace and then led a trump to the queen. He returned to his hand with the king of spades and claimed the contract, as he could now discard all his losing cards on dummy's diamonds.

In the closed room, the contract was six diamonds, with North as declarer and East on opening lead. The one-club opening bid and one-heart response again were artificial and, as in the open room, the only unbid suit was clubs. Garozzo chose to lead the unbid suit rather than cash the ace of hearts, but he would have done just as well to lead the ace of hearts and lead the unbid suit. Belladonna won the opening club lead and returned the two of diamonds. Jim Jacoby never had a chance, as he was always going to lose a second trick to the ace of hearts.

Somebody might suggest that had the players been using the Blackwood Convention, it might have proved quite helpful on these hands, but modesty forbids me to point this out.

If you took a poll of expert players to see what pair is considered the strongest in the world today, Bobby Wolff and Bob Hamman would either come in number one, or close to it. In spite of that, they got to a six-club contract with the opponents holding two cashable aces. I am not sure what that proves, if anything, for they made their contract. The deal is from the 1973 World Championship, in which the Aces Team was playing as defending champions. There was also another team representing North America, plus teams from Brazil, Italy, and Indonesia.

Both vul., dealer North.

```
                    NORTH
                    ♠ 9 8
                    ♡ K Q J 7
                    ◇ A Q 9
                    ♣ K 10 7 3
     WEST                          EAST
     ♠ A Q 10 2                    ♠ 7 5 4
     ♡ 10 6 5 4 3                  ♡ A 8 2
     ◇ 6 4                         ◇ 10 8 7 5 3 2
     ♣ 9 5                         ♣ 2
                    SOUTH
                    ♠ K J 6 3
                    ♡ 9
                    ◇ K J
                    ♣ A Q J 8 6 4
```

The bidding:

SOUTH	WEST	NORTH	EAST
Wolff	Becker	Hamman	Rubens
		1 NT	Pass
2 ◇	Pass	2 ♡	Pass
3 ♣	Pass	3 ◇	Pass
3 ♠	Pass	4 ♣	Pass
4 ◇	Pass	4 ♡	Pass
4 NT	Pass	5 ♡	Pass
6 ♣	Pass	Pass	Pass

You will see from the bidding sequence that the famous pair did use a 4NT bid, but, according to their announced system, 4NT was Blackwood only when it was a jump bid or when obvious. Otherwise, it was "declarative or interrogative". Apparently, there was one thing it did not inquire about. It did not inquire about the number of aces in the North hand.

B. J. Becker, West, made the only lead that could beat the slam contract by two tricks. He led a heart. Had Jeff Rubens returned a spade, B. J. would then have cashed two spade tricks. Unfortunately for the defenders, Rubens did not return a spade. He returned a diamond, hoping that B. J. was void.

On the opening heart lead, Wolff played low from dummy and East won with the ace. Wolff won the diamond return, and pulled trumps. Now he had three discards coming on hearts, plus one on diamonds. That was just enough to take care of all four of his losing spades.

If you look at enough defensive hands played by the experts, you begin to think they are better at promoting and developing tricks than they are at simply cashing the ones the dealer gave them.

The last of the hands, where the opening leader and his partner each had an ace, is from the 1976 World Championship, with North America playing Italy.

E-W vul., dealer East.

NORTH
♠ K 7 6 4
♡ A 10 8 3 2
♢ K
♣ K J 6

WEST
♠ A 10 9 8 5
♡ 6 5
♢ 10 8 7 2
♣ 10 5

EAST
♠ Q J 2
♡ K Q J 9 7 4
♢ A J 9 5
♣ None

SOUTH
♠ 3
♡ None
♢ Q 6 4 3
♣ A Q 9 8 7 4 3 2

The bidding:

SOUTH	WEST	NORTH	EAST
Forquet	Hamilton	Belladonna	Eisenberg
			1 ♡
5 ♣	Pass	6 ♣	Pass
Pass	Pass		

Instead of leading his partner's suit, Fred Hamilton laid down the ace of spades. If a heart lead was necessary, he still would have time to make that lead after seeing the dummy. When the dummy came down and he saw five hearts there, including the ace, it looked like the lead of a heart would get him nowhere. Hamilton led a diamond and the defenders took the first two tricks.

Then there are times when your side has a trick other than an ace which will not disappear, but your ace will disappear unless you lead it. Look at this hand from the 1965 World Championship, in the qualifying rounds with Great Britain playing the United States.

E-W vul., dealer West.

NORTH
♠ A K J 9 8
♡ A K J 7
♢ 7 2
♣ 8 5

WEST
♠ 5 4 3
♡ 10 8 5 3 2
♢ 10
♣ A 10 7 2

EAST
♠ 7 6 2
♡ 9 6 4
♢ Q J 6
♣ Q 9 6 3

SOUTH
♠ Q 10
♡ Q
♢ A K 9 8 5 4 3
♣ K J 4

The bidding:

SOUTH	WEST	NORTH	EAST
Becker	Rose	Hayden	Gray
	Pass	1 ♠	Pass
3 ♢	Pass	3 ♡	Pass
4 ♢	Pass	4 NT	Pass
5 ♢	Pass	6 ♢	Pass
Pass	Pass		

Albert Rose, of London, England, was on lead with the West hand. Although he didn't know it, his side had a trump trick as well as the ace of clubs. The defenders got both of their tricks. Rose led the ace of clubs and then switched to a heart. B. J. Becker, for the United States, cashed the ace and king of trumps, and then conceded down one when the diamond suit failed to break.

You will see that, had Rose led any other card, Becker could have taken twelve tricks. He would have won the opening lead and led the ace and king of trumps. Upon discovering the trump loser, he would have cashed the queen of hearts, led a spade to dummy, and discarded his three clubs on dummy's high hearts,

391

as East ruffed the last heart. The trump trick would be the defenders' only trick.

The very first match which is recognized as having been for the World's Championship was held in Bermuda in November, 1950. There was one team from the United States, one from England, and one team which was called the European Team, consisting of players from Sweden and Iceland. The next hand is from that event. It was played in the match between the United States and Great Britain. Sidney Silidor held the West hand for the United States, while Leslie Dodds, from Great Britain, was South. The final contract was six spades by South.

E-W vul., dealer West.

```
                    NORTH
                    ♠ J 10 3 2
                    ♡ 8
                    ◇ A Q 10 9 8
                    ♣ 10 8 2
        WEST                        EAST
        ♠ Q 6                       ♠ 9 7
        ♡ A 5 4 2                   ♡ Q J 10 7 6 3
        ◇ J 5 2                     ◇ K 7 3
        ♣ 9 7 6 4                   ♣ 5 3
                    SOUTH
                    ♠ A K 8 5 4
                    ♡ K 9
                    ◇ 6 4
                    ♣ A K Q J
```

Silidor led the deuce of diamonds. However, Dodds went up with dummy's ace and laid down the two top trumps. He then cashed his four clubs, discarding dummy's heart. After losing a diamond, he claimed twelve tricks and his contract. If the defenders had cashed the heart ace at trick one, they would have taken a second trick with the king of diamonds. The diamond trick could not disappear, but the heart trick did.

The classic situation, where you lead an ace against a small slam contract, is where you believe you have a trump trick in your hand. The next hand is a good example of this. It's from the World Championship Olympiad Games in 1962, with a team from the United States playing against the Italian champions.

None vul., dealer West.

NORTH
- ♠ J 10 6
- ♡ K 7 2
- ◇ Q J 9
- ♣ K J 10 3

WEST
- ♠ Q 7 4
- ♡ A Q J 4 3
- ◇ 10 4
- ♣ 5 4 2

EAST
- ♠ 2
- ♡ 10 9 8 5
- ◇ K 8 7 6 2
- ♣ 9 8 6

SOUTH
- ♠ A K 9 8 5 3
- ♡ 6
- ◇ A 5 3
- ♣ A Q 7

The bidding:

SOUTH	WEST	NORTH	EAST
Manca	Schenken	Bianchi	Ogust
	Pass	Pass	Pass
1 ♠	Pass	2 NT	Pass
6 ♠	Pass	Pass	Pass

From the bidding, it sounded like Howard Schenken's queen of spades was going to take a trick. Had he been playing against only a game contract, there would have been no reason to lead the ace of hearts from his tenace holding. The chances would be good that he or his partner would have another chance to lead the suit. However, it is different in a small slam contract; too often you never get another chance. Schenken led the ace of hearts, and eventually got his spade trick to set the hand one trick.

With any other lead, the declarer would make the contract by pitching his heart on the fourth round of clubs, and smothering West's diamond ten by leading the queen and jack from the dummy.

The last hand to demonstrate the situation where the opening leader must lead his ace to get it, and where there is a second trick in the partnership that will not disappear, is taken from the 1958 World Championship, with Italy playing Argentina.

E-W vul., dealer East.

```
                    NORTH
                    ♠ A Q
                    ♡ K Q 10 6 4 3
                    ◇ K Q 6 5
                    ♣ 4
        WEST                      EAST
        ♠ 3 2                     ♠ J 10 8
        ♡ J 9 7                   ♡ 8 5
        ◇ 10 8 4 3                ◇ J 7
        ♣ A 10 9 7                ♣ K J 8 6 5 2
                    SOUTH
                    ♠ K 9 7 6 5 4
                    ♡ A 2
                    ◇ A 9 2
                    ♣ Q 3
```

The bidding:

SOUTH	WEST	NORTH	EAST
Cabanne	Avarelli	Lerner	Belladonna
			Pass
1 ♠	Pass	3 ♡	Pass
3 ♠	Pass	4 NT	Pass
5 ♡	Pass	6 ♠	Pass
Pass	Pass		

When the Italian team was North-South, they arrived at a six-heart contract, played by North, and took twelve tricks with no trouble. East got off to the club lead. West won and returned a club, but declarer was able to trump with a small heart, and then take the balance of the tricks.

Where the Argentine team had the North and South hands,

they reached a contract of six spades. Actually, the lead of the ace of clubs resulted in the second trick by promoting a trump trick for East. In 1958, the Italian players were playing odd-even signals instead of high-low. Belladonna played the five to encourage a heart continuation, and Avarelli continued the suit. Cabanne had to trump in the dummy or go set at once. When he trumped, he established the setting trick for Belladonna.

The next hand illustrates two earlier themes. First, that a singleton is not a good lead against a slam contract when you hold an ace. Second, aces themselves should be led against slam contracts.

N-S vul., dealer East.

```
                    NORTH
                    ♠ K J 5
                    ♡ Q 7
                    ◇ A K 8 7 3
                    ♣ K 10 5
        WEST                    EAST
        ♠ 10 7                  ♠ Q 9 3
        ♡ 9 5                   ♡ 8 4 3 2
        ◇ 6                     ◇ 10 9 5 4 2
        ♣ A Q J 9 8 6 4 3       ♣ 2
                    SOUTH
                    ♠ A 8 6 4 2
                    ♡ A K J 10 6
                    ◇ Q J
                    ♣ 7
```

The bidding:

TABLE ONE

SOUTH	WEST	NORTH	EAST
Weichsel	Brachman	Sontag	Passell
			Pass
1 ♠	5 ♣	Double	Pass
5 ♡	Pass	6 ♠	Pass
Pass	Pass		

TABLE TWO

Soloway	Russell	Goldman	Freeman
			Pass
1 ♠	5 ♣	5 ♠	Pass
6 ♠	Pass	Pass	Pass

The deal is from the 1976 Vanderbilt Team of Four game. At Table One, Malcolm Brachman gave his team a boost by the simple expedient of cashing his ace of clubs. From then on, Peter Weichsel had no way to make the hand, as he always had to lose a trump trick.

At Table Two, Cliff Russell led the six of diamonds. Paul Soloway handled that one neatly. He won the jack. As it was unlikely that Russell would have led a singleton if he had three trumps to the queen, Soloway laid down the ace and king of spades, rather than take the finesse. He then played two more rounds of diamonds, discarding the club from his hand, conceded a trump trick, and claimed his slam.

Reese and Dormer put it well. They said, "Players who lead a singleton against a small slam when holding a certain trick in their own hand should be studied carefully but not imitated."

Although more slams are made because an ace is not led than the other way around, there are still times when leading an ace is a disaster. Let's take a look at some hands where this would have been true, and see whether we can find any clues which might tell us that the hand in question is one of those exceptions.

The next hand illustrates an obvious case. It is taken from the 1966 World Championship, in the match between North America and The Netherlands.

E-W vul., dealer North.

```
                    NORTH
                    ♠ 9 8
                    ♡ A J 9 6
                    ◇ K Q 7
                    ♣ Q 10 5 4
        WEST                      EAST
        ♠ Q                       ♠ J 10 7 6 2
        ♡ K Q 7 3                 ♡ 8 5 2
        ◇ A J 10 8 3 2            ◇ 9 5 4
        ♣ 7 6                     ♣ J 2
                    SOUTH
                    ♠ A K 5 4 3
                    ♡ 10 4
                    ◇ 6
                    ♣ A K 9 8 3
```

The bidding:

SOUTH	WEST	NORTH	EAST
De Leeuw	Kehela	Blitzblum	Murray
		1 ♡	Pass
2 ♣	2 ◇	3 ♣	Pass
6 ♣	Pass	Pass	Pass

In addition to his diamond ace, Sammy Kehela had a heart holding where he could establish a trick after one lead. There was nothing to indicate his diamond trick would go away if he didn't cash it at once. Chances were excellent that he could establish a heart trick in his hand and still be able to regain the lead and cash it. So Kehela led the king of hearts, and could not be denied his two tricks.

If you look at the hand, you will see that had Kehela cashed his ace of diamonds, he would have established dummy's diamonds for a discard of declarer's losing heart.

The next hand is a variation on the same theme. The hand is from the match between the United States and Brazil in the 1978 Olympiad Games.

None vul., dealer East.

```
                        NORTH
                        ♠ J 4 2
                        ♡ 10
                        ◊ K J 9 3
                        ♣ K J 10 4 2
        WEST                            EAST
        ♠ K Q                           ♠ 10 8 7 6
        ♡ 8 7 5 3 2                     ♡ A J 9 6
        ◊ None                          ◊ 10 6 4
        ♣ A Q 9 7 5 3                   ♣ 8 6
                        SOUTH
                        ♠ A 9 5 3
                        ♡ K Q 4
                        ◊ A Q 8 7 5 2
                        ♣ None
```

The bidding:

SOUTH	WEST	NORTH	EAST
Branco	Wolff	Cintra	Hamman
			Pass
1 ♣	2 ♣	Pass	Pass
2 ◊	2 ♡	3 ♡	4 ♡
5 ◊	5 ♡	6 ◊	Pass
Pass	Pass		

In the Precision Club System, which the Brazilians were playing, South's opening one-club bid was supposed to show 16 or more HCPs. Branco modified that by one point because of his excellent distribution. Bobby Wolff was able to show both of his suits at a low level. After the diamond fit was uncovered, Cintra, North, became bullish about the hand, and, in a competitive auction, the Brazilians finally ended up in six diamonds.

One thing that terrifies players about leading aces against small slam contracts is the possibility of finding that one of your opponents is void in the suit, with the other one holding the king. That may not occur too often, but this hand is an example of what would have happened if Bobby Wolff had decided to lead his ace of clubs. It is not so much that establishing dummy's king of clubs would have made this play disastrous, but rather that it would have destroyed the timing needed by the defenders. Declarer would trump the ace of clubs and go to the dummy with a trump to lead the singleton heart. If East rises with the ace, the declarer discards two spades on his hearts. He then discards one of his spades on dummy's king of clubs and trumps the other two in dummy. If East doesn't go up with the ace of hearts, things would still work out all right for declarer. He trumps two hearts in the dummy, discards one spade on the king of clubs, pulls trumps, and leads the ace and a spade. Dummy's jack would become the twelfth trick.

But, Bobby Wolff removed all of this speculation. He established the spade trick for his side before declarer got to establish his tricks. He led the king of spades. Now the defense was able to take one trick with the queen of spades and a second trick with the ace of hearts.

There are times when your partner is given an opportunity to tell you about a trick that needs to be established before you turn loose of your ace. Take a look at this hand from the 1955 World Championship, when Great Britain represented Europe against the United States.

```
                    NORTH
                    ♠ Q J 8 7
                    ♡ K 3
                    ◊ A 8 6 5 3
                    ♣ A J
        WEST                    EAST
        ♠ 2                     ♠ None
        ♡ A 9 6 4               ♡ Q J 10 7 5 2
        ◊ Q J 4                 ◊ K 9 7
        ♣ 9 8 7 4 2             ♣ K Q 6 3
                    SOUTH
                    ♠ A K 10 9 6 5 4 3
                    ♡ 8
                    ◊ 10 2
                    ♣ 10 5
```

The bidding:

SOUTH	WEST	NORTH	EAST
Konstam	Moran	Meredith	Mathe
		1 NT	2 ♡
3 ♠	4 ♡	4 ♠	Pass
4 NT	Pass	5 ♡	Double
6 ♠	Pass	Pass	Pass

OPEN ROOM

Ellenby	Reese	Rosen	Schapiro
		1 ◇	1 ♡
1 ♠	2 ♡	2 ♠	3 ♡
4 ♡	Pass	5 ♣	Double
Pass	Pass	5 ♡	Pass
6 ♠	Pass	Pass	Pass

Lew Mathe's attempt to suggest a sacrifice by doubling five hearts backfired when John Moran took it as a lead directional double. He laid down the ace of hearts. After a look at dummy, he switched to a club. It was too late. Kenneth Konstam, South for England, was able to establish his tricks before the defenders could establish theirs. He won the club switch with the ace and discarded a diamond on the king of hearts. Now the ace of diamonds, a diamond ruff, back to dummy with a spade to trump another diamond, back to dummy with another spade and his losing club went off on the established diamond.

In the open room, Milton Ellenby and Bill Rosen, for the United States, took the cue bid route to six spades, rather than using the Blackwood Convention. The five-club cue bid gave Boris Schapiro something worthwhile to double. Although he had bid hearts two times, his double of five clubs told Reese that he had something important in clubs. It turned out to be a high card which needed to be established before Reese released his ace of hearts. After the lead of the nine of clubs, there wasn't much Ellenby could do. He won dummy's ace, and came to his hand with a spade to lead his singleton heart. Terence Reese went up with the ace and led a club to Schapiro's queen for the setting trick.

On the next hand, Carlos Cabanne, from Buenos Aires, did not lead an ace against a slam contract. Had he led his ace, the contract would have been made. Let's examine the hand and see whether we can determine what influenced Cabanne to reject the ace lead.

None vul., dealer South:

                    NORTH
                    ♠ A 9 8 6 3
                    ♡ J 9
                    ◇ A Q
                    ♣ K Q J 5
    WEST   EAST
    ♠ J   ♠ 4
    ♡ K 6 5   ♡ Q 10 7 2
    ◇ K 10 6 3   ◇ J 9 8 4 2
    ♣ A 10 8 6 3   ♣ 9 7 4
                    SOUTH
                    ♠ K Q 10 7 5 2
                    ♡ A 8 4 3
                    ◇ 7 5
                    ♣ 2

The bidding:

SOUTH	WEST	NORTH	EAST
Murray	Cabanne	Coon	Berisso
1 ♠	Pass	3 ♣	Pass
3 ♠	Pass	4 NT	Pass
5 ◇	Pass	6 ♠	Pass
Pass	Pass		

The hand is from the 1962 World Championship, with the Argentines playing against a team from North America.

Charlie Coon, North, had bid clubs. That fact surely made the lead of the ace of clubs questionable. You don't lead aces of suits where you are almost certain you will be setting up the suit for the opponents. As a matter of fact, Cabanne held five clubs, which made it not at all unlikely that, if he laid down his ace of clubs, he would run into that terrible situation where North had a suit headed by the king and South was void. Instead, Cabanne went for an attacking lead in one of the red suits. The king in a three-card suit is more likely to stand up as a second round winner than is the king of a longer suit, so Cabanne led the five of hearts. That was the killing lead. A heart had to be led before clubs to beat the contract. When a club was led, Cabanne jumped up with his ace and cashed his king of hearts.

So here we have another exception to the rule that you "always" lead aces against slam contracts. Be wary of leading an ace against a slam when the opponents have bid the suit.

Now let's look at one more exception before we attempt to summarize. This hand is from the United States versus Italy match in the 1968 World Championship.

Both vul., dealer North.

```
                        NORTH
                        ♠ A K Q J
                        ♡ K Q 8 3
                        ◇ J 9 3
                        ♣ A J
        WEST                            EAST
        ♠ 10 9 5 4                      ♠ 8 7
        ♡ 6 2                           ♡ J 7 5
        ◇ A 10 2                        ◇ Q 8 7 6
        ♣ Q 7 6 5                       ♣ 9 4 3 2
                        SOUTH
                        ♠ 6 3 2
                        ♡ A 10 9 4
                        ◇ K 5 4
                        ♣ K 10 8
```

The bidding:

SOUTH	WEST	NORTH	EAST
Forquet	Jordan	Garozzo	Robinson
		1 ♣	Pass
1 NT	Pass	2 NT	Pass
3 ♣	Pass	3 ◇	Pass
3 ♡	Pass	3 ♠	Pass
3 NT	Pass	4 ♣	Pass
4 ◇	Pass	4 ♠	Pass
4 NT	Pass	6 ♡	Pass
Pass	Pass		

Arthur Jordan, West, opened the four of spades. Forquet won, led three rounds of trumps and cashed the balance of his spades. He then discarded a small diamond from his hand and led a small diamond to his king. Jordan won the ace and returned a diamond, letting Robinson take the setting trick with his queen.

This simple hand has a very important lesson. To understand why an ace should not be led on this bidding, let's examine why an ace is frequently led against small slams.

Occasionally, your partner will have a king to go with your ace. If you don't lead the suit, the opponents will often have twelve tricks in the other three suits. More often, if you don't lead your ace, your opponents will be able to discard any losers they have in that suit on some long suit of their own. For them to accomplish this, there are two things they need: shortness in the suit where you hold the ace and a long suit on which they can discard those losers. Under these circumstances, if you don't take your ace, you may never get it.

If these conditions don't exist, that is if you are convinced your opponents have neither short suits nor long suits, the urgency to cash the ace is not present. Now you get to the rule that aces were meant to catch kings and queens, and not deuces. You lead something else, confident that the trick you have in the ace will not disappear. You just wait and hope your opponents will have to lead the suit and your ace will indeed catch a high card.

You can't always tell when your opponents have either long

suits or short suits, but there are some bidding methods in common use which advertise that fact for all who care to listen. In the Neapolitan Club System, which was being used by the Italian pair, North-South advertised that they did not have long suits, and almost certainly neither of them had a singleton. This made it unlikely that they could discard all of their diamonds in either hand.

The opening one-club bid said nothing about the club suit, but simply showed that Garozzo had 17 HCPs or better. South's 1NT bid showed nothing about distribution, but simply said that he had four controls, with each ace counting as two controls and each king counting as one. At this point, the Italians were forced to game and there was no necessity for any jump bids. In their careful exploration, the 2NT bid by Garozzo, North, indicated that his hand was suitable for notrump, without a long suit and without a singleton or a void. The three-club bid by Forquet was the Stayman Convention, and denied that South had any long suits. Not only did this long sequence of bidding show that both the North and South hands were balanced, but it also suggested that they had approximately 30 HCPs. They showed an interest in playing in 6NT until they discovered their 4-4 heart fit and chose to play in their eight-card major. On this basis, West judged that his partner had very little indeed, and that even if his partner happened to have the king of diamonds, they would still probably get both tricks before the hand was over. So he had no fear that his diamond trick would disappear when he opened a small spade. Now that we have had a good look at the record, I suggest that we make a new rule for ourselves: "Lead an ace when you have one against a small slam contract, unless the available evidence indicates a specific reason why the lead should not be made."

At times, a lead may be made at matchpoint duplicate simply to keep your opponents from making an extra trick. At International Match Points, or any form of total match scoring, the ace is led on the theory that it offers the best chance to defeat the contract. Of course, this rule has exceptions. The casual player will do well enough if he just forgets the exceptions and follows the rules. The more serious player will make every effort to discover the exceptional cases. I do not know exactly what odds will favor this procedure, but let us assume for a moment that it is as high as 3:1; that is to say, 75% to 25%. The problem on each hand is to determine whether the particular hand is or is not one of those that belongs in the 25% group. If it is, the serious player will want to avoid leading the ace.

He will avoid leading the ace under three conditions:

1. He has reason to feel that he or his side have some other trick which needs to be established before the ace is relinquished.

2. The opponents have bid the suit in which he holds the ace.

3. The opposing bidding has clearly indicated that the opponents have no long suits and no short suits and, hence, there is no great hurry about cashing the ace.

I have spent a lot of time on this subject. My excuse is that nowhere else has the subject been adequately covered in bridge literature. The loss when you fail to set a slam contract which could be set is one of the largest penalties you are likely to experience in an average bridge game. In addition, the subject is naturally a tough one because, like all opening lead problems, the evidence you have to go on is so limited. It would always be easier if you could see the dummy before you made the lead. Unfortunately, when the opponents are in a slam, the crucial decision must usually be made before you have any evidence except the bidding and the cards you see in your own hand.

CHAPTER 11:
OPENING LEADS AGAINST PRE-EMPTIVE BIDS

LEADS AGAINST THE GAMBLING THREE NOTRUMP BID

Is the so-called gambling 3NT bid really a pre-emptive bid? It certainly has some of the characteristics of a pre-emptive bid. It has a long, strong minor suit, and one of its purposes is to keep the opponents from bidding. However, it differs from other pre-emptive bids in two respects. The 3NT opening bid guarantees that the minor suit is completely solid, and usually indicates something like a six- or seven-card suit headed by the three or four top honors. No such guarantee goes with other forms of pre-emptive bids. In addition, while some people play that there will be virtually no strength outside of the one suit, others play that the hand might be quite strong.

The bid was first played in the ACOL bridge club in London, and was a part of the ACOL bidding system. In the early days, the hand could be quite strong, and one of the requirements was that you must hold "controls" in two side suits. The term "controls" seems to be rather loosely applied, as examples exist where one of the controls was something like the queen doubleton. Some players still follow the requirement of having controls in two side suits to make the bid. The majority of players today, however, have reduced that requirement to the extent that most players guarantee no more than a side queen when the bid is made in the first or second seat. Before deciding what to lead against the players who use gambling 3NT, it is wise to find out just what variation the partnership is playing.

Literature on the subject is limited, but most authorities recommend that if you have an ace against a gambling 3NT bid, lead it to take a look at the dummy. The assumption is that as soon as the declarer gets the lead, he can cash about seven tricks in his minor suit, but that he may well be wide open in one of the other suits. After looking at dummy, you can better judge whether it is the suit where you lead the ace, or some other suit. A review of the hands played in World Championships, where the gambling 3NT bid was used, certainly supports this opinion.

Actually, the bid is rare. I have checked ten years of World Championship books, from 1968 through 1977, and have found only four occasions where the gambling 3NT bid was used. On only two of those occasions was the final contract 3NT. Because of this scarcity, I have added some examples from tournaments other than the World Championship.

Of the four hands to be presented, three represent triumphs for the defenders. The last represents a stunning disaster for the defense.

The first hand is from the European Championships of 1956, in a match between Great Britain and Ireland.

Unknown vul., dealer South.

```
                    NORTH
                    ♠ A K 8 5 2
                    ♡ K 6 5 3 2
                    ◊ J 4
                    ♣ 10
         WEST                      EAST
         ♠ J 10 9 6 3              ♠ 7
         ♡ 4                       ♡ Q 10 9 7
         ◊ A Q 10 8 6             ◊ K 9 7 5 3
         ♣ 5 3                     ♣ J 9 4
                    SOUTH
                    ♠ Q 4
                    ♡ A J 8
                    ◊ 2
                    ♣ A K Q 8 7 6 2
```

In the room where Great Britain had the North-South hands, Rockfelt opened the South hand with 3NT. The hand seems to meet the qualifications for the gambling 3NT bid, as it was originally used. He certainly could believe the club suit was a favorite to bring in seven tricks, and he had some kind of high cards in two additional suits. He played it there. The Irish defender followed the normal procedure against this bid and led the ace of diamonds. As a result, the defenders took the first five tricks.

In the room where the Irish players had the North-South hands, they were represented by Bridburg and Cohen. South opened one club and North responded one spade. South jumped to three clubs and North bid three hearts. South bid 4NT and, when North responded five diamonds, showing one ace, South went to six clubs. With the suit breaking normally, the declarer had twelve tricks on top.

On the next hand, the jump to 3NT was an overcall. It was played in the 1970 World Championship. The Italian team consisted of six players substituting for the famous Italian Blue Team, who had "permanently" retired from World Championship bridge, until they returned in 1972. Opposing them were the Aces, representing North America.

Both vul., dealer East.

```
                  NORTH
                  ♠ A K 8 6 5 3
                  ♡ J 7
                  ◇ 6 4 3
                  ♣ 7 5
      WEST                      EAST
      ♠ J 4                     ♠ 10 9
      ♡ K 6 4 2                 ♡ A 10 8 5
      ◇ Q 9 8 5 2               ◇ A K J 10 7
      ♣ 4 3                     ♣ 9 8
                  SOUTH
                  ♠ Q 7 2
                  ♡ Q 9 3
                  ◇ None
                  ♣ A K Q J 10 6 2
```

The bidding:

SOUTH	WEST	NORTH	EAST
Cesati	Jacoby	Tersch	Wolff
			1 ♡
3 NT	Pass	Pass	Pass

CLOSED ROOM

Hamman	Barbarisi	Lawrence	Morini
			1 ♡
3 ♣	Pass	3 ♠	Pass
4 ♠	Pass	Pass	Pass

Cesati's 3NT overcall, in the open room, was somewhat less than a success. Jim Jacoby, West, didn't have an ace, so he followed the old-fashioned practice of leading the suit his partner had bid. Bobby Wolff won the ace and switched to the king of diamonds. The defenders cashed five diamond tricks, while Cesati suffered agony at the discards he had to make. He simply could not afford to turn loose of a second heart. So the defenders took the first seven tricks, and Cesati was down three.

In the closed room, the Americans were playing intermediate jump overcalls, and Bob Hamman simply overcalled three clubs. When Mike Lawrence showed a spade suit, Hamman was pleased to raise. The final contract was four spades. Against an opening lead of the king of diamonds, the Americans took all thirteen tricks.

The next hand is not from a World Championship team game—it is from the Olympiad pair games of 1978. In this drama, Jean-Marc Roudinesco, of Paris, France, is featured as the hero. When he started playing tournament bridge, he was usually referred to by his opponents as "the little genius." While the authorities all tell us to lead an ace against a gambling notrump bid, it is not that common to lead a singleton ace. That is what Roudinesco did.

N-S vul., dealer West.

NORTH
- ♠ 10 7 3
- ♡ 10 9 8 6 5 3
- ◇ J 10
- ♣ K 8

WEST
- ♠ Q J 6
- ♡ A
- ◇ 4 2
- ♣ J 10 9 7 5 3 2

EAST
- ♠ A 8 5 4 2
- ♡ K J 7 4 2
- ◇ 8 5
- ♣ 6

SOUTH
- ♠ K 9
- ♡ Q
- ◇ A K Q 9 7 6 3
- ♣ A Q 4

The bidding:

SOUTH	WEST	NORTH	EAST
Mauri	Roudinesco	Perron	Stoppa
	Pass	Pass	1 ♠
3 NT	4 ♣	Pass	Pass
4 NT	Pass	Pass	Pass

Roudinesco knew his opponent well, as Mauri is also from France. He had no doubt that Mauri's notrump bids were of a gambling nature, based on a long solid diamond suit, and he knew Mauri to be a sound bidder. Mauri had said that he thought he could take ten tricks at notrump against a lead of a spade or a club, and Roudinesco respected Mauri's opinion. However, Mauri had said nothing about his ability to take ten tricks against a heart lead, so Roudinesco decided to lead his ace, in spite of the fact it was a singleton. When the queen fell out of Mauri's hand, he was unable to continue the suit, but he was able to give his partner the lead by shifting to a spade. East won and cashed two heart tricks. I would say down went McGinty, except that his name was Mauri.

Let's give our sympathy to Mauri. Bidding and making 4NT

is a better match point score than bidding five diamonds and making it. That is, provided you can take ten tricks at notrump. You will see that against a player unwilling to lead a singleton ace against a notrump contract, Mauri would have made his contract. You will also see that no matter how good the defenders were, eleven tricks at diamonds were there for the taking, so long as East held the ace of spades.

Now we come to the story which has a tragic end. Like life, bridge hands do not always have happy endings. And, again like life, what is anguish to one competitor can be sheer joy to the other. The deal is from the Round Robin of the 1971 World Team Championship, with the North American team playing the Australian team.

None vul., dealer.

```
                    NORTH
                    ♠ 9 6 3
                    ♡ Q 8 7 6 4 3
                    ◊ 4
                    ♣ J 6 5
        WEST                      EAST
        ♠ K 5 4                   ♠ J 10 8 7
        ♡ K J 9 5                 ♡ A
        ◊ A 9 8 3 2               ◊ K J 10 6 5
        ♣ 9                       ♣ 10 3 2
                    SOUTH
                    ♠ A Q 2
                    ♡ 10 2
                    ◊ Q 7
                    ♣ A K Q 8 7 4
```

The bidding:

SOUTH	WEST	NORTH	EAST
Seres	Kaplan	Cummings	Kay
		Pass	Pass
3 NT	Pass	Pass	Pass

It is apparent that Tim Seres still plays the old-fashioned

ACOL variation of the gambling 3NT bid, which allows considerable strength in two suits other than the solid minor suit. Actually, the club suit doesn't look all that solid to me, but maybe when I was as young as Seres was when he made this bid, the suit looked stronger.

Opposing the Australians was the pair of Edgar Kaplan and Norman Kay, who have been winning major events for years. I would have thought that long years ago they had worked out all partnership understandings, but for the fact that on this hand something went wrong. Kaplan's opening lead was the ace of diamonds. Kay played the jack. Kaplan switched to a small spade!

With dummy's club holding, that suit looked good for six tricks, but Seres still had only eight tricks after the spade switch. Apparently, he decided his best chance to find his ninth trick was to add to the confusion. Instead of winning the trick with the queen of spades, he won it with the ace. From then on, it appears that Kaplan was convinced that Kay had the queen, and Kay was convinced that Kaplan had the queen.

Seres now ran his six club tricks, discarding three hearts from the dummy. Kaplan had to make five discards. He chose to discard three diamonds and two hearts. Now Seres led a small heart toward dummy's queen. Kaplan won that for just a moment with his king, but he didn't hold the trick very long, as Kay had to win with his singleton ace. Kay now led a small spade to what he thought was his partner's queen. Seres played the two. Kaplan decided he had to unblock so Kay could run the suit, so he played his king and returned a spade. It was Seres, and not Kay, who won it with the queen, and Seres still had two good heart tricks left in the dummy.

Where he could have lost the first seven tricks, he ended up losing only three altogether. He made 4NT.

OPENING LEADS AGAINST
PRE-EMPTIVE BIDS OF FOUR OR MORE

There is not a great deal in the literature on this subject. In his book *Killing Defense at Bridge,* H. W. Kelsey makes this statement: "Usually it is a good idea to have a look at the dummy when the only bid has been pre-emptive." Other authorities tend to ignore the subject.

One reason for this scarcity of material is that these hands seldom appear. In the approximately two thousand hands I examined in the decade 1968-1977, I found exactly fifty-two hands where there was such an opening bid. One of these was an opening six-bid, four of them were opening five-bids, and forty-seven of them were opening four-bids. Only in seventeen instances were these hands played with no further bidding. Six times the opening bid was doubled, and in twenty-nine cases it was either played in a different suit or at a different level.

Sometimes, when the hand was played against the opening bid, the opening leader had an ace-king combination from which he generally led. In others, the opening leader didn't have an ace. However, in those few where the opening leaders did have suits headed by an ace, but without a king, they tended to lead aces with good results. Notice this hand from the North America versus Brazil match from the World Championship of 1973.

None vul., dealer North.

```
                    NORTH
                    ♠ Q 9 5 4 2
                    ♡ J 6 5
                    ◊ K 8 7 4 2
                    ♣ None
      WEST                        EAST
      ♠ 10 6                      ♠ A K 8 7 3
      ♡ A Q 10 9 8                ♡ 7 2
      ◊ A Q 5 3                   ◊ J 10 9
      ♣ A 5                       ♣ J 10 2
                    SOUTH
                    ♠ J
                    ♡ K 4 3
                    ◊ 6
                    ♣ K Q 9 8 7 6 4 3
```

Where the North Americans had the North and South hands, Bobby Goldman opened the South hand four clubs after two passes. M. C. Branco, of Brazil, doubled, and P. P. Branco bid four spades where he played the hand, going set two tricks. When the Brazilians had the North and South hands, South's opening bid was five clubs which was doubled.

Assumpcao, South, was due to take a beating no matter what Bobby Wolff led, but it is interesting to note that his opening lead was the ace of hearts. At first sight, it appears that this lead cost a trick, but on further examination of the hand, you will see that it cost nothing. Wolff switched to the ace of diamonds. His partner followed with the nine, but Wolff knew that was the smallest diamond in the East hand, as he could see all of the diamonds from the two through the eight. Now he led the ten of spades to his partner's king. East switched back to a heart, and the defenders still had to get another heart trick. They always were going to get two club tricks, and so the Brazilians went down four tricks doubled for a score of − 700.

In the room where the Americans played North and South, they scored + 100 points, while in the room where they were East-West, they scored + 700 points, for a net total of 800 points.

On the next hand, it was necessary to lead an ace against an opening four-bid to defeat the contract.

E-W vul., dealer South.

NORTH
♠ None
♡ K Q 9
♢ A K 8 7 6 5
♣ K Q 9 7

WEST
♠ A Q 3
♡ A 6 4 3
♢ Q 10 4
♣ J 5 2

EAST
♠ K 4
♡ J 10 7 2
♢ J 9 3 2
♣ 8 4 3

SOUTH
♠ J 10 9 8 7 6 5 2
♡ 8 5
♢ None
♣ A 10 6

This deal is from the North America versus Nationalist China match in the World Championship of 1970. When the North American players held the North-South hands, Bob Hamman, South, opened four spades. M. F. Tai doubled and led the ace of hearts. Hamman had to lose three trump tricks and went set one. When the Chinese held the North and South hands, Conrad Cheng bid three spades. His partner raised to four, and when it got around to Bobby Goldman, West, he doubled. Unfortunately for the American players, Goldman apparently did not go along with the idea of leading an ace against a pre-empt of only three. His opening lead was the four of diamonds. The two losing hearts in the South hand were discarded on dummy's diamonds, and Cheng lost only three tricks, making four spades doubled.

The last few hands were intended to illustrate the importance of taking your tricks quickly when an opponent has shown a very long suit. The next hand is a bit livelier.

E-W vul., dealer West.

```
                    NORTH
                    ♠ Q 3
                    ♡ 3
                    ◇ A K 8 6 4 2
                    ♣ 9 7 6 2
        WEST                    EAST
        ♠ 8 6                   ♠ A 10 9 5
        ♡ A K Q 10 9 8 6 4      ♡ J 7
        ◇ Q 3                   ◇ J 7
        ♣ 5                     ♣ A K Q 10 4
                    SOUTH
                    ♠ K J 7 4 2
                    ♡ 5 2
                    ◇ 10 9 5
                    ♣ J 8 3
```

The bidding:

SOUTH	WEST	NORTH	EAST
Tularak	Fahss	Somboon	Bedros
	4 ♡	4 NT	Double
5 ♣	Pass	Pass	Double
Pass	Pass	Pass	

The hand is from the match with Lebanon against Thailand in the Olympiad Games of 1968. The Lebanese West opened four hearts, and Somboon, for Thailand, trotted out his secret weapon. His secret weapon was the Unusual Notrump bid, asking partner to select his better minor suit. I am not sure that the inventor of the convention meant for it to be used on hands like this North hand. However, Somboon was at the helm, and I was not. East doubled, ready to double five of either minor, and now it was up to Tularak, in the South seat. Which suit was better, the diamond or the club suit? He must have decided that a suit headed by the jack is better than a suit headed by the ten, and so he bid five clubs. I suspect that when it got back to East, he couldn't believe his ears. He certainly saw no reason to change his original intentions to double. When the bidding got back to Somboon, he decided that he had asked his partner to show his better minor suit, that his partner had done so. For better or worse, he was going to stick with his Unusual Notrump Convention, and he passed.

West led a top heart and, after looking at dummy, switched to a trump. East pulled trumps, cashed his ace of spades, and then led his remaining heart. West took the balance of the tricks. The Thailand pair had bid to take eleven tricks, and had gone set eleven tricks.

The Thai players met disaster in both rooms. In the other room, West opened with four hearts, and East went straight to six hearts. North did not forget to lead both the ace and king of diamonds, which neatly disposed of that contract. This gave the Lebanese players a plus of 2200 points. If that is not the record in a World Championship match, it must be pretty close to it.

OPENING LEADS AGAINST
WEAK THREE-BIDS

In America, and throughout most of the bridge-playing world, three-bids are opened with hands which generally have seven-card suits and fewer than ten HCPs. Nobody sticks too closely to these requirements. Six- and eight-card suits abound, and the high-card strength varies considerably with the vulnerability, position at the table, and partnership agreements. Not-vulnerable-against-vulnerable, third-seat three-bids have a tendency to be particularly weak.

We are interested in seeing what experts lead against opening three-bids when there is no further bidding, and when their hands do not have a well-defined choice. These situations are not frequent. More often, when someone opens with a three-bid, there is further bidding to give additional clues to the opening leader.

When there are no such clues, there is a tendency on the part of the experts to lead aces or unbid major suits. The old adage about laying down the ace so you can have a look at the dummy is more common against slams and against auctions in which there has been only one bid.

E-W vul., dealer South:

```
                    NORTH
                    ♠ K Q J 6 4
                    ♡ J 9 4 2
                    ◊ None
                    ♣ A K 10 3
      WEST                        EAST
      ♠ A 7                       ♠ 10 9 5 3 2
      ♡ Q 8 6 3                   ♡ A 7 5
      ◊ 10 8 4                    ◊ K J
      ♣ 8 7 6 4                   ♣ Q J 5
                    SOUTH
                    ♠ 8
                    ♡ K 10
                    ◊ A Q 9 7 6 5 3 2
                    ♣ 9 2
```

This hand was played in the semi-final round of the 1974 World Championship, with Brazil opposing North America. M. Branco, South for Brazil, dealt, and bid three diamonds. There was no further bidding. Notice North's disciplined pass.

Bobby Wolff chose the ace of spades as his opening lead. One look at the dummy told him it was time to quit leading spades, so he switched to a heart. Eventually, the defenders came to their diamond trick, when Branco took the correct view after seeing the jack of diamonds fall on the lead of his ace.

The Americans were unlucky on this deal. In the other room, where Bobby Goldman had the South hand, he chose to pass. After his partner opened one spade, he kept bidding until he reached five diamonds. If his partner had held one diamond so that he could finesse the suit, he would have had a play for his contract. However, he took the same ten tricks that Branco took in the other room, and went set one trick.

There is a lesson for us in the opening lead made by Belladonna in the next deal, from the 1976 World Championship.

E-W vul., dealer North.

```
                    NORTH
                    ♠ K 7 5 4
                    ♡ J 6 4 2
                    ◇ J 9 8
                    ♣ A 6
       WEST                        EAST
       ♠ A J 8 6                   ♠ Q 9 2
       ♡ A Q 10                    ♡ K 8 7 5 3
       ◇ 7 4 3                     ◇ K Q 2
       ♣ J 9 8                     ♣ 7 3
                    SOUTH
                    ♠ 10 3
                    ♡ 9
                    ◇ A 10 6 5
                    ♣ K Q 10 5 4 2
```

After two passes, Paul Soloway, South for North America, bid three clubs. There was no further bidding.

Belladonna had two aces. Which one should he lead? In practice, he led the ace of hearts. Many inexperienced players avoid leading from this combination. One good reason for leading it was that it was the shorter of the two suits.

Although on this particular hand Soloway held only one heart and two spades, the preemptor is less likely to be void in opener's shorter suit than in his longer suit. When you lead an ace, it is in the hope that you will retain the lead after seeing the dummy. Soloway trumped the second heart and led a spade towards dummy's king. Belladonna rose with the ace and led a third heart, also trumped by Soloway. Soloway went to dummy with the king of spades and led the jack of diamonds. East covered, and Soloway won his ace. He pulled trumps and, conceding one more trick to the king of diamonds, he claimed the balance of the tricks. He had taken ten tricks.

The next hand occurred in the 1972 Olympiad Games, where we again find Paul Soloway opening a three-bid against the Italian Team.

E-W vul., dealer South.

```
                    NORTH
                    ♠ Q 8 5 3
                    ♡ 6 3
                    ◊ K Q J 6 5
                    ♣ Q 10
        WEST                      EAST
        ♠ A 9 6                   ♠ K J 10
        ♡ K 4                     ♡ 10 8 5
        ◊ 9 8 7 3                 ◊ A 4 2
        ♣ K 9 7 4                 ♣ A 8 5 2
                    SOUTH
                    ♠ 7 4 2
                    ♡ A Q J 9 7 2
                    ◊ 10
                    ♣ J 6 3
```

This time, Soloway dealt and opened the South hand three hearts. Pabis Ticci led a diamond. East won the ace and led back the ten of spades. West won the ace and continued the suit. The defenders cashed the ace of clubs, the king of spades, and the king of clubs before giving Soloway the lead by leading another club. When the heart finesse failed, Soloway had been set three tricks. The defenders had won three spades, one heart, one diamond, and two clubs.

Why did I choose this hand where the opening leader did not lead an ace of spades? You will notice that the lead of the ace of spades would have been just as effective. Pabis Ticci was lucky when he led a diamond in that he found his partner with the ace, so the defenders still got to inspect the dummy before they planned the rest of their defense.

OPENING LEADS AGAINST
WEAK TWO-BIDS

It is rare that an opening weak two-bid concludes the bidding when you are playing in the big leagues. On those occasions, and when the opening leader does not have an obvious lead (such as an honor sequence or a singleton), the lead of an ace is recommended. The following hand demonstrates this principle in expert competition. The hand is from the 1972 Olympiad Games, with the United States playing Canada.

N-S vul., dealer East.

```
                    NORTH
                    ♠ 5
                    ♡ A J 8 5 4
                    ◊ A 9 6 3
                    ♣ Q 7 5
      WEST                        EAST
      ♠ A 9 7 2                   ♠ 4 3
      ♡ None                      ♡ K Q 6 3 2
      ◊ K 10 7                    ◊ J 4 2
      ♣ A 10 6 4 3 2              ♣ K 9 8
                    SOUTH
                    ♠ K Q J 10 8 6
                    ♡ 10 9 7
                    ◊ Q 8 5
                    ♣ J
```

After a pass by East, Bob Hamman, for the United States, chose to bid two spades with the South hand. There was no further bidding. Bill Crissey, of Canada, was on lead with the West hand. He had no honor card sequence. He led the ace of clubs. Hamman played small from the dummy and East followed with the nine. Crissey continued with the ten of clubs, ducked in the dummy and by East. Hamman trumped. Hamman now started leading spades. West won the second spade lead, and continued a third club to dummy's queen, East's king, and Hamman trumped again. At this point, West and South each had two trumps. Hamman led one more trump, and saw that in order to exhaust West of trumps, he would have to use all of his own trumps. He switched to the ten of hearts.

Crissey discarded the seven of diamonds as Hamman let the heart run to the queen. East led back a small diamond covered by the eight, ten, and ace. Hamman led a diamond from the dummy and ducked it into the West hand. Crissey led yet another club, exhausting Hamman's trumps. Crissey still had the nine of trumps. Crissey claimed the balance of the tricks with his outstanding trump and his two good clubs. Hamman had gone set 200 points.

CHAPTER 12:
DOUBLING FOR A LEAD

When a player doubles the opponents in a bid which they obviously do not mean to play, he is requesting a lead of that suit. This applies to doubles of cue bids and artificial bids. The hand that demonstrates this principle could be called a "might have been" hand. It is from the 1974 Vanderbilt Team Game, held at the ACBL National Tournament in Vancouver.

E-W vul., dealer North.

```
                    NORTH
                    ♠ A J 8 7 6
                    ♡ A J 4
                    ◇ K Q 5
                    ♣ 6 4
    WEST                        EAST
    ♠ 9 5                       ♠ K Q 10 4
    ♡ K Q 10 9                  ♡ 8 6 3 2
    ◇ 9 8 4                     ◇ J 10
    ♣ 9 8 7 5                   ♣ J 3 2
                    SOUTH
                    ♠ 3 2
                    ♡ 7 5
                    ◇ A 7 6 3 2
                    ♣ A K Q 10
```

The bidding:

SOUTH	WEST	NORTH	EAST
Silver	Feldman	Kokish	Goldstein
		1 ♠	Pass
2 ◇	Pass	3 ◇	Pass
4 ♣	Pass	4 ♡	Pass
5 ♣	Pass	5 ♠	Double
6 ◇	Pass	Pass	Pass

When Eric Kokish supported diamonds, the diamond suit became established as the trump suit, and subsequent bids were cue bids. When Steve Goldstein doubled North's five-spade bid, he did not expect his opponents to play in spades. He was simply indicating a good lead. Unfortunately for the defense, Mark Feldman thought he knew better. He led a high heart.

Joe Silver let Feldman hold the first trick, won the diamond shift in the dummy, came to his hand with a club, and finessed dummy's jack of hearts. Now he led the king of diamonds, a club to his ace, and ruffed a club. He cashed the ace of hearts, discarding a spade, led the ace of spades, and trumped a spade to get back to his hand. He pulled the last trump and claimed twelve tricks. A spade lead would have given the declarer no chance. Goldstein was right and Feldman was wrong.

These lead-directing doubles apply not only to the cue bids. They apply to most doubles of artificial bids, other than artificial opening bids of one club. This includes Stayman, Blackwood and Gerber responses, Jacoby transfers, artificial two-club bids, etc. Some pairs extend this to include artificial bids which show short suits, such as Splinter bids (a response of four in a minor suit to an opening bid of one in a major suit indicates a game-going hand with strength in a major suit and either a singleton or a void in the minor suit). As you don't get much mileage leading an opponent's short suit, many players reserve doubles of Splinter bids to show great length in the minor suit bid. It suggests the possibility of a sacrifice if partner has length in the Splinter suit and suitable distribution.

LEAD-DIRECTING DOUBLES AGAINST NOTRUMP CONTRACTS

Doubles of notrump contracts are often lead-directing.

LEAD-DIRECTING DOUBLES OF NOTRUMP CONTRACTS

1. If the defenders have bid only one suit, the double requests the lead of that suit, whether it was bid by the doubler or his partner.

2. When both defenders have bid a suit, the double strongly suggests that the opening leader lead his suit. The theory is that you would tend to lead your partner's suit in the absence of instructions to do otherwise.

3. When neither of the defending players has bid a suit, the double usually asks for a lead of the first suit bid by the dummy.

4. If no one has bid a suit, the double usually says, "I have a suit in my hand which will defeat this contract. I hope that your hand is such that you can determine what this suit is." If the contract is only a game contract, this indicates that the doubler holds a solid suit which will take five or more tricks, while if the contract is a slam, the double suggests that the doubler can defeat the contract with aces and kings, if you can figure out in what suit he has such a holding. There are other ways to use this double when no suit has been bid, which will be discussed later on.

Charlie Goren contributed the following hand, describing it as having occurred "in real life". The hand illustrates #1 in the box; i.e., the doubler was requesting the lead of the only suit bid by his partnership.

None vul., dealer West.

NORTH
♠ 4 2
♡ A 6 2
♢ K J 10 9 8 4
♣ K 2

WEST
♠ K J 8 6 3
♡ K Q J 3
♢ A 5
♣ 6 5

EAST
♠ Q 10 5
♡ 8 7
♢ 6 3 2
♣ Q J 10 4 3

SOUTH
♠ A 9 7
♡ 10 9 5 4
♢ Q 7
♣ A 9 8 7

The bidding:

SOUTH	WEST	NORTH	EAST
	1 ♠	2 ♢	Pass
2 NT	Pass	3 NT	Double
Pass	Pass	Pass	

Had East not made his lead-directing double, West probably would have opened the king of hearts. This would give declarer time to establish his diamond suit. He would take five diamonds, two clubs, and his two major suit aces before the defenders could do him any harm. However, East had two honors in his partner's suit and, in spite of his weak hand, he risked a double to encourage his partner to lead a spade. Against a spade lead, declarer's situation was hopeless. The defenders were going to take four tricks in spades and one in diamonds because their suit was established before the declarer's suit.

The next hand is a "teaching" hand. Only the doubler had bid. He urged his partner to lead his suit in spite of the strong bidding by the opponents.

425

Both vul., dealer West.

NORTH
♠ A 5 3
♡ 9 4
◇ K Q 9 7 2
♣ A K 5

WEST
♠ Q J 10 9 6
♡ 6 5 3
◇ 8
♣ J 10 9 2

EAST
♠ 7 4
♡ K Q J 10 7 2
◇ A 6 3
♣ 6 3

SOUTH
♠ K 8 2
♡ A 8
◇ J 10 5 4
♣ Q 8 7 4

The bidding:

SOUTH	WEST	NORTH	EAST
	Pass	1 ◇	1 ♡
1 NT	Pass	2 NT	Pass
3 NT	Pass	Pass	Double
Pass	Pass	Pass	

East thought that he would beat 3NT with a heart lead, so he doubled the final contract to ensure getting that lead. It's a good thing he made this request. Had he not done so, West well may have led the queen of spades. That would have given declarer time to knock out the ace of diamonds and come home with ten tricks. After his double, the defenders were assured of six tricks.

When you and your partner have both bid suits, and your partner doubles the final contract of 3NT, the standard agreement is that he is asking you to lead your suit, and not his. The theory is that his double asks you to do something which you had not planned to do. Without the double, the opening leader is likely to lead his partner's suit rather than his own because, in general, it is better to lead up to partner's strength, rather than

426

to lead away from your own strength.

The hand that illustrates this point was played at a sectional tournament in Dayton, Ohio, in 1970. Best scores were made by those pairs who bid 3NT and took eleven tricks against an opening spade lead. Some pairs played the hand in four hearts and took either ten or eleven tricks. Two unfortunate pairs played 3NT, got doubled on the sequence of bidding shown, and ended up going set one trick, for a two-way tie for the bottom score.

N-S vul., dealer South.

```
                    NORTH
                    ♠ 8 7
                    ♡ A K J 9 5
                    ◇ K 3 2
                    ♣ 6 5 2
        WEST                    EAST
        ♠ 4 3                   ♠ K J 10 9 6 2
        ♡ 8 6 2                 ♡ 10 7 3
        ◇ A 10 8                ◇ 9 7
        ♣ A J 9 7 4             ♣ Q 3
                    SOUTH
                    ♠ A Q 5
                    ♡ Q 4
                    ◇ Q J 6 5 4
                    ♣ K 10 8
```

The bidding:

SOUTH	WEST	NORTH	EAST
1 ◇	2 ♣	2 ♡	2 ♠
Pass	Pass	3 ◇	Pass
3 NT	Pass	Pass	Double
Pass	Pass	Pass	

East's double was a bold bid. He held an honor in the suit his partner had bid, and the bidding suggested to him that his partner did not hold an honor in the suit he had bid. Had the distribution of the club suit or diamond suit been a bit different, his double would have been a disaster for his side, but, as the cards lay, he had to have the club lead to defeat the contract. After the club lead, the defenders had the suit established, and there was not way declarer could take nine tricks without getting a diamond trick. When he led a diamond, West rose with the ace and took the setting tricks in clubs.

In his book *The Play of the Cards,* Fred Karpin tells how he was the beneficiary of a misunderstanding on the part of his opponents concerning doubles of 3NT when neither of the defenders had bid.

Dealer South.

```
                    NORTH
                    ♠ J 8 5 4
                    ♡ J 5
                    ◇ K J 7 2
                    ♣ 8 6 3
        WEST                      EAST
        ♠ 3 2                     ♠ A K Q 10 7
        ♡ K Q 9 6 4               ♡ 7 3 2
        ◇ 9 6 5 3                 ◇ 8 4
        ♣ 10 4                    ♣ 9 5 2
                    SOUTH
                    ♠ 9 6
                    ♡ A 10 8
                    ◇ A Q 10
                    ♣ A K Q J 7
```

The bidding:

SOUTH	WEST	NORTH	EAST
1 ♣	Pass	1 ♠	Pass
3 NT	Pass	Pass	Double
Pass	Pass	Pass	

East's double of 3NT said, "Partner, please lead the highest card you have in the suit bid by dummy." West was a non-believer. He led the six of hearts and Karpin was looking ten tricks squarely in the face. The extra heart trick made it eleven. Obviously, had West led the three of spades, the defenders would have taken the first five tricks.

Now I have a bit of advice for you. Don't double in those sequences where your side has not bid unless you want dummy's suit led. Look what happened when Von Der Porten violated this principle in the 1975 play-off among four teams competing for the right to represent North America in the World Championships.

None vul., dealer West.

```
                        NORTH
                        ♠ K 4
                        ♡ Q 3
                        ◇ Q 9 5
                        ♣ K J 10 8 6 4
        WEST                            EAST
        ♠ 10 7 3 2                      ♠ Q J 9 5
        ♡ K 9 8 5                       ♡ A 10
        ◇ 8 3 2                         ◇ 10 7 6
        ♣ 9 3                           ♣ A Q 7 2
                        SOUTH
                        ♠ A 8 6
                        ♡ J 7 6 4 2
                        ◇ A K J 4
                        ♣ 5
```

The bidding:

SOUTH	WEST	NORTH	EAST
			Von Der
Ross	Stansby	Paulsen	Porten
	Pass	2 ♣	Pass
2 ♡	Pass	3 ♣	Pass
3 NT	Pass	Pass	Double
Pass	Pass	Pass	

Until Von Der Porten doubled, the bidding seemed to call for a spade lead. Paulsen's opening two-club bid showed 11-15 HCPs with a good club suit. Ross's two-heart bid showed a five-card suit, and Paulsen's three-club rebid showed that he had support neither for hearts nor spades. Ross had not explored to see whether his partner had four cards in either major, as he might have done by responding an artificial two diamonds to the opening two-club bid. Therefore, it looked like neither opponent had a great deal in spades.

Stansby, West, was on the verge of leading a spade until he heard his partner's double. Had he done so, the defenders would have established their spade tricks before declarer set up his club tricks. The defense would have taken two spades, two hearts, and two clubs. A two-trick set would have been an adequate score, in view of the fact that the defenders held only 40% of the high-card points. However, after Von der Porten's double, Stansby decided that he was requesting a club lead in spite of the fact that North had rebid the suit. He led the nine of clubs, and now declarer was on the road to getting his club suit established before defenders got their spade suit established. The first trick went nine, ten, queen, five. Von der Porten now switched to a spade, but it was too late. Ross won dummy's king and led a club, getting that suit established. He still had the queen of diamonds in the dummy for an entry. He took four diamonds, four clubs, and two spades, making an overtrick.

This hand is a vivid example of the difference between defending against a slam contract and a game contract. For a moment, let's imagine that East does not have the queen and jack of spades, nor the ace of hearts. Let us say that the declarer has reached a contract of 6NT, instead of 3NT, after two clubs had been bid and rebid. Now the double would be in order. Taking two clubs against a 6NT contract is a great victory. However, against a 3NT contract, getting a lead in a suit where you have two tricks may be just the thing you don't want. Sometimes, as in this hand, you don't want to take your two tricks too early. Your first priority is to get your own suit established.

Both vul., dealer North:

```
                    NORTH
                    ♠ A 7 6 5 2
                    ♡ 7
                    ◊ A Q 9 5
                    ♣ K 8 3
        WEST                    EAST
        ♠ 3                     ♠ K Q J 10 9
        ♡ K 10 8 5 4            ♡ Q 3 2
        ◊ 8 6 3                 ◊ K 7 4
        ♣ 10 6 4 2              ♣ 7 5
                    SOUTH
                    ♠ 8 4
                    ♡ A J 9 6
                    ◊ J 10 2
                    ♣ A Q J 9
```

The bidding:

SOUTH	WEST	NORTH	EAST
		1 ♠	Pass
2 ♣	Pass	2 ◊	Pass
3 NT	Pass	Pass	Double
Pass	Pass	Pass	

Here North has bid two suits, but the double by East requests the lead of the first suit bid by the dummy. In view of the bidding, East can hope that his king of diamonds represents an entry, and he has every right to feel that the opponents are going to romp home with nine or more tricks unless he gets a spade lead. You can see that, should West make the normal opening lead of a heart, declarer would have no problem getting his diamond suit established, and would have at least four club tricks, three diamond tricks, and his major suit aces. However, with a spade lead, the timing passes over to the defenders. It is East who is going to take four spade tricks and a diamond trick.

I mentioned earlier that not too many hands from genuine play resemble the hands we teachers use. In the actual hands, the situation often is more obscure. Here is a deal on which

Belladonna lucked out, though if you will examing the hand carefully, you will see that he should not have gotten by with it.

Both vul., dealer East.

```
                        NORTH
                    ♠ A K 9 7 6 3
                    ♡ K 8
                    ◊ Q
                    ♣ K J 9 7
        WEST                        EAST
    ♠ 8                         ♠ Q J 10 4 2
    ♡ A 10 9 4 3 2              ♡ 7 5
    ◊ 6 3                       ◊ A 9 7 5
    ♣ 8 6 5 4                   ♣ A 2
                        SOUTH
                    ♠ 5
                    ♡ Q J 6
                    ◊ K J 10 8 4 2
                    ♣ Q 10 3
```

The bidding:

SOUTH	WEST	NORTH	EAST
K. W. Shen	Avarelli	Kovit	Belladonna
			Pass
Pass	Pass	1 ♠	Pass
2 ◊	Pass	3 ♠	Pass
3 NT	Pass	Pass	Double
Pass	Pass	Pass	

The deal is from the finals of the 1969 World Championship, with Nationalist China playing Italy.

In spite of the fact that North had bid and made a jump rebid in spades, Avarelli led the eight of spades after Belladonna doubled the final contract. This turned out to be the only opening lead which had a chance to beat the contract.

Shen won in dummy and led the queen of diamonds. Belladonna saw no reason to get impatient about diamonds, and let the diamond queen win the trick. Shen next led a low club from the table, and Belladonna ducked that one as well. Shen won in his own hand with the ten and then continued the king of diamonds. Belladonna won his ace and led the queen of spades. Dummy won and, in an effort to get back to his hand to cash his diamonds, Shen led dummy's small club. Belladonna won the ace, and cashed the jack and ten of spades. Next, he led the heart to his partner's ace for a one-trick set.

It seems that Shen gave up when he won the opening lead. Had he played dummy's nine of spades, he would have come home with nine tricks. After Belladonna won the first trick, the defenders could have brought in only their three aces. Of course, the heart distribution might have been such that Belladonna could have switched to hearts and gotten a couple of heart tricks for the defenders. However, this depended not only on the switch to hearts, but also on the suit being divided in such a manner that a second heart trick could be established and cashed.

A double when no suit has been bid says, "Partner, I have a suit in which I can take enough tricks to set this contract. I hope you can determine what suit this is, and lead it for me."

If the bidding has gone 1NT-2NT-3NT, and your partner now doubles, he is telling you there is a suit in which he can take at least the first five tricks. Should you happen to hold

♠ J 7 4 3   ♡ Q 5 4   ◊ 5   ♣ J 7 5 4 2

lead a diamond. In none of the other three suits could your partner guarantee five winning tricks.

If the bid is 6NT, then your partner needs only two tricks in his hand to assure the defeat of that contract. Where no suit has been bid, he probably has the ace and king of some suit he hopes you can locate, or conceivably he has two aces. It's not always as easy to identify the suit in which your partner has an ace-king, as it is to identify one in which your partner has five or more winning tricks right off the top. In such cases, the Fisher Double, developed by Dr. John Fisher, of Dallas, has been helpful.

The convention was designed to be used against game contracts in notrump, as well as against slam contracts. The double where no suit has been bid asks for the lead of a minor suit. If the Stayman Convention has been used by the opponents, then the double asks for the lead of a diamond. Had the doubler wanted a club lead, he would have doubled the club response to the opening NT bid. On the other hand, if the Stayman Convention has not been used, then the double asks for a club lead.

An extension of this convention scored a sensational triumph in the play-off for the right to represent North America in the 1979 World Championship.

E-W vul., dealer South.

NORTH
♠ K Q J 8 6
♡ K Q 6
♢ Q 3
♣ K 5 4

WEST
♠ 10 9 2
♡ 9 8 3 2
♢ 10 6
♣ Q 7 6 2

EAST
♠ 4 3
♡ 10 7 4
♢ A K 9 7 5 4
♣ 8 3

SOUTH
♠ A 7 5
♡ A J 5
♢ J 8 2
♣ A J 10 9

The bidding:

TABLE ONE

SOUTH	WEST	NORTH	EAST
Goldman	Wolff	Soloway	Hamman
1 NT	Pass	4 ♣	Pass
4 ♢	Pass	6 NT	Double
Pass	Pass	Pass	

TABLE TWO

SOUTH	WEST	NORTH	EAST
Smith	Kantar	Wold	Eisenberg
1 NT	Pass	4 ♣	Pass
4 NT	Pass	6 NT	Double
Pass	Pass	Pass	

At Table One, Soloway's four-club response was Gerber, and not Stayman. Goldman's four-diamond response was Roman Gerber, showing either three aces or none. For those who sometimes ask how you can tell whether your partner's response shows three aces or none, just common sense would tell North, who holds three kings and three queens, that South could not have opened 1NT if he had no aces at all. For the real beginners, there is even a simple mathematical verification of this. There are 40 HCPs in the deck. The four aces come to 16 HCPs. Therefore, there are 24 HCPs in kings, queens, and jacks. North has 16 of these HCPs. If South didn't have any aces in his hand, then he had opened 1NT with no more than 8 HCPs.

I throw this in as a little bonus for you. There are hands where this will be helpful. Right now, our problem is deciding what Bob Hamman's double meant. It is obvious that to Bobby Wolff, it asked for a diamond lead. That pair seems to have been playing the Fisher Convention. When Hamman did not double the club bid when he had the chance, his double called for a lead of the other minor suit. Wolff led a diamond and the defenders took the first two tricks.

Eddie Kantar and Billy Eisenberg were not playing the Fisher Convention. At Table Two, the four-club bid by Eddie Wold was not a club suit, but again was the Gerber Convention. Some players, who do not use the Fisher Convention, use a double of a 6NT contract to ask that the lead be the first suit bid by the dummy. On the basis of this reasoning, Kantar led the two of clubs. Not only did the defenders fail to cash their two quick winners, but Curt Smith played clubs to lose no club tricks after that opening lead, and came home with twelve tricks.

Of course, one hand never proves anything, but I do find this one impressive. In my regular partnerships, I like to play that the Fisher Convention is used only against slam contracts. Against game contracts, I use the old-fashioned method; namely, that a double of 3NT when no suit has been bid by either side shows a solid suit and asks partner to try to find that suit. My partner usually should have no trouble identifying such a suit, for it would not be one where he had any honors, nor would it be one where he had great length. However, identifying a suit in which I hold an ace and king would be more difficult, and that is the suit I want identified when I am defending against a slam contract. To a certain extent, the Fisher Double does ask your partner to lead something he probably would not have chosen to lead. When the opponents have reached a high-level notrump contract without bidding a major suit, the tendency is for the opening leader to choose a major. The reasoning is that if the opponents had a major suit, they would have bid it. While this is not always true, it is true often enough so that, generally, the double can be used to ask for a minor suit lead. The request can be to lead that suit which the doubler has not had an opportunity to double during the bidding.

THE LIGHTNER DOUBLE

Doubling When Your Partner Is On Lead

In the early days of contract bridge, players found that penalty doubles of freely-bid slams to gain points simply did not gain many points. Strangely enough, they seemed to lose more points than they gained. At times, the double would tell the declarer how to play the hand, and he would make a slam contract which he would not have made except for the double. If the double was based on a trump stack, the opponents might go into some other suit where trumps were not adversely distributed, or into a makable notrump contract. At times, the doubler would have the slam set in his own hand as long as he had the opening lead, but the declarer would change the contract in such a way as to change the opening leader, and the partner of the player who had the contract set would lead the wrong thing and the slam would come home.

In addition, the odds just seemed to be against such doubles. Rarely would a freely-bid slam contract be set more than one trick. In that case, the gain from the double would amount to only 50 points if the opponents were not vulnerable, and 100 points if they were vulnerable. Even if the contract went set two tricks, the gain from the double would be 200 points when they were not vulnerable, and 300 points when they were. On the other hand, when the doubler made his contract, which he sometimes would make redoubled and with an extra trick, the double would turn out to be very expensive. The following table details the extra rewards the declarer gets over and above his normal profit if he doubles a small slam in a major suit, and he makes his contract.

BONUS FOR MAKING SIX OF A MAJOR DOUBLED		
	Not Vulnerable	Vulnerable
Contract made	230	230
Contract with extra trick	330	430
Redoubled and made	590	590
Redoubled and extra trick	790	990

In 1929, one of the early stars of contract bridge, Theodore Lightner, of New York, proposed a better way to use doubles of freely-bid slams. Occasionally, an unusual lead will defeat a slam, and Lightner suggested that when the partner of the opening leader doubled, he was requesting that the opening leader make a lead which he would not otherwise have made. This was one of the earliest conventions of contract bridge. It is known as the Lightner Double, and is in general use the world over. While occasions for its use are rare, the gain when it is successful is considerable. If you set them in a non-vulnerable small slam contract, which they would have made but for your opening lead, you have picked up something in the neighborhood of 1000 points. This includes the bonus you collect for setting your opponents. If they are vulnerable, you have picked up around 1500 points. And, of course, if it is a grand slam which you set by telling your partner what to lead, the gain is even greater.

Let me introduce this convention to you by giving you an example from Lightner himself, as presented in *The Encyclopedia of Bridge,* edited by Ely Culbertson and published in 1935.

Dealer North.

NORTH
♠ K 10 9 6 2
♡ Q 7 6 5
♦ A Q
♣ A Q

WEST
♠ 8 5 4 3
♡ 10 8 4
♦ 8 7 6
♣ 8 7 6

EAST
♠ A Q
♡ 9 3 2
♦ 10 5 4 3
♣ 10 5 4 3

SOUTH
♠ J 7
♡ A K J
♦ K J 9 2
♣ K J 9 2

The bidding:

SOUTH	WEST	NORTH	EAST
		1 ♠	Pass
3 NT	Pass	4 NT	Pass
6 NT	Pass	Pass	?

Here is what Lightner had to say about his double:

"If East now passes, West will have to guess, and as a
lead of four small of opponents' bid suit is about the
worst that can be imagined, the slam contract will almost surely be fulfilled. But note the difference with
my convention. Double by East! This tells West, 'I
have the contract beaten if you do not make the normal opening.' As any opening other than opponents'
suit may be West's normal lead, the double here definitely advises West a spade lead will beat the hand."

You will see that the Lightner Convention does not differ
greatly from the modern lead-directing double, which asks for a
lead of the first suit bid by the dummy when the opponents have

freely bid game in notrump. Most players make the same request of their partner that dummy's first suit be led when the final contract is 6NT.

The matter is considerably more complicated when the final slam contract is in a suit. Now there is the added possibility that the doubler is void in a suit which he wishes to have led, and which probably will not be led unless he specifically requests it. Your doubling partner may have a void, which he hopes you can identify because you have great length in that suit, or because you have some length and the opponents have bid it. When he doubles a freely-bid slam in a suit, he is asking you for an unusual or unexpected lead. Specifically, he is saying, "Do not lead trumps, do not lead a suit either of us has bid, and, unless you have exceptional length in one of the unbid suits, do not lead an unbid suit." Instead, he is asking you to do one of the following:

LIGHTNER DOUBLE VERSUS SUIT CONTRACTS

1. Try to locate the suit in which he can trump the opening lead.

2. Lead a suit which the opponents have bid. If declarer has bid a second suit, this may ask you to lead that suit, as that suit would be the most unexpected of all.

3. If your hand and the bidding make it unlikely that your partner has a void, and when the declarer has bid no suit other than trumps, your best chance is to lead dummy's first-bid suit.

Even if you don't plan to use the Lightner Double yourself, it is well to know about it, so that you'll be able to protect yourself against players who do use the convention. The late Sonny Moyse used to play and kibitz at the famous Cavendish Club, in New York City, to get material when he was editor of the *Bridge World* magazine. He reports the following disaster by a declarer who did not know about the Lightner Double. For fear of reprisal, Moyse refused to give the names of the participants of the game.

Both vul., dealer North.

```
                         NORTH
                     ♠ K Q J 6
                     ♡ J 8 7
                     ◇ Q
                     ♣ A Q J 7 3
        WEST                           EAST
    ♠ 7                            ♠ 5 4 2
    ♡ K 9 6 5                      ♡ 10 4 3 2
    ◇ K 10 7 4                     ◇ J 9 6 5 3 2
    ♣ K 9 8 2                      ♣ None
                         SOUTH
                     ♠ A 10 9 8 3
                     ♡ A Q
                     ◇ A 8
                     ♣ 10 6 5 4
```

The bidding:

SOUTH	WEST	NORTH	EAST
		1 ♣	Pass
1 ♠	Pass	3 ♠	Pass
4 NT	Pass	5 ◇	Pass
5 NT	Pass	6 ◇	Pass
6 ♠	Pass	Pass	Double
Redouble	Pass	Pass	Pass

Let's check the double by East against the requirements for
the Lightner Double. In the first place, the double said do not
lead spades—they are trumps. Do not lead an unbid suit. That
eliminated the two red suits. Leading a suit bid by the opponent
is an unusual lead. That is what I want. The only side suit bid by
the opponents is the clubs. Therefore, lead clubs.

Probably, East thought that winning the first trick would get
the defenders off to a good start, and doubled in hopes his partner might find an additional trick somewhere. Actually, the
double should have cost the defenders points, because declarer
should have had no trouble at all taking twelve tricks after the
club lead. All he had to do was play small in the dummy and let

East ruff. Now he would win whatever card East led, pull trumps, and discard his queen of hearts on dummy's long clubs.

The double should have helped the declarer on the score sheet, in spite of the fact that, by playing with reasonable care, he could have taken thirteen tricks with any lead except a club. All he had to do was be sure that he attacked clubs by leading the ten from his hand for a finesse. By doing so, he could have brought in the entire club suit. However, the hand turned out to be a disaster for South, who apparently knew nothing about the Lightner Double.

West's opening lead was the eight of clubs. He saw no reason to make the situation clear to South by leading his fourth-best. The correct play should have been clear to South, no matter which club was led. East was not likely to be doubling for a club lead if he held three clubs to the king. Experienced players always look around to see if a void suit is likely when they hear the Lightner Double. Seeing nine clubs between his hand and dummy, declarer should have guessed the true situation. However, he seemed to think that East might hold the club king and West a singleton. If that were the distribution, and he ducked the first club trick, East would win the king and return a club for his partner to ruff. The poor fellow played the ace of clubs from the dummy. East trumped with pleasure, and returned a heart. There was a chance to hold his losses to one down if the heart finesse worked, so declarer played the queen. West won the king and returned a second club for East to trump. West still had to make a trick with his king of clubs, and the declarer went set 1600 points on a hand where he could have made a vulnerable slam doubled and redoubled.

The next hand was played in a match in London, in 1952, where Norman Squire said, "After years of waiting, they dealt me a Lightner Double."

E-W vul., dealer East.

NORTH
- ♠ A
- ♡ A Q 4
- ◊ A 9 8 6
- ♣ A K 8 4 2

WEST
- ♠ J 5 4 3
- ♡ 10 9
- ◊ Q J 10 5 4 2
- ♣ 10

EAST
- ♠ K Q 10 9 6 2
- ♡ K 7 3
- ◊ None
- ♣ 7 6 5 3

SOUTH
- ♠ 8 7
- ♡ J 8 6 5 2
- ◊ K 7 3
- ♣ Q J 9

The bidding:

SOUTH	WEST	NORTH	EAST
Meredith	J. Tarlo	Reese	Squire
			Pass
Pass	Pass	1 ♣	1 ♠
2 ♡	2 ♠	3 ♠	Pass
4 ♣	Pass	4 ◊	Pass
4 ♡	Pass	6 ♡	Double
Pass	Pass	Pass	

Squire's double said, "Don't lead the suit we bid, partner."
Joel Tarlo's choice lay between clubs and diamonds, both of
which had been bid by his opponents. Both opponents had bid
clubs, and only one had bid diamonds, but Tarlo seems to have
had no trouble deciding that a diamond lead was called for.
With Tarlo holding only one club, it was difficult to imagine
that Squire was void in that suit, as the opponents would then
have had twelve cards in clubs. So although only Reese had bid
diamonds, Tarlo chose to lead from his six-card holding, as this
is the suit in which his partner was most likely to be void.
Squire's report of the hand says that Meredith went three

down trying to make twelve tricks after the opening diamond lead, and that Reese reproved him gently for not cutting his losses.

The following hand is a more modern example of where the doubler wanted a lead in a suit in which he was void.

N-S vul., dealer South.

NORTH
♠ Q 7 6
♡ A
♢ 9 7 4 2
♣ A K 8 7 5

WEST
♠ 2
♡ 10 8 2
♢ A 6 5
♣ Q J 10 9 6 4

EAST
♠ 8 5 4 3
♡ K Q J 9 7 5 4
♢ J 10
♣ None

SOUTH
♠ A K J 10 9
♡ 6 3
♢ K Q 8 3
♣ 3 2

The bidding:

SOUTH	WEST	NORTH	EAST
Bianchi	Lawrence	Forquet	Goldman
1 ♠	Pass	4 ♣	4 ♡
4 ♠	5 ♡	5 ♠	6 ♡
Pass	Pass	6 ♠	Double
Pass	Pass	Pass	

This hand allows me to clear up another point about the Lightner Double which may appear obscure. It appeared that North and South were bidding because they thought they had values to bid, while East and West were bidding to take a sacrifice. The Lightner Double applies only when used against the players who appear to expect to make their contract. In other words, a double by North or South of a six-heart bid by

Goldman would not have requested a specific lead. It simply would have said either "Let's take a sure profit by doubling rather than speculate on a questionable slam," or "I think the points we can score doubling this contract will be worth more than the slam even if we bid and make it." On the other hand, the double by Goldman did ask for an unusual lead because it was evident that North and South, holding most of the high cards, had bid their slam in the hopes of making it. This may not be exactly the same thing as the freely-bid slam which the books all call for, but it is the sense in which the double is usually made in competitive auctions.

The hand was played in the finals of the 1973 World Championship, by the Aces from America versus the Italian Blue Team. The Italian pair was using their own version of the Precision Club bidding system. Forquet's four-club response was a slam invitation. As usual, the double said, "Don't lead the suit we have bid." It also asks that an unbid suit not be led. Again, this eliminated the red suits, and it was easy enough for Lawrence to see that the choice was clubs. He was so confident of this that, instead of leading the queen of clubs, he led the four of clubs as a suit preference signal. Goldman trumped the opening lead and led a diamond back to Lawrence's ace, so that another club could be led and trumped. The Italian pair ended up down 500 points.

It seems that history does sometimes repeat itself. In the 1970 World Championship, we find almost a repeat of the situation which Sonny Moyse reported from New York's Cavendish Club in 1961. Here we find the Aces, representing the American Contract Bridge League, playing against Nationalist China, representing the Far East Bridge Federation, in the qualifying rounds.

Both vul., dealer East.

NORTH
♠ A Q 9 6 5 2
♡ K 5 3 2
♢ A K 2
♣ None

WEST
♠ K J 4 3
♡ 10
♢ J 9 5 4
♣ K J 5 4

EAST
♠ None
♡ J 9 7
♢ Q 10 8 7 3
♣ A Q 9 7 6

SOUTH
♠ 10 8 7
♡ A Q 8 6 4
♢ 6
♣ 10 8 3 2

The bidding:

SOUTH Lin	WEST Hamman	NORTH Cheng	EAST Lawrence
			Pass
Pass	Pass	1 ♣	2 ♣
2 ♡	5 ♣	6 ♡	Double
Pass	Pass	Pass	

The Chinese were using the Precision Club bidding system. North's opening one-club bid guaranteed 16 or more HCPs, and said nothing about his distribution. Against that artificial method of bidding, the Americans were playing that Lawrence's two-club bid showed length in both minor suits. Lin's two-heart bid guaranteed a five-card or longer suit and promised 5-7 HCPs. Holding a fit in both minor suits, Hamman decided to put the pressure on the Chinese by going all the way to five clubs. To Cheng, North, it looked like the opponents had all of the clubs, so his void in clubs was not a duplication of values. With his many controls, he accepted the challenge by bidding six hearts. Now we come to Lawrence's double. Again, this said, "Don't lead what we have bid." Remember that his two-club bid showed that he held both clubs and diamonds, so the double in effect said don't lead a minor suit. Hamman got the message and led the three of spades. While Lin, South, had been given a written statement of the methods used by the Americans, he must not have fully understood the implications of their bidding. Had he simply played low from the dummy, Lawrence would have been able to trump a spade, but that would have been the end of the story for the defenders. However, Lin went up with the ace of spades. After that, he could not make his contract.

Not all lead-directing doubles are made because the doubler has a void suit, by any means. Here is one reported by Jose Le Dentu, which was played in a rubber bridge game in the French-American Club in Paris.

Both vul., dealer East.

```
                    NORTH
                    ♠ J 10
                    ♡ A
                    ◊ K Q J 8 3
                    ♣ A Q 10 7 4
     WEST                          EAST
     ♠ 8 7 2                       ♠ A K 3
     ♡ 10 8 6 4 2                  ♡ Q J 9 7 5
     ◊ 7 6 2                       ◊ 4
     ♣ K 2                         ♣ J 9 8 6
                    SOUTH
                    ♠ Q 9 6 5 4
                    ♡ K 3
                    ◊ A 10 9 5
                    ♣ 5 3
```

446

The bidding:

SOUTH	WEST	NORTH	EAST
Renaudin	du Pasquier	Renier	Le Dentu
			1 ♡
1 ♠	2 ♡	3 ♡	Pass
4 ◇	Pass	6 ◇	Double
Pass	Pass	Redouble	Pass
Pass	Pass		

It was obvious that North bid the slam because he thought he could make it. Let's see what Le Dentu's double told his partner:

1. Do not lead trumps. That took care of the diamond suit.
2. Do not lead the suit I bid. That cancels out a heart lead.
3. Do not lead the unbid suit. That took care of clubs.
4. Make an abnormal lead.

Nothing is much more abnormal than leading declarer's second suit. Du Pasquier duly got the message and led a spade, and Le Dentu took the first two tricks.

You can see that with any other lead the slam would have been made. Declarer would discard one spade from dummy on the king of hearts, finesse for the king of clubs, and trump two clubs. He would lose only one spade trick.

In the qualifying rounds of the 1969 World Championship, Benito Garozzo got himself into a trap with a lead-inhibiting psychic bid, but got by with murder when one of the Brazilian defenders failed to recognize a Lightner Double.

E-W vul., dealer West.

NORTH
♠ K 9 7 6
♡ K J 10 8 6 5 4
♢ K 5
♣ None

WEST
♠ A 5 4
♡ 9 7
♢ Q J 7 2
♣ 8 7 4 2

EAST
♠ Q J 10 8 3 2
♡ Q 2
♢ A 10 9 4
♣ 6

SOUTH
♠ None
♡ A 3
♢ 8 6 3
♣ A K Q J 10 9 5 3

The bidding:

SOUTH	WEST	NORTH	EAST
Garozzo		Forquet	
	Pass	1 ♡	1 ♠
2 ♢ !	Pass	2 ♡	Pass
2 ♠	Double	Pass	Pass
6 ♣	Pass	6 ♢ !	Pass
7 ♣	Pass	Pass	Double
Pass	Pass	Pass	

Boys will have their fun, and Garozzo responded two diamonds, hoping to stop a diamond lead when he finally arrived at a high-level contract in clubs. It may have seemed like a good idea at the time, but after he bid six clubs, it sounded to Forquet like Garozzo had a powerhouse in the two minor suits and wanted him to choose the trump suit. Naturally, he preferred diamonds to clubs, and this made Garozzo go to seven clubs to buy the contract. By this time, Forquet caught on to what had happened, and passed. East also caught on to what had happened and doubled. He hoped his double said to his partner, "Yes, that diamond bid by Garozzo was just what you

448

think it was. This is a lead-directing double, so don't lead spades. I bid them. That leaves you a choice between hearts and diamonds, and, as leading a diamond would be a more abnormal lead than leading a heart, please lead a diamond." You will see that, had West led the queen of diamonds, the defenders would have taken the first two tricks. Not all of my stories have a happy ending, and I'm forced to tell you that West led the ace of spades. Garozzo trumped and led all of his clubs. During this process, West discarded two hearts, and Garozzo didn't even have to count the suit. He now knew that the queen of hearts was bound to fall. He ended up running hearts and discarding his three bad diamonds.

If you are beginning to think that the Lightner Double is an accident-prone convention, history suggests that you are right. It has led to some disastrous results for both the defenders and the declarers when used by some of the world's finest players. There is one aspect we have not yet touched upon. The Lightner Double sometimes lets the declarer escape from a contract he cannot make into one which he can make. It seems that the old-timers may not have been aware of this danger. The next hand is in the article in the old Culbertson *Encyclopedia,* and is supposed to have been written by Lightner himself.

Dealer North.

```
                    NORTH
                    ♠ K J 10 7
                    ♡ Q J 8
                    ◇ A K J 8 7
                    ♣ 9
        WEST                    EAST
        ♠ 6 5                   ♠ 8 2
        ♡ 9 7 6 4               ♡ 10 5 3 2
        ◇ 10 9 6 5 4 3          ◇ None
        ♣ J                     ♣ A Q 10 8 4 3 2
                    SOUTH
                    ♠ A Q 9 4 3
                    ♡ A K
                    ◇ Q 2
                    ♣ K 7 6 5
```

The bidding:

SOUTH	WEST	NORTH	EAST
		1 ♦	2 ♣
2 ♠	Pass	4 ♠	Pass
6 ♠	Pass	Pass	?

The *Encyclopedia* article suggests that East can find his salvation by doubling. This will tell West he should not lead what East has bid, trumps, or an unbid suit. This would leave diamonds, which would set the slam contract.

In these more sophisticated days, the double would be salvation for the declarer, and not for the defenders. South would simply get out of a contract where he was going set into one he was sure to make. He would have bid 6NT and now there would have been no way to defeat the hand. The only chance East had to defeat the hand, and that was not a very good chance, was to pass. He would hope that, with his six diamonds, West would come to the conclusion that his opponents had clubs under control when they bid a slam. The best chance to set the hand was that his partner would be void in diamonds, and his partner had been unable to use the Lightner Double for fear declarer might escape into notrump. However unlikely it was that this would have happened, hindsight tells us this was the only chance the defenders had, and a small chance is better than no chance at all. With a thinking partner that chance can materialize. Look at the next hand. It was played in the trials which chose the North American team for the 1973 World Championship.

E-W vul., dealer East.

```
                      NORTH
                      ♠ A K 9 8 5
                      ♡ 10 9 8 5 4
                      ◊ A 4
                      ♣ 4
        WEST                      EAST
        ♠ 10 7 6 2               ♠ None
        ♡ J                      ♡ 7 3
        ◊ K Q 9 8 3             ◊ J 10 7 5 2
        ♣ 6 5 3                 ♣ K Q J 10 9 8
                      SOUTH
                      ♠ Q J 4 3
                      ♡ A K Q 6 2
                      ◊ 6
                      ♣ A 7 2
```

The bidding:

CLOSED ROOM

SOUTH	WEST	NORTH	EAST
M. Becker	Kemp	Bernstein	Russell
			3 ♣
Double	Pass	4 ♣	Pass
5 ♣	Pass	7 ♠	Pass
Pass	Pass		

OPEN ROOM

Greenberg	Rubens	Smith	B. J. Becker
			Pass
1 ♡	Pass	1 ♠	Pass
4 ♠	Pass	4 NT	Pass
5 ♡	Pass	5 NT	Pass
6 ◊	Pass	7 ♡	Pass
Pass	Pass		

The cue bids made by Andy Bernstein and Mike Becker, in the closed room, after Cliff Russell opened three clubs, showed that both North and South had length and strength in both major suits. Actually, Bernstein could have cue-bid a second time had he wished to do so, but he wisely decided to play the hand from his side, rather than let the hand be played by South. Russell had opened a pre-emptive bid with adverse vulnerability, and there would be nothing at all unusual about finding him with a void. Had the hand been played from the South side, West would have been on lead, and might have led that suit. With the hand played from the North, the player who was more likely to have a void was himself on lead. Taking thirteen tricks with spades as trumps involved only trumping the losing diamond in the dummy, and created no problems.

In the open room, B. J. Becker made some exemplary bids, which turned out well. Probably that last statement is incorrect. Technically, a pass is not a bid, and it was the excellent passes made by B. J. Becker which served his side well. His first pass gave the opponents room to make a lot of bids, and those bids helped Becker and Jeff Rubens to find the defense to defeat the grand slam contract. You will see that, after the opponents bid seven hearts from the South, Becker could have called on the Lightner Double. With this sequence of bidding, the double would have called for a spade lead. But if you will review the bidding, you will see that Becker did not double. He passed when they got to seven hearts. Had he doubled, almost certainly the opponents would have switched to seven spades, West would have been on lead, and the grand slam would have come home.

An article written by Jeff Rubens entitled "Honor Your Partner" has become deservedly famous. That is exactly what B. J. Becker did. He figured that Rubens could work out what to lead without the double. Rubens came through. He had heard North bid one spade and South go directly to four spades. He figured that the spades in the opposing hand were either divided 5-4 or 4-4. If they were 4-4, it probably would do no harm to lead a spade. But if they were 5-4, then Rubens just added his four to that total and knew how many spades Becker had. Rubens led a spade. In choosing this lead rather than the routine lead of the king of diamonds, Rubens demonstrated that listening and thinking are better than leading by formula.

It should not be necessary to caution against doubling a freely-bid slam contract unless you want an unusual lead, but the record shows that it probably is necessary. Here is another hand which Sonny Moyse watched in a high-powered game at New York's Cavendish Club. Again, Moyse did not have the courage to name the participants.

N-S vul., dealer North:

```
                    NORTH
                    ♠ A Q
                    ♡ A J 9 6
                    ◇ K J 4
                    ♣ K J 9 8
    WEST                        EAST
    ♠ 10 8 5 2                  ♠ 9 4
    ♡ 7                         ♡ 8 3
    ◇ 10 8 6 5 3                ◇ A Q 2
    ♣ 7 6 4                     ♣ A Q 10 5 3 2
                    SOUTH
                    ♠ K J 7 6 3
                    ♡ K Q 10 5 4 2
                    ◇ 9 7
                    ♣ None
```

The bidding:

SOUTH	WEST	NORTH	EAST
		1 ♣	Pass
1 ♠	Pass	2 NT	Pass
4 ♡	Pass	6 ♡	Double
Redouble	Pass	Pass	Pass

Had East simply passed, the odds are good that West would have led the unbid suit. You can see that with a diamond lead the defenders will take the first two tricks. Maybe East got a little excited. His double requested that his partner not lead an unbid suit. West led the first suit bid by the dummy. Declarer simply trumped the first trick, pulled trumps, and discarded all three of dummy's diamonds on his spade suit.

On the next hand, did Mrs. Evans, in the East seat, really want her partner to lead clubs?

N-S vul., dealer South:

NORTH
♠ K Q 7 6
♡ J 9
♢ J 9
♣ A Q J 6 3

WEST
♠ 9 2
♡ 10 6 3 2
♢ K 8 7 6 5 4
♣ 10

EAST
♠ 8 5
♡ 8 5
♢ A 10 3 2
♣ K 8 7 5 4

SOUTH
♠ A J 10 4 3
♡ A K Q 7 4
♢ Q
♣ 9 2

The bidding:

SOUTH	WEST Mrs. P. Williams	NORTH	EAST Mrs. R. Evans
1 ♠	Pass	2 ♣	Pass
3 ♡	Pass	4 ♠	Pass
4 NT	Pass	5 ♢	Pass
6 ♠	Pass	Pass	Double
Pass	Pass	Pass	

The British writers on bridge do not pretend that their players are some sort of supermen who never make mistakes. Not only do they tell about those plays which did not work out, but, in their writing, they also tell who made them. If they want to be gentle about it, they say that their player "took the wrong view," instead of simply saying a mistake was made. This is a more realistic attitude than that taken by some American writers, who try to sell us the idea that there is an expert class who have achieved perfection.

The deal is from the Women's European Championship of 1952. The report is by Ewart Kempson, who was editor of the

Bridge Magazine, published in England, and the non-playing captain of the British women's team. The match was the English ladies versus the Norwegian ladies.

With the club lead, South had no problem making the hand. She played dummy's ace, cashed two rounds of trumps and five heart tricks, discarding two diamonds and a club from dummy. Conceding a club, she now claimed her contract.

Mrs. Evans' double said not to lead diamonds, the unbid suit, but to lead one of the suits the opponents bid. Had Mrs. Evans been void in hearts, the opponents would have had nine cards in that suit, and probably would have been playing their slam in hearts, rather than in spades. So, Mrs. Williams did not lead a heart. Instead, she obediently led a club, the other suit bid by the opponents.

Mrs. Williams would have led a diamond if Mrs. Evans had not doubled. After careful consideration of the East hand, we must say that, if the defenders had a club trick, it was not likely to disappear, while if they had a diamond trick, it was likely to disappear with South bidding both majors strongly. So we agree that Mrs. Evans should have passed, and that had she done so, she probably would have gotten the diamond lead which would have set the hand.

Now that I have said that even the experts will sometimes make errors, let me point out that they also will dream up unusual actions to take in unusual circumstances. Such actions require imagination that would not occur to many players of less than international rank. Look at this double of a game contract made by Nicola Gardener, of Britain, in 1972. At that time, Miss Gardener was only twenty-four years old, but for three years she had been Britain's youngest Life Master, and had represented her country in international competition on several occasions.

Both vul., dealer West.

NORTH
♠ 10 2
♡ A K 4 3
◇ A 5 3 2
♣ 9 8 7

WEST
♠ A 3
♡ 9 8 7 6 5 2
◇ 10 9 8
♣ Q 2

EAST
♠ 7 6 5
♡ None
◇ K 7 6
♣ K J 10 6 5 4 3

SOUTH
♠ K Q J 9 8 4
♡ Q J 10
◇ Q J 4
♣ A

The bidding:

SOUTH	WEST	NORTH	EAST
	Bob		Nicola
	Rowlands		Gardener
	Pass	Pass	3 ♣
3 ♠	Pass	4 ♠	Double
Pass	Pass	Pass	

Miss Gardener's opening three-club bid said that she had a hand
with little or no defense. Why then would she double a four-
spade bid, when her partner had refused to open the bidding
and had refused to act over South's three-spade bid? To Bob
Rowlands, her partner, the bid must have said, "Don't lead
clubs, but I do have something I can trump if you can figure out
what it is." Rowlands tried his longest suit, hearts, and Miss
Gardener trumped it. Later, when West got the lead with the ace
of spades, he led a second heart and that also got trumped. The
defenders had to come to a diamond trick to set the contract.

DOUBLING WHEN YOU ARE ON LEAD

If you are on lead when your opponents bid 7NT and you have an ace, go ahead and double them. They have nowhere to run. Otherwise, when you are on lead against a slam contract and you have it set in your own hand, it may be wise not to double. Your opponents may put the slam in some other denomination and put your partner on lead instead of you. And he may not know what to lead.

Bobby Nail and John Hathorn, in their book *How To Play Championship Duplicate Bridge,* tell us, "When the opponents wander into the only slam contract you have a chance of setting, don't run them somewhere else with a double. Pass and take your fifty points with a sigh of relief."

The following hand is from that book. It was played by Bill Hanna and Doug Steen in a national championship.

None vul., dealer North.

```
                    NORTH
                    ♠ 10 4
                    ♥ Q 6 3
                    ◇ 4
                    ♣ A K Q J 6 5 2
        WEST                        EAST
        ♠ 8 7 6 3 2                 ♠ J
        ♥ 8 4                       ♥ A K 10 9 5
        ◇ Q 10 8 5 3               ◇ J 7 2
        ♣ 7                         ♣ 10 9 8 3
                    SOUTH
                    ♠ A K Q 9 5
                    ♥ J 7 2
                    ◇ A K 9 6
                    ♣ 4
```

The bidding:

SOUTH	WEST	NORTH	EAST
Hanna		Steen	
		3 NT	Pass
6 NT	Pass	Pass	Double
7 ♣	Pass	Pass	Double
Pass	Pass	Pass	

Hanna and Steen were playing the gambling opening 3NT bid, where the bid guaranteed a long, absolutely solid minor suit. Hanna thought 6NT would be a good shot, until East doubled. At this point, Hanna could just see the ace and king of hearts in the East hand. What else had he doubled on? Hanna also knew that West could not see the ace and king of hearts in the East hand, so he decided to put West on lead. He bid seven clubs, knowing from his hand that the long, absolutely solid suit that North held was clubs. East must have doubled again out of frustration, but that still didn't tell West what to lead. Poor West led a small spade. Hanna was sitting there looking at fourteen tricks off the top after East followed suit with the jack.

Great Britain's team came in second in the 1958 European Championship. They did not do too well on the next deal, which is taken from their match against Belgium.

N-S vul., dealer North.

```
                        NORTH
                        ♠ J 8 6 2
                        ♡ None
                        ◇ A Q J 9 6 5 2
                        ♣ K 7
        WEST                            EAST
        ♠ K 10 9                        ♠ A 7 4
        ♡ K 9 7 6 4 3                   ♡ 10 8 5 2
        ◇ 4                             ◇ 10 8 7 3
        ♣ 10 8 2                        ♣ 6 5
                        SOUTH
                        ♠ Q 5 3
                        ♡ A Q J
                        ◇ K
                        ♣ A Q J 9 4 3
```

The bidding:

SOUTH	WEST	NORTH	EAST
Van			Harrison-
Baanteghen	Truscott	Savostin	Gray
		1 ◇	Pass
3 ♣	3 ♡	4 ◇	4 ♡
4 NT	6 ♡	Pass	Pass
6 NT	Pass	7 ◇	Double
7 NT	Double	Pass	Pass
Redouble	Pass	Pass	Pass

In 1952, Alan Truscott was still living in England and was
playing on Great Britain's team. He shoved the Belgian players
around until they didn't know what they could make, but it is
obvious they bid a slam, hoping they could make it. Harrison-
Gray had an ace, which the bidding seemed to indicate he could
cash with no difficulty, so when the Belgian players reached
seven diamonds, he doubled. Van Baanteghen, South, believed
that Gray knew how to beat seven diamonds, so by bidding
7NT, he put Alan Truscott on lead. Truscott doubled, but he had
no idea that a spade lead was called for. He led a diamond, and
the Belgians had seven diamond tricks, six club tricks, and the ace
of hearts for a bonus.

CHAPTER 13:
DECEPTIVE OPENING LEADS

The art of deception is sometimes called the fourth dimension of bridge. It is an essential part of the play of both the declarer and the defender. However, you will find more deceptive opening leads in textbooks than in championship play. The plain truth of the matter is that until you've seen the dummy, you simply don't know enough about the deal to make the odds favor some sort of coup. By and large, master players stick with stodgy old mathematical probabilities until they know enough about a deal to make their deceptive play an odds-on favorite. That time comes after they've seen more cards than their own thirteen. Until then, the chances are simply too great that any deceptive play they make will fool partner more than declarer.

However, there are a few cunning opening leads which seem to succeed more often than they fail. Many years ago, Al Morehead suggested that the lead of the nine from the 10-9, with or without other cards, is more likely to deceive the declarer than the leader's partner. The hands I have found where this lead was made support Morehead's claim. It was tried by Howard Schenken in a men's team championship game in 1949.

Dealer South.

```
                    NORTH
                    ♠ J 6 3
                    ♡ 8 5
                    ◊ A Q 7
                    ♣ K 9 5 4 2
        WEST                      EAST
        ♠ 10 9 5                  ♠ K
        ♡ A 7 4                   ♡ J 10 9 3 2
        ◊ 9 5 4 2                 ◊ K 10 6
        ♣ A Q 6                   ♣ 10 8 7 3
                    SOUTH
                    ♠ A Q 8 7 4 2
                    ♡ K Q 6
                    ◊ J 8 3
                    ♣ J
```

The bidding:

SOUTH	WEST	NORTH	EAST
1 ♠	Pass	2 ♣	Pass
2 ♠	Pass	3 ♠	Pass
4 ♠	Pass	Pass	Pass

Schenken led the nine of spades. Declarer decided this probably was a singleton, which would leave East with the K-10-5.
Left to his own devices, declarer would somehow have managed
to get to the dummy and would have led a small spade. When
East followed with a singleton king, declarer would have no
spade losers. However, if East did have the spades which
declarer credited him with, the situation was different. The jack
had to be played from the dummy. East would have to play the
king. When declarer got back to dummy, he would lead a small
spade and finesse the eight against the presumed ten in the East
hand. But after the declarer played the jack of spades from the
dummy, the ten of spades in Schenken's hand was going to take
a trick. The defenders were also due one trick in each of the
three side suits. Therefore, the trump trick made the difference.
    The same lead was made with equal results in the Olympiad

NORTH
♠ Q 10 9 3
♡ A 3
◇ J 7 6 5 4 2
♣ K

WEST
♠ J 8 4
♡ K J 6
◇ 10 9
♣ A J 9 4 2

EAST
♠ 2
♡ 10 9 8 7 5 2
◇ K 3
♣ 8 6 5 3

SOUTH
♠ A K 7 6 5
♡ Q 4
◇ A Q 8
♣ Q 10 7

When the Italian Blue Team held this hand against Sweden, they reached a doubtful six spades, played by South. The opening lead was the ace of clubs, followed by a heart switch. Garozzo rose with dummy's ace. Aided by the fact that East held the doubleton king of diamonds, Garozzo came home with twelve tricks.

This hand was from the qualifying round, and was played in all of the matches. South Africa arrived at the same contract when playing against Germany, but the result was different. The German West did not lead the ace of clubs. He led the nine of diamonds. South credited East with the K-10-3. He played dummy's jack and won with the ace when East played the king. He then pulled trumps in three leads ending in the dummy, and led a small diamond, finessing the eight. West won with his now-singleton ten. He lost no time cashing the ace of clubs.

It is well-established that when you lead from a doubleton, you lead the higher of the two cards. This is true no matter what the two cards are. Experience has taught us that leading from Qx or Jx in a suit our partner has not bid is often a losing proposition. Nonetheless, there are times when the bidding seems to demand a lead of a suit where you have this holding. In those circumstances, thought should be given to leading the small card rather than the high one. This seems to be one bit of deception which fools the declarer more often than it fools your partner. This is particularly true when the declarer happens to be a player who carefully counts out every hand.

On the next hand, the Sharples twins, James and Robert, were on a powerful British team playing against four British ladies for the Crockford's Cup.

Dealer South.

```
                    NORTH
                    ♠ A K 10 7
                    ♡ A
                    ◇ J 10 7
                    ♣ K J 8 7 2
        WEST                    EAST
        ♠ Q 3                   ♠ J 9 8 5 2
        ♡ J 7 6 3 2             ♡ 9 8
        ◇ 9 4 2                 ◇ 6 5 3
        ♣ 9 5 3                 ♣ Q 10 6
                    SOUTH
                    ♠ 6 4
                    ♡ K Q 10 5 4
                    ◇ A K Q 8
                    ♣ A 4
```

The bidding:

SOUTH	WEST	NORTH	EAST
1 ♡	Pass	2 ♣	Pass
2 ◇	Pass	3 ♠	Pass
6 NT	Pass	Pass	Pass

Mrs. Nell Kahn, Mrs. Lena Litante, Mrs. F. North, and Mrs. Steve Hunt won the cup. This hand contributed to their victory.

The opening lead was the three of spades. When the dummy came down, South could count eleven tricks off the top. There were numerous possibilities for the twelfth trick. A successful finesse against the queen of clubs would do the job. If the club finesse failed, then the hand could be made if the clubs broke

463

3-3. If that did not work, there was always the chance that the jack of hearts would fall out after three leads. Players who don't count would probably decide to use these three lines of play, in this order. When the opposing clubs broke 3-3, it would be all over. Robert Sharples was in the South seat, and he is a counter par excellance. The lead of the three of spades could have been from either a three-card, four-card, or longer suit. Sharples set out to find out. He played dummy's ace; East dropped the five. He cashed the ace of hearts, the jack of diamonds, and a small diamond to his hand. Now he cashed the king and queen of hearts, discarding a club and a small spade from the dummy. On the queen of hearts, East discarded the two of spades. So Sharples knew that West had started with five hearts. By first playing the five and then the two of spades, East had indicated that she had an even number of cards in that suit. It was also clear that West did not have five spades, because he would have had to hold the deuce. It was now pretty clear that West had started with three spades, and not four or more. Sharples now took a third round of diamonds and when everybody followed suit, he knew that West started with three spades, five hearts, and three diamonds, and hence, with a doubleton club. He led his good diamonds and discarded the ten of spades from the dummy. On this diamond, West discarded one of his clubs, and East discarded the nine of spades. Sharples now had a neat end-play all worked out. He cashed the king of spades, on which East played the eight and West played the queen. It looked like West was up to some sort of monkey business in the spade suit. West was, but not the kind of monkey business Sharples thought. Now he took the ace of clubs and led a club toward dummy. When West showed up with three clubs, it appeared that West had started with fourteen cards—three spades, five hearts, three diamonds, and three clubs. Sharples knew something was wrong, but it was too late to do anything about it. He had planned to duck the club to East, on the assumption that East had nothing left but clubs. If that were true, he would have to lead a club back into dummy's king-jack. Instead, East won the trick with the queen of clubs and cashed the jack of spades.

The next hand is only a story of what might have been. This hand is also from a Crockford's Cup finals.

N-S vul., dealer South:

NORTH
♠ Q 10 4 3
♡ 8 7 6 4
◇ A 10 5
♣ 8 3

WEST
♠ None
♡ J 2
◇ K Q J 8 6
♣ Q J 10 9 7 6

EAST
♠ 9 2
♡ K 5
◇ 9 7 3 2
♣ A K 5 4 2

SOUTH
♠ A K J 8 7 6 5
♡ A Q 10 9 3
◇ 4
♣ None

The bidding:

SOUTH	WEST	NORTH	EAST
2 ♠	2 NT	3 ◇	6 ♣
6 ♠	Pass	Pass	7 ♣
7 ♠	Pass	Pass	Pass

Boris Schapiro reports this hand in his book *Bridge Analysis*.
The 2NT overcall by West showed great length in the minor
suits. As West's bid had shown diamonds, the three-diamond
bid by North was a cue bid, indicating control of the diamond
suit and the acceptance of spades as trumps. East pushed once
too often, and South got to a grand slam contract somewhat
against his will.

It turned out all right for South when West led the queen of
clubs. Declarer trumped and pulled trumps in two leads. He
then led a heart and finessed his queen. Shapiro points out that
that was the proper play, as it would have succeeded if West had
a singleton jack of hearts or if the hearts were distributed as in
the actual hand. As the hand was, when the king fell on the second round of hearts, it was all over.

Shapiro wonders just what would have happened had West

led the two of hearts. Presumably, East would play his king, and it would then be up to South to decide if West started with a singleton deuce, leaving West with the K-J-5. If that were the distribution, he would have to take a finesse in hearts. With the actual holding, he would lose to the singleton jack. We will never know. It does seem likely that declarer would have played East for both missing honors.

In his *Red Book On Play,* Ely Culberston claims that when you are reduced to leading a suit which is a doubleton headed by a jack or higher honor, leading the small card can deceive your partner, but can really do him no harm even if he is fooled. He gives this hand to illustrate his point.

NORTH
♠ K J 8 5 2
♡ 7 4 3
◇ K Q
♣ A 10 7

WEST	EAST
♠ 9 7	♠ 3
♡ Q 8	♡ A 9 5 2
◇ 10 8 6 4 2	◇ A 9 7 3
♣ 8 6 5 3	♣ J 9 4 2

SOUTH
♠ A Q 10 6 4
♡ K J 10 6
◇ J 5
♣ K Q

Ely says, "With Q-8, if I must lead it at all, I much prefer the lead of the 8." Against South's four-spade contract, the situation looked almost hopeless to West, and he decided that only a miracle could set the contract. Ely says that since miracles rarely follow an orthodox lead, he selected the eight of hearts. East won the ace and returned a heart. After some thought, South decided that the lead of the eight was possibly a singleton, so he put in the ten. To give you the full flavor of Culbertson's narrative style, I quote him.

"West gathered the queen to his bosom, led the diamond four to East's ace hand, chuckling diabolically, and ruffed the third round of hearts for the setting trick."

Culberston goes on to say that his favorite irregular lead is a low trump from Kx when the declarer is on his right. He states this lead has never failed him, and in many instances has saved the day. It is known that Albert Morehead sometimes assisted Culbertson with his writing, and you wonder whether Morehead had something to do with that statement, as here is a hand which Morehead defended.

None vul., dealer South.

```
                    NORTH
                    ♠ A 9 6
                    ♡ 7 6 5
                    ◇ A 10 9 4 3
                    ♣ 8 3
        WEST                        EAST
        ♠ Q J 3 2                   ♠ 8 7 5 4
        ♡ K 4                       ♡ 10 3 2
        ◇ J 6                       ◇ Q 7 5
        ♣ A 7 6 5 2                 ♣ Q J 10
                    SOUTH
                    ♠ K 10
                    ♡ A Q J 9 8
                    ◇ K 8 2
                    ♣ K 9 4
```

The bidding:

SOUTH	WEST	NORTH	EAST
1 ♡	Pass	2 ♡	Pass
4 ♡	Pass	Pass	Pass

This time, the lead of a small diamond would have proved disastrous. Of course, Morehead, with the West hand, had no reason to believe that a diamond should be led. However, a lead from either black suit would also give declarer an unearned

467

trick. Leading the four of hearts looked like that also might give up a trick, but actually it was the play that set the hand. Declarer overtook East's ten with his jack, and was now absolutely convinced that East had the king of trumps. He went to the dummy with the ace of spades and led a heart to repeat the finesse. This time, Morehead won with the king. Now he had a safe exit card. He led the queen of spades. Declarer finished pulling trumps and led a low diamond. He put in dummy's nine, hoping against hope that East would lead back a spade. But, East led the queen of clubs and the defenders took two club tricks to set the contract.

I can't give you any testimonial about this opening lead from my personal experience. Frankly, I've always been too nervous to try it. Some day, if I happen to get just the right hand in one of the ladies' afternoon tea parties where nothing is at stake, I may test it.

Fred Karpin reports a hand where he underled a king against a grand slam for a different reason.

Dealer North.

```
                    NORTH
                    ♠ 3
                    ♡ A J 10 9
                    ◊ A Q J 10 2
                    ♣ 8 6 4
        WEST                    EAST
        ♠ J 10 9 7              ♠ 8 6 5 4 2
        ♡ 6 2                   ♡ 8 7 5 4 3
        ◊ K 9 8                 ◊ 7 4 3
        ♣ J 7 5 3              ♣ None
                    SOUTH
                    ♠ A K Q
                    ♡ K Q
                    ◊ 6 5
                    ♣ A K Q 10 9 2
```

The bidding:

NORTH	EAST	SOUTH	WEST
1 ♡	Pass	3 ♣	Pass
3 ◇	Pass	4 NT	Pass
5 ♡	Pass	7 NT	Pass
Pass	Pass		

The bidding made it sound like South had a long solid club suit with which he expected to take a lot of tricks. Karpin knew what the declarer couldn't know: the club suit was not going to break. From the bidding, it sounded like North held the length and strength in diamonds. If so, Karpin knew the diamond finesse would work. He decided he had better attack diamonds before the declarer found out about the bad club break. He led the nine of diamonds.

Of course, the declarer could not risk a finesse at the very first trick, especially when it looked like he had thirteen tricks without the finesse. Declarer played dummy's ace, and promptly led a club. When East discarded a small spade, declarer saw that he was doomed to go set. Holding his losses to a minimum, he won the club trick in his hand and led a diamond toward dummy to let whoever had the king win a trick with it. Karpin played his king for the setting trick.

It is not unusual for a player who has already seen the dummy to lead the ace from A-K-x to deny holding the king. It is unusual to see this play made as an opening lead. The following hand was played by Gloria Reysa (formerly Gloria Turner).

Dealer South.

NORTH
♠ Q J 10 6
♡ A 9 5 4
♢ K Q 10
♣ 7 3

WEST
♠ A K 7
♡ 10 8 6
♢ 5 2
♣ 8 6 5 4 2

EAST
♠ 9 5 4 3 2
♡ K Q J
♢ 8 4 3
♣ 10 9

SOUTH
♠ 8
♡ 7 3 2
♢ A J 9 7 6
♣ A K Q J

The bidding:

SOUTH	WEST	NORTH	EAST
1 ♢	Pass	1 ♠	Pass
2 ♣	Pass	3 ♢	Pass
5 ♢	Pass	Pass	Pass

North and South missed the ironclad contract of 3NT to reach five diamonds on the sequence shown. Mrs. Reysa wanted to lead one of her top spades to give her a chance to look around and decide how to proceed, but she decided that if she did so, she should not reveal to declarer the fact that she had both of the top honors. Playing standard leads, her lead of the ace denied the king. At trick two, she switched to a low heart.

South won dummy's ace and cannot be faulted for thinking East held the king of spades. He led the queen of spades for a ruffing finesse against East. When East did not cover, declarer discarded one of his hearts. Mrs. Reysa won with the king and promptly led a heart to set the contract one trick.

Had Mrs. Reysa opened the king of spades and then switched to a heart, declarer could have won with the dummy's ace and established a spade in the dummy for a discard by trumping

470

spades twice, a play which he could have made after Mrs. Reysa led the ace of spades had he known she had the king as well.

Earlier, I mentioned the advantages of leading the ace from A-Q-x of trumps, but on the next hand, Tony Sowter, of England, improved on that idea.

Dealer North:

```
                    NORTH
                    ♠ K J 5 4
                    ♡ A
                    ◇ K J 6 2
                    ♣ A Q J 5
        WEST                      EAST
        ♠ A Q 3                   ♠ None
        ♡ 9 7 2                   ♡ K Q J 8 6 4 3
        ◇ 8 4 3                   ◇ 10 5
        ♣ K 9 8 7                 ♣ 10 4 3 2
                    SOUTH
                    ♠ 10 9 8 7 6 2
                    ♡ 10 5
                    ◇ A Q 9 7
                    ♣ 6
```

The bidding:

NORTH	EAST	SOUTH	WEST
1 ♣	3 ♡	3 ♠	Pass
6 ♠	Pass	Pass	Pass

The hand was played at the International Festival of Bridge, in Paris, late in 1978. We have Sowter's own words explaining why he chose his lead.

"The standard view in this type of position is that you should try leading out the ace and another (when the king appears in dummy). The idea is that declarer may opt to try and fell your partner's doubleton queen. When I held this hand (the West hand) I felt that this bold policy was likely to come rapidly unstuck, for it struck me that declarer would have no problem at all were my partner to have no trumps. This leap to six spades seemed to suggest a very good hand with four-card trump support, which made it very likely that the three-spade bid was based on a long rather than a strong suit. Accordingly, I kicked off with a small spade. Declarer went into the tank—obviously I was more likely to have A-x than Q-x, but could I just have A-Q-x? After an agonizing pause, he arose with the king.''

Before I leave this subject of deceptive opening leads, let me add a word of caution. I recommend that you do not go out of your way looking for a holding where you can make a deceptive lead. If you do, you're going to lose a lot of marbles, or points, or whatever your stakes are, for a small amount of happiness and a large quota of grief. It has been said that first you decide what suit to lead, and then you decide what card to lead from that suit. However valid that advice might be, it certainly is correct when it comes to the matter of deciding to make a deceptive lead. When the suit you have chosen offers the combination of cards which lends itself to a lead which has more chance to fool your opponents than your partner, that is the time to try a deceptive lead.

CHAPTER 14:
CONCLUSION

There is more written about opening leads than about any other aspect of defense. This is because we know so little about the thirty-nine cards other than our own when we make an opening lead. The scarcity of clues as to how we should proceed leads to the multiplicity of options. Shortly after we see the dummy we are going to know how right, or wrong, we are. If we try to imagine too much about what we're going to see in the dummy, we all can be terribly wrong at times.

Adam Meredith is called "one of the brilliant players of the world" in the *Encyclopedia of Bridge*. He moved from London, England, to New York City in 1957, after having won about everything that could be won playing for Great Britain. He was European champion, he was world champion, on five different occasions he was on the team that won the Gold Cup, which is the Knock-Out team championship of Great Britain played under the auspices of the British Bridge League. Shortly after he moved to New York, his team had reached the semi-finals in Gold Cup play and, with all vulnerable, Meredith, as dealer, picked up this hand.

♠ 6   ♡ A K Q 10 7 6 5   ◇ Q 10 9   ♣ K J

Meredith, West, was dealer. He opened two hearts. Harold Franklin narrates the story, telling how this drama unfolded.

The bidding:

WEST	NORTH	EAST	SOUTH
Meredith	Lee	Juan	Booker
2 ♡	Double	4 ♡	5 ♣
Pass	Pass	5 ♡	Pass
Pass	6 ♣	Pass	Pass
Double	Pass	Pass	Pass

Franklin relates, "Meredith was on lead, and he is a player with the courage of his convictions. On this occasion, his conviction was that North, the original doubler, must be void of hearts and have a good spade suit, which, given time, would produce vital discards. So his best hope was to develop a diamond trick before he came in with his club. Without a backward glance at the secure heart suit, he led the ten of diamonds."

Here is the entire hand.

Both vul., dealer West.

```
                    NORTH
                    ♠ A K 3
                    ♡ 2
                    ◇ A J 8 3
                    ♣ A 10 4 3 2
        WEST                        EAST
        ♠ 6                         ♠ J 9 8 7 5 2
        ♡ A K Q 10 7 6 5            ♡ 9 8 3
        ◇ Q 10 9                    ◇ 7 6 4 2
        ♣ K J                       ♣ None
                    SOUTH
                    ♠ Q 10 4
                    ♡ J 4
                    ◇ K 5
                    ♣ Q 9 8 7 6 5
```

Terence Reese, editor of the magazine in which Franklin told his story, said, in a typical British footnote, "a memorable play". I leave it to you to decide how closely the dummy conformed to Meredith's expectations. Booker let the diamond ride to his king and cashed the ace of clubs. When he found that he had to lose a trump trick, he came to his hand with the queen of spades and successfully finessed dummy's jack of diamonds. He led the ace of diamonds, discarding a heart, and cashed the eight of diamonds, discarding his last heart. Meredith got to trump with his king of clubs for the one and only trick taken by the defenders.

Let this hand demonstrate how much you know after you see the dummy compared to your knowledge before you see it. Had Meredith seen the dummy, he would have known that he had a trump trick. He would have reason to fear that if he did not take his heart trick right now, he might never get it. So he would have cashed a high heart immediately.

Consider for a moment the possibilities when there are thirty-nine unseen cards, as compared to when there are only twenty-six or fewer hidden cards. The more cards you have seen, the fewer possibilities remain. Your best chance when on opening lead is to try that play which is favored by the odds. Of course, if the odds are only seventy percent to thirty percent in favor of your play, then three times out of ten you're going to make the wrong play. As the play progresses, you see more cards, so the number of possibilities is reduced. You can eliminate many hands and may determine that the actual hand is part of the group that was only thirty percent before the opening lead. That is hard to determine when you are making the opening lead.

Of course, there are things you can learn from the bidding. The very odds I am talking about can at times be based on the bidding. You can make a reasonably good estimate of the high card strength of your partner's hand. If your partner has been in the bidding, you have a pretty good idea where his strength lies. You can spot a shortage in your partner's hand when both opponents have bid a suit where you have length. Your opponents may advertise long solid suits, making it necessary for you to cash or establish your winners without delay. Just don't count too much on information supplied by the bidding. At times, you may find yourself as far off as was Meredith.

Before looking at the technical defensive plays which are used by the experts in the middle and end games, we are going to take some time out to study the language of the defenders. There are codes which the defenders use to give each other important information about the cards they hold. These codes are perfectly legal. Most of them have to do with the size of the card played or with the order in which they are played. The declarer knows these codes as well as do the defenders, making it occasionally advisable to withhold information which might be more helpful to the declarer than to your defending partner. Most of the time, however, this information is more valuable to the defenders than it is to the declarer. The messages sent by these codes are called signals. These signals will be the subject of Volume Two of this series.

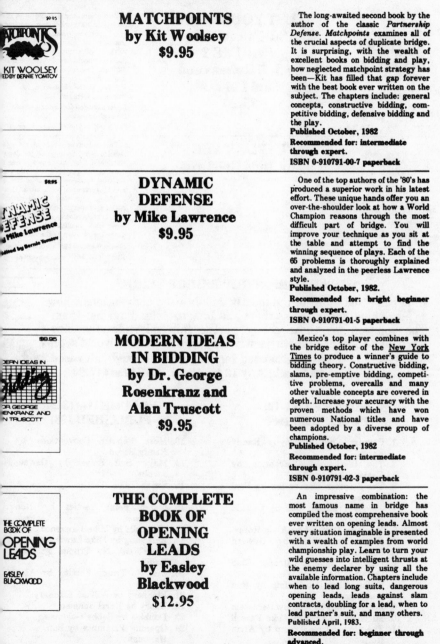

THE BEST OF DEVYN PRESS
Newly Published Bridge Books

A collection of the world's premier bridge authors have produced, for your enjoyment, this wide and impressive selection of books.

MATCHPOINTS
by Kit Woolsey
$9.95

The long-awaited second book by the author of the classic *Partnership Defense*. *Matchpoints* examines all of the crucial aspects of duplicate bridge. It is surprising, with the wealth of excellent books on bidding and play, how neglected matchpoint strategy has been—Kit has filled that gap forever with the best book ever written on the subject. The chapters include: general concepts, constructive bidding, competitive bidding, defensive bidding and the play.
Published October, 1982
Recommended for: intermediate through expert.
ISBN 0-910791-00-7 paperback

DYNAMIC DEFENSE
by Mike Lawrence
$9.95

One of the top authors of the '80's has produced a superior work in his latest effort. These unique hands offer you an over-the-shoulder look at how a World Champion reasons through the most difficult part of bridge. You will improve your technique as you sit at the table and attempt to find the winning sequence of plays. Each of the 65 problems is thoroughly explained and analyzed in the peerless Lawrence style.
Published October, 1982.
Recommended for: bright beginner through expert.
ISBN 0-910791-01-5 paperback

MODERN IDEAS IN BIDDING
by Dr. George Rosenkranz and Alan Truscott
$9.95

Mexico's top player combines with the bridge editor of the <u>New York Times</u> to produce a winner's guide to bidding theory. Constructive bidding, slams, pre-emptive bidding, competitive problems, overcalls and many other valuable concepts are covered in depth. Increase your accuracy with the proven methods which have won numerous National titles and have been adopted by a diverse group of champions.
Published October, 1982
Recommended for: intermediate through expert.
ISBN 0-910791-02-3 paperback

THE COMPLETE BOOK OF OPENING LEADS
by Easley Blackwood
$12.95

An impressive combination: the most famous name in bridge has compiled the most comprehensive book ever written on opening leads. Almost every situation imaginable is presented with a wealth of examples from world championship play. Learn to turn your wild guesses into intelligent thrusts at the enemy declarer by using all the available information. Chapters include when to lead long suits, dangerous opening leads, leads against slam contracts, doubling for a lead, when to lead partner's suit, and many others.
Published April, 1983.
Recommended for: beginner through advanced.
ISBN 0-910791-05-8 paperback

THE BEST OF DEVYN PRESS
Newly Published Bridge Books

A collection of the world's premier bridge authors have produced, for yo[u] enjoyment, this wide and impressive selection of books.

TEST YOUR PLAY AS DECLARER, VOLUME 2
by Jeff Rubens and Paul Lukacs
$5.95

Two celebrated authors have coll[ab]orated on 100 challenging and instr[uc]tive problems which are sure [to] sharpen your play. Each hand emp[ha]sizes a different principle in h[ow] declarer should handle his cards. Th[ese] difficult exercises will enable you [to] profit from your errors and er[?] learning at the same time.
Published October, 1982.
Recommended for: intermediate through expert.
ISBN 0-910791-03-1 paperback

TABLE TALK
by Jude Goodwin
$5.95

This collection of cartoons is a jo[y to] behold. What Snoopy did for dogs [and] Garfield did for cats, Sue and her g[ang] does for bridge players. If you wa[nt a] realistic, humorous view of the cl[ubs] and tournaments you attend, this [will] brighten your day. You'll meet [the] novices, experts, obnoxious know[-it-] alls, bridge addicts and other cha[rac]ters who inhabit that fascina[ting] subculture known as the bridge wo[rld].
Recommended for: all bridge playe[rs]
ISBN 0-910891-04-X paperback

THE CHAMPIONSHIP BRIDGE SERIES

In-depth discussions of the mostly widely used conventions...how to play them, when to use them and how to defend against them. The solution for those costly partnership misunderstandings. Each of these pamphlets is written by one of the world's top experts. **Recommended for: beginner through advanced.**
95 ¢ each, Any 12 for $9.95, All 24 for $17.90

VOLUME I [#1-12] PUBLISHED 1980

1. Popular Conventions by Randy Baron
2. The Blackwood Convention by Easley Blackwood
3. The Stayman Convention by Paul Soloway
4. Jacoby Transfer Bids by Oswald Jacoby
5. Negative Doubles by Alvin Roth
6. Weak Two Bids by Howard Schenken
7. Defense Against Strong Club Openings by Kathy Wei
8. Killing Their No Trump by Ron Andersen
9. Splinter Bids by Andrew Bernstein
10. Michaels' Cue Bid by Mike Passell
11. The Unusual No Trump by Alvin Roth
12. Opening Leads by Robert Ewen

VOLUME II [#13-24] PUBLISHED 1981

13. More Popular Conventions by Randy Baron
14. Major Suit Raises by Oswald Jacoby
15. Swiss Team Tactics by Carol & Tom Sanders
16. Match Point Tactics by Ron Andersen
17. Overcalls by Mike Lawrence
18. Balancing by Mike Lawrence
19. The Weak No Trump by Judi Radin
20. One No Trump Forcing by Alan Sontag
21. Flannery by William Flannery
22. Drury by Kerri Shuman
23. Doubles by Bobby Goldman
24. Opening Preempts by Bob Hamman

THE BEST OF DEVYN PRESS ♣

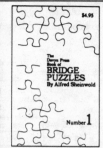

DEVYN PRESS BOOK OF BRIDGE PUZZLES #1, #2, and #3
by Alfred Sheinwold
$4.95 each

Each of the three books in this series is part of the most popular and entertaining collection of bridge problems ever written. They were originally titled "Pocket Books of Bridge Puzzles #1, #2, and #3." The 90 hands in each volume are practical and enjoyable—the kind that you attempt to solve every time you play. They also make perfect gifts for your friends, whether they are inexperienced novices or skilled masters.
Published January, 1981. Paperback

Recommended for: beginner through advanced.

CKETS TO THE DEVIL
Richard Powell $5.95

is is the most popular
dge novel ever written
the author of Woody
en's "Bananas," "The
ung Philadelphians,"
d Elvis Presley's "Fol-
v That Dream."

ets has a cast of characters
ing from the Kings and Queens of
nament bridge down to the deuces.
ng them are:

e McKinley, famous bridge col-
nnist who needs a big win to
store his fading reputation.

role Clark, who lost a husband
cause she led a singleton king.

bba Worthington, young socialite
o seeks the rank of Life Master to
ove his virility.

e Dukes and the Ashcrafts, who
ve partnership troubles in bridge
d in bed.

ny Manuto, who plays for pay,
d handles cards as if they were
ives.

ell shuffles these and many other
ers to deal out comedy, violence
drama in a perfect mixture.

jblished 1979. . .Paperback
ecommended for: all bridge
ayers.

PARTNERSHIP DEFENSE
by Kit Woolsey
$8.95

Kit's first book is unanimously considered THE classic defensive text so that you can learn the secrets of the experts. It contains a detailed discussion of attitude, count, and suit-preference signals; leads; matchpoints; defensive conventions; protecting partner; with quizzes and a unique partnership test at the end.

Alan Truscott, Bridge Editor, New York Times: The best new book to appear in 1980 seems certain to be "Partnership Defense in Bridge."

The author has surveyed a complex and vital field that has been largely neglected in the literature of the game. The player of moderate experience is sure to benefit from the wealth of examples and problems dealing with signaling and other matters relating to cooperation in defense.

And experts who feel they have nothing more to learn neglect this book at their peril: The final test of 20 problems has been presented to some of the country's best partnerships, and non has approached a maximum score.

Bridge World Magazine: As a practical guide for tournament players, no defensive book compares with Kit Woolsey's "Part-

nership Defense in Bridge" which is by far the best book of its kind that we have seen. As a technical work it is superb, and any good player who does not read it will be making one of his biggest errors of bridge judgment.

The author's theme is partnership cooperation. He believes there are many more points to be won through careful play, backed by relatively complete understandings, than through spectacular coups or even through choices among sensible conventions. We agree. If you don't, you will very likely change your mind (or at least modify the strength of your opinion) after reading what Woolsey has to say.

Published 1980. . .Paperback
Recommended for: Intermediate through expert.

DO YOU KNOW YOUR PARTNER? by Andy Bernstein and Randy Baron $1.95 A fun-filled quiz to allow you to really get to know your partner. Some questions concern bridge, some don't — only you can answer and only your partner can score it. An inexpensive way to laugh yourself to a better partnership.
Published 1979   paperback
Recommended for: all bridge players.

DEVYN PRESS
1327 Walnut St.
Shelbyville, KY 40065
Phone (502) 633-5344

VISA AND MAST
CARD ACCEPT

ORDER FORM

Number
Wanted

_____	MATCHPOINTS, Woolsey	x $9.95 = [___]
_____	DYNAMIC DEFENSE, Lawrence	x 9.95 = [___]
_____	MODERN IDEAS IN BIDDING, Rosenkranz-Truscott	x 9.95 = [___]
_____	COMPLETE BOOK OF OPENING LEADS, Blackwood	x 12.95 = [___]
_____	TEST YOUR PLAY AS DECLARER, VOLUME 2, Rubens-Lukacs	x 5.95 = [___]
_____	TABLE TALK, Goodwin	x 5.95 = [___]
_____	PARTNERSHIP DEFENSE, Woolsey	x 8.95 = [___]
_____	DEVYN PRESS BOOK OF BRIDGE PUZZLES #1, Sheinwold	x 4.95 = [___]
_____	DEVYN PRESS BOOK OF BRIDGE PUZZLES #2, Sheinwold	x 4.95 = [___]
_____	DEVYN PRESS BOOK OF BRIDGE PUZZLES #3, Sheinwold	x 4.95 = [___]
_____	INDIVIDUAL CHAMPIONSHIP BRIDGE SERIES (Please specify)	x .95 = [___]
_____	TICKETS TO THE DEVIL, Powell	x 5.95 = [___]
_____	DO YOU KNOW YOUR PARTNER?, Bernstein-Baron	x 1.95 = [___]

---

*QUANTITY DISCOUNT
ON ABOVE ITEMS:
10% over $25, 20% over $50*

*We accept checks, money
orders and VISA or MASTER
CARD. For charge card
orders, send your card number and expiration date.*

SUB TOTAL [___]

LESS QUANTITY DISCOUNT [___]

TOTAL [___]

_____ THE CHAMPIONSHIP BRIDGE SERIES
VOLUME 1 .... x $9.95 (No further discount) [___]

_____ THE CHAMPIONSHIP BRIDGE SERIES
VOLUME II .... x 9.95 (No further discount) [___]

_____ ALL 24 OF THE CHAMPIONSHIP
BRIDGE SERIES .... x 17.90 (No further discount) [___]

ADD SHIPPING:
   60¢ for 1 ITEM   TOTAL FOR BOOKS [___]
  $1.00 FOR 2 ITEMS OR MORE   SHIPPING ALLOWANCE [___]
  SHIP TO: AMOUNT ENCLOSED [___]

NAME _____

ADDRESS _____

CITY _____ STATE _____ ZIP _____